MW01249233

Liberty
in My
Soul

Autobiography

ARPAD GAAL

ISBN 978-1-68197-368-5 (paperback)
ISBN 978-1-68197-648-8 (hardcover)
ISBN 978-1-68197-369-2 (digital)

Copyright © 2016 by Arpad Gaal
All rights reserved. No part of this publication may be reproduced, distributed, or transmitted in any form or by any means, including photocopying, recording, or other electronic or mechanical methods without the prior written permission of the publisher. For permission requests, solicit the publisher via the address below.

Christian Faith Publishing, Inc.
296 Chestnut Street
Meadville, PA 16335
www.christianfaithpublishing.com

Printed in the United States of America

This book is dedicated to my grandchildren,

Jacqueline Rosemary Gaal
and
Thomas Jacob Rogers.

CONTENTS

PREFACE

This autobiography is about my boyhood memories in Hungary from 1945 to 1956. It is a true story of survival in difficult times—growing up without Mother and Father, living under Communism, and later fleeing my country. When I reached my new country, I dropped my face to the ground and kissed the beautiful land of the United States of America. I had become a free boy at age seventeen.

The story unfolds the challenging events that impacted growing up on my own and fighting against poverty and hunger and at the same time against the tyranny of Communism.

Being too young, I didn't understand what hardship meant until something better came along. I learned that poverty was a force that pushed my mind to find ways to improve myself. Because I had a strong will, I thought nothing seemed impossible; but my mistakes proved it otherwise. Along the way, I gained a lot of common sense. That, I believe, was the most essential part of my survival, for I learned not to make the same mistakes again.

I was born in Hungary. It is here my story takes place. In 1956, after the collapse of the Hungarian Revolution, I escaped to the United States. Most of all, I was seeking freedom from persecution as I was an active member in the uprising, fighting to overthrow Communistic socialism. I had skillfully escaped the gallows that waited for those who couldn't.

Basically, my life story is a success story but not without misery, not without pain and hunger, and not without the domination of other people. It shows that I had the will to endure it all because I never gave up hoping for a better life. I was not a bystander but my own pioneer.

The book is not a translation. Learning the English language was my paramount requirement for staying in the United States of America. I learned the language on my own from a dictionary and, along the way, translated the New Testament and a few classics for myself in order to better my talking skills. Today, I think, that was the best thing I ever did, as I not only learned the accurate meaning of words but also their grammatical usage. And I also became very familiar with the parables of Jesus, the guiding light to my earthly reasoning.

Translating the Bible revealed the inescapable truth: God created my soul, and it is his own, regardless of my free will. But if I don't call on him, the *devil* would snatch my spirit and fill it with worldly ingratiation for one reason only—to deny his existence. Hence, liberty to choose the right course of action was in my soul, guiding my faith to believe in myself and in God.

The names of most actors in the story, I changed. Although they are all dead, I still want to protect their survivors who are of Jewish background. The names of my relatives and those interacting with me in the story without having Jewish heritage, I left unchanged. They are also dead. I am not Jewish. It just so happened that a lot of my friends were. So I have now rejoined everybody in spirit to relive the past with me in order to present the story of my boyhood years. The story itself is presented, as much as possible, in plain English so as to allow the younger generation to understand it without having a dictionary at hand. There is one special word in the story for which I could not find a suitable replacement: *undulating* (to rise and fall gracefully in volume, as when the wind makes waves over the top of tall grass in the wilderness.)

What can my grandchildren learn from this book? Many, many examples of how to or not to do things in life. They can learn the value of willpower and positive thinking to fight against doubts. They can learn the power of faith to overcome failure. And they can learn self-assurance, the mover of the soul to reach the seemingly impossible.

Beyond all this, there is a primary phase to the events as the story unfolds reality—the onslaught of Communistic socialism in Hungary. That alone is worth to stir the minds of those readers who forgot that history is about to repeat itself. This time in the United States of America. Could it be that I would have to relive part of my boyhood again to fight off the onslaught of Communistic socialism? I wonder.

It is a fact that presently the social order in the United States of America is in disorder. The mass distribution of wealth to those who are lazy to earn their keep is just one example. Furthermore, the incremental loss of individual liberty and democracy and the loss of individual choice are other examples. All of these are, slowly but surely, taking place now under the very eyes of those who forgot to check the background of the current president of the United States of America and elected him. He is partially driven by the philosophies of those *idiots* who lied to the people (and killed millions) in order to implement Communistic socialism against their own will (Marx, Lenin, Stalin, Hitler, and many others). Moreover, a background check on the president definitely would have revealed that the teachings of Saul Alinsky's philosophy—how to dupe the masses with falsehood—is solidly imbedded in Mr. Obama's head. Know this for sure that the background of every man is his moral fiber through which he builds his ambitions. (*Obamacare* is full of that.)

"Get on your feet, Magyars!" said the great Hungarian poet Sandor Petofi. He fought together with Kossuth in the 1848 Hungarian Revolution against Austria to gain freedom and independence for the country. Lajos Kossuth, the great Hungarian general, was the second foreign dignitary who addressed the United States Congress. He foretold Congress that "if you don't help those who fight for freedom, you will lose your own."

I say the same thing to you: Get on your feet, America! Unite to defeat the charlatans! I don't want to be a freedom fighter with guns again. Let's get rid of them peacefully while there is still time left to do it. This is our last real opportunity to do so. Right now, the ballot box should be our weapon.

And finally, the story exemplifies how my will coupled with my faith overpowered every obstacle in my quest to become a better person today than I was yesterday, to become free and independent from the coercion of evil people—be it in government or in misguided society.

INTRODUCTION

Yes! I do have the courage to tell my grandchildren that I was the poorest kid in town and I recognized it when I became an orphan. So I go from here to tell them that what had happened was pioneering work, the kind that tried my faith in God and self.

So I'll also tell my grandchildren, "Read about what I had done for myself. Then, *crack the whip* (so to say) and conquer your world."

I thought that it would be a good thing to mention a few mind-piercing events that painfully impacted my life in my growing years. This is a threefold impact: The first is the capture and deportation of Father to the Gulags in Russia, then the death of my mother; the second is the *Communist* takeover of Hungary; and the third, the relatives who had abandoned me. Destiny had shuffled me around from one extreme to the other within these events, forcing me to decide, eventually, what I should or shouldn't allow others to do with me.

Let me start first by telling you the position of Hungary in world affairs. Its geographic location made it the crossroad between Eastern and Western Europe. World War I decimated the country, and World War II almost destroyed it. It was the undefeatable will of its people to be free that preserved the nation's identity, even today. No nation fought harder and longer for its independence and freedom than Hungary—on and off for over a thousand years. The beginning of its true independence and freedom should be earmarked from the beginning of the great Hungarian Revolution of 1956. And I took part in it.

* * *

In most wars in Europe, Hungary is in the center of the battles because of its location. It stood the test of time, however, for it was a bastion against invaders from the east, moving west to conquer it. Or fighting off the invaders from the west, moving toward east to dominate it. In different times, Hungary was occupied by invaders. From the east came the Mongols, the Tartars, the Turks, and the Russians. From the west came the Germans. All wanted Hungary for itself; all massacred the innocent and stifled liberty. All occupied the land because of its distinct military location and agricultural advantage. Hungary was the real battleground, the central position from which to defend frontiers. The country provided the best geographical defense, for the mountains, the Carpathian Mountains on the one side and the Alps on the other, ensured the relative safety of the invaders. This was the corridor west to east and east to west. More than likely, this was the main reason as to why Arpad, the leader of the seven tribes of the Magyars, also settled here in 865 AD.

Inside the country, Hungary had different nationalities deep within its borders (Slavs, Serbs, Romanians.) Each wanted to be independent from Hungarian subjugation; therefore some form of insurrection was brewing in their hearts all the time, waiting for the right moment to erupt. To maintain its territorial grip that at times comprised almost half of Europe, Hungary formed alliances with previous enemies. This was just one reason as to why the Austrian-Hungarian monarchy was formed. One thing, however, the kings of Hungary did not do was give freedom to the oppressed nationalities within its borders. That had to be granted to them by force. In 1920, after World War I, old Hungary was downsized to its present borders. It lost three-fourth of its territory.

After World War I, in accordance with the terms of the Treaty of Trianon (1920), the opportunity for the big powers (Russia, Great Britain, France, United States) was never riper than now to slice up Hungary. So small they carved it up that it could never be in the center of wars or cause trouble to anybody inside or outside of its new borders, again. All the oppressed nationalities became free at last and were allowed by the treaty to establish their own identities and countries. Hungary lost its centuries-old territories and also lost more than half of its Hungarian population. The map of Europe had been redrawn, but only temporarily until Hitler rose to power. In 1938 Hitler formed an alliance with Hungary, and as part of that pact, part of the lost territories in Slovakia had been returned to Hungary. But it lasted only until the end of World War II (1945). The Allied Powers (United States, France, Great Britain, and the Soviet Union) reversed everything back at the Yalta Conference, the way it was before.

Because Hungary was allied with Germany, it also lost the war as Germany did. From the arms of one devil, Hitler, Hungary now had been thrown into the arms of another devil, Stalin. These two leaders were like the leaders of all the evil empires throughout history. They made agreements and formed treaties only to break them in order to advance their own conquests, conquering their targeted parts of the world with the eventual aim to conquer the world.

Now the Nazis had been defeated on the battleground in 1945. As a result, Europe became divided almost evenly between the Allies and the Soviet Union. Barbed wires separated the two halves. Winston Churchill named it the *Iron Curtain*. Stalin was free at last to exercise his brutal treatment of the people in all those countries that fell on his side of the fence. Millions of people died in labor camps and millions more died through torture and persecution in order to subjugate all opposition. This was how Stalin forced his Communist-style socialism on every country within the *Iron Curtain*. Henceforth, two giant powers with different social orders controlled the world, the United States of America ("In God We Trust") and the Soviet Union ("In No God We Trust").

Then in 1948, Hungary fell under the complete domination of Communism. I was then nine years old—a ripe age to bend the mind of a stubborn child toward a Communistic ideology. How that turned out to be, you shall know it shortly.

Section One

CHAPTER ONE

The Impact of WWII

World War II swept through Polgardi, Hungary, in 1945. The Nazis were just retreating from the town but not without fighting the Russians. Only a few months ago, my family moved here from the town of Ercsi, where I was born in 1939.

We were now taking shelter in the basement of a railroad house, bundled up and lying on layers of potatoes as the bombardment could still be heard from afar. We ate raw potatoes. Daring to go outside was equal to capture or death as the Russian soldiers replaced the Germans. At times, we heard heavy noises upstairs. They were rummaging for food and destroying furniture in their fury for not being able to find any. They didn't know that we were in the bunker below. The entrance to it was camouflaged by folding pantry shelves, reinforced inside with steel plates.

We spent almost four days in this shelter during the bombardments as the Germans kept fighting the Russians. But the Germans couldn't withstand the massive onslaught and retreated. It was April. The balmy weather signaled the beginning of new life. I couldn't figure out what was happening or how things were going forward.

The Russians captured many able-bodied men and deported them to Siberia because Hungary was allied with the Nazis. My

Father was one of those deported. I have not seen or heard from him ever since. He was a railroad worker in this town and wore that type of uniform. It made him a suspect, spying for the Nazis.

When finally we surfaced from our bunker, we saw live as well as spent ammunition littering the landscape like snails in the garden after rain. Destroyed cannons and tanks stood almost side by side, abandoned for looting or toying by curious men and restless children.

One by one, we crawled out our shelter and looked for my father. Neighbors said that they saw a group of men being forced by bayoneted soldiers into railroad cars and Father was among them. We embraced Mother and cried together.

The railroad house we lived in was about five hundred yards away from the railroad station where my father was in charge of switching the tracks in order to control rail traffic. The Russians took that over, too. Of course, there wasn't much to control anymore, as everything was at a standstill, except the prison train that carried the captives.

Above the shelter was the main floor of the house. Inside, it looked much like a place that thieves rummaged through. One could tell that savage people were there—earmarks of the brutal Russian soldiers. Out of the broken furniture, we rebuilt the beds, the kitchen table, the chairs, and the cabinets so that we could sit and eat somewhere. Foremost in mind now was not the surrounding destruction but something that we could eat.

Over the main floor was the attic that served as our food storage. Here we kept all the dry and smoked goods. Mother was always mindful of tomorrow. She used to say, "What you didn't splurge today was your safety net for tomorrow."

She stored in the attic everything from sun-dried herbs and fruits to grains, beans, and nuts; flour; and smoked ham, slab bacon, and pork fat. This part of the house was untouched by the wild soldiers, for they couldn't get to it. The entrance to the attic was from outside, from the gable end of the house. The Russians weren't smart enough to figure out why a ladder was hidden close by inside a just budding chestnut tree.

Now, my older brother pulled the ladder from the tree and leaned it against the attic's entrance. One by one, the four of us climbed to the attic. There, we ate smoked sausage and shriveled apples. After we had our full, Mother called us to sit around her in order to talk about what we should be doing next.

"Let's pray together first," she said. We clinched her hands and listened as she thanked God for saving us. We also prayed for Father's return, safely and soon.

Moving from Polgardi to Balatonkeresztur

During the following month, we packed our meager belongings onto an open-top railroad car and left town. Father never returned. We moved back to Balatonkeresztur to the house my grandfather bought for Father and his sister, Matild. It was a duplex; half of it was Father's, the other half Matild's.

(The name *Balaton* signifies the biggest lake in central Europe and most of the towns that surround it are prefixed with that word. And *keresztur* means the intersection of two main roads through the town. At the intersection stands a prominent Catholic church visible miles away from any direction.)

For the next eight years, my life was revolving around this town. It was here that I learned to love and hate, experienced good and evil, and took on bad habits. It was here that I endured miseries and worked my way out of them. Additionally, it was here where I met a man who told me all about America and the opportunities it offered to all who dared to face the challenges going there. It was here where the best memories from my childhood brought forth the stories of my adventures worth telling others.* * *

World War II ended in 1945. The Russians conquered the entire Eastern Europe and subjugated every country within it. They introduced the ideologies of Marx, Lenin, and Stalin, known as *Communism*. By 1948, Hungary became completely under Russian domination. Rakosy (the Communist boss) became the puppet of the Russians in Moscow. Disaster befell the country as Hungary had to pay war reparations to the Russians because it was allied with the now defeated Germans. The *Secret Police* became the most feared and hated agents, supporting at all cost the Communist government. They carried out the atrocities ordered by Rakosy. The society became layered. The poor was labeled the *proletariat,* the rich became the *kulaks,* and the professionals became the *intelligentsia.* Those who sided with the government were the *Communists*; those who didn't were the enemy.

Within these three groups of people, another group emerged. And by far, this was the greatest group of people who became Communists, but in name only. In their hearts, they held onto the traditional values of the nation. At work, they mingled with the Communists and worked side by side with them. This was the only way to work and earn the daily bread. Nobody really knew who was who, except in their closest circles. To try to find out *who was who,* the Secret Police established the biggest network of informers within all layers of the society at large. Those who were caught as *underground saboteurs* were persecuted and sent to hard-labor camps or otherwise eliminated without mercy. Not being able to trust anybody, fear had gripped the hearts of millions.

As the peasants raised their animals and grew their crops, the Secret Police came and confiscated everything they could lay their hands on. So the peasants, being very smart, buried everything that they could or hid things off their premises.

Those who resisted, the Secret Police rounded at night, and they disappeared. Any who came back had part of his body bitterly bruised and even mutilated. The wealth of the rich was over; it became the collective property of the government. Those with professional status, resisting the government, were sent to hard-labor camps.

But those who accepted the Communist ideology were highly favored. They were indoctrinated to become the teachers of the new society. The biggest enemy of the Communist government was the Roman Catholic Church. (Cardinal Mindszenty escaped to the US Embassy.) The churches' property was confiscated, the priests jailed, their parishes closed. Under the Communist ideology God had no name. But faith in him was another matter, solidly kept in the hearts of believers in the whole country. It was then practiced all the more underground.

* * *

Now, I was six and a half years old, and we had already moved into my father's house in Balatonkeresztur. It was an old house with two rooms, a kitchen, and a bedroom for the four of us. It was a rather neglected duplex structure with no electricity. Mother maintained an absolute discipline among us regarding manners, respect, and courtesy toward each other. She was also strict regarding work assignments for each of us. I was often disobedient and, for that, received the wooden spoon.

My perception about life, living conditions, and the people in the village was mostly upbeat. Since I was always inventive in spirit, I was flying high above the crowd to overlook the miseries of life that others thought impossible to live through. This type of disposition was the strength of my soul, wanting to know more than what I was seeing before my eyes, wanting to be extraordinary in my own way—without understanding reality.

It was time for me to attend school, although a year late, because my birthday was in October. In the first three years after the war ended, the Catholic Church was still holding onto the reins in educating most children. My teacher was a middle-aged white-robed Augustinian priest. His hands were freely flying over my butts, for I couldn't recite the basic prayers and didn't do my homework. For the first time, I had realized that there was an *authority* over me and I had to obey. The Catechism was followed to enforce it.

Settling Down in Balatonkeresztur

After moving to Balatonkeresztur from Polgardi, I saw everything in disarray. I didn't know anybody and was not familiar with the surroundings. Since I was not in school yet and it was already late spring, I had plenty of time to get acquainted—first with all my relatives, then with the girls and boys in the neighborhood. For over a whole year now, I had the time to help Mother to do odds and ends. And it seemed that she never ran out of orders. By doing all the errands as well, I met both the good and the bad people. Pretty soon even the dogs stopped barking at me. They noticed that I was smiling at them.

Ella, my older sister, was also at Mother's side in order to help her with cleaning the house, baking the bread, and washing the clothes. My older brother, Laszlo, who was now fifteen, assumed the man-of-the-house role. He was strong. He was the only one, I thought, who could dig the land for planting the vegetable seeds. But it turned out that I could do it just as well. My strength exceeded my imagination.

This parcel of land we shall prepare for plantation was a mile away from our house. It overlooked the village as well as the surroundings. From there, the panorama of Lake Balaton was breathtaking. I used to stop working just to marvel the changing colors of the water as it reflected the high hills from the north side of the lake, especially when the sun declined over the horizon. It took us a couple of days to turn the soggy clay over with a shovel. By the time we finished, I had blisters all over my palms where the shovel handle rubbed the skin. My brother was cruel.

"Get used to it. We have one more piece of land in the meadows. Put on a pair of worn-out socks over your hands tomorrow."

Because of the lack of proper farming tools, we were digging manually. We owned two shovels, one handsaw, one ax, one hammer, and one screwdriver. If we needed nails, we pulled them out wherever we found them. If we needed boards or posts or planks, we had to go to the forest first for the logs, carry them home, and hew them with ax to the size needed for the purpose. Since the forest was state property, cutting down trees was forbidden. Who cared, everybody else did the same thing.

After the war, few, if any, could afford to buy anything. There was no money. When money was finally printed, a kilogram of sugar (two pounds) had a price tag of one million forint (about twenty dollars). It took a heap of paper money to buy that one kilogram of sugar. Inflation killed the value of everything. Everybody was forced to do business by bartering. Mother was doing it all around town in order to obtain salt and spices. She bartered lard for spice. Lard was one commodity we had extra.

Our food supply quickly ran low, especially the cured meats. We were good eaters. Fresh meat, we had not eaten for months already. It was for this reason my brother said, "We'll make wire loops and set them in rabbit trails. As they make their run in and out of the woods through them, they will choke themselves to death."

So we found a coil of wire in our shed, and within a couple of hours my brother had the traps ready-made. I was observing every step of it just in case I would have need for such a thing one day. The next thing we did was hewing out small stakes to which to fasten the wire traps. Then we went with the traps to the edge of the forest and looked for the rabbit trails. Their trails were easily recognizable as the grass was trampled from their frequent back-and-forth running.

We drove the small stakes in the ground about six inches away from the edge of the trails and placed the traps so as the rabbits could just crawl through the loops. (Good to know that rabbits seldom ever walked backward.)

The next morning at dawn my brother kicked my side and yelled, "Get up! The rabbits are squealing in their traps." Of course, all this happened in his dreams. Nevertheless, I jumped out of bed and dragged him out, too. I couldn't sleep any longer from the excitement. While Mother and Ella were still sleeping on the other bed, we left the house quietly. It was the crack of dawn. I carried the shovels on my shoulder, whereas my brother carried a jug of water and a bag of corn for seeding. We were going to turn over a portion of the land in order to plant corn seeds. This was the main project for the day. The land was situated close to the forest. As we got closer and closer to the land, we had a better idea. The thought of rabbits in the traps captured our attention, and we went there.

We left the shovels, the bag of corn, and the jug of water on the property and went straight to the traps at the edge of the forest. Eight traps were empty, while four traps had noosed rabbits in them. They were already dead. *This was a tremendous success*, blitzed through my head. I repeated the words a hundred times on my way home as I lugged the rabbits to Mother.

The joy of seeing four fat rabbits turned Mother into prompt action, flaying them without hesitation. She promised me that by the time I returned again from the field, she would have prepared a sweet and spicy stew for me.

The thought of it gave me the extra energy to rush back to my brother, who stayed behind in the field to turn over the ground. By noon we had prepared the rows to plant the kernels in them. This part of the work was easy. We evened the top of the soil with the tip of the shovel and made furrows with the shovel's handle, three feet apart. Then we dropped the seeds one by one into the furrows, twelve inches apart. Now, we used the tip of the shovel again and gently covered the furrows even with the rest of the ground. Crows were flying in circles above us because they either smelled the corn or saw it as we were dropping them into the furrows. Had we not leveled the furrows even with the ground, they would have dug up the corn as soon as we had left the place.

By three o'clock in the afternoon, we finished and were heading home.

The dirt road on which we walked was lined with flowering acacia bushes. The locks of flowers on them were full of nectar. So the bees, the birds, and the kids alike had gathered around them in order to suck the honey from the flower clusters. We had our share of it, too. We washed the sweet stuff down with the little water left over in the jug. The fragrance of these flowers was so strong and pleasant that I could have stayed there for hours, not only to enjoy the pleasant smell and relish the honey, but also to watch the partridges feeding their little ones with the same stuff, yonder. About one more week, I thought, I would come back and take them home and fatten them for a great meal.

At home, Mother and Ella were marveling at the size of the four jackrabbits. At the same time they were moaning over the tough job flaying them, for their skin were practically glued to their bodies. Mother decided to dunk them in hot water for a few minutes so as their skin would peel off easier.

Now, each of these jackrabbits weighed anywhere from ten to fifteen pounds, too much to eat all at once. So Mother decided to make a business deal with the neighbors. She kept two rabbits, one for stew that day and the other for broiling tomorrow. The other two she bartered away, one with Matild, my aunt next door, and the other with the third neighbor. She received in return ten chicks from Matild and a piglet from the neighbor. This deal provided the opportunity to raise these animals for future provisions and, at the same time, lessened her worry where to get meat for later.

My brother and I were now fast approaching home. The stew's smell pervaded the air a good distance from home. That alone was enough to quicken our steps to get home sooner, for we were now exceedingly hungry. As we met Mother at the kitchen door, she was already feeding the new chicks with crushed corn meal. She greeted us as a good mother would—always loving, smiling, and caring for the next right thing to do.

"Will you nook more rabbits again?"

She wasn't thinking of food, but rather to do more bartering for other things we needed in the kitchen. My brother quickly replied, "We'll be checking the traps every dawn, Mother."

Up to now, she didn't reveal that she bartered two rabbits away. It was obvious, though, that the chicks didn't fly in from the field overnight. When I saw the small, wobbly chicks, I knew right then where they came from. Matild's yard was full of them. I concluded that tomorrow as I come back from the meadows, I would be bringing the partridge chicks back with me and would put them together with these chicks. They would accept each other and grow up together.

Now, I quickly stepped inside the kitchen and found the pot of stew still simmering on the stove. I held the lid in my left hand and spooned the juice into my mouth from the pot with my right hand.

"That's not the way to eat, Arpad," Mother said. "From now on, you'll wait until I dish it out for you!"

Of course, I had heard that a hundred times already before. My hunger was always stronger than words, and I could never break that habit even to this day.

But now, we had enough rabbit stew left over that we could share it with others. So Mother asked me to invite the closest neighbor's family. They were good people. They allowed us to bucket water from their well every day. In return, Mother was now very much glad that she could return their kindness.

While I did the invitation, Mother hurriedly washed the plates in order that she could serve stew out of them again for the guests. The whole family of four came and ate at our table. We moved out of the way and sat on the edges of the two beds we had in the same room. They all had their full, and more was still left over. That we gave to Matild, our aunt next door.

Eight of us had gathered in this small room that we used now as our bedroom as well as our kitchen. We were practically elbowing each other. Yet we talked and laughed over our miseries and short-comings without showing any sign of ill-comfort about our lives. Good people we were and had gotten along just fine.

Our far neighbors, all around, were better off than we were. We were the newcomers in the village and had little of anything else other than what we brought with us from Polgardi. Everybody else was well established and had the means to support themselves from the crops they grew and the animals they raised. The lasting ravages of the war, however, were everywhere. There was no real money. The stores were empty and the local government corrupt.

In Need of a Friend

Even though I became quite familiar with the people in town, I had no real friends, first of all, with whom I could talk things over, share my secrets, and escape the real world—just dream as children do about things the world seldom offered. But finding such a friend had to come naturally between two people seeking the same thing. I'm thinking about Laszlo, a boy about my age, who lives next door. He was already at our house before, eating rabbit stew with us.

Within a few days, chance brought us together again. As I was going to draw water from his father's well, Laszlo watched me passing by. He was standing next to the clothes line trying to tie it together. I passed him. I didn't know how to start talking to him inasmuch as I saw that he wanted to say something to me also. I thought it would be just a matter of time before the two of us would find the way to say something to each other.

The next day, I did the same thing again. But this time the rope with which I was bucketing the water broke in half and fell in the well, taking my draw bucket with it. Before I could even recover from the surprise, Laszlo already brought a long ladder and lowered it into the well. "I'll go down to get it for you," he said.

I knew it in that instance that by his earnest move, Laszlo revealed his brotherly feeling toward me in my helplessness. We became the best of friends after that without even saying a word about it to each other. His full name is Laszlo Szalado, a Jewish boy, totally opposite from me in character, religion, and courage. A very exciting relationship developed between the two of us after that.

About the Village Where I Grew Up

World War II did little damage to Balatonkeresztur. It was occupied by the German soldiers for only a short time because the Russians pushed them westward with relentless firepower. As a defensive measure, the Germans blew up all the bridges over a nearby canal that drained the backwaters into Lake Balaton. This stopped the quick advance of the Russians for a while from moving west.

The church at the intersection of the two main roads crossing the village suffered substantial damage from the Russians, bombarding the Germans from the east side of the canal. It was an easy target. Its tower was the highest point visible from the surrounding areas. The Germans used it for observation until the Russians blew it off.

Balatonkeresztur is bordering the shores of Lake Balaton. It is hugging the southern side of the water, and from there it stretches southward for about two miles. The village is surrounded by farm-land on all sides from the lake. It is located one hundred miles south-west of Budapest, the capital of Hungary.

Before World War II, the nobility and the Catholic Church owned half the farmland. The other half belonged to individual farmers; some of them were very rich. After 1948, the Communists confiscated all the land from the nobility and the church and started the collectivization in farming. The land that was still in the hands of the rich farmers, they couldn't yet confiscate, for their opposition to collective farming was overwhelmingly rebellious. Small plots of land, here and there, were allowed in private hands, however, for gardening purposes, especially if there was a house on it. This was how we owned two half-acre plots in separate locations.

(Even today, the residence and the granary of the baron who lived on the land are still standing in the village. They are now historical monuments of the past era. It was in the baron's residence where I attended my first three years of elementary school. My teacher was that Augustinian priest of uncommon discipline, who demanded that I learn the catechism almost cover to cover.)

Mother and Her Early-Bird Advice

Now, spring was at hand. So was the work in the fields. I could never understand why weeds grew faster than plants did. Pulling weeds was never a favorite time for me, especially when the sun was scorching my back. Mother always believed that if I wanted to get rid of the weeds, I shouldn't let them grow. Since I didn't understand how her thinking worked in practice, I was looking for the proof of it.

"I will prove it to you tomorrow" she said. "We'll get up before daybreak and go to the garden in the hills and lightly hoe the top of the soil everywhere in between the plants.

"You see, the weed seeds are close to the surface, and they germinate very fast. Their roots grow quickly and deeply. When lightly hoeing the surface, you're cutting in half the just germinated weeds, and as soon as the sun shines on them, they quickly wither. The roots may or may not grow back. That depended on what type of weed grew in the soil.

"Now, if you do this early in the morning, you really save the rest of the day for yourself to do other things in the shade. Maybe even sleeping. There is a saying from early times: 'Those who rise early, discover gold.'" (*The early bird gets the worm.*)

In the afternoon on the same day, I went back to the hills in order to check Mother's idea of weeding. I couldn't find any weeds in between the plants where she hoed the soil. The sun dried every weed that was shaved off. This was a good lesson I learned early in my life. Do my work as early in the day as I could, and thereby finish the day's planned work by the time others struggle to do theirs in the scorching sunshine.

The good thing that I gained from getting up early was the fact that I acquired the habit of it. I have become an *early bird* ever since that time. By getting up early, I'm full of energy, ready to grapple the most difficult tasks of the day first. But the best of it is the stress relief I gain from it every day. Look around yourselves and notice that most of the successful people are *early birds*, too.

Textbooks Didn't Teach Common Sense to Me

If I had been born just a month earlier, I would have finished my first-grade school about now. My Jewish buddy Laszlo was ahead of me; he had just finished his first grade. Although he never said he was smarter, I felt that he was, but only from textbooks. And that bothered me a lot. The basic courses were language, mathematics, and grammar. So I asked him to show me his books in order that

I simply page through them and maybe even catch up to him. Of course, that was more from my curiosity than learning. I recognized immediately the formality that book study required—discipline. I didn't care for that at all. Formality and I were strangers as I was a common-sense-type kid, capable of doing things while others were still learning how to do them from textbooks. Then, I gave the books back to him and said: "You do things your way. I do things my way."

So the lack of formality followed me during all my years in elementary school. I flunked the first grade and barely made passing grades later. It never bothered me though as I was street-smart and surpassed my schoolmates in the practical things in life.

Hardship was my teacher, as destiny ordered it that way. It forced me to think quickly. In hardships I couldn't wait for calculations. They required quick responses in order to get over them. And I made plenty of mistakes, too. But, through them, I gained common sense so as not to make the same mistakes again. Mistakes I made in my boyhood were, of course, free of cost; but the lessons I learned from them were priceless in the long run. It honed my mind to think clearly, for every mistake stood before me was an example for improvement. Few things could have been equal to those experience-based mistakes, for my mind had a lasting fix on them.

CHAPTER TWO

Cherry Picking, the Fun and the Pain

As I grew older, the daily chores my mother piled on increased by leaps and bounds. I had very little time now left for fun and play, for scouting around Lake Balaton, or for picking cherries from trees that lined both sides of the main road just south my village. So I began combining work with fun. At this time my work was to gather wild clover, alfalfa, and soft weeds early in the morning at the roadsides in order to feed the pig, the rabbits, and the chickens. I hated to walk barefoot early mornings in the wet grass. But barefoot I had to walk because I had one pair of shoes only, and that I saved for special occasions.

So I decided to go cherry picking first while the dew dried up in the bright sunshine. The trouble was, however, that the low-hanging fruits were already picked by the gypsies. But I didn't mind that at all, for I knew that the best and most luscious cherries were on the top branches that couldn't be reached by ordinary means. That's where the sun hit them first.

I loved climbing trees for good reasons. From the top of trees I could see the world around me far away. I could fill my lungs with fresh air, gently blowing in my face. I could even examine how little birds behaved in their nest. And I could see also the flowering meadows, the grazing cows, the working peasants, and who was coming or going to mind their business. But now I couldn't wait to stretch my hands and pluck the luscious cherries from the outer limbs of this tall cherry tree. Higher and higher I climbed until I reached the top where I could pick and choose the sweetest and crunchiest cherries. And I did. These cherries were extra large, the kind that when I crushed in my mouth, the juices squirted in all directions.

After a while I couldn't eat anymore, and my attention leaped to far places to the breathtaking views of the mountains on the north side of Balaton. Momentarily, I forgot where I was. While I wished to be there, my body slipped a few feet onto a thicker branch below. The thick branch on which I landed hit my testicles, and the pain knocked me out for a few seconds. But I was lucky because as I was sliding down, the baggy bottom of my canvas shirt got caught in a dry branch. Now being clinched between the trunk and the limb of the tree, I couldn't move up or down from my position. Finally, after my pain subsided, I squeezed myself through my shirt and climbed down. My original plan failed.

I couldn't bring Mother the nicest cherries from the top of the tree anymore, for my shirt was waving at me from the top as I was looking at it from the bottom. At the same time, I couldn't bring greens to the animals either for my baggy shirt could no longer serve as my apron. I walked home empty-handed, stood before Mother, and waited for the consequences.

"Who scratched you all over? Were you fighting with gypsies? What happened to you? Tell me!"

When I did tell her what happened, instead of being sorry for me, she chased me out of the kitchen.

"Go, get your shirt back. Don't come back without it!"

Instead of being let down, I was as happy as a just released dog from his chain. I was free to do anything I wanted. So I ran back to the cherry tree and climbed it as a monkey would in order to get my shirt. I paid no attention to anything else. Within an hour I was home with my shirt and all the greens wrapped in it for the animals.

If you wonder why all the fuss about my shirt, well, that's the only one I had for ordinary use.

* * *

Now climbing up a tree was not the same as climbing down. I had already learned that from kittens. Looking upward I could see the branches. Coming down, however, I had to memorize the same braches I stepped on upward. Furthermore, I also learned that I couldn't just step anywhere on a branch. I had to examine it and determine whether that branch was living or dead, wet or dry, and most of all, strong enough to hold me close at the trunk's joint. Anyway, I'm a great climber, and the news of it spread all over town. People came asking to fetch their kittens chased up the trees by dogs, or to throw down crows' nests. The crows are especially nasty birds as they pluck chicks one by one from where they are roaming. At first, I climbed free; but, then, my Jewish buddy Laszlo called me a fool for doing it free. So after that, I charged one dollar for each climbing.

The Unexpected Cherry Picker

The next day I went picking cherries again. Since there were different types of cherry trees planted on this road and each was ripening at different times, I was taking my time and walking from tree to tree tasting the cherries to find out which ones were ready. The tree that I found bore yellow cherries. They were as big, crunchy, and juicy as the dark-red cherries were. Somehow, though, they didn't appeal to me as the dark-red cherries did. Even the starlings avoided them, for they couldn't pinch them as easily as they did the dark-red cherries. I didn't know this until a pretty-eyed gypsy girl told me so.

She was already in the tree eating them, as well as filling her basket. I climbed close to her.

"Are you a good climber?" I asked.

"Not as good as you are. I saw you yesterday on that other tree. You were on the top of it, and I was scared to even look at you. Weren't you dizzy up there?" she asked.

"Heights don't bother me, but distractions do. The world looks so much different from above. I could even see a mouse running across the road, and of course, from my eagerness to keep looking at it, I sometimes forget that safety should be my foremost concern."

I didn't tell her anything about my accident, for her criticism would have been embarrassing to me. It would have been like second opinion after the fact that wouldn't change what already had happened.

"You should be a mountain climber," she said. "There, you would be on land all the time. What's your name, anyway?" she asked.

Being back on the ground already, I didn't respond. I acted as if I didn't hear her. My handbasket was already full of cherries, and I was ready to run home with it. So I left the gypsy girl on the tree without saying anything. Truly, I was afraid of her. I didn't want her to question me about where I lived and so on. Gypsies weren't liked in my village because they were constantly begging and snooping around to snatch something when nobody was looking. They abhorred working to earn their living.

It was now sunset. The mosquitoes were out and were all over my body. They had no problem catching up to me as I was running away from them to get home quicker. In my hurry, I stumbled over a fallen branch, as I attempted leaping over it, and spilled about a third of the cherries. I left the beads there scattered all over the place. As the sun now disappeared, I decided to take a shortcut in order to lessen the distance. I still had about a mile to run. I crossed over fields of corn, potatoes, and small gardens. A lot of rabbits crossed my path as they sensed danger from my pounding the ground. I thought that I would get them tomorrow using my slingshot.

As I was approaching home, I noticed that a campfire was blazing in the middle of our small yard. The bright flame threw the light on several faces, making visible my mother, my brother, my sister, and my buddy Laszlo. The folks were sitting on short logs, cut for the occasion. I couldn't believe what I was seeing in that split second. They were roasting a rabbit that my brother fetched from the traps while I was away picking cherries.

Now, it was almost dark, and the only light that lit the small circle came from the campfire. As I finally appeared in the light, Mother scanned my whole body. I couldn't tell whether she was smiling or crying over what she saw. The others were looking at me also and suddenly started laughing. They saw that my lower body was covered with smudge from the wet plants I trampled over and that my upper body was full of bloody patches from the mosquitoes I smashed with my hand.

My mother didn't say anything. Quickly, she ran inside the house and brought with her a bottle of vinegar and a white rag. Then, she fully wetted the rag with the vinegar and wiped my torso with it. While rubbing me all over, she kept saying, "Stay still. I know it stings." The others laughed as I hissed and wiggled nonstop. That made me angry. To quiet them, I poured the cherries over their heads. So now they had to pick them up from the ground if they wanted any. Mother finished dabbing every bump with the vinegar-drenched rag. The rag was no longer white but looked more like somebody just wiped a dirty floor with it. Then, she ordered me to wash myself completely in a large vat full of sun-heated rainwater.

While I was privately washing myself, the rest of the family gathered all the cherries and joyfully spitted the pits in all directions, or shot them at each other for fun. In the meantime, the rabbit was roasting on the open pit. I kept my eyes on its state of readiness from the vat.

My brother was good at roasting rabbits in this fashion. He already skillfully cut the roast apart and handed a piece to everyone. He kept the hind legs to share them with me. I joined him soon after I washed myself. "The bigger chunk is yours, Brother, because I'm full of cherries," he said.

The bigger chunk, of course, had part of the back attached to it. I ripped apart the juicy pieces with my teeth and shoved them down without a morsel of bread.

While eating, Matild, my aunt, looked at us from her side of the fence. Mother invited her to join us to eat a piece from this huge roast. She came, and peace prevailed between them for a few days.

It was now about ten o'clock in the evening. Mother and Matild stayed by the fire, gossiping about the latest hearsay in the village. Ella, my sister, went to sleep. My brother, Laszlo, went for a walk to the shores of Lake Balaton, looking for a date. The other Laszlo, my neighbor, and I went for a short walk on the street in front of our house, for sharing our secrets required privacy to do so.

One-of-a-Kind Serenade and the Aftermath

Soon we joined a group of young men, clumsily carrying a fifty-foot-long pine pole on their shoulders. Laszlo and I decided to stay close to them as we had never before seen such an event take place.

The young men were sipping wine in between the activity. One of them had a gallon jug and kept passing it from one to the other in order to keep the good mood going and the energy flowing. Being courteous, the man passed the jug to me, and I took a gulp from it. Laszlo refused to have any, being afraid of his father.

This pine pole had its top branches untrimmed and was already decorated with colorful ribbons. The boys would erect it at midnight in front of a girl's house as a sign for her to become the fiancée to one of the young man in the group. As soon as they erected the pole, they would serenade at the girl's window. And if she accepted the invitation, she would open her window and show herself to the fiancé as a sign of availability. Within a few days after that, the decorated pole with wine-filled bottles dangling on top of it would be taken down amid a big party honoring the engagement.

(It is a custom in many villages in Hungary to do this, especially in the month of May.)

Suddenly, my brother showed up, coming back from Lake Balaton without meeting any girl there. He gently knocked our heads together and stuck his head between ours and remarked, "Don't you think this is not for you to stick around watching? Let's go home. I'll go with you as I'm afraid if I don't, you are going to receive a whack or two on your ass for staying out this late."

We went home together. Sure enough, Laszlo would have been slapped by his father had not my brother stood up for him. He explained to Laszlo's father what was going on and that he was with us toward the end.

"Kids needed exposure so that they learn the fun part of life, too," Brother emphasized.

Laszlo's father knew what most parents knew: Night revelry was a tremendous opportunity to copy bad habits from others leaning toward having a *kick*. Not knowing the difference between what's good or bad, kids, of course, would opt for the wildest kick of the moment.

Being a little more than ten years old, I had every inclination to go for the wildest rides. It was my nature to be curious, daring, and fun-loving.

CHAPTER THREE

The Tourist on Lake Balaton

Lake Balaton was a great lure for tourists during summertime. From all over Europe, people of all nationalities come here to spend their vacations, for the waters of this lake was exceptionally warm, shallow, and the clearest and cleanest among the few lakes located in Europe. Best of all, it was about fifty miles long. The shores were dotted by resort-type villages. They offer all types of very reasonable lodging, including camping for the young and villas for the rich. On top of that, the Hungarian cuisine and the palatable wines from the volcano-enriched soils were served at a very modest price that make a whole family's vacation a choice spot even in hard times after the war.

Special attention was given by the government to provide the best entertainment in restaurants, cafes, and bars. Singers, comedians, even film stars are invited from Budapest and other major cities in the country to come to Lake Balaton in order to entertain the people. I could hear from my house in late evenings the sound of music, which was at times accompanied by a vocalist. The quiet waters of the lake, backed by mountains, echoed the sound miles away. No wonder why my brother wanted to spend his evenings here. It was no wonder either why I was itching to go there whenever I saw my brother go. The only other way I could go there was without permission. And many times, I did just that.

It looked as if the youth of the world had congregated to the shores of Lake Balaton. This was in fact the reality. After the war, Europe was split in half by the so-called *Iron Curtain*. Eastern Europe became under the control and influence of the Soviet Union; Western Europe became under the influence of the United States. Two great enemies were now the biggest threat to world peace. The friends and relatives in Western Europe had friends and relatives in Eastern Europe; therefore, they anxiously spent their vacations together on Lake Balaton in order to see each other. There was no other way to see the separated friends and families. Lake Balaton became the meeting point for the two different groups of people. From these international vacationers the overwhelming majority were the folks from East and West Germany.

Since my grounding was limited to the nighttime, I and my buddy went together during afternoons to the local beech; and we were surprised that we could hardly find anyone speaking Hungarian. Now we were able to speak freely without paying attention to those who might hear us, making opinions about how the girls were dressed or which one was prettier than the other. We, of course, stood out like a sore thumb as we walked around in worn-out, patchy shorts and barefoot. My haircut was much like the haircut on a shaggy dog, uneven and curly, while Laszlo's hair was flat and cut back with scissors. I had a bronze-colored complexion and light-brown, curly hair. My body was evenly tanned. Not because I'm sun-tanning it, but because I had to work in the fields, whether it was sunny or cloudy.

Now we ran into the shallow waters to join the same age-group of boys and girls already playing volley ball. The ball occasionally bounced out of control, and either I or Laszlo jumped after it and threw it back. We hung around the players and finally became part of the group. Not knowing the rules of the game, we were tossed out within minutes. The captain of the group yelled at first, but we didn't understand him. He was German. Then, he came close to us and pointed with his hand to get out. The sign language he showed was probably crueler than the words he uttered. I didn't know at the time that sign language was the only way to communicate one's way of getting around when one was ignorant of another man's language.

Summertime was now gradually coming to a close. By the end of September, the waters of Lake Balaton cooled off quickly. The north wind steered up four-to-five-foot-high waves that made me imagine I was surfing on top of it. Laszlo and I were watching the seagulls picking up clamshells and dropping them on the red stones that lined the shore. It was a scene of rivalry among these birds. The one that dropped the clamshell was not the one that ate the shattered contents. It was the one that skillfully stole it. I knew they weren't playing games. It was a survival event much like mine was.

The evening sun was about to disappear from the horizon. I persuaded Laszlo to stay at our present spot for ten more minutes until it disappeared. We were facing north and were looking at the disappearing sun on the left. We weren't talking now, as I was completely overtaken by the beauty of sunset. Not only the sky bathed in hues of red, but also the waves rolled different hues of this color before my eyes. I was sure that Laszlo was seeing the same thing. When I finally explained to him what was happening, he said that I was imagining it. He didn't see what I saw. Nevertheless, I took note of this event, as I just realized that I had a different personality than Laszlo. This difference accounted for my keen sense in recognizing the beauty of sunset in the making. It set the stage before me to realize also that being able to recognize the beauty in nature, I was a different person. For a fleeting moment I had become one with it.

It also set the beginning stage in my life to realize that the most important part of me was to recognize who I am. What I mean is who I am inside. For what I am inside shall eventually come outside in my reactions. And those reactions shall determine what I like or dislike in people, in culture, and in the environment.

CHAPTER FOUR

Mistakes Happen without My Knowing It

As summer came to a close on Lake Balaton, the farmland was ready with its bounty for harvest. The potatoes needed to be dug up, the corn shucked, and everything else besides that was green and someway storable had to be picked and preserved from the heavy frostbite looming on the horizon in a few weeks. These were the works I couldn't shirk off or improvise my way out of them. So Mother ordered Laszlo, my brother, and I to sit down at the kitchen table and plan the work schedule for the fast approaching harvest.

"By the end of October, nothing should be left unattended in the field," she insisted.

First on the agenda was digging the potatoes with a pointed hoe. Mother sent me alone to do this on the hill property. She knew exactly what to do, and as always was the case, she thought that I did, too.

But I didn't have the slightest clue about potato digging. The rows I saw, all right, but the potato stalks were already dried and decayed. Nothing indicated where the potatoes were lodging in the soil. It was already late October. So I started at the beginning of the first row, thinking of pound-size potatoes and lots of it. I used the hoe as I always did, scraping the surface of the soil. There were fifteen rows, each about thirty feet long that I had to do. Occasionally a small potato rolled out from the ground as I was shaving the top of it. It took me about three hours to finish the fifteen rows. When finished, I carried home a sack of potatoes, thinking that I did a great job.

"Mother, the work wasn't as bad as I thought it would be," I declared.

"Did you gather the potatoes in a neat pile, Arpad?" Mother asked.

"Yes, Mother, I put the potatoes into my burlap bag, and here they are." And I dropped the bag in front of her.

"Where are the rest of the potatoes?" Bouncing her eyes at me back and forth from the bag.

"That's all I found, Mother, that's all."

"Tell me, my son, how did you do the digging?"

"I took the hoe and shaved the ground with it where the rows were," I answered.

"I have the inkling that you didn't go deep enough, or else the gypsies dug it up," she remarked.

Now, I became confused all of a sudden.

"How deep you think they are buried in the ground?" I asked.

"Anywhere from six to ten inches deep," she answered.

"Mother, you really did not tell me how to dig potatoes. So I took my tool and blended the top of the soil even. Here and there a potato rolled out, and I thought that was it," I told her.

It was now about two o'clock in the afternoon, cloudy and cool and otherwise pleasant to do potato digging. So Mother decided to drag me back to the field in order to prove her point. But she could only prove her point by words rather than by digging. She couldn't bend down to do this kind of work on account of her having a high blood pressure. So she directed me instead to dig potatoes for real this time.

It was my time now to prove how wrong my previous thinking was. Sure enough, the potatoes were between six to ten inches deep, buried in the ground. I dug out pound-size potatoes and lots of it.

The work was a backbreaker. And that was what I really needed to learn my lesson: Ask when you don't know how to do something. Taking things for granted lead to painful redos.

CHAPTER FIVE

A Priestly Lesson

I was already attending third-grade elementary school in a place that was known as the Baron's Residence. (The baron escaped to Austria from the onslaught of Communism.) Out of eighteen students, I was the strongest, the tallest, and the slowest learner; but otherwise, I was the wisest and the shrewdest. I never did my homework, and my classmates knew it. They practically handed me the handwritten copies of their homework assignments. My physical strength was intimidating to them. Since I was always smiling, they couldn't figure out what might lurk behind it. So they were choosing the safer side instead.

Being in class now and no written homework to hand in on account of oral examinations, I was put on the spot. I couldn't answer any question the priest asked me. I became the laughing stock of the whole class. I stood in the classroom like a scarecrow in the garden, allowed the other side to laugh at me. The Augustinian priest gave up hope to keep drilling me for improving my grades, my prayers and my attendance.

"You are going to be the saddest failure in your life unless a heavenly call strikes you," he said.

"I hope it does. Will you be embarrassed then, *Father?*" I asked.

He was very much puzzled from hearing something that sounded like a prophecy. I really didn't know what I was saying, but what I said came without thinking. He ordered me to sit down. What the priest said didn't bother me at all; for I already heard similar words from him a hundred times before. That heavenly call, however, turned out to be a call from hell instead. In a few days, the Secret Police locked the church and took away the priest.

The school years went without improvement in my attitude or my test scores. As far as being troubled in front of my class, I considered that to be a good thing. It strengthened my mind to withstand more of it from others as the time went by. I never withdrew from my classmates. On the contrary, I was on good terms with most of them. When it came to play tactful fighting or soccer, I was a team player. When I saw that bullying was underway, I stepped in and made the bully-minded kid shake hands with the bullied one.

The lesson here was that my stubbornness worked in my favor. It gave me the strength to disregard my ignorance of academic matters, even when I was embarrassed by others. And later when I realized it, it also gave me the strength to improve my character from it.

Bullying My Gypsy Friend

We had a gypsy kid in our class, whose name was Tony. He often needed my protection as he was being bullied by the other boys. Even our teacher, the priest, was shunning him. He assigned Tony to the last seat, all by himself. My classmates avoided him because he smelled like a dirty rag shoved in the corner of a smokehouse. The reasons, of course, were obvious.

Gypsies, who lived close to my village, were the poorest of the poor. They lived in their camps in the outlying area of town and did mostly hired work for little money or food in exchange. Their homes were styled somewhat like ice-cream cones. They fabricated them from secondhand timber. After leaning the pieces together, they covered the exposed areas inside as well as outside with layers of well-meshed straw and clay packs. In the center was the fireplace that was nothing more than a pit dug in the ground. The fire provided the heat for cooking and heating. But they also slept around it on the ground. So it was no surprise that Tony smelled as he did and looked soiled all over. Besides, Tony spoke broken Hungarian as it was not his mother tongue. Gypsies speak their own dialect that Hungarians don't understand.

I had great compassion for Tony because I was only a few steps above him being the poorest of the poor. The differences in culture and tradition between the two of us didn't matter to me one bit. The areas in which we vastly differ from each other, however, related to cleanliness and living conditions. I could neither stand foul smell on my body nor on others near me. Neatness could be my second nature, for in it I saw that my thinking and my behavior were impacted by it.

My ultimate aim now was to change Tony's habits to become cleaner and more organized, thinking that if he cared to be a good friend of mine as I feel that I was a good friend of him, he would follow me. After all, true friends love to imitate each other.

Otherwise, Tony was exceptionally kindhearted. He accepted all that bullying, shunning, and isolation with a meek attitude. Both of us were poor and easy targets to be shunned for different reasons, of course. While he accepted his fate, I rebelled against mine for the better.

As he walked barefoot to school, he passed by my house and I often joined him, also barefoot, till the winter set in. Tony repeated the first grade thrice. He was in school because it was mandatory. What he lacked in schooling, however, he made up in the experience gained through ordinary gypsy life, which was loose, carefree living, bordering on total irresponsibility.

(This, of course, is not characteristic of all the different classes of gypsies. Some are highly educated, especially the musicians and singers. Others are highly skilled artisans. My experience with gypsies related only to the lowest class, mostly to the ones that basically lived from doing as little work as possible, to the ones that did a lot of begging and shrewd stealing instead. Unfortunately, the majority of the gypsies around a lot of villages fell into this category in Hungary as of 1948. I witnessed their actions as I traveled around.)

On my first visit to Tony's hut, it became evident that his mother was that pretty girl whom I saw early summer on that cherry tree. I ran away from her then because I didn't want to tell her where I lived. Tony was her illegitimate child.

Now Tony was bullied one day. On that occasion I purposely stayed away from school in order to skip the midterm examinations. The following day he cried to me over it. He asked me if I had ever been bullied and what I did do about it.

"I was bullied only once, Tony. One of my classmates repeatedly made fun of my wavy, uneven, and messy-looking haircut. He cajoled a couple of other kids to do the same thing. Of course, I laughed off the whole thing as if nothing had happened. But inside, I couldn't bear the pain. I said to myself that I shall get even with this kid. Yes, I shall get even with him tomorrow.

"You see, Tony, getting even is the right thing to do, for he wouldn't have stopped otherwise. This kid should have received deserving punishment long ago, but there was no one brave enough to do it. Ever since he labeled me as *Curly Burly*, I was fuming inside to get even with him.

"I'll tell you now what I did to him. Since he was not a local kid, he bicycled to school every day from the neighboring village. I was now on the lookout for him to find the exact time when he bicycled back. I knew that at the end of my village both sides of the road had ditches dug to drain off the surface water. The left side of the ditch was deeper than the right side and had about a foot of standing water in it. I also knew that this kid bicycled home on that side of the road. So when he reached the ditch, I jumped from behind a cherry tree and pushed him into the water. Then, I jumped right next to him and grabbed his long, bushy hair and pulled his head under water. I held his head underwater until he drank a good amount of water. Then, I pulled his head back and said to him, 'Remember me—from now on my name is Arpad.'"

As I explained this whole thing, Tony's eyes rolled from excitement. He gained courage from my reliving the moment of retribution I did to this kid. His name was Tibor.

"Arpad, don't skip school anymore, or at least tell me when you would do it again. I don't want to be in school when you are not there," Tony said.

This Tibor wasn't much of a figure. He was about five inches shorter than I and was almost half my waistline. But he was a noisy, boisterous daredevil. Everything changed in his behavior after I almost drowned him; for in the following days in school, he behaved as if he had attended boarding school.

Tony wanted to know more.

"Did you really want to drown him?" he asked.

"Of course, I wouldn't have drowned him. But I wanted to keep him underwater so that he would feel what I felt from his insults. I'm sure he was suffering, too. After he regained himself, he said, 'I'll always look up to you from now on. I'm afraid of you.'"

Tony came closer to me now and said, "I'm your friend, and I want to be like you—brave and daring to do things."

Long ago a Hungarian writer said: "In the shadow of a brave man, even the weak becomes strong." Tony well fitted this truism.

I wasn't yet a brave man, only a brave boy, able to foresee sooner than my friends did the coming events. I was smarter, too, than most kids around me because I wasn't bragging all the time as they were. I was listening to them and observing them instead. This way when I had to respond, I had a daring attitude to do so; for I had the facts.

So I replied to Tony:

"You want to be as brave as I am? Well, you cannot be. Every person is different in his own ways. But you can come close to me or even surpass me. Here is how you should begin. Do daring things on your own. If you carry them through, you gain courage. You are now ready for the next one, and the next one. By doing this, you would start believing in yourself and also would build confidence in yourself. But should you make small mistakes along the way, don't stop. Rather, run for the next try. Those who stop and moan over small mistakes lose faith in trying to do it again. Try not to be an imitator, Tony! For imitators are followers of others. Try to be a pioneer of your own making! I'm telling you what I am doing.

"Tony, make a commitment to yourself, if you want to be as I am. However small that commitment is, keep it. Or else, you have deceived yourself. You see, I make small commitments to myself all the time, besides those imposed by my mother. One of those commitments is that I keep myself clean from top to bottom. Sometimes, I lack warm water, so I use cold water. Other times, I don't have soap, so I mix a little bit of lye from the ash pot into my bathing water. I keep this up every day. You should, too. Wash your hands, your face, and your feet every evening, and wash everything else in between at least twice a week.

"Look at yourself now! Wash yourself and look at yourself again! You would feel so good being clean all over. You would surprise everybody else around you, too. You would hear words like 'Tony, you smell clean.' Promise me that from now on you won't show up in school being soiled everywhere. Your nails, too. They look as if you just scraped the soot off the wall in your hut. Remember, Tony, I am your friend. And friends usually follow each other. I am very mindful how you look."

I really meant every word I said to Tony. Even though he felt that I was trying to impose things on him, he wasn't insulted. He was in deep thought now, trying to figure out how he would be able to change himself so that I would like him all the more.

"Arpad, I will try to wash myself, I promise. I'll do that even if I have to do it in the creek along the way to school. I'll clean my nails, too. I'll rub fine sand under my nails to remove the soot. But I don't know what to do with my shirt and pants. I don't have extra ones. You are right. They are soiled."

"Tony, I don't have extra clothes either. But I try to keep my shorts, my shirt, and my pants clean. And how do I do it? I wash them myself once a week. I do it after everybody goes to sleep. They dry by the morning. In earnest, I do this for my own satisfaction because I think the clothes I wear are my feathers. You know, Tony, even birds wash their feathers."

This time I didn't go with Tony to his hut after school. We parted from each other at my house. He had about two miles walk ahead of him. On his way home, he figured out what he would do to clean himself. He decided to skip school until he had found the way to fulfill his promise. Being alone now, he realized that what I said to him about "being dirty all over his body" was true. He felt very embarrassed. At home, his mother was waiting for him as she always did. Tony asked her:

"Mother, do you love me?"

"That's stupid what you just said. Which mother wouldn't love her only child?"

"Well, if that is so, then find the way that I can wash myself every day and my clothes, too. Everybody hates me in school because I smell like an outhouse. You know, Mother, I am beginning to hate myself on account of this. I don't want to live like this. Put me away for good. Then, my embarrassment would be over." Tony cried in his mother's lap.

What Tony said to his mother was a shock to her, for she was soiled all over, too. He took example from her. She didn't know now what to say to Tony. The shock, however, sent her mind spinning, thinking, *This kid of mine is really teaching me a lesson that would take me some time to figure out how to solve.*

Tony stopped crying and jumped away from her mother as if it were ordered that way by me, his closest friend. He said to her loud and clear:

"My crying cleared my mind how to fix my dirtiness. Look, Mother, it is not that hard. The two things I need most, we already have. There is the pail, and there is the big vat outside, full of rainwater. Now, I only need soap—can you get that for me, Mother?"

"I don't have any money, but I'll go to the village and beg for homemade soap. Come to think of it, the place I worked a little bit yesterday just made soap from pork fat and ash lye. Maybe they can spare me a little," she answered.

My ghost was prompting Tony to find ways to do things on his own, after all he remembered me. The necessity to clean himself was on his mind like craving for water in the desert. He was ready to find the shortest way to it—rainwater.

CHAPTER SIX

Looking for Soap in the Gypsy Camp

There are twenty huts and two small shed-type structures in Tony's gypsy camp. Tony wants to look at every one of them during the time he was out of school. He wants to find out what they do, how they live, but mostly, how they wash themselves. Before even having a good look round, he met the head of the tribe and his son midway to the camp. Each was carrying an oblong vat, hewed out from a large trunk of an elm tree. The hollow part of the vats covered partially their heads, and the rest hid their backs down to their knees. They were going to a village oppositely located from my village.

From an overall view, Tony noticed that this settlement had no regular pattern to it. Dirt roads were winding like a snake from hut to hut in short distances. It had one outhouse and one dug well. There were no trees anywhere nearby as they were cut down for firewood.

As the father faced Tony, he set his vat on the ground and started questioning Tony.

"Who are you, young fellow?"

"I'm Tony, and I live in the first hut at the other end. I'm looking for someone who might have soap."

"Wrong place! We don't use soap around here. Go to the city. They need to wash themselves every day because they can't stand each other," said the old gypsy.

"How do you wash yourself then?" Tony asked.

"I don't. I jump in a pool of water, yonder, in the creek and whirl around a few times. The water removes the dirt but leaves the oil on my skin. And that's good. It protects my skin from chapping," said the old gypsy. Then, he paused and took a deeper look at Tony and continued, "You say you live here. How come that I don't know you and haven't seen you here before?"

"I moved here with my mother a few weeks ago before my school started. The hut is not ours. It belonged to her boyfriend who hung himself a month ago. You heard that, haven't you?"

"I did, but I didn't pay attention to it because he didn't belong to our clan. Every hut here in this camp, except the one you live in, is owned by my family, my sons and daughters. That guy, whose name was Bane, was an outcast here. He wanted to marry one of my daughters, but I disapproved the marriage because he was always drunk. But most of all, he was from a different bloodline. So, as far as I'm concerned, you are also an outcast here. Turn around and run back to your place and look elsewhere for a soap maker." He swung his cane at Tony.

The old man waited at the same spot until Tony disappeared. Tony was disappointed. He didn't expect this kind of rejection and much less expected to learn that the whole camp belonged to one family.

"What's a bloodline?" he pondered.

On his way back he was considering that he, too, should try to jump into this pool of water in the creek until his mother has found soap.

The creek was the same creek he passed by whenever he went to school. The pool of water the old man was talking about was somewhere part of this meandering creek. It was hidden in the woods and wasn't visible from the dirt walkway on which Tony travels to school. Thick bush covered the edges of the creek in this area, and it was almost impossible to break through it. He would have to stoop down almost to a crawl to reach the creek. But he found the courage to clear a path through the briars and wild rose bushes to reach it.

Some of the thickets he uprooted with his hands; some he broke off. The wild rose bushes he sidestepped, for the thorns on them had already pricked his hands all over. When he finally reached the creek, he got scared. The water in the pool was so clear and clean and deep that he didn't dare to step into it, thinking that he might drown, or it would outright swallow him. He also saw that the creek meandered next by the gypsy camp; thereby the gypsies had unhindered path to it.

There are no lily pads or wild grass growing at the edges of the pool, and it couldn't be reached from anywhere else except through the creek. The size of the pool was only about half an acre, and the water in it was slowly emptying itself into the creek. Now, Tony stepped into the creek which was only a few inches deep and was dotted with small stones, big enough though that the water churned over them. He was scared to death to go close to the pool, for he didn't know how to swim. As he tiptoed in the creek, he realized that the water was lukewarm. It was unreal for him to accept the fact that in late October the water in a gently flowing creek could be so warm. He should have guessed it, however, from the steam that whirled ever so gently over his head.

It turned out that the pool of water was fed by a warm spring that emptied itself into the shallow creek and rather quickly cooled off in the shallow basin downstream.

Tony lived only a half a mile from the pool. It was a great joy for him that he found water, for he could now forget about the soap and all that fuss that would involve washing himself inside the hut where even elbow room had to be negotiated. The pool area was also very private, but for now, he could only linger at the mouth of it, where it emptied into the creek. His next thought was to tell me about his pleasant discovery and urge me to come with him to it so that I could teach him how to swim.

It was toward evening when he arrived back to his hut from the pool. Good news awaited for him there. His mother received tree bars of homemade soap from a peasant for whom she worked today.

"These peasants exploited me today." She said, "I did the hardest and dirtiest work for them. I had to clean out the outhouse for three bars of soap. The whole neighborhood rushed to the place just as I was finishing it; they chased me off the job on account that the reek from the waste spread through the air like smoke. The good thing was that I already had the soap in my bag. I ran out of that village as if a wild dog were chasing me. I was lucky, though, I didn't lose the soap along the way. Now, we have soap to wash ourselves—tell me, Tony, what did you do all day?"

"I went walking through this camp today. As I did, I met this old gypsy and his son midway to the camp. He was rude and unkind to me. He also chased me away because, by his account, I had no business being there. He said that the whole camp, except our hut, belonged to his family and, furthermore, that everyone there was from his bloodline. 'Strangers were outcasts,' he said as he chased me. Can you tell me what *bloodline* means?'"

"I don't know what it means. But what I heard from Bane when he was still alive was that this whole bunch of gypsies married each other within the same family. And I think that's why there are so many of them crippled or otherwise crazy. Anyway, why did you go there?"

"I wanted to look around the whole camp because I wanted to help you find a bar of soap. As it turned out, the old man told me that they don't use soap, that they go to a pool of water nearby and wash themselves in it. He sent me to the city to look for soap. 'They were the ones needed to wash themselves,' he said. Then, he chased me off with his walking stick, swinging it at me.

"Then, I wanted to find this pool he was talking about, but he chased me off. Thereafter, I didn't dare to go to the end of the camp from where the gypsy approached the pool. So I turned around and went the other way, the way I go to school. It took me quite a while to reach the pool as I had to clear a path to it. I just finished it."

* * *

It was unbeknownst to Tony that the pool of water was only a side pocket to the creek. The creek itself does not start at the pool. It was slowly churning from north to south through the old man's family camp. Even though the creek's water was cold at the camp, the old man and his family had enough water from it to satisfy their needs. But to take a bath, they had to wade in the creek a few hundred feet south in order to reach the pool.

Now, Tony became worried that he may someday encounter the gypsy at the pool. The thought filled his mind with resentment toward the old man. He would have to be on the lookout now for him if he wanted to avoid him.

A few days after the old man chased him off the camp, Tony was playing with his dog in front of his hut when he heard loud cries and wails coming from the direction of the camp. At that same moment, his eyes caught the sight of my jogging on the dirt road toward him. In his joy seeing me, he and his dog ran toward me to bring me the good news, that he found a pool of warm water in which he could bathe himself until his skin wore off, but only if I would teach him how to swim.

Because I didn't see Tony ever since I upbraided him for his soiled body and clothes, I was very much concerned about him; and for this reason, I came to visit him. As soon as we reached each other, we practically fell into each other's arms. The joy of seeing each other kept our hands on each other's shoulders, and we both erupted at the same time to tell what went on with us in the past few days. As I was still gasping for air after my long jog, I was happy to let Tony to do the talking first. Let me tell you that he had so much to talk about that he didn't know where to begin or where to end his stories.

Suddenly, we both heard the same loud cry followed by wailing. Tony rushed to say, "Let's check this out. Something funny is going on there. I'm hearing the same cry repeatedly. It could only be of two things, Arpad,—either a wedding or a funeral."

"No. It could also be an engagement celebration," I replied.

So we turned around. Tony led me to the pool of water through the path he cleared, telling me nonstop how hard he worked at it and also his worries about drowning in it—unless I would teach him swimming.

I held back my promise to teach Tony how to swim, for promising something meant that I would have to keep it. Now teaching Tony how to swim was a very difficult thing to do. Unsuccessfully healing his fears of drowning meant that unknowingly he could face death itself. So I let Tony keep talking about it for talking about it, in itself, was overcoming the fear of drowning.

The round stones on the bottom of the creek prevented us from finding steady footing, so we dragged our feet from stone to stone as we passed by the pool. I switched my position now to the poolside so that Tony wouldn't accidentally stumble into it and drown. For the strength of a drowning person could easily outweigh the strength of the rescuer, unless he knew what he was doing. I know this from rescuing my sister, Ella, from drowning in Lake Balaton in two feet of water. So we passed the pool without incident although Tony kept persuading me that I should teach him swimming in this pool. We barely passed the pool, however, and Tony turned around.

"Although I don't know how to swim, I am thinking from the beginning that inviting you here might give me a peace of mind and the courage that upon seeing you swim, I, too, might try to follow you. You see, Arpad, I desperately want to clean myself as I hate myself being smelly. But now, I feel that I have to choose between life and death on account of your hesitation to teach me swimming. Would you please change your mind and teach me how to swim, now?"

"Of course, I'll teach you now. We shall start first right here in the creek—the safe way. That was the way I learned how to swim also, first in shallow waters. You have the same problem I had. Panic took over my mind before I even stepped into the water. So ease your mind now and think that you are a dog, walking and paddling in the water at the same time.

"Look, this creek has a few small pockets of water, here and there. You see it? Let's go to that one over there. Now, get down on your knees and reach the bottom with your hands right here in this pocket of water. I'll do the same thing so you can feel confident. But look at me first. I'll show you the breathing technique that you must understand and do now. Your body will not sink underwater as long as it is full of air. So let's practice that first.

"Take a deep breath and hold it for as long as you can. Let the air out now and take another breath. Hold that longer. Practice this a few times so as you understand why you have to do it. Now, let's sit down in this knee-deep pool here. Okay? Now take another deep breath and hold it this time as long as you can. Lie down now with your back completely in the water while holding your breath. Don't panic! My hand is under your back to hold you up. You see, you're floating like a dry stick. Let the air out now completely, and you'll sink. Do it! I'm holding you up, just enough that you realize what's going on. Keep practicing this a few times alone as I'm watching you doing it from the side. And keep alternating your body in the water, belly up, belly down. Make sure, you practice the floating and sinking of your body as you let the air in and out," I emphasized.

I stepped aside and watched him. I noticed, however, that Tony was cheating himself. Of course, he didn't know that he was doing it. It was his subconscious mind doing it. While he was doing the floating and sinking practice, he kept touching the bottom of the water, making sure that nobody pulled it away from under him. I waited a while longer to see if he would realize what he was doing, but he didn't. So I interfered and stopped him.

"Tony, you really don't need your hands to do this practice, you know. Why are you continually wanting to support your body by touching the bottom?"

"I have that fear that I'm going to drown, Arpad."

"Now, look at me. I'm going to show you that you won't sink. I'm going to take a deep breath and hold the air in my body and lie on the top of the water motionless. My hands will be firmly held at my sides. You just keep watching me. My head will never sink underwater so long as my body is full of the air."

Tony watched as I showed him how the inhaled air kept me floating. He was completely relieved. His fear of drowning subsided, and he immediately jumped next to me to imitate me. We kept practicing until Tony became completely sure of himself.

Tony successfully finished the first step—the control of breathing. And he did it very well because he wanted to learn how to swim, no matter what....

"This was so simple that I feel outright stupid realizing that it took me almost two hours to make my body float just by holding the air in it. Where did you get this idea, anyway?" he asked.

"This is not an idea, Tony. It's a fact. Take a ball and throw it in the water. It will float unless the air is pushed out of it and replaced with something heavier than water. Now, to answer your question, I learned this breathing technique and swimming from my brother. He is a lifeguard at the local beach at Lake Balaton."

Tony was so excited from the gained confidence that he wanted to go swimming right of way in the pool, but I held him back. "You are not yet ready to swim, Tony. If you try swimming now, you would drown. Tomorrow, I shall come back and teach you the next step, how to combine two swimming techniques, the control of your breathing with the movements of your hands and feet. Watch me as I give you a foretaste of it."

So I jumped into the deeper part of the pool and swam there like a frog, showing my skills to Tony as to how the two techniques when coordinated worked to make my body a plaything in the water. From seeing what I did, Tony realized that learning to swim was a lot more than just jumping in the water. The thought of tomorrow boosted his confidence like that of a fledgling bird, frequently flapping its wings in his nest, practicing to fly out of it tomorrow.

* * *

The crying and the wailing that we heard before kept our curiosity alive as we left the pool area. This time, we walked to the place, following the edge of the creek that bordered the gypsy camp. We became afraid, however, as we approached the camp site.

"Let's go up this hillside, and we shall see from there what these gypsies are doing," Tony remarked.

As we walked to the top of the hill and looked back, we saw that there was a small cemetery with a fresh grave in the center of it, already covered with lots of fresh flowers and wreaths. We were convinced that somebody died.

"The old gypsy may have died. If that would be the case, I wouldn't have to worry anymore seeing him at the pool." Tony was highly relieved.

It was almost sunset on the horizon. So I had to run home to my worried mother because I didn't tell her where I went. In fact, my visit to Tony meant to be only a stopover. Instead, it lasted more than three hours. I was supposed to gather kindle wood in the forest that was located between my house and Tony's hut. But that did not happen, because of the unexpected swimming lessons I gave to my friend.

Seeing Tony again tomorrow never came to pass. Tony's hut was burned down that very night by the gypsies from the old man's family. It was always regarded by the members of the clan as an outcast place. Tony's dog perished in the fire. He and his mother were not aware of the fire, however, as they were out in the field somewhere, hand-digging (stealing) potatoes for the winter months.

After realizing that their hut burned to the ground, both of them ran away from the site and hid themselves in the nearby forest, fearing for their lives. At dawn, they decided to go back to Romania without saying anything to anybody. Tony's mother came from Romania. Her family had their own gypsy camp already established there.

I came back to revisit Tony the following day as I promised it. What I saw at the site put me in a state of shock. I sat on top of that stump to which Tony's dog used to be tied. There, I lamented awhile over losing my friend forever.

Longer Than His Passing

I cried my eyes out for a good friend.
He had his trust and faith in me.
Forget now his looks and manners,
But don't forget what he left behind:
Enduring memories of a kind gypsy boy,

Evasive tears will not fade my love for him,
Lasting shall be his friendship that time shall not erase.
A good friend stays in my heart longer than his passing.

CHAPTER SEVEN

My Father, Gal Laszlo

Most of the information written here about my father is collected from those who knew him; therefore it is secondhand information. I personally don't remember him. Whatever took place before I was six years old, I have no accurate recollection of those events. My oldest sister, Iren, who is sixteen years older than I am and with whom I had many times discussed the life of our father—she revealed to me most of the stories written here. The rest of the information, I received in tidbits from others who either knew him or heard about him. In order for me to create from this fragmented information a believable story about my father's life, I added my own consequential interpretation and placed them in contextual order.

As a father, he was a great provider to sustain a good life for us while he was with us. He had no inkling whatsoever that the Russians were nabbing the able-bodied men they could find and transport them to *labor camps* in Russia in order to keep Stalin's war efforts in high-gear operation against the Nazis. My father became one of them.

Father was born around 1903 in Savoly, Hungary, into a peasant family. He was the oldest of three children, two girls and a boy. *Matild*, a major player in my early life, is one of the girls.

My grandfather on Father's side was a peasant in Savoly; but he was also a shepherd in a neighboring village, where the land belonged to a baron, hence to the nobility. My father and his sisters grew up in Savoly. When my father was about to become married to my mother, his father went to Balatonkeresztur and bought there a duplex house. He gave the smaller half to my father, who was at that time about twenty-two years old, and the bigger half he gave to Matild, my aunt, who stayed unmarried for a long time, probably till her early sixties.

Before Father married Mother, he already had a full-time job at the local railroad station. He worked there as a manual laborer, maintaining the tracks and looking out for the safe operation of those tracks. That was his main responsibility, manually switching tracks to control the safe movement of rail traffic. He stayed with the National Railroad Corporation until his disappearance in 1945.

In return to the employees, the National Railroad Corporation provided the best fringe benefits for life. The whole family received free medical and hospitalization services, and accidental insurance. In addition to that, we also received free travel allowance and free pension benefits had he died early. Moreover, the corporation also provided free housing allowance wherever Father was transferred. For unknown reasons, he was transferred several times, and as such, the family moved with him—hence the reason as to why we moved so often to different locations.

Father was about six-foot-three-inch tall with a medium-size torso, long legs and hands. I have one picture of him, showing his body features. He doesn't appear to be a handsome man. He had a well-groomed, short mustache and looked much older than his age. Conceivably much wine drinking took its toll on him. The picture also reveals his Roman nose on a long, skinny face with a small mouth and almost pointed chin. His hair was black and very neatly combed. The color of his eyes was also black—so says my sister—and the way he looked with them suggested that they were beady and pointedly piercing.

Two of his avocations caught the attention of all those who met him or had anything worthwhile to do with him. These were wine drinking and poaching, his most outstanding and aggressive pursuits.

He had avidly pursued both of these destructive habits; but for him, they were pervasive hobbies that nothing, except death, could have erased. And eventually in a Russian labor camp, he died.

Certain areas of Hungary is wine-growing country and, appropriately believed, wine-drinking country as well. In Balatonkeresztur I didn't know any peasant who didn't have a small vineyard planted somewhere on his property. While wine is an alcoholic beverage, it is also part of the food chain here and consumed with gusto at any time of the day. I grew up believing this as everybody else did. So Father drank wine more perhaps than he should have, but he was not an alcoholic. He was perfectly fine when he didn't put his lips to the bottle. But when he did, he was aggressive.

Although he didn't have a vineyard, he always had wine available to him through his circle of friends within the boundary of at least seven villages. His best friend was my godfather. Sticking together as buddies, they were the biggest poachers in the whole county. There weren't enough rangers in the county that could have been assigned for their capture. And those who were looking for them were also their buddies, collaborating and drinking together and sharing the wild games they caught.

They never left evidence behind themselves that could have been used as material witness against their poaching activities. And their friends wouldn't dare to turn them in. Within their territorial expanse, they kept several guns hidden. So whichever direction they went hunting, they had a gun with ammunition available. In return for this cooperative spirit, their friends received plenty of wild games, such as rabbits, pheasants, deer, and boars. Who were actually these friends? Nobody really knew it because the two kept it a top secret. Besides, their activities took place during night hours, the best time to gun down wild game.

Surely, they had plenty of wine flowing that kept their nerves charged to pursue poaching. One thing, however, could have easily revealed how broad their circle of friendship was—the number of keys they had in their possession. Everyone with whom they cooperated had given a key to them to their wine cellars in exchange for wild game. This way, they could freely enter their friends' cellars, where both the guns and the wine were kept. In return, a wild game or two was left behind every time a cellar was visited. The amazing part of this whole episode is that they were never apprehended.

In due time, as my father was transferred to different locations in his employment, the circle of friends on his side had slowly dwindled with one exception: the relationship between my father and godfather. That had lasted until my father was deported to Siberia. (Later, I shall recount both the most thrilling and the most amazing part of my youthful life with my godfather.)

My Mother, Baranyai Julianna

On my mother's side, I didn't do any research as to who were her parents. Those who had intimate knowledge of them died before I had the opportunity to ask them. And I was no longer interested in secondhand information. Although on a couple of occasions, I met her mother and her three cousins. It would be unfair, however, to write only impressions.

But I must mention here the fact that after mother's death, it was my grandmother who tenderly took care of me and my sister, Ella, for a week at our house. I said "*tenderly took care*" of us for a very good reason. This grandmother had such loving and caring personality that no other member from my entire family equaled it. She never gave me anything without a smile and a kiss on my cheek. And she never missed a day waiting for me with cooked food and serving it after giving thanks to God. She never put me to bed without saying a prayer over me and giving me a good-night kiss. Sixty years later, I still see her as vividly in my soul as on that day when Mother died. So impressive her personality was that I followed her examples with my own children in later years.

Nothing else I needed more after Mother died than the tender love and care my sweet grandmother gave me. The year was 1950. Words didn't mean much to me then. But rather, it was her silent crying, meek behavior, and undivided attention in caring for me and Ella, my older sister, that carried us through our grief.

My mother had a number of physical features inherited from my grandmother. She was six feet tall. That immediately revealed she was in command. With black, slightly recessed eyes and somewhat pointed, long nose, featured on an oblong, puffy face, she meant every word she said. Her rosy cheek and always pleated black hair riveted even her enemies to marvel her beauty. She had subdued smiles, occasionally showing her perfectly formed teeth between her even lips that were created more to keeping them shut than expressing gossip. Her composure demanded quick response in action from others and less talk doing it. My oldest sister, Iren, is her unmistakable replica in looks and actions. Iren is a major cast in the story, and through her actions a lot could be surmised about my mother.

After the war, getting medical attention to treat mother's high blood pressure was next to impossible to find. Doctors were scarce. Four to five villages had one doctor, but without the means of transportation to reach them. Medicine was unavailable. As a result, Mother suffered a stroke while she was at home. Somebody called the doctor to come, but he didn't come. Instead, he called an ambulance that took her to the nearest hospital, ten miles away. There, the doctors let her recover on her own strength. But she couldn't. The second stroke completely paralyzed her, and the next day she died in the hospital. She died at age forty-six. I was at that time eleven and a half years old. Her final resting place is located in the monumental cemetery of Keszthely, Hungary. In order to keep her grave sacred to me, I encased the entire grave site in ornamental concrete and added on the top of it a fitting headstone in 1965.

CHAPTER EIGHT

After Mother's Death

It was the same doctor who sent Mother to the hospital who notified us of her death. Since there was no telephone available, this doctor waited almost a day before he drove his car to our house to let us know that she died. It was the beginning of July 1950, very hot summer days. Our concern was that the decaying body had to be buried fast in order to prevent stench. To this day, I don't know who called on all my relatives as to what had happened. But within two days, everybody gathered for her funeral at the morgue of the cemetery in Keszthely.

There was no funeral, however, because Mother was not yet in the coffin. So everybody went back home to wait another day for the funeral. The big problem was that nobody had money to buy the coffin. In desperation, Iren, my oldest sister, had to borrow it from the local grocery-store owner on promise of quick repayment. The man trusted my sister, for she was a well-respected young woman in town. Everybody knew her from the early days before she got married. It was now four days before Mother could finally be buried. Many of the relatives who showed up the first time for the funeral didn't show up the second time. So it happened that only a few of us were present at the cemetery's chapel for the burial ceremony.

After the funeral, everybody traveled back to where they came from. I and my two sisters, together with Matild, went back to Balatonkeresztur. Only my grandmother from my mother's side was waiting for us at home. She was waiting for all of us with cooked meals. We sat down with cried-out eyes and were looking at each other through the still-trickling tears, slowly waning. My oldest sister, Iren, had the strongest will and realized that too much thinking and speaking about our miseries thwarted her determination from planning our future. Besides Ella and I, she had her own five children back in Rackeresztur, waiting for her return. She now waited for us to finish our food before she would begin talking about what to do with the two of us.

That decision had to be made between her and Matild for there was no one else around who could care and watch over us. My only brother, Laszlo, was in the army who otherwise would have taken care of us. In order to keep the atmosphere calm and discrete among us, Matild invited Iren to go to her side of the duplex. In the meantime, we spent the next few hours with my sweet grandmother.

The calmness and discreteness, however, lasted only until they closed the door behind themselves in Matild's kitchen. The wall that separated the two sections of the duplex was not soundproof, and any louder-than-normal voice could be clearly heard on our side. I, of course, kept my ears close to the wall in order to hear everything discussed about us. Although I had my own idea about what would happen to us, there wasn't much that I could do about it. I couldn't earn my living and didn't have as yet the experience in making sound decisions.

As I was uselessly trying to figure out how the two decision-makers on the other side of the wall would settle the course of our lives, I became convinced that we would be like two fledglings, losing their mother—learn to survive on your own. I heard how they were fighting over us. They handled the matter as if we were merchandise at a farmers market, being evaluated as to which one of us would be more useful or less problematic than the other. I thought how cheap our life is. The value of our souls, the very essence of our beings, has been totally disregarded. The two cared about the material ownership of our bodies only.

The perception of truth about human nature began to dawn in my mind wide open at that moment—how cruel the nature of men is.

"I'll take both kids with me!" Iren said.

"I have a better idea. You take the girl and leave the boy with me," replied Matild.

Iren wanted us to stay together for a while. That way it would have been easier for her to convince the authorities to grant her official guardianship over us and thereby enable her to receive our father's pension to support us.

Matild wanted me to stay with her instead. That would have given her an extra worker to exploit as her husband was half-crippled.

The haggling now moved into a new phase. They were trying to read each other's mind. Each wanted to collect some sort of windfall from our misery. My sister insisted that we stay together, while Matild desisted that we don't. Finally, they called each other *viper*.

"The two kids are mine, and I'll take them home with me tomorrow," said Iren to Matild.

For now, it didn't exactly happen that way, because my brother was already on his way home from the army. He hoped that Mother was not yet buried. He missed the funeral by two days however.

For about an hour, while he locked himself in the bedroom, my brother bitterly cried over Mother's death. Ella and I commiserated with him as we sat on the kitchen floor. We waited there for everybody—for Brother to stop sobbing, for the other two to stop the subterfuge.

We were just sitting and gazing at each other, blindly trying to read each other's mind. We didn't know what to say or how to say what we had in mind. Ella and I were the center pieces in their eyes, while they were the centerpieces in ours. Feeling that another storm was looming, I became restless and testy and yelled: "What are you two going to do with us this time?"

My brother sensed that I had already asked this question before in response to a previously revved up conversation. He didn't know, however, that Matild and Iren had already torn each other apart over us for hours. He didn't know either that I was hearing through the kitchen wall all of it and yelled over in my anger the same question at least twice before. But their deeply set schemes blocked their hearing it. This time, I said to my brother that the two were harboring deep jealousy and greed over our future. Finally, he broke his silence and said, "Let them kill each other over you."

My brother was not even an iota different from the other two. Had the two abandoned us, he would have collected Father's pension. His plan was to convince the army that he was our guardian now; therefore he should be excused from serving and be allowed to come home to take care of us.

* * *

While Mother was still living, my life was a great joy. I cared the least what happened in the world or, for that matter, in the village. The flowers by the roadside looked more beautiful than they really were. I used to make arrangements from them for her to turn her anger to forgiveness, as I didn't always do what I was supposed to do for her.

The singing larks over the wheat fields invited my spirit to dance in circles amidst the wild flowers. Nobody saw it; nobody knew it how beautiful life was as my caring mother always forgave my mischief.

Now, I was hearing the church bells mournfully peeling at the cemetery's chapel. The imaginary sound crushed my heart. My tears were pouring over my mother's casket being slowly lowered deeper and deeper into that everlasting darkness. Thank God that I had been daydreaming. The great joy of this boy had ended with it. Many times I relived that burial event, for that alone kept me sane from burying myself in dissolution.

I couldn't bring back the joyful past and replay it again. I could only think about it. In times of sadness what I did wrong to her haunted me more than anything else. But it was time now to settle it in my mind that whatever had happened in the past should only be a reminder for correcting my ways as I was moving forward. There wasn't much to correct, however, for I was only eleven and a half years old when Mother passed away.

My future was at a standstill now waiting for others to shape it in the right or in the wrong direction. I could only listen and guess what was coming into my life by the two decision-makers. Nevertheless, I was seldom more alert and more attentive as to what Iren and Matild wanted to do with us. Since the future was not mine to tell and the past was not possible to relive, I was more in despair than ever before. It brought about the most boring moments in my life. I was much like a dog, waiting for his owner to give him directions. However, my owner was dead now, and sound direction was not coming either from Iren or from Matild. All the trouble caring for the two of us was perhaps never more difficult than now because there wasn't much food or money around to feed additional mouths. The Communist takeover of Hungary (1948) deprived the people of their freedom and independence to plan their future.

* * *

As a young kid, I already went through brainwashing at the hands of my school teachers, trying to convince me that the truth about what's right and what's wrong was proclaimed only in the *Communistic ideology* of Marx, Lenin, and Stalin. They, too, as well as the rest of the Communists, regarded the humans as animals in the field, ready to be herded and moved to different pastures. Those pastures, of course, are now in a new field—the Communistic ideology. When I witnessed how the Communist agents (the Secret Police) persecuted the innocent peasants in my village, I realized that the truth was not what man had in his mind, but rather what he did with it in his actions. Similarly, Ella and I would soon find out what kind of action Iren and Matild would exercise over us.

Grandmother had already returned to her home which was located in the next town, Balatonbereny.

Now both Matild and Iren heard the heart-rending cry from Laszlo, my brother, resonating through the wall with such a touching feeling that they, too, were moved to tears. That sound instantly transformed their bitterness toward each other to peaceful behavior, thinking momentarily that nobody would feel sorry for them should they die tomorrow. So they agreed, instead, to let my brother decide what should happen to us. They also agreed that Ella and I should have some say in this matter because, after all, we were the ones who would have to adjust ourselves to the new way of living from now on.

My brother, Laszlo, had by this time evaluated the gravity of the situation and had determined that he couldn't do anything for us— even if he wanted to—on account of being a soldier far away from home. So he abruptly got up and picked up his meager belongings and packed them into his army bag. Then he hugged and kissed us and said: "Go back to Iren and Matild. They will take care of you. I shall always treasure both of you in my heart."

And he left without saying as much as *good-bye* to Iren and Matild. For unknown reasons, he disliked both of them. He shut the door behind himself without looking back. He returned to the army.

We didn't go back to join the two next door for we didn't want to hear the outcome of their decision. I said to Ella that no matter how things are going to turn out, we'll always be united, even if only in spirit.

* * *

We knew that hardship would be waiting for us as soon as we left our home. Ella and I were now in that predicament. Tomorrow, we would be leaving our house to join a bunch of unknown kids, the sons and daughters of our oldest sister, Iren. It had become a fact what Iren previously said to Matild: "The two kids are mine, and I'll take them home with me tomorrow."

That unknown world that would be coming upon us would now be a never-ending journey. It would be the biggest change in our lives that would alter everything we have gotten used to in our home to something else that would be frequently changing. Now that we are orphans, our life would be guided by others, without hugs and kisses that orphans needed, too.

While we were fearful of the unknown, we were at the same time hoping for the better. And I said to Ella that we must have steadfast courage to withstand everything for that was the secret of survival. My steadfast courage drove me to catch rabbits, drove me to pick cherries, and drove me to climb trees to throw down the crows' nests for pennies to enable me to buy candies. "Don't you worry, Sister, I'll show you the way!" I hugged her.

Ella and I had no say now in our moving away. We were under Iren's control, who made the decisions for us. And the outcome of those decisions happened very quickly. Just as Iren told Matild what she will be doing, she told us the same thing. She ordered us to pack all our clothes and shoes tightly in burlap bags, one bag for each. She would then make backpacks from them that we could easily carry on our backs. This was the easiest thing to do, for we barely had anything to pack.

After I finished packing, I looked for Iren, who was at that moment with Matild, ironing out any unfinished business. The last part of their heated discussion reached my ears as I moved closer and closer to her: "Don't you even think to rummage through their house and vacate its contents and turn it into your barn!" Iren threatened.

What I had in mind now was to ask the two the same subject matter they were fighting over. What will happen to our possessions inside the house after we left?

But after hearing the ugly skirmish between the two, I lost whatever politeness I had in my disposition. The thought of coming back here later at the end of summer and finding everything missing or even destroyed troubled me. I was afraid that Matild would do just such a thing. So I wanted to reassure myself that that wouldn't happen.

"The reason why I want to break up your bickering is I want both of you to understand that I also have my own say in this matter as to who would be taking apart our belongings after we left our home. I say it to both of you now. Nobody! My heart is attached to our belongings. I'll be a threat to that person who dares to do otherwise." And I left both of them in shock.

Afterward, I was wondering whether what I said meant anything. Would Matild take it as a joke, coming from such a young kid? But I took no chances. I turned around and went back to the two and looked into their eyes, swinging my head back and forth so they notice my anger.

"I just want to make sure that you understood what I said before. Now, I want to add one more thing to it. I'll shutter the bedroom window, and I'll lock the bedroom door in order to keep my belongings safe, for I'll be back at the end of summer. And if I find that the lock was destroyed, that hand that did it better be hidden because I'll reshape it with a stick."

My sister Iren knew that what I said was directly intended to warn Matild. She was doing the same thing to her in different ways.

Matild finally realized that what I said was a serious matter and responded: "Arpad really has his own mind. I'll do as he said. I'm beginning to be afraid of him."

"No, you don't have to be afraid of Arpad," Iren retorted. "He senses what's right and what's wrong. You are old enough to know what's right. Do what's right then, and he will love you for it."

Iren finished saying all that she wanted to say to Matild for now. The next thing on her mind was to decide what to do with the animals and the two separate properties we owned.

* * *

Iren wanted to get rid of all the ducks before we left, but she needed help to kill so many of them at once. Therefore, she ordered us to help her. We now would have to kill fifteen ducks, one by one. Then, we would have to scald, de-feather, and clean them. This would be a real teamwork among the three of us, I thought.

Here, I would learn that individual attention to the details meant everything to a mistake-free outcome even though killing ducks did not amount to much of anything. Still, there was a routine process to it. So it was Iren now who laid out the most important details—the planning. What I took for granted before had become a disciplined, step-by-step approach now, for planning required total knowledge of the entire project. And only Iren had that kind of experience. First, the detailed steps and the sequences of those steps she so laid out that the whole project would become an integrated effort.

Otherwise, we would have been correcting each other in confusion all day long. The second part was training us how to carry out the verbally laid-out steps.

So Iren said to Ella: "Just as I explained before, you must get rid of all your attachments toward these ducks—about slaughtering them. That's why the Almighty created them. I know that you regard these ducks as your pets, but we don't raise pets because we don't have room for them, or the money to feed them."

I had no problems slaughtering animals to be cooked for a hearty meal, for that meant my survival. It was Ella who was confused about whether animals were created for pets or for food. When these ducks hatched, she fed them and cuddled them. They thought that Ella was their mother. They followed her everywhere. When she stopped, they stopped; when she ran, they ran. Ella loved these ducks more than any other animals and wanted nothing to do with slaughtering them. Now, she was crying. The whole episode left in me something to remember forever—don't regard animals as you regard humans for your heart would break when you have to part from them.

Killing one duck or a chicken would not have been hard to accomplish, but now, we would have to do it to fifteen ducks. I thought my fingers would wear off from plucking feathers after scalding. Just the thought of it tired me already. On top of that, I hated the smell of scalded feathers. I was ready now to face the spitball.

I was hoping that Iren would give up the whole project and that she would leave the ducks alone for me and Matild to worry about them later, after I returned from Rackeresztur at the end of summer.

So because of Ella's crying, Iren decided to give up killing fifteen ducks in one day. She reached a compromise with her and settled on three ducks instead.

"My wish came through. Lucky me!" Ella happily exclaimed.

"One, two, three. I'll do it all by myself," Iren quipped. "It will be faster than troubling myself to show you what to do. Learn it on your own, the hard way."

Within an hour she returned to the kitchen. A wooden bowl she carried was full of duck parts, cleaned and ready for frying. She then lit the potbelly stove. Then, she placed the fatty pieces first in a large frying pan, added a half a cup of water to it, and let the whole thing simmer. After enough fat exuded, she added the legs and breast and slowly fried them till they turned into a crispy-looking delicacy. The odor reached Matild's nose, and she followed the smell. She used the occasion as a ruse to investigate the latest in our preparation for traveling tomorrow. She didn't know as yet that twelve more ducks would be left until I returned at the end of summer.

Before Matild entered the kitchen, however, I stepped outside and turned her around, embracing her shoulders with my right arm and saying to her: "Iren is upset because we didn't help her kill fifteen ducks. So she only killed three of them. The rest, you and I will take care when I return at the end of summer. You and I will have a feast. Sounds great, doesn't it?"

"Not exactly. I haven't figured out yet how you and I will get along, never mind living together. Taking care of you, suddenly, would be on my shoulders."

"Why should you worry yourself over that? I'm strong and handy and am willing to help you. Besides, I can take care of myself if you let me," I whispered it in her ears.

Iren interrupted our seemingly cozy relationship by calling us back. She had the ducks fried and was ready to serve dinner early.

"Come, Matild, and sit at the table in the other room. Consider this as our farewell dinner. Tomorrow morning, we are leaving you alone for a long time," she said.

Matild didn't reply. Her mind was busy figuring the consequences of what "leaving you alone for a long time" meant.

Eating together for the last time gave Iren the opportunity to nail down the final arrangements with Matild regarding our moving away. The stillness during eating was disturbed only by the many houseflies zooming from plate to plate to have their share of the tasty stuff. Chasing them off prolonged the time and allowed Iren and Matild to think about what to say and how to say the last words without rancor toward each other.

Iren couldn't stand the eerie silence any longer. She couldn't sit aimlessly anywhere very long, for her mind was urging her to do the next thing. The many things still needed to be done were on her mind like a memorized shopping list she would only add to as the occasion presented itself.

After eating, she wished everybody would move out of the area so that she could clean up the mess. But at this time nobody moved; we just sat there as if another course would be served. So she raised her voice and said: "Don't just sit there and look like peacocks on a fence doing nothing except looking for something to happen. Pick up your plates and put them in the wash bowl and push your chairs back. Ella, you wipe the table and wash the dishes. Arpad, go and feed the animals for the last time. Matild, you come with me. We are going for a short walk to iron out reminders."

* * *

It was evening now. I could still see the only rooster we had, ushering the hens to get inside the coop. Then, I chased him inside to the hens and shut the coop's door tight. Otherwise, the foxes would have grabbed them by morning, as they already did it before.

Next, I went and sat on a stump outside of the property line close to the fence. Here, I was listening to, thinking of, and observing everything that was happening at the moment. The two women were moving away from me, took a few steps and stopped. They did this over and over again. Every time they stopped, I could still see their hands fanning the air and their fingers pointing at each other.

I could hear that a hectic discussion went on over our lives in the otherwise quiet moments of the evening twilight. Ella was still washing the dishes, as the sound of clinking of the porcelain plates reached my ears. For some reason, she didn't light the petrol lamp as yet. Probably, she didn't want any mosquitoes to swarm into the kitchen. The bats were out en masse also and flew very close to my head. To prevent them from swooping so close, I held a tomato stick above my head to guide them away. Owls were hooting nearby also, probably looking for mice, which traversed the road right in front of me. It was an awesome mid-July evening as the stars began to light the sky.

Although my sorrow over Mother's death was as if it just happened, I couldn't help noticing the busy life around me. In a way, this was what I really needed at this time to stave off melancholy from taking over my feeling. While all this was going on, I was also very alert knowing that this evening I have to say good-bye to everything here. A new beginning, a new life full of uncertainties, would be coming as early as tomorrow morning.

Then I heard Matild saying to Iren, "This untamed kid will be a big trouble for me when he comes back."

The two were now on their way back on the dirt road for the last time. They didn't see me sitting on that stump next to the fence. They didn't know I heard everything they said.

"Don't exaggerate something that didn't happen yet, Matild! It may turn out to be a blessing for you. Look, you are overlooking the fact that all the animals will be yours. And all the crops in the field will be yours also. I think you have a grudging mind and an ill-filled heart toward Arpad," Iren responded.

"What about when he returns? What will I do with him?" Matild asked.

"You should act like a mother to him. Love him, always love him, even when you discipline him. But of course, you never had any children of your own and faking love would only create the opposite effect. Sooner or later, Arpad would discover your ruse behind it, and he would hate you for it. One thing, though, you can always do. Tell him the truth. Telling the truth doesn't need love. It only needs a backbone. Do you have a backbone, Matild?" Iren asked, holding back past examples of her cheating and lying.

Iren knew Matild very well from her early years when she was still a young lady. She was certain even now that Matild would have a problem telling the truth—as hardcore habits don't take respite for anybody.

"Judge for yourself, Iren," Matild retorted.

They reached the house now and each went inside her side of the duplex.

* * *

Iren had spent almost two weeks with us since Mother died. She stayed a few days longer than she wanted to. But now, she was anxious to head back home to her own family in Rackeresztur.

We all said *good-bye* to Matild even though we distrusted and disliked her. I thought this was the better way to part from her than saying *go the hell*. I envisioned that I would need her help later when I returned.

So while Ella and Iren rushed to the railroad station, I lingered a bit longer with her in order to tell her very nicely that she can count on my helping her when I returned. She didn't say anything but tipped her head as a sign of concurrence.

Iren and Ella were already a few hundred feet ahead of me, rushing to the rail station.

As I rushed after them, I encountered my buddy Laszlo. He was coming home from the general store, and instead of going home, he turned around and accompanied me all the way to the railroad station. I felt good about that, for we could share our last minutes together, encouraging each other as friends do, how to keep our relationship on track during my absence.

In parting, we hugged each other. Then, I gave him the key to my room for safekeeping. I had just enough time now to jump onto the slowly moving last wagon. With one hand I held the handrail; with the other, I waved as the train pulled out of the station.

Getting Along with Iren's Children

Iren's family was large, two boys and three girls. They were born quickly in succession; only a year or so separated them. Ella was about the same age as Iren's firstborn, Maria. And I was the same age as her first son, Janos.

Soon after we arrived, John, Iren's husband, gathered us around a bench outside under a huge walnut tree. This gathering was to introduce Ella and I to the family and, at the same time, set some rules into motion for all of us to follow.

Now, all the kids in this family were, at the moment, unknown to us. We weren't smiling at them, and they weren't smiling at us. The aura suggested a keen sense of aloofness, especially among us boys. On the other hand, Maria and Ella acted as if they already knew each other. They were giggling and sitting by each other, talking things over.

I sat across from the boys and looked at them when they weren't looking at me, and they looked at me when I wasn't looking at them. I knew they were confused, for they quickly took their eyes off me, not knowing where else to look, except in the air. Their looks revealed that they weren't in any hurry to accept me into their circle. Maybe I looked to them the same way.

John, the boys' father, sat next to me. He noticed the fidgety composures of his two sons, Janos and Laszlo, and said to them: "You boys are to like Arpad because I accepted him as my own. He will spend the summer with us. Might as well, do things to one another that point to a *brotherly* behavior. Any questions?"

They didn't have any. They didn't dare to have any, for knowing that their father was a straight-shooter, one word said it all, *brotherly*.

Then Iren, the mother, spoke: "You kids don't know yet that your grandmother died. That's the reason why Arpad and Ella are here with us. There will be no change regarding house rules and manners. Except, Arpad will be with you boys and sleep on the upper bunk bed. On the other hand, Ella, will do the same thing in the girls' bedroom."

Rules and manners meant that Ella and I will have to learn them as we go on living here. Neither John nor Iren explained them to us in detail. But I know there would be many, for even their dog knew where to lie in wait during a commotion—in the corner. This type of regimented living must have had a well-founded meaning, I thought. When finally we scattered, I asked Iren why everything has to have a place, why everybody has to follow set rules and manners in this family.

She smiled at me and said: "There is an inside order or disorder in every person formed by his habits. How that order or disorder was arranged depended on how that person was raised. If you don't learn certain rules regarding behavior while you are growing up, it would be the cruelest awakening when you have grown up and discovered the wrong in yourself. Life would be the cruelest teacher for you. It would force you to reshape your inside if you wanted to be normal. You see, my young brother, we live by certain habits. The good ones are those that please us as well as others. The bed ones hurt everybody. We want our children to learn all the good habits during their growing years. And while you are here, you should be part of it."

"Where did you learn these good habits?" I asked Iren.

"Some of it, our mother taught me; some of it, I learned from my husband, your brother-in-law. You see, when I married him, I was only sixteen years old and he was then fifteen years older. He learned the good habits in life through hardship. So John and I agreed that we will raise our children as the Good Book tells us. Let's go inside the house now, and I'll read it to you so you would remember that we were warned what could happen when we don't raise our children with discipline in mind."

And we went inside the house. Iren pulled out the *Black Book* from the bottom shelf of her kitchen cabinet, opened it where the book marker was. At this moment I said to her: "Sister, you stop right here. I don't want to hear it. I hate forced discipline. So far, that's all I have heard from you and John. I don't want to go through with it. Forced discipline means to me that I would have to be on a leash, like a dog that you and John would yank in all directions until you have subdued me. I have decided that I'll head back home tomorrow to Balatonkeresztur. Your way of disciplining me sounded highly artificial. Love was missing from it. I already went through this type of forced discipline from a priest in catechism class. He was drilling my mind to remember prayers. But because I couldn't, he belted my butts for it. I have a feeling that's what you would be doing, too."

"Well, how else would you learn the ways we suppose to live if we don't drive it into you?" Iren asked me.

"So far, besides what Mother told me, I learned what's right by seeing other people doing things wrong. Moreover, I learned also from making my own mistakes. Lately though, I have realized that the best way to avoid making mistakes is to ask nice people how to do things the right way," I answered.

Iren became altogether confused hearing my refusal of her steadfast explanation about disciplining children. She couldn't imagine that I had such a gift of being able to decide right from wrong at my age. I didn't tell her as yet that I was very much relying on my instincts also to choose right from wrong. I gave her one example from the many I had.

I told her that one day I was watching crows trying to figure out how to grab corn from under a wicker basket that I propped up as a trap. They circled the basket several times from left to right, then from right to left before they would stretch their necks forward to snatch a kernel. Their bodies were never under the rim of the basket to be caught inside, as I would have then yanked on the cord that was tied to the prop stick holding up one side of the basket. They sensed the danger, for their instincts guided them.

Then, Iren replied, "Animals don't have anybody to guide them, but you have me, for example, to teach you."

"I don't want to become your "*yes, Mom,*" "*no, Mom*" as I see your children are. You force your children into silence even though they want to say something. I want to be able to see the world through my eyes as well, not just through yours only. How else could I, then, face the world? Lopsided? You have to give me a chance to see things my way as well. I think that would be the right way to weigh things one way or the other," I said.

"All right, I won't talk about discipline anymore. In some ways you are right. You can see and hear others going in the wrong direction if you watch them closely. Stay with us a while longer, at least, until you become acquainted with my children," Iren asked.

As it turned out, I didn't leave the next day. Not because of Iren, but because of Ella.

She heard of my wanting to go back home. She heard it from Maria, Iren's oldest daughter. Ella was now crying over it. Maria consoled Ella since by now they had begun forming a friendship that would last forever. I, on the other hand, couldn't establish any kind of bond between myself and Iren's two boys, other than figuring out strategic moves how to stone them, returning the stones they had thrown at me.

The three of us boys were of puberty age, and the only privacy we could assure each other was by turning ourselves back to back to show self-respect. We were sharing a ten-by-ten room.

The two boys were shy, the result of heavy-handed raising by John and Iren, limiting their exposure to the outside world and forcing them to look down when they were receiving behavioral discipline.

As for myself, I was completely the opposite in my comportment with others. Shyness was far from my attitude with people, for it was natural to keep my head up and face people and the world without hiding my emotions. The hardships that confronted me from all directions erased from my attitude all doubts and hesitations to do things my way first—others' later. I learned very early in life that doubt and hesitation in myself were signs of being unsure of myself—the stigma of lackluster motivation. My survival in an otherwise cruel world demanded that I match my actions with others in like fashion regarding attitudes and manners.

The next day, I called on Ella in order to tell her a few things from my observations and plans that I thought would be fitting for the occasion. Since privacy was a remote possibility in this house and since we were newcomers into this family, all eyes were fixed on us, and all ears were widely open as to what we did or said about the other members of the family. Anything we did or said out of the ordinary was swiftly suppressed. Mostly though, it was I who couldn't adjust to the ways the other children were following orders. These incidents revealed to Iren that it would be better for me to go back home alone. So without any doubt she said, "I sense that you want to talk to Ella about what's on your mind. Go and take a long walk in the garden to talk things over with her. But don't step on my plants there and don't touch my peaches and don't—"

"Here we go again!" I exclaimed. "'Don't step on my plants. Don't touch my peaches.' Was there anything else on your mind that would allow me to do without your don'ts? I'm not going to your garden. I can tell you right here what I wanted to say to Ella in private. I'm ready to go back home tomorrow without Ella, and stay with Matild. Whatever will happen between me and Matild shall be better than having my mind and body squeezed between your yeses and nos," I said.

So it happened that the following day I picked up the same stuff I brought with me only a few days ago, shoved them all in the same sack, and said *good-bye* to the whole family just as we had finished breakfast together.

"What a gutsy kid you are, Arpad," remarked John, my brother-in-law.

"No, it has nothing to do with my being gutsy. I have a clock ticking inside of me that says, 'Move on, kid. Don't trifle your precious time here.'" I replied.

I don't know why I said what I said, but I did know that something always prompted my mind to do what was beyond my understanding. So I followed my conscience.

Ella ran after me as I was about to close the front gate.

"Wait! I want to talk to you," she yelled after me. "When will I see you again, my sweet brother?"

I stopped at the gate and waited for her. She gave me all her pocket money she occasionally received from Iren and said, "Come back for me as soon as you settle down, for we truly belong together."

"I'll come back for you, no matter what happens to anybody. Stay close to Maria, for she is the most loved one by her parents. That way you would be sweetly treated. Occasionally write to me, especially when things don't go your way. I love you."

Just as I was about to close the gate again, Iren, my oldest sister, ran to me.

"Hold on a minute! I have to say a word or two before you take off on us. It's a darn shame that you can't tame your will to stay here with us. Do you realize the hardships you're facing?"

"I sure do. The hardship you imagine is not the hardship I imagine. I love to face hardship for that's the only way to know the worth of myself.

"Don't you realize that from your own sacrifices you do every day to your family, you don't think of them as hardships? Do you? That's because you love your children. Well, I love you, too. But I love myself more. And for that reason, I want to do willingly what comes my way. So that way, I could be very proud of myself. You see, Iren, things that you do for me are very good, but they don't move my will to improve myself. They nurture laziness in me, and I lose my self-initiative."

"Arpad, you put me in high regard, and I don't know what to say to you anymore. But, here, I have prepared food for you for the road, and, here, I give you some money, too."

By the time I and Iren finished, the whole family showed up behind us, all at once. It was my brother-in-law, John, who ushered all the kids to the gate in order to say good-bye to me. The goodwill that was sparkling from everybody's eyes sent joy to my heart, for now I realized that they loved me. I also realized that the everyday skirmish we did to each other was an ordinary thing to do within a family and had nothing to do with what they held in their hearts for me.

I became perplexed to the point of thinking that I should stay with this family for a while longer. But, then, my conscience prompted me to stay the course I chose in the first place. I recognized at this time how my feelings could trip me if I allowed it. Only to regret it later that I took the wrong step. So I hid my feelings, thanked everybody for their good wishes, and left the whole crowd behind. At a bend in the road, I could see that they were still looking. I decided to jog my way out of their sight.

In about ten minutes, I would reach the main road that led to the railroad station. It was mid-morning now. The sun has already lifted most of the dew pearls from the grass. It looked as if all the farm animals gathered along the roadside to watch me running away. But I realized that they were only feeding on the fresh, cool grass at the roadside. Dogs were quiet, too, as they sat at the gates of almost every house I passed by. Only the cats sitting on top of the fence posts decided to evade my presence as I swiftly ran by them. Soon, I had to stop running as my backpack was painfully rubbing my back from the steady knock-knock.

As soon as I reached the main road, I sat on the bench at the bus stop and waited there until the next bus came. Nobody was there waiting. That indicated that I was either early or missed the bus. Either way, I had now plenty of time to reach the twelve o'clock train leaving Martonvasar to Lake Balaton.

Now, as I sat there on the bench and let the world go by, I was busy figuring out the meaning of my unfettered freedom that I suddenly gained. My positive outlook about my future sustained my spirit now. It lifted my hope for the better. I was now imagining my aunt Matild living next door to me in Balatonkeresztur. How to set up a good relationship with her, how to outsmart her craftiness, how to stay free from her. Suddenly, the bus came, and I forgot everything about Matild.

CHAPTER NINE

A Day Packed with Unexpected Events

My bus ride from Rackeresztur to the railroad station was definitely an eye-opening event. The bus was full of gypsies. They were riding to go to work at a Collective Farm two miles away. They carried with them their flimsy hoes and were already drinking and chewing tobacco. I didn't understand their language, but I understood from the tone of their voices that they were bickering among themselves. I also saw that they are spitting tobacco-filled saliva at each other. I hid myself behind a fat gypsy woman to take cover in order that the juice wouldn't land on me. Others were spitting onto the floor, and still others were spitting straight out the open windows, just to have the draft suck it back onto my back two windows down. The whole event lasted only about five minutes, as all the gypsies left the bus at the next stop. I am the only one who stayed behind. The bus still had one more stop to make before reaching the rail station.

After I entered the railroad station, the first thing I wanted to do was to find the bathroom and change my clothes. I couldn't find any booth with a door on it. So I resorted to change over in one of the booths that was not so near to the entrance door, thereby avoiding the frequent in-and-out traffic. Since I had only one extra shirt and one short pants in my backpack, I didn't have the problem which one to wear in exchange with the one I'm wearing. So I turned toward the back wall of the boot and changed my shirt first, thinking that it will cover my butts in case somebody was looking. Then, I exchanged my shorts quickly that not even a fly could catch a glimpse of me. Now I grabbed my smelly clothes and shoved them in my backpack and turned around. Suddenly I bumped into a young male soldier. "I like to touch you, would you…," he said. I couldn't say anything in my shock. But the strength of my angel took over my whole being. I tore off the wooden toilet seat and jammed it over the soldier's neck and ran out from the toilet, dangling my backpack in case I had to swing it around in my defense.

For the first time I became aware which side I really belonged. From this time on, I was ready to look at girls a little more than just their pictures. Needless to say, this episode was a stark reminder for me that from now on I would have to add another milestone to my growing worries—eying the motivation of weird people in order to protect the most important part of my being. My mind was more on this part of my body at this age than on anything else because I had reached those curious times of puberty.

As I rushed out through the exit door from the waiting room, I saw that my train was just about ready to pull out. The conductor's whistle signaled that the boarding ended and that the train would imminently leave the station. I really didn't care and swiftly jumped onto the closest wagon's stairs. There, a watchful girl of about my age grabbed my right hand and pulled me up to the platform next to her. We smiled at each other longer than usual, not as passersby do, but rather as someone wanting to say something. That was the beginning of our getting to know each other.

She stayed on the platform while her parents moved somewhere inside the cabins. They had stopped here at Martonvasar in order to visit the famous Beethoven Gardens and had boarded the same train a little earlier.

In no time at all, we started talking to each other as there appeared to be no hesitation between us to do so.

"My name is Ildiko. What's yours?" she asked.

"I'm Arpad. Where are you traveling, Ildiko?" I asked.

"We are going to Balaton to our usual vacation spot. The place is Balatonkeresztur."

Hearing the name of my hometown arrested every part of my senses. Ildiko was the most beautiful girl on earth that I had as yet seen in my entire adolescent life. And now, she would be staying in my hometown. Not much time needed for my imagination to roll—we could even be swimming together in Lake Balaton. Since I'm almost shaking from excitement, I couldn't say another word, and she noticed it.

"How come you are so excited all of a sudden?"

"Balatonkeresztur is my hometown!" I'm looking at her and smiling. "It would be very nice if you could be my friend during your stay in town. Would that be possible, you think?"

"Why not! I'm bored there anyway most of the time. Besides, you asked me so nicely. How can I refuse?" she answered.

I remembered what my mother told me: "If you can say what you want to say nicely, your listener will look at you twice before answering."

Ildiko didn't look at me twice. Her eyes didn't leave mine ever since she grabbed my hand as I leaped onto the train. And as for me, it wasn't my eyes that were looking at her. It was my heart. My mind became numb, my eyes stopped seeing, and my ears blotted out all voices. It was my heart that took over everything. I never felt anything like this before. I knew instantly that I was in love with her.

My utmost concern now was how to hide my feelings from her. It was impossible to fake my feelings as I was so young to act artificially. One needed a lot of finesse to do that. And that came about through wheeling and dealing. Convinced, I was not there yet.

My face, however, revealed the whole truth. She noticed that I was looking at her with yearning eyes and was speechless. That prompted my right hand to gently touch her face for a moment. She returned it by touching my chin and slightly pushing my head up so as she could really look into my eyes. They were hazy and filled with telling signs of love.

Nobody saw us as we were standing alone on the platform. The train was now picking up real speed. The cross draft stifled our voices. So we went inside, looking for her parents in order that she could introduce me to them.

My emotions slowly subsided as my attention turned to pushing my way through the center aisle in order to stay close to Ildiko. I hate to be so close to people, squeezed and pushed around. Nothing turns me off more than standing close to people and smelling their foul breath. This time I couldn't help it. I was always repulsed by foul smell, whether it's mine or others'. This time, however, I held my breath until a fresh draft from the open windows fanned my face, again and again. But I never took my eyes off Ildiko as she was also jostling her way through the crowd a few feet ahead of me. We passed through two wagons and didn't find her parents. Now we entered the first-class wagon with only a few passengers in it. Ildiko noticed her parents and ran to them. It looked as if she was telling them already that I was with her. She then quickly turned, took my hand, and pulled me to her parents in order to meet them.

I didn't need to be introduced as I had more courage to introduce myself than a beggar on a city street. With the pressure of a strong man's handshake, I pressed mine into theirs, one by one, looking into their eyes and smiling as if I had just found a lost pearl. My forthrightness surprised them to the point that they didn't know what to say to me. And they couldn't say a word because Ildiko hurriedly told them how I had leaped onto the train and kept her company ever since.

"Guess what, Dad?" she said. "Arpad is living in the same town we're staying."

"How come we haven't seen you in town before?" he asked as he scanned my body from head to toe at the same time. His frowning look invited me to say more than perhaps a gossiper would tell him tomorrow.

"I come from a poor family and live at the end of town. When I go somewhere, as when I go to Lake Balaton, I take the back road. I am keenly aware of the fact that I am poor and am an orphan. People look at me with disdain, thinking that I am less important than any other peasant in town. But I tell you, I'm the richest man in the world, for I have the faith and the courage to introduce myself to anybody with a strong handshake to subdue his superior feeling, be it a man or a woman. I shall not be a peasant forever. Someday, I shall be more than that because I am on my own."

"And what do you think you want to be, Arpad?" he asked.

"That, I don't know yet. What I do know, however, I will walk to the end of the world to find my rightful place in life," I answered.

"Wunderkind!" (wonder boy) his wife, being a German, exclaimed.

With my straight and bold remarks, the stage was now set, whether they would accept me into their company or turn me away. Then they looked at my backpack, and I knew right of way that if anything would turn people off, it would be that. My backpack was unseemly to say the least. A burlap sack—tied at the corners with a heavy string, then tied to the mouth of the sack—held all my belongings. It must have suggested to others that I was either a vagabond or a gypsy. Only I knew that I was neither.

Then, they eyed me all over again. They saw that I was wearing clean clothes—sky blue shorts with a matching dark blue shirt and a pair of sporty-looking, almost-worn-out sandals. My nails were as clean as a clamshell just washed ashore, and my hair, a bit covering my ears, was wavy but neatly combed and parted on the left side. They suddenly turned and were smiling at me.

Now, the mother of Ildiko kept tapping the top of the seat next to her, inviting me to sit there. I, in turn, invited Ildiko to sit there, as I felt that she would be asking a lot of questions that I wouldn't be able to answer, for I was not a city boy.

They were living in Budapest, where people dress differently and speak differently than I, a village boy, did. And I knew in my heart that sophistication didn't flourish in cornfields. So I stopped telling anything more about myself. They would hear plenty about me from the village folks, once they reached Balatonkeresztur. With this in mind, I listened more and talked much less.

Ildiko, however, noticed from my use of the Hungarian language that I, without knowing it, assimilated the style of a very much liked and popular poet, Sandor Petofi. Inasmuch as I was a lousy learner in school, I was eager to read Petofi's poems. He set my heart aflame with his love songs—love songs not just about girls, but about nature, patriotism, and revolutionary fervor (1848). Moreover, his folklorist expressions, I was eager to emulate when I talk with others. Because of this, I was able to express myself when the need arose in a concise, meaningful way in responding to the questions of nosy people.

The steam-powered locomotive pulled one freight and eight passenger wagons with unusual speed, as if it wanted to reach Paris almost nonstop. It was the Oriental Express, running essentially between Bucharest and Paris. It only stopped at major hubs with heavy rail traffic. Budapest and Siofok were two of them. I had no idea about the fame of this train 'til Ildiko reminded me of it. So Siofok would be the last stop on Lake Balaton, where we would have to change trains because it would not stop at Balatonkeresztur. Siofok was the biggest resort town on Lake Balaton.

* * *

I never heard of Paris before. In fact, I knew very little about world geography. I had no idea of its significance in worldly matters. Ildiko explained it all. Her father had traveled all over Europe when he was young and single. He told her everything about Europe, especially the places where he hid himself from being captured by the Germans. He was a Jew.

It was during that time that he married Ildiko's mother in Berlin, Germany. She was a German national. This was the reason as to why she couldn't speak fluent Hungarian. So any conversation between me and her needed translation, and that would have been burdensome because I sat at one end of the compartment's bench and the father, the translator, at the other end of the bench. In between, next to me, sat Ildiko, then her mother.

On the opposite side of our bench sat four young foreigners who were, of course, intently watching and laughing at us as we mumbled over trying to make sense out of the meaning of words. They were laughing because we used our hands more than our lips in giving sure meaning to the words we intended to convey to each other. So we stopped talking altogether. The parents fell asleep from boredom; Ildiko and I went from the compartment to the hallway. Through the open windows, we watched the beautiful panorama of Lake Balaton unfolding before our eyes as the train swished toward Siofok.

The time quickly passed, and the train pulled into Siofok without our knowing it. Just as it stopped, the parents were already behind us, telling that we must depart with all our belongings and change to another train, which was already waiting at the adjacent track.

"Follow me," Ildiko said. "We must get our bicycles from the freight wagon right now!"

All this had happened within seconds. It caught me off guard, so much so that in the hustle I forgot my backpack under my seat.

"Get it after we fetch the bicycles," Ildiko said. "You have ten more minutes before the train leaves this station."

By the time I recovered my backpack, the Oriental Express slowly started rolling out from the station. It was a must to get off the train immediately as it was accelerating. So I forced the exit door open and jumped out the moving train. Unexpectedly, I landed straight in the face of a middle-aged man who was waving to his relatives. I knocked him to the ground, as my weight must have been doubled over him. Then, I helped him recover and apologized for the mishap. He looked and punched me in the face, being angry. "You stupid kid, you!" he yelled. Now my nose was bleeding from the fistful punch, and the blood was dripping onto my shirt. As I realized it, I leaned forward and let the drops fall on the ground.

Ildiko saw me jump out the train and came over to check if I was all right. She didn't see that I landed on a man and knocked him down and that he punched me in the face. By the time she reached me, the man ran away as I was ready to return what I have received. Ildiko took her white scarf and asked me to moist it with my saliva in order for her to clean the blood off my face. We didn't waste time pitying over the incident as our next train was almost ready to depart from the station. Since the conductor saw what had happened, he waited, not letting our train depart until we recovered ourselves.

The event caused an instant confusion among us—what to do with the bicycles. The train was about to leave the station, departing to Lake Balaton. It was Ildiko who quickly solved the problem.

"Mom and Dad, you board the train! Arpad and I will ride the bicycles to Balatonkeresztur. We will be there about the same time you arrive. You agree or what?" Ildiko made her point.

"That's a smart thing to do. Don't leave the bicycles unattended! We'll be waiting for you," said her father. Both parents boarded the train in a hurry.

This train was a commuter train, and as such, it stopped about thirty times between Siofok and Balatonkeresztur, a distance of no more than thirty-five miles. Ildiko and I were riding our bicycles now alongside the train for a few hundred feet and were waving to the parents. They were amused seeing us happy and smiling.

At the outskirts of Siofok, the tracks veered off the bicycle path. We now followed the main road from village to village. In each village, there were more bicycle riders on this road in both directions that I cared to count. In addition to that, there were the horse-drawn carriages, the tractors, and of course, all kinds of animals in between, running all over trying to avoid being killed.

Ildiko was very familiar with the entire area as in previous years she and her father zigzagged with their bicycles the whole shoreline between Balatonkeresztur and Siofok, searching for the cheapest rentals for their summer vacations. After about thirty minutes bicycling, we reached Balatonlelle. This was the place with the largest camping center on the south side of the lake, easily accommodating a thousand children who were members of the *Communist Youth Organization*. Ildiko spent a couple of previous summers here and now wanted to ride through it and visit a few of those people who were managing it.

All the children here were required to attend classes, learning how to glorify the Communist leaders *Marx, Lenin, and Stalin* and how to praise the *Communist ideology*. In addition they were brainwashed how to change those who opposed it.

We stopped at the entrance gate in order to obtain permission to visit the campsite. I guarded the bicycles while Ildiko went inside the office. Everybody remembered Ildiko, for she was not only smart but also knew how to use her wits in order to obtain favors. Remember, she had a Jewish heritage from her father's side—a well-suited heritage to be nice but pushy.

Waiting for somebody is not at all my favorite pastime. But in this case, it didn't bother me, because what else could have been nicer than waiting to see Ildiko again? After about twenty minutes, she returned, saying that she had good news for me.

"We are invited to have lunch with the staff."

"That's not possible, Ildiko. Your parents would be very upset if we delayed," I replied.

"But we have to eat something. I'm starving."

"Come on, Ildiko, I have food to eat. My backpack is full of it."

For a few seconds, she thought about it. Then, she went back to the office, declining the invitation on grounds that she was with me and that her parents were waiting.

We still had a good ways to bicycle. Anyway, she promised them to return in a few days for a whole day's visit.

All the while Ildiko was inside the camp's office, I was sitting on a long bench next to the office at the entrance gate. I set the bicycles against the backboard and watched everything that my eyes could take in.

The campsite was enormously sprawling in all directions. There were several pavilions built a few hundred feet apart, and tent sites surrounded each building. Not too far from these pavilions, I saw two tennis courts, three volleyball courts, and an open field where kids were playing soccer. What else was here waiting for me to discover, if time allowed? I just wished to come back here one day with Ildiko to see it.

The whole area was enveloped by the shades of tall elm trees, cooling the air on this mid-summer day. Garden flowers were circling each tree, and humming birds were flittering over the red blossoms, relentlessly feeding themselves. They must have been as hungry as I am.

While my eyes were scanning the territory and watching all the different activities going on, I was sadly reflecting on my own situation—I had no parents to send me here.

Ildiko returned from the office and sat next to me. The joy of seeing her again sent my imagination soaring. I was dreaming about being with her every day during her stay on Lake Balaton. Without even knowing, my head was already touching hers.

"I want to see you every day, Ildiko, while you are staying in town."

She didn't reply. But she put her arm around my waistline. I, in turn, put my arm around her shoulders, carefully embracing her. We stayed like that awhile as we watched afar the many kids playing in the open fields—soccer, tennis, and volleyball.

"You know, Ildiko, I have nothing to compare to these kids in this camp. I have no parents and have no money. But I have something they don't have. I have unlimited time and freedom."

"Then, you can see me every day while I'm in town. You don't need money for that."

"Thank you, allowing me to do that. You just made my dreams come through."

*   *   *

Almost every kid at this campsite was a son or a daughter of Communist Party member parents. The children had been inveigled to come here, for the parents wanted them to excel in sports and other promotions. They were growing up under the Communist system in which they shall play the most important role—the future of *Communism*.

Of course, by now, the government had confiscated all the business properties and nationalized most of the arable lands in the country. It had locked up the opposing owners or forced them to labor camps. From the stolen wealth, the government suddenly could grant all the enviable privileges to those who were the loudest and cruelest advocates of the Communist ideology. And here was I, who witnessed the ruthless persecutions of the peasants in my hometown, seeing now with my own eyes the children of those brutal people having a good time, while their parents promoting Communism. How easy it was for them to spend the wealth of other people and send their children here to trifle it away. Of course, these children didn't really know how this had come about. They were having a good time. I was only jealous of the fun part of it.

Suddenly, I hated this place, but I had to hide my feelings. Ildiko noticed that while I was embracing her, my mind was somewhere else. I stood up from the bench now, stepped forward, and stretched my hands into hers. I wanted to kiss her.

"Not in public," she whispered.

So we now picked up our bicycles and left the campsite. We had the same purpose in mind. Find a place so as we could unwrap my bag's contents to eat.

Before I left Rackeresztur this morning, my sister packed enough meat, fruits, and vegetables for me to last at least a week. She took my backpack and put the wrapped stuff in it.

"There is enough food here for you, and even to share some with the hungry," she said.

(I acquired her habit and am doing it to this day cooking extra for a guest. "It is heartwarming to be able to give from the abundance I have been blessed with." she used to say.)

And now, it was so good to have Ildiko with me and share with her everything I received.

The question now was where could we find a place to spread that food out and sample everything? In this beach town, we could hardly take a few steps without running into somebody. For that reason, we decided to keep biking until we left town and found a weeping willow tree somewhere off the main road where under its huge canopy we could hide ourselves.

(Weeping willows are beautifully shaped, quite tall trees. Their branches droop to the ground, while their inside stay hollow and shady. They are growing everywhere here at the shorelines of Lake Balaton.)

"One tree would completely hide us from the world and also shade us from the scorching sun," I said to Ildiko.

"That would be the perfect spot. Let's find that tree."

On we went to find that tree. The month was August 1952. So we pedaled until we found that perfect willow tree that would hide us from everybody.

"Let's take this road down to the shoreline. I know a huge pasture land there where willow trees grow tall and beautiful." Ildiko directed the way.

I followed her because she was familiar with the entire surroundings of Balatonlelle. Within minutes, we found a place just as she thought it would be. It was a grazing field that was cut off on both sides by wide man-made ditches, draining the surface water off the grazing field into Lake Balaton. And at the same time, it also supplied the drinking water to the cows. Many willow trees were growing here that dotted the field. The ones that were close to the water supply provided plenty of shades to the thirty or so cows now hiding under them.

Close to the road, we had the pleasure of choosing a tree with broadly spread limbs drooping down to the grass below it. Here, we settled down. We were able to look out from under the branches. Nobody could see us there from the outside. We pushed our bicycles under the tree and leaned them against its trunk.

I had now untied my backpack from my bicycle's luggage rack and emptied its contents right on top of the velvet-soft grass under the tree. Besides my slingshot, there was the wrapped bundle full of the goodies my sister provided.

The outside wrapper was a large hand-woven tablecloth and was perfectly suitable for this occasion. The several smaller bundles within it were also wrapped in dishcloth-sized towels, and they unrolled themselves as I spread the tablecloth open. The bundles contained the fried meats, the fruits, and the vegetables, wrapped again in wax paper. There were no plates and no utensils with it, however. Apparently, my sister forgot them as she hurried to give me food for the road.

So now, we sat side by side and fed each other. I held a duck leg, took a big bite, and let Ildiko take her share from it. She did the same thing with the cucumbers, a bite for me, a bite for her. In this manner, we ate our lunch and quenched our thirst with fresh peaches. All the more, we enjoyed each other's company.

As soon as the smell of food spread around, we had a great company coming out from the tree's trunk. A whole family of chipmunks showed up, circling in haste all around us, begging for a piece from our food supply. We ended feeding them from our hands, as they had become the friendliest creatures I had ever seen. After we finished eating and feeding, I pulled the tablecloth to the open field and let the chipmunks finish the leftovers there.

I noticed, however, that a skirmish erupted over the leftovers. Ravens swooped from the sky and grabbed, not only the leftovers, but also the innocent chipmunks. One by one, they grabbed all of them and flew away with them. Not one of them returned. I felt terribly sorry seeing how *nature* provided for both friends and foes alike. I didn't say anything to Ildiko.

Now, this allowed us uninterrupted peace to enjoy each other's company. We leaned side by side against the tree's trunk and dosed off, holding each other's hands.

Soon, we were awakened by a crackling sound coming from close by. It was the cow herder's dog, crunching on the leftover bones that the ravens didn't pick up. Soon after that, we heard the cow herder talking to himself.

"What's this rag doing here, spread out like a blanket?"

"That rag is mine, and you leave it alone!" I yelled from under the tree.

The young fellow became scared from my ghostly sound and ran off the scene.

We stayed there for a few more minutes and dreamed coming back again. I was thinking that few things were better in life than revisiting the place where I really discovered that I was in love.

Since we still had plenty of time left before sunset, we decided to stay on the inner roads spanning the shores of Lake Balaton, instead of going home on the main road on which the travel was unsafe. We still had about ten miles to go before reaching our hometown.

So we bicycled from beach to beach, instead of one stretch straight home. The distance seemed longer, but it was safer to go this way. It was my idea to go this way, as I had cramps in my legs from all that pedaling and wanted to stop here and there to relieve the pain. The last time I bicycled any distance was when I was six years old. That was in Polgardi just before the war. For almost seven years, I had not sat on a bicycle until now.

Midway at the town of Balatonfenyves, we reached the train carrying Ildiko's parents. We talked to them through the train's open window and assured them of our being safe. The train left the station; so did we. From here, there were only four more stops before arriving at the home station.

For me, the remaining stretch was very familiar. I already knew this part of the lake and its sparsely populated areas. My best friend's father worked here at a canal's pump station. On visiting him, Laszlo and I used to run around here, eating fresh plums we plucked from branches overreaching the fences along the way. The owners knew that we were doing it, and they didn't mind. Anybody could have done that, for the branches leaned over the fence to the outside of the property.

Back to our bicycling, we reached an area where the edge of the lake was about five hundred feet from the train stop. I needed to take a break as the bicycle's seat rubbed rashes all over my crotch. I was embarrassed to say this to Ildiko. So instead, I said: "Let's stop here and take a dip. I'm sweated all over and don't want to go home smelly. Come, Ildiko, take a dip with me. Nobody is here. We leave the bicycles at the edge of the water. We also have a good view from here, watching the train go by."

"I don't feel like taking a dip, Arpad. I don't know this part of the lake, and I'm afraid."

"Afraid of what, Ildiko? I'm with you and know this part of the lake. Come?"

"No, I don't want to. You go alone. I'll stay here and watch you swimming around. When you return, I'll tell you why."

So I went alone and swam with butterfly strokes far out and hid myself behind the reed banks. Then I removed my shorts and washed the salty sweat off my rear. Nothing felt better than being clean and knowing it. I swam out to the shore as fast as I swam in from it. I was very anxious now to find out why Ildiko didn't come swimming with me. But before I could say a word, she yelled: "The train just went by. It didn't stop. Let's go after it so that we could get to the station in time to meet Mom and Dad."

"Yes, let's do that. But tell me first, why you didn't come swimming with me?"

"I don't know how to swim."

I couldn't believe what I heard. I couldn't believe that none of my close friends knew how to swim. Yet they lived so close to the shores of Lake Balaton. *This shall be a great challenge for me tomorrow to teach both Laszlo and Ildiko how to swim,* I thought.

Upon arrival at the railroad station, we saw the train already parked, awaiting the passage of an oncoming nonstop train. The passengers were told to stay put until the other train passed. After it did, I hurried to the parents to lift their luggage off the train. In the meantime, Ildiko guarded the bicycles on the safe side of the tracks.

Soon, we left the train station and headed to the rented place where the family would be staying for the next two weeks. Only one thing was on my mind now: impress the parents good enough so as to allow me to hang around Ildiko while they stayed in town.

For me, this was the most important moment because now we would be separated from each other. I would be going to Matild, while Ildiko would be staying with her parents. The distance from my home to her place was about a third of a mile.

"Thank You, Arpad" was their last words as I dropped the two suitcases on the living room floor next to them. Then, I looked in the eyes of the father and said, "I had a great joy to be in your company. I thank you for allowing Ildiko to be with me all this time. Would it be possible to see her again during the time you're staying in town?"

The father looked at his wife instead. While she understood everything I said, she responded in German, "Naturlich!" She said it with a broad smile. Ildiko quickly smiled after translating what her mother said—*naturally!*

"I'll be waiting for you. I'll be sitting on the bench in front of the house. Come tomorrow. Come after seven in the evening."

I was overwhelmed with joy and couldn't hide it either. My face reflected what my heart was singing—after seven, tomorrow.

After that I walked home. During my way, I had plenty to think about. The problems I had with Matild just a few days ago returned to bother me. For sure, I wouldn't be able to escape them.

Don't Hide Problems, Face Them

Close to home now, I remembered the time when I attended catechism classes. What I heard from the priest then vividly rang in my ears now: "God created heaven and earth and then let men do the rest… and finessing entered into their hearts," he said.

This would be the best advice for me to follow also. *Why not?* I thought. I had learned enough nastiness from Matild already that it would cause a mouse to run back to its hole in order to save his life.

This shall the beginning of my applying a little bit of ruse to my thinking as far as Matild is concerned.

The time was about seven o'clock in the evening, and I was terribly hungry. I was away less than a week from home and would be glad now to touch the doorknob and enter my room to feed myself fried ducks that I kept preserved in fat for the rainy days. But Laszlo had the key to my room, and he wasn't around.

My hunger pangs lifted my imagination. Why not cook something fast and easy? There were plenty of chickens running around, right in front of me. Grab two of them and cook a real good stew for everybody. Since Matild's kitchen was open, I found everything needed for the cooking.

By eight o'clock that evening, I prepared a big pot of chicken stew with potatoes. Just as I finished it, Laszlo dropped in to greet me. He had the key to my room in his left hand and extended the other to embrace me. I invited him to eat with me, and while eating from the same plate, we talked about what had happened while I was gone. I couldn't stop telling him about the beautiful things that happened between me and Ildiko.

"It looks like you are looking for some kind a trouble. Girls don't know what they want at this age. They use two mirrors, one in the front and one in the back, and their eyes are glued to them, imagining the impossible. Are you planning to see her again?"

"Tomorrow evening at seven o'clock."

"Is she going to stand between us now?" Laszlo asked.

"Never! Friendship between me and her is not the same as between you and me. I like you, but not the same way as I like her."

"I don't understand what you're saying."

"That's because you haven't been crazy about a girl before."

"What does that mean?"

"She is always on my mind. My heart tells me that I'm in love with her."

Laszlo and I parted company for the rest of the day. He left home, confused. As he passed the kitchen door, I heard him mumbling the same words—"always on my mind, always on my mind." I would find out tomorrow why he repeated my words.

While the sun was still hiding low behind the trees, I set my mind to help around a little bit. Matild and her husband were still working in the wheat field.

First, I cleaned the pig's pen, for I couldn't stand the stink any longer. Then, I fed all the animals; and finally, I swept the yard. In between I was thinking that when Matild comes, I would hug her and kiss her and say to her: "I would be helping you from now on." And I meant every word of it. This would be one way to lure her into letting me to do the one thing I wanted to do most now—spend time with Ildiko.

After I finished the works outside, I unlocked the door to my room and saw that everything was the same way as I left it before I went to my sisters at Rackeresztur. I decided now to wash myself and put on fresh clothes, but I didn't find any clean clothes to put on.

So I filled a wooden vat with sun-heated rainwater and brought it inside the kitchen and washed myself. After, I wrapped myself in a tablecloth, as there wasn't anything else at hand at the moment. I threw the grey water out to the front yard and refilled the vat again and added a cup of ash lye to it. Then, I picked my dirty clothes, including the ones I had in my backpack, and dunked them in the silky water in order to soak them awhile. I gave it just enough time to soak in the lye and water mixture so as the smell and the soiled spots would disappear. Then, I took a smaller vat and filled it with fresh water and rinsed everything with it. Now, I squeezed the excess water and hung them all over in my room to drip-dry. They were hanging on nails that I hammered into the wooden beams that supported the ceiling in my room. By morning, I had dry clothes again. Whatever water dripped out, the dirt floor soaked it in. This chore I repeated every three or four days in order to keep myself and my clothes always clean.

It was now around ten o'clock in the evening. There was no sign of Matild or her crippled husband anywhere. I was so tired already that if the wind had blown the house away, I would have been still sleeping undisturbed. I blanked out without knowing it. My naked body fell on the straw mattress; consequently, my weight broke the supporting boards as I landed on them. I had no knowledge of it until the following morning.

A New Beginning

So now I woke up from the deepest sleep I ever had. The early sunrise was coming through the only window I had in my bedroom. As I was looking out, I saw Matild standing idly and looking around in the middle of the front yard, trying to figure out who dared to move things around, upsetting the chaos she had there before. I yelled out to her through the open window: "*My dearest*, your nephew came back!"

"No place like home, ha—" she responded and headed to my kitchen door to meet me.

"Don't come in, Matild. I'm naked. I'll be out in a second," I yelled.

I grabbed my dried shorts from the nail, slipped it on, and rushed out from the kitchen to meet her. I didn't dare to hug her, because she was smelly. She probably slept in the same close she had on yesterday, and may be even the day before. Otherwise, she looked amused over what I did for her. She knew now that I was the one who cleaned the yard.

I asked her, "How things are going with you, Matild, without the need of having your eyes on me?"

"I didn't miss you as a person, but I missed your helping. Are you staying now? Am I going to be your guardian now? Are you… now?" There was no end to her are yous.

"You are throwing these questions at me as if you had a list already made. I have hardly opened my eyes yet. Can't you just wait until I'm ready, too, with my plans? Be glad right now that I'm back to live here; for tomorrow, I may be living somewhere else."

I was thinking of my *godfather,* who wanted to adopt me while Mother was still living. Should things get unbearable here, I would go there. What the hell—there was no place for an orphan, except may be in heaven, if there is one. My soul had recoiled from anger without any visible signs as I responded to Matild. Then, she continued: "Tell me, what's on your mind for today? I really need your help at my husband's place. You know that he is half-crippled with his hips and can't walk straight. Every step he takes forward, he has to make a quarter circle with his legs to do it."

Matild knew that I had a compassionate heart, and if she would mention her husband's walking pains, I would help him without the slightest hesitation. She used this pitying tactic on me many times before. Her husband's name is Joseph Magyar.

"As far as what's on my mind for today, well, you already decided for me. But not all day. I have something very important to do in the evening, and don't ask me what it is 'cause I won't tell you." Then I continued, "Give me a few minutes until I wash my face. Why don't you go, too, and clean yourself? You stink."

In about five minutes, I went back to Matild's kitchen and ate the leftover chicken stew I cooked yesterday. After that, I went to help Joseph. Matild was still in her bedroom, giving herself a serious scrub, for she was rather embarrassed when I said, "You stink."

(Joseph's house was in a separate area, built on a couple of acres of land. The land was narrow in width as compared to other house lots on Main Street, but it was about nine hundred feet long. Two families lived there in the same house. The front part was occupied by his son, and the back part by a couple named Mr. and Mrs. Joseph Forro. This was the couple who returned from the United States just before the war. They bought this place, then resold it to Joseph Magyar for a lifetime homecare in the same house. Attached behind was Joseph's stall for cows and horses. And behind that was the barn, now half full with hay. From my house to Joseph's place, I walked about seven hundred feet, crossing Main Street before I reached the stall.)

Now it was about seven o'clock in the morning as I crossed over Main Street, going to help Joseph. Farmers were already coming and going to and from their fields. It was a traditional gesture to greet people, if nothing more than just a nod or lifting a hand. Sometimes I didn't feel like seeing the same people and doing the same greeting over and over again. I was keenly aware that everybody knew me. For being an orphan, I was watched by the whole village. This was the main reason as to why I was running most of the time. The least I wanted from anybody today was to ask questions about my life.

As I entered Joseph's stall, he was leaning on a fork and wailing for his first wife who really loved him, helped him, and took care of him. The marriage between Matild and Joseph was for reasons of opportunity and convenience. Matild declared to the whole world that "I'm no longer an old maid." There was very little else between them besides field work and lots of bickering.

(Matild always looked for opportunities to take advantage of people. This time she figured that it would be the perfect time to initiate me to do her work by my helping her husband. Until now, I had endured just about anything to let the time pass by. But, from now on, I would be following the teaching of my catechism teacher, the priest, "and finessing entered into their hearts." In other words, I would be outsmarting Matild for the sake of having fun, proper to my age, and a lot more.)

Joseph suddenly stopped wailing and went back to forking the week-old manure from under the cows. He noticed from the corner of his eye that someone had stepped inside the stall. I yelled to him, "Joseph!" My voice had a sweet ringing to it, inviting a smile in return. I couldn't tell, however, whether he smiled or not, for he had a funny-looking imperial mustache covering everything below his nose. But the fork dropped out of his hand, and he jolted to reach me and hug me much like a father would upon finding his lost son. I gave him a tight hug in return even though he smelled like cow dung. For once, I didn't care. My love for him was stronger than the smell of manure.

It was only natural that he would have the smell of cows, for that was what he handled. But not the way I thought he should have. His cows where filthy as they wallowed themselves in the manure-soaked straw under them. Their hair was shedding off their backs, falling on everything nearby as the draft blew it.

"These cows need a real good cleaning, Joseph. Don't you think so?" I reminded him.

"Not only they need cleaning, this whole place too, including myself. After you left town, I gave up. I couldn't keep up with everything, and your aunt wouldn't come near these cows. They hated her and poked her back. I suppose they felt that she hated them, too. But I know that they love you because you love them, too," he replied.

"Now that I'm back, I'll help you again."

So now, we removed all the dirty straw that was mixed with the droppings and replaced it with fresh straw. Then, we led the two cows outside and washed them clean. Joseph washed one, and I washed the other. These cows knew what we were doing. My cow occasionally looked back at me and gently nudged my rear and all the more pressed her side against my hands as I brushed her dusty fur with a hand-held bristle brush. I could not have imagined that a cow would be able to feel who loves her, or who hates her.

For the first time in my life, I smelled like a cow also, and the only way to remove it was by taking a complete bath. I told Joseph I was running to the canal to take several dips there until all the smell wore off my body.

The canal was about five hundred yards from the back end of the property. For me that was a two-minute run. Within a half an hour, I was back to continue helping Joseph. Only one more thing was left to do before I could quit for the day—milking the cows. The time was now about ten o'clock in the morning.

While I was in the canal, Joseph took a hint from me. He filled with water one of the wider troths from which the cows drank, dabbed several rags into it, and threw them in a pail. He then went inside the barn with it. There, he scrubbed himself with the rags several times. He repeated this one more time and put on clean clothes. Matild kept an extra pair of pants and shirts in the barn for him. That was the only way he could keep himself clean.

Nobody in the village had bathrooms; therefore, they washed themselves with sun- or stove-heated water. For me, the canal was the quickest way to wash up. From early spring till late fall, I ran there often to clean myself. Only on special occasions, I heated water to get a thorough soaking. Now, of course, I had that special occasion to clean myself in addition to dipping myself in the canal. Ildiko was in town.

So now this last thing, milking the cows, had to be done. I had no idea how to milk a cow with my bare hands. On the other hand, Joseph was master at it. "I'll teach you. Just look at my fingers," he said.

His fingers were squeezing one nipple at a time with an in-and-out motion, and the milk was oozing into the bucket held tight between his knees.

Could this be part of my survival? I was wondering. *Yes, I'm going to learn how to milk a cow.* Anything new and useful for my survival, I would gladly learn from now on, for I didn't know when my life would depend on it. This was how I pondered my immediate future.

My fingers were now mimicking the movement of Joseph's fingers. Finally, I said to him, "Let me try it." So Joseph handed me the milk bucket, having the foam on top of it dancing as I walked with it to put it on the bench.

"Take the other bucket and let's go to the other cow 'cause I emptied this one," he said.

This other cow was the one that I washed clean before. So friendly she was that I kissed her forehead and whispered to her: "Give me some milk 'cause I'm very hungry." And I sat on Joseph's stool and started milking her. Two or three times I pumped the milk onto the floor, and after that I pumped it straight into my mouth. Joseph laughed as loud as he could and said, "My boy, you never go hungry!"

When I was full, I asked him to take over the rest of the milking.

In a few minutes, Matild showed up with two enameled cans in order to collect the milk. She looked around with amazement how neat and clean the place was. Then she poured the milk from the buckets into her large cans. Her eyes jumped back and forth from me and Joseph. "How come I don't have more milk? These cans used to be full every morning."

"Next time I'll add water to fill up the milk buckets. Guess what, Matild, I drank it."

"You'll be here every morning then from now on helping Joseph! That's the price for the milk," she stressed.

Matild was dressed in black. She looked like a witch, moving quickly with her eyes and body. She left the place so fast carrying the milk cans that I couldn't even talk to her.

"She is nasty, a very demanding creature," Joseph remarked. "The trouble is, she's doing this all the time. I'm shivering when I have to go home in the evening. That's why I sleep here a lot of nights. If you come tomorrow morning, don't be alarmed finding me here in my straw bed."

As he finished saying this, I hugged him and ran away.

"So long, Joseph, 'til tomorrow."

CHAPTER TEN

The Tentacles of Love and Hate

By the time I arrived home, Matild was nowhere. A passerby said, "She dropped off the milk at so and so and went to the funeral of Mr. Suttogo." Now, I got the answer to my inkling from one mouth, Matild's cousin, Helen, who was the mouthpiece for the Communist Party secretary in the village. And she was always on the go from street to street—talking, listening, and prying information that would be useful against someone. She was the informer.

She was blacklisted by every decent peasant in the village for what she did. The inevitable revenge for the dirty works that the Communists did was looming on the far horizon. It was to erupt without warning in the whole nation. But now, it was slowly but surely surging to that boiling point in the hearts of every terrorized citizen in the country. It was certain to happen, for food to eat and place to worship are less and less available. The year now was 1952, and I was thirteen years old. I was too young to know the political side of events or understand why some people were ruthlessly wanting Communism while others were ruthlessly opposing it. As I witnessed already both to take place, I formed a real good impression where I stood in the current demise—nowhere at the moment.

Who was right or who was wrong, I couldn't figure it out, until later when I was inducted into the Communist Youth Organization. Here, I was taught to hate wealth and freedom. Wealth was associated with Capitalism and freedom with acquiring it. *Who cares!* I said to myself. I had neither wealth nor freedom now. So I was growing up between the old mentality and the new ideology. Neither directly impacted my daily life now.

After I finished talking with this *passerby* (Helen), I ran home on the other side of the street, as I didn't want to meet another passerby who was heading in my direction on the same side of the street. Village folks had the same trend of thought—minding the affairs of others.

In contrast, I was mindful of my own things to do only. If I really thought of it, I should say I hated gossipers. So I avoided them as much as possible.

Less and less of it occupied my mind now as to what others said or did. For the next two weeks, I shall be deaf to listen to anybody who might want to alter my thinking about Ildiko. She was my dream, she was my life, and she was the fulfillment of all I wanted to do now.

Preoccupied with this, I had some daunting questions to answer myself. What was I going to wear? How was I going to approach her? Who would be around her this evening?

Now, a fearless courage replaced my trepidation, and I answered myself: Clothes would not make me a different person, for my inside would be the same. However, how I looked on the outside had a lot to do how I felt on the inside. Hence, I would have to be charming. Furthermore, I would approach her the same way as I parted from her yesterday. I would have more smiles than words, for my smiling face had already revealed my positive attitude. And who would be around her? Definitely not the altar boys from the other side of town and not the dull boys from the neighborhood. They didn't have what

I had—fearless courage. Furthermore, they weren't in love with her; they were there because she was different from the village girls.

So, in my final stand, I concluded: Being in love, I should always have fearless courage to defend my own thinking and actions; and this will be the way I would meet Ildiko tonight with courage. This would be my first date to prove it.

* * *

It was not right to wear the same clothes I wore yesterday even though they looked clean enough. Then, I remembered that Iren, when she came to my mother's funeral, brought with her two bagfuls of clothes and shoes that her sons didn't want to wear. The clothes were too colorful, and the shoes too stylish. Her children thought that.

I pulled the first bag from under my bed and emptied it. These clothes were colorful, all right, but solid colors. Individually, each piece looked sensational in my eyes, for pastel is my favorite color. I picked out a light blue shirt and matched it to a pair of light brown pants. Since I didn't have a mirror, I couldn't look at myself dressed up. So I imagined myself in it. I looked now just like a city boy. And that was what I wanted in the first place. I wanted to be different from the peasant boys in the village. They don't wear light clothes, for dirt was cream thick everywhere in the village.

Now, I pulled out the other bag that was full of shoes. They were only slightly worn, but they were shiny, black and brown dress shoes. I chose the brown shoes that matched the pants. I was certain that now I would be looked upon by any villager as a stranger in town. For all practical purposes, I was. I was an orphan.

All the clothes were as wrinkled as those that man pulled out of a jam-packed suitcase.

"Where is the iron? Where is the iron?" I cried out. I was looking for it all over the house. I couldn't find it anywhere. Then, I went to the attic and found it there. It was hidden at the end of a cross beam with its top open. Being in a hurry for lack of time, I slammed the top shut and carried it downstairs. I put the iron right on the stovetop in order to heat the bottom hot enough to press my pants and shirt with it.

While the iron was warming, I laid the wrinkled pants on the table and dabbed it with water here and there and smoothed it so that the iron would slide with ease over it.

Occasionally, I looked at the stove to make sure the fire was still alive in it. Then suddenly, I noticed flickers of shine reflected here and there through the slits of the iron. I went closer and realized that the shine came from the eyes of mice. A whole family of mice were locked inside, feverishly trying to escape the heat. I grabbed the handle of the iron and rushed outside with it. When I opened its top, I counted one mom and eight little mice escaping the iron.

It looked to me that the iron press had not been used for years, as the bottom was rusty all over. Common sense told me that if I pressed my shirt and pants with it, the rust would not let the iron do its intended purpose. Not only that, it would not slide over the cloth, but it would discolor it also. Since I didn't have any sandpaper or the like to remove the rust, I ended up sliding the thing back and forth on the ground until the rust disappeared. Then, I checked the inside. That, too, had to be cleaned, for the mice didn't run out of it to do their business elsewhere.

So now, I had to start everything all over again. As I judged the time by the sun's standing in the sky, it was about 3 p.m. I decided to repack the stove and cook my supper. The iron press had plenty of time now to become hot in the meantime. I still had four more hours left before my first date with Ildiko.

* * *

Matild came home now, and she noticed the swirling smoke coming through my chimney. She walked straight to my kitchen. "Hope you are cooking my supper," she said.

"Of course, I am. I always cook extra servings. You know me, I always expect a friend to drop in. Where were you anyway?"

"I went to the funeral of Mr. Suttogo, who had no relatives and who was secretly a Communist Party member. But only a few people knew that until the funeral attendees were invited by a member to honor him with a burial feast at the town hall. There, the party secretary addressed the crowd and praised the poor man for his staunch support of *party* activities. Then, the secretary changed the subject and agitated the crowd to support collectivization of private land in the village," Matild explained.

Hearing this said I sensed that she was a sympathizer with those who supported the collectivization of farmland in the village. It became also clear that the milk that she carried away in the morning was the drink served to the children at the burial feast. Matild noticed that I was troubled over her participation in a Communist-sponsored meeting and asked, "What's your problem, kid? Why your face suddenly look angry?"

"How could you support something that most of the peasants in town oppose? Haven't you seen what the *Secret Police* did to those who were openly against collectivization?"

"I don't want to be one of those who were taken away by these agents and beaten for opposing collectivization. I rather joined them and kept quiet about it," she answered.

"You know, Matild, you have the same nerve that they have. You actually enjoy taking over things that don't belong to you. While I was away, you killed all my ducks and chickens. You have torn down my fence and have taken over my shed as well. Why?" I asked her.

"I figured that after you left a few days ago, you wouldn't have need for them anymore. I figured that after you returned at the end of summer, you would be living with me. You would be working for me, and I would be looking after you that you do."

"You mean you would be looking to it that I did what you are supposed to be doing, helping your husband. Go and see what he's doing and leave me alone. Don't you see that I have my own things to do now? I already had finished what I said I would do for you today," I snapped back.

Matild didn't want to leave my kitchen. So I said to myself that I was going to smoke her out of there. And I removed a still burning log from the stove and dropped it on the earthen kitchen floor, acting as if it was an accident. In a few seconds, she ran out, rubbing her eyes and yelling, "Now my funeral clothes are going to smell like a chimney." She ran to her kitchen, apparently to change her clothes.

Because she was standing, the smoke covered her head; but because I was stooping down, I felt nothing. Smoke doesn't settle low; I was convinced of that. Now I took the iron from the stovetop and dropped into it the amber pieces that broke away from the burning log. Then, I picked up the still smoking log and threw it back into the stove. The rest I swept outside the kitchen and locked the kitchen door. Now, the hot amber would keep my iron hot enough 'til I would finish ironing my shirt and pants. And I entertained myself uninterrupted.

Before I started ironing, I strained the noodles and ate. Noodles, potatoes, beans, and corn were my food supply day after day. Once a week, I had meat that I cooked into a stew and served it with one of the mentioned foods. For dessert, I loved noodles with a topping of crushed, sugar-packed walnuts.

My stomach was full now. Nothing could have pleased me more than that. All the things I could think of looked nicer after having a full stomach. My work went easier, and my dreams, loftier. And now,

I was dreaming of having a good time with Ildiko, for tonight would be the beginning of many joyful *tonights* with her.

I wanted to know the time now, so I unlocked the kitchen door. Before I could even step outside, Laszlo stepped into my face.

"Where you standing here all this time, Laszlo?" I asked him.

"No. I just ran over now 'cause I didn't see you outside all afternoon. I wanted to know why."

Having my freshly pressed clothes on already, he scanned me from top to bottom. "You look cool, very cool indeed. I bet I know where you're going. You have a date tonight."

"You hit it right on, Laszlo." I felt cocky, then asked, "What time you have?"

"About six o'clock. Can I at least follow you, Arpad? I want to see your encounter with her," Laszlo begged.

"No. Don't follow me. Come with me instead, and when we get there, keep walking," I said.

"But I can't go like this! Let me run back home, and I'll put on my best clothes. I want to look different, too, as cool as you are."

My First Date with Ildiko

Laszlo came back in a few minutes and ate his share of the noodles. He looked cool, too. He wore sporty clothes while I had on what young men wore for casual dates. The loose stuff.

It was time now to leave the house and find the place where Ildiko said she would be waiting for me. As we started walking on Main Street, I saw a number of boys gathered in front of her house, where I suspected Ildiko would be waiting for me. Since the distance was about a thousand feet, I could hear the meaningless laughter and gibberish coming from a group of peasant boys gathered around her. They weren't doing anything more than horseplay because Ildiko kept her distance from them. These boys, after seeing me coming, one by one, cleared from the place. They knew who I was and also remembered from last year that I sank one of their bullying friends into the ditch water. When they saw me, they must have been thinking that I would bounce them off like a fly. Ildiko already spread the word that I was the one for whom she was waiting.

By the time we arrived to the place, Ildiko was alone. She took my hand and pulled me to sit next to her. She then kissed my lips. I returned that kiss with matching fervor. Seeing all this, Laszlo stepped back. He thought that he would also get a kiss. But Ildiko took his hand and pulled him to the other side of her. She knew already that he was my best friend. I told her yesterday that he was. Therefore, Laszlo didn't need a formal introduction. I also told Ildiko that he was a loner. His Jewish tradition kept him from mingling with non-Jews. I was the only exception. That was all I said about Laszlo although I knew practically everything about his Jewish background. Laszlo asked me to keep everything he told me locked away in my head forever. "Past persecutions could be repeated anytime. That was our fate," he said. I vowed that whatever he said to me will go down to the grave with me.

It was good that Laszlo came along. Ildiko had a terrific plan momentarily put together.

"Tomorrow, my best friend is coming here to be with me. Her name is Lisa. She will stay with us until we return to Budapest. I thought that Laszlo would be a good company for her, and the four of us could go dancing at the Lake's festivities," Ildiko explained.

Laszlo turned to Ildiko and started inquiring about Lisa, nonstop. I could tell that his blood churned from the excitement. He couldn't sit still, he couldn't stop talking, and he couldn't keep his hands still. Since he hadn't faced a girl before, hearing that he would be facing one now, he became overexcited. He thought that this would be the greatest moment in his life too, dating a girl for the first time. She would be close enough to him to quench that burning desire naturally surfaced in every boy.

Ildiko, in the meantime, was nudging my side to calm him down. And I did. I got up and stretched myself, hinting to Laszlo that I had enough of him. Seeing what I did, he got up also and stretched himself. Now Ildiko got up also, and we decided to take a walk.

We passed the other boys, who were eyeing us from the other side of the street. We also passed a lot of other people coming in from the fields, for working outside was almost over for the day. Some were walking, carrying their forks and hoes; others were sitting on horse-drawn open wagons.

Walking and talking and more walking and talking, we lost track of time, place, and people. We almost reached the shores of Lake Balaton before we realized where we were. Then, we turned around and headed home. All this time I was firmly holding Ildiko's hand. With my other hand, I waved a short corn stalk in order to keep the mosquitoes at bay. Only one thing interrupted everything. The walkway was as gritty as freshly spread pebbles on a newly tarred sidewalk. My dress shoes rolled all over on it.

We were now discussing tomorrow's activities. Everything depended on Ildiko. She led the conversation that attracted every bit of our attention.

"We'll be on the beach from ten to three tomorrow. At five o'clock, we'll pick up Lisa at the railroad station. And again, at seven o'clock, I will be waiting for you in front of my house."

It was my turn now to explain my schedule. "I'll be helping Joseph from six to ten in the morning. Then, I'll be looking for you on the beach and spending all my time with you—maybe even doing a little swimming together."

Then, it was Laszlo's turn to fold himself into our schedule. "I know that I'll have some time available. I'll make Papa realize that I need a time-out from reading *holy books* all summer. He thinks that I'm still holding onto my mother's skirt."

Ildiko became perplexed over what she heard from Laszlo. She didn't know Laszlo's Jewish background, which I knew but couldn't explain it to her—no matter how much I loved her.

Slowly, we returned to the same spot we started, and I said to Ildiko, "Look for me tomorrow on the beach around eleven-thirty in the morning. I'll come with or without Laszlo." Then, I gently hugged her and kissed her on her forehead and kept on walking home with Laszlo. It was still somewhat light at around nine-thirty in the evening.

Laszlo accepted Ildiko's invitation without thinking that his parents might not agree to it. He was once grounded for breaking curfew rules. On the way home now, we talked about that, and I consoled him.

"I'll go with you to your parents and talk to them. They will listen to me, as they know I am your best friend. I'll convince them that you need to see a little more than the fences around your house. I'll tell them that I need you to be with me, for good friends watch out for each other. Also, I would tell them that we would be talking with girls. It would be perfectly natural that boys at this age talk to girls. Don't you think this would be persuasive enough?"

I volunteered to do this for my own benefit also. *A good company would interact when ideas run short,* I thought.

(Laszlo was the only one of the three of us who already had instructions from his father as to what to do every day during the summer recess. First of all, he had to understand the general meaning of the Torah, which contained the Word of God through the five books of Moses, known as the Pentateuch [the Old Testament]. On top of that, his father assigned him special sections that dealt with significant events in the life of the Jews that every Jew had to remember. One of these is the Ten Commandments.)

Then, Laszlo added, "I'll make my own pitch also. I'll talk to Father separately and tell him that nowadays I think a lot about girls, and if I could just touch one, it would set me free—at least in my dreams. I will also tell him: 'Remember, Father, last February when I turned thirteen, you initiated me into adulthood (bar mitzvah). Now give me the opportunity to practice it.'"

Laszlo's Angry Father

This was the moment when reality opened our eyes and minds. Laszlo's parents were anticipating his homecoming. They were up in arms that he left house again without any trace as to where he went.

I knocked on the door and heard Laszlo's father say, "It's open. Come right in!" I stepped in, and Laszlo was right behind me, being afraid that if he were to step in first, his father would slap him. But upon seeing me dressed in clothes he never saw on me before and also saw that Laszlo was very nicely presentable, he stood up and said: "I can smell that you were in the presence of woman. Now, which of you is the peacock here?"

I stepped close to him and said, "I asked Laszlo to come with me. You know, good friends always hang around each other. So I'm telling you the truth. I met a beautiful girl yesterday on my way home from my sister and wanted Laszlo to meet her today. I had a date with her at seven. We were there and talked so much that we forgot the time. You know, when girls are involved, time picks up speed. The reason as to why I am here with Laszlo is to ask you to overlook our daring to talk to girls. We have a need to talk to girls since we are boys of that age. Anything else is boring stuff to talk about. We feel that it is better to be open about it, instead of hiding what cannot be hidden long enough before you would know about it. Besides, I supported Laszlo, and he supported me when we were not sure about something," I said.

Laszlo's father answered, "I am amazed over what the two of you did. I'm amazed, simply amazed. As I look back when I was your age, you are now at least thirty years ahead of me. I can't force you not to do what you are doing, but I can demand that you don't act silly with girls. The consequences when young boys and girls are engaged in sex could be a very damaging act. It could mean the devastation of your lives and the ruin of your future."

We were silently hearing the father's talk. Even the houseflies weren't zooming from place to place. I was weighing the consequences of what he said and knowing that Laszlo was doing the same thing. After the father quit talking, I replied, "My body at my age goes through a hell of a combat wanting to fulfill its cravings. And if my mind would be a weakling, what you said could happen. But on the other hand, I'm sure of myself that I wouldn't reach that point. I have relentless self-control over myself. Nevertheless, what you said was a smart thing to keep in mind."

Now, Laszlo turned toward his father and said: "Dearest Father, I carefully listened to every word you said, and I understand everything. In between the lines, you were really thinking that I would do *silly* things with girls. How many other nice things there are that a boy like me could do with girls besides that *silly* thing? How come you never talked to me about this before? You know, in all my readings from the Book of Moses, I haven't got any clear warning about this. So where did you get the idea that I would do such a thing as knocking up a girl?"

"Parents resort to thinking the worst when their sons or daughters delay coming home. You are at that age when boys think of things that are in many ways forbidden. It is true that I haven't prepared you for it. I thought it was better that you find these things out on your own. I won't mention it again. I trust in your judgment from now on."

"Does that mean that you would allow me now to have some free time and go with Arpad during the remainder of the summer—seeing and talking to girls?

"Yes, provided that you tell us where you going and what you doing."

Now, it's up to Laszlo to figure out how to work out his allowed free time and how to make it fit my schedule.

What Laszlo said about the Book of Moses planted the seeds of curiosity in my mind. How much did he really know about what was written in those books? For sure, I would like to find it out, not so much reading it, but rather talking about it. That time shall come.

(The Szalado family, Laszlo's grandparents, lived in Croatia and were richer than most folks in the town where they lived. Fearing the ruthless persecutions against the Jews across Europe, they secretly sold their properties in Croatia and moved to Palestine. Before they left, they converted their young son, Lajos [Laszlo's father], to the Baptist religion and adopted him into a Baptist family. They left behind quite a bit of gold and silver money as an inheritance for Lajos. Lajos was not circumcised as it was a well-known fact that a male Jew's real identity was his circumcision. When Lajos turned twenty-one, he moved to a different location within Hungary and married a Christian Jewish girl and bought a house in Balatonkeresztur. He still had quite a bit of silver and gold money buried somewhere on the new property. In order to remove any suspicion of his Jewish background, Lajos joined the Communist Party, but only in name. This was a thinly condensed form of Laszlo's background, who now was my next door neighbor.)

Breaking a Promise Once

It was now about eleven o'clock in the night, and I was rushing home to my house next door only to find that Matild had locked my bedroom door and took the key with her. So I went to her, took my right shoe off, and banged her door with it so much so that the heel of it fell off. I was discomforted, and Matild was shaken hearing the loud noise and was afraid that I might do something to her. She threw the key out, shut and locked her door so fast that the door squashed a big moth against the door jam. All the body juice from that fly landed in my face and on my shirt. When I got back and lit my petrol lamp, I saw that it wasn't a big fly at all but something much bigger. My shirt and face had blood squirted on it all over. It must have been either a mouse or a bat that got caught by the door that Matild shut in a split second. The next day she told me it was a bat.

Falling asleep this night wasn't as easy as I thought it would be. *How can so many events pile on each other?* I asked myself.

First, Matild's affair with the Communist Party, then the Collective Farming issue, then Laszlo's entanglement with his father and the Book of Moses. And now Matild again, locking my door and harboring a rotten feeling over my hiding something from her. I don't know how many times I turned and rolled in bed before I jumped out of it. I decided that I would take each event and think about its value. In so doing, I tossed out everything as rubbish, except the Book of Moses. *Something is in that Book for me for guidance,* I thought. *In due time, I might learn it from Laszlo,* I answered.

Then, I went back to bed and lulled myself to sleep, repeating, *Something was in that Book for me.*

When I got up the next morning, I was more tired than before I went to bed. But I thought of my commitments and didn't go back to sleep. I had a promise to fulfill—help the half-crippled Joseph with his cows. I would not break my promise, no matter what.

Laszlo told me the other day, "Breaking a promise once meant that breaking it again would be much easier, and the third time, it would mean nothing. When you lie to yourself, you also lie to others just as easy."

Laszlo learned about lying from the Book of Moses. And that was just one of the myriad things in that book I shall now remember. My question had been answered.

Getting to Know a Mysterious Person

So I was on my way to help Joseph just as I promised I would. Although I was a few minutes late, I didn't disappoint him. He was already waiting for me and was cleaning the manure from under the cows. As he finished piling that stuff onto a flatbed cart, I pushed it out for him to a pile set aside for that purpose. Before long, we finished with that chore. It was time now to wash the cows' udders and milk them.

Before I squeezed any milk into the bucket, I filled my stomach first. Matild didn't show up this morning to carry the milk away, and I didn't really care. After a couple of hours, Joseph gave it to the couple who lived in the middle section of the house, Mr. and Mrs. Joseph Forro.

Although I saw Mr. Forro almost daily as he was moving around the backyard cultivating his own garden, I didn't pay attention to him. I didn't know him and he didn't know me until just a few minutes ago when Joseph introduced me to him.

This encounter with Mr. Forro began a year-long friendship between the two of us. It was the beginning of my learning about the United States of America. In the coming months, he talked to me more about America than I wanted to hear. But later, when I really wanted to know everything, he died.

He lived in America for many years before the war. He regretted coming back with increasing alarm, for the Communists soon encroached on his freedom also. He was regarded now as an enemy of the state, the bourgeois. (Details shall come later.)

Bees Tell You Something

As we finished the work with the cows, Joseph asked me to help him to top off the grapevines in his small vineyard located just behind Mr. Forro's garden. He had there one thousand individually planted grape bushes, some table grapes, others wine grapes. Two to three times a season, these bushes needed to be topped off, or else the vines on them would creep too high and fold over each other. Should that ever be allowed to happen, the life-giving powers of the sun would not reach the grapes on the lower parts of the vines. That would deprive the grapes from producing the necessary sugars needed to maintain a naturally balanced alcohol content of the wine. Otherwise, processed sugar would have to be added to the still unfermented must in the barrels.

"The more processed sugar added during the fermentation process, the worse hangover I would have from it later when it turned to wine, should I feel like tipping the bottle all day," explained Joseph. He knows it best from self-experience.

"How many times a day you tip the bottle?" I asked him.

"Oh, I drink wine all day after lunch. My wine doesn't have processed sugar added to it, so I don't have a hangover the following day. I drink a quart of wine every day. Sometimes two. It all depended on what Matild said or did to me that day. Nice days, I sing to high heaven. Bad days, I curse to low hell and Matild with it."

I enjoyed listening to him as we moved along cutting off the vine suckers.

I kept pace with him, cutting off every sucker that grew on each vine from the bottom to the top. Joseph gave me a very sharp pocketknife, and with it I had no problem slicing off each sucker. Each grape bush had four stalks allowed to grow five feet high. And at that height, it was topped off. Each stalk had clusters of grape, three or four of them, growing not far from each other. To prevent these long stalks from bending to the ground, Joseph drove stakes in the ground to each bush and tied the vines together to it. The stakes were spaced four feet apart in any direction to maintain a straight layout.

It was now the beginning of August, and the white table grapes were turning yellow, indicating that they were ripe. I had no idea when certain type of grapes were ripening. But now, I noticed the gathering of bees around these table grapes. So I asked Joseph, "Why are these bees flying around me?"

"They aren't flying around you, Arpad. They want to get to the grapes. They are telling you, '*Get out of my way.*' After a while, they will get used to you. Don't try to fan them though. If you do, they will sting you. Look here, they already know me."

(Joseph proudly displayed his attraction to the bees. These bees were swarming all around the rim of his hat, for it was saturated with wine sugar. This whole thing happened because, a couple of days ago, Joseph pulled the bottom tap out of one of his large oak barrels in order to flush out the bottom sediments into a hand-held oak vat. His hat accidentally fell into the vat. As he sun-dried it, the liquid evaporated, but the wine sugar stayed deposited in the cloth. Now, as he wore his hat while being in the vineyard, the bees had an instant feast on the rim of it. Eventually, he had to drop it to the ground, for the bees were blocking his sight from being able to work. They never stung the old man.)

"But they will eventually eat all your grapes. Don't they?" I asked.

"No, they won't. We'll harvest them pretty soon. That's why I have you here."

It was now about nine o'clock in the morning. The sun was burning my back. I was sweating from two sources, the sunshine on my back and the work ahead of me. Just about now, I reached the end of my row. Joseph was about ten feet behind on account of the bees. So I stepped next to him and helped him to finish his row.

"You have a good nature, boy, and I don't think you even know it," he remarked.

The Power of Care is in Sharing

I was thinking about what Joseph just said. I really didn't pay attention to the fact that I had a good nature—helping others. That was part of me, I supposed; I was born that way. That I have a good nature was more of an instinct of mine, rather than a soldier's drill. I would push a loaded wheel barrel uphill for an old man. Or lead a blind person across the street. Or give a beggar half of my sandwich. Or even my shirt—without being asked for it. Compassion automatically surfaced in me without realizing it.

"Half the trimming is done. The other half would have to wait 'til tomorrow," I said to Joseph. "I have to go now. I have another promise to attend to. This one is more important than anything else. I fell in love with a girl a couple of days ago and promised her that I would be with her today, sometime between ten and eleven o'clock," I explained.

"You fell in love! How can that be? You are only thirteen years old."

"Does age have anything to do with falling in love, Joseph?"

"I suppose not. Is your heart gripped by it? If it is, you are in love. I want to say only that you are too young. Walk away from that stuff. In due time you would be happy that you did. You are too young. Another girl will solve your problem," Joseph said.

I didn't listen to Joseph. How could have I listened to him? Love was not a pancake that only lasted till I swallowed it. Love was more like heaven; I kept it because my soul had been captured by it. Loving

Ildiko was something that now lived in me, whether I wanted it or not; I could not forget her even if I wanted to. She was in my soul, and I was willing even to die for her.

Joseph took the next row of gapes and kept trimming the suckers. He saw me now running toward the canal as I always did after being dirtied on the job. I did this from spring to fall in order to wash myself clean.

Laszlo saw me running, too. He came to look for me to tell that his father granted his wishes, and was now ready to come to the beach. He carried a fancy handbag. Packed in it was a blanket, two towels, and a body-tight swimming trunk for me. He knew that I had nothing of the sort in my possession. While I bathed in the canal, he helped Joseph as good neighbors would do at times.

"This buddy of yours is in love. I could tell 'cause his mind is in the clouds, daydreaming and smiling without saying anything to me," Joseph commented.

"I know. He told me all about it. He also said, 'The next two weeks I'll be with Ildiko as often as I can be and nothing else will matter.'" Laszlo responded.

Both Joseph and Laszlo were looking toward the canal while trimming the vine suckers. They were already halfway done with one row. Suddenly, they noticed my head, appearing in the midst of the tall grass that covered most the field down to the canal.

I was coming back through the tall grass this time, instead of the beaten path I used to take before. I was curious as to what type of animal would jump out from his hiding place in the tall grass. While I was wading through it, my hands were swaying the spikes of the tall rye grass. I was trying to imitate the way the wind was *undulating* the top of it in waves.

I didn't chase any deer out, but I saw pheasants and partridges flying out in front of me, sensing the danger as my feet shuffled the grass. Toward the end of the field, I saw that other animals were moving forward to stay ahead of me. Rabbits, hedgehogs, prairie dogs were running in all directions when they reached the open field. "With this many wild animals I would never go hungry" ran through my mind.

I didn't have my slingshot with me. I bet if I had, no game would have flown or ran by me. *This is a missed opportunity*, I thought. It would be a good thing to remember that I should never leave my hunting tools behind, for opportunities seldom, if ever, repeat themselves in similar fashion. But I had no regrets. It was just a reminder for the next time.

I looked at the grass field again and enjoyed the lovely colors of the different wild flowers interwoven with the rye grass. How lovely it would be if Ildiko could see it.

Nature was so beautiful, colorful, and peaceful. I should just leave it that way even as I count my troubles ahead of me. *An orphan has very little else besides trouble and hardship,* I thought. *Better to accept it than fight it.*

As I left the grass field, I looked up the slope ahead of me and vaguely saw that Joseph had company. I picked up pace so as to get there faster. In a short time, I recognized that it was Laszlo, who was helping Joseph trimming the suckers off the grape vines.

"Good timing, Laszlo. Fun is waiting for us on Lake Balaton. It's good that you helped Joseph, for I have less to do tomorrow," I said.

Now, Joseph was wondering about us as he remembered his time of youth, when he was dating his first wife. He was still in love with her to this day even though she died ten years ago already. I know this because I overheard him many times crying after her in secret.

He looked at us and said, "I like both of you, for you are full of life. It gives my soul a lift back to my youth. Don't ever give it up! It will keep you young in mind and spirit. I still love my first wife.

Now, before you leave, take your bag and fill it with grapes from the bushes you see in front of you. Take enough and share it with others in your company."

Laszlo ran for his bag, threw out the bulky blanket in order to make room for the grapes. Then, we went to the grape bushes and, cluster after cluster, filled the bag. Joseph didn't mind if we took all he had, for the bees were out in great numbers, sucking on the sweet and aromatic nectar.

As soon as we left the premises, we sat down on Joseph's front bench that faced the street and started stripping these juicy, sweet beads off their stems straight into our mouths. They were the size of Bing cherries and as crispy as when cherries are picked in the early morning hours.

The sweet taste and the aromatic smell invited the honey bees to us perhaps from as far as the end of the village. I enjoyed watching them sipping the juice from the beads held in my hand. Conversely, Laszlo couldn't stop chasing them away. He was flicking them off with his middle finger. Finally, he got stung on his arm. Then, another and another attacked him in defense of their colony. Nothing serious happened; he ran off to avoid the next sting. I sent him to Joseph who dabbed a few drops of his wine over the sting. In a few minutes, both the pain and the swell eased. The acid in the wine was the good medicine that did the cure.

"Next time, Laszlo, let the bees do their own business undisturbed, for they are mind readers and know their enemies in mysterious ways. Know also that bees attack in company when sensing the threat of being killed," I reminded him.

* * *

It was noon now as Laszlo and I passed the local church. The bells were ringing again as they did every day at this time. There wasn't much human traffic in the village now, for most peasants took their siestas wherever they are, inside the house or outside in the fields. As we came closer and closer to Lake Balaton, we saw the vacationing crowd, mostly foreigners, walking back to their beach blankets, carrying their lunches.

Since there was only one restaurant close to the shore, most folks were eating food that was made available at almost every house that faced the street alongside the shore of the lake. There was nothing like home-cooking on their minds. It was inexpensive and delightfully tasty. Just by walking up and down the street, they can pick and choose many different dishes. The smell of stews here and the smell of pastries there made these folks even hungrier than before.

There was no place to sit at these open kitchens facing the street, so these foreigners carried their food back to the beach area, where they could sit on their blankets and eat.

Being on the beach now, we were wondering, where could Ildiko and her family be sitting in this crowd? So we decided to go all the way to the edge of the water and stand there, turning and looking back over the crowd to spot Ildiko somewhere. She was nowhere in sight. After a while, I asked Laszlo to sit on one of the many benches facing the water and wait there while I walked around the whole beach in search of her.

The beach area was about five acres in size. Grass covered the beachfront almost to the water's edge, while the back was wooded to provide shade to those who dislike sunbathing. Next to the water's edge was a narrow sidewalk on which elegantly carved benches were placed at random. Sitting here provided the perfect view of the eye-catching beauty of the other side of the lake. On nice days, the beach was full by noon. The majority of the people here were from East Germany. They knew only a few words of Hungarian, just enough to greet people. No wonder as to why Ildiko's parents loved to come here every day. Both of them spoke fluent German.

So Laszlo sat on one of these benches and enjoyed the beautiful panorama being displayed on the other side of the lake. The different shapes and sizes of the mountains captured his attention, for in this calm weather he could almost touch their tops as they were reflected in the water. In the meantime I was searching for Ildiko.

She wore a mint-colored bikini that perfectly matched her suntanned body. She had blue eyes and a slightly pointed nose. Her lips were even with the curvature of her face. Her long blond hair covered most of her full face, especially when she was reading. She had a paperback on her blanket that she was reading while waiting for my coming.

First, I walked along the shore, thinking that Ildiko would be there somewhere. Then, I turned right toward the soccer field and saw her there. I also saw that she noticed my coming. She got up and waved and walked toward me. As soon as we were close enough, she jumped into my arms, and I caught her and swung her around. There was no other way to release my joy and happiness to be with her again. Then, I put her down, and hand in hand we looked at each other as if we had just returned from a faraway place to visit each other. Her beauty completely sank into my soul—the undeniable sign that I was in love.

We now walked back to her blanket and sat there for a few moments until our passions subsided. Her parents were sitting about twenty feet away on a different blanket. I asked her, "Why are you sitting separately?"

"They always have company and talk German that I don't understand. The language sounds to me as if they are bickering over something. So I made up my mind that I would have a separate blanket and just stay nearby them. And now that is very good 'cause we can be here together separated from them."

My eyes now noticed that the south wind picked up her book marker and blew it away a few feet toward the direction of her parents. It landed not there but on the fourth blanket away. Two boys and two girls were tanning themselves on that blanket. I went after the book marker but didn't know what to say to them in German. So I smiled as I always do when meeting strangers and extended my right hand to receive the book marker from one of the girls. And I tipped my head expressing my thank-you. Then, I went to Ildiko's parents and warmly greeted them. On my way back to Ildiko, I looked at the book marker. It had an angel printed on it, and I wondered, *Why?*

Ildiko noticed what I did and said, "My sister is a nun." I didn't say anything, for I didn't know what to say. In my silence I figured that her sister had a religious impact on her. So I tucked the book marker inside the book and forgot about the whole thing.

A good half an hour must have slipped by when I realized that Laszlo was still waiting for me where I left him.

"Come with me, Ildiko. I have completely forgotten that Laszlo is waiting for me at the other side of the beach."

She was pleasantly surprised. "Why didn't you tell me? I would have reminded you. You know, Lisa is coming today."

We left the blanket and, hand-in-hand again, went to meet Laszlo.

The time now was about one o'clock in the afternoon. Half the crowd was in the water, and the other half was on blankets, amusing themselves on the velvety grass in the open part of the beach. The sun was blazing equally on both groups. The south wind helped, however, to cool the air just enough so that everybody was enjoying the day. While Ildiko blended perfectly well into this crowd and could easily be taken for a German, I stuck out like an abandoned child. My shorts and shoes were worn, whereas everybody else seemed to have colorful-looking, new clothes on. This didn't bother me one bit. My good looks and manner and my sporty body features caught the attention of all those who cared to look at me. And lots of people were looking as we passed by them to the place where Laszlo was. I was convinced now that they were looking at Ildiko being so beautiful, instead of me, being the oddball on the beach.

While Ildiko's head turned in all directions looking for Laszlo, mine was only turned on her. I couldn't help but wonder as to what would happen to her after she returned to Budapest. Who would snatch her away from me? For separation held the seeds of temptation. A beautiful girl that she was had no chance, not even for a moment, to think about me when a hundred other boys fancied themselves close to her in wanting to have her. How good it was that she couldn't read my mind now. How good it was that I was only deluding myself. Hurriedly, I swept the delusion away and turned back to reality.

Laszlo was standing at the bench where I left him. He was looking toward us. It was easier for us to see him than for him to see us in the multitude. When we finally noticed him, we waved, and while waving, all of a sudden, he waved back.

After a couple of minutes of idle talk, we decided to go to the bathroom facility in order to change our clothes. Laszlo handed me the brand new swimming trunk, saying it was too big for him. I pulled the thing on, and it fitted me perfectly. It was more colorful, however, than I would have liked. But in this crowd, I also looked like a German now. Besides, his trunk looked almost identical to mine. Now, we rejoined Ildiko outside the facility and went back to her blanket. I could tell on her face that she enjoyed seeing my new outfit.

Her mother waited for us there, worrying where in the world we had disappeared. We didn't tell her that we went to look for Laszlo.

Now, Laszlo emptied the ten-pound-worth grape clusters from his bag onto Ildiko's blanket. Ildiko's mother, Mama Clare (her nickname), voicing her pleasure, immediately joined us. Then, all her friends there followed. Soon enough, folks from the nearby blankets were curious and, one by one, filtered over and joined the circle, wondering what was going on. It was a novelty, the earliest grapes of the season, and everybody enjoyed themselves taking part in the feast. The honey bees didn't show up this time. They lost the trace of smell, for the wind blew it toward the lake.

I said to Laszlo and Ildiko, "Let's break this up. Let's go swimming 'cause we don't have any more grapes."

As soon as we stepped into the already disturbed water, Ildiko and Laszlo hesitated to go deeper from the shore. The thought of drowning made them fearful and arrested their bodies to the spot. They sat on the red stones that lined the shore and looked at me being uncertain—what will I say or do now?

While I knew that they couldn't swim, I didn't expect them to have such a rigid mindset about it. Now, I was confronted with the task of persuasion, how to go about explaining or even showing that this type of mindset could only be changed by learning how to swim. So I sat between them, having my feet dangling in the water.

"You know, guys, swimming starts right here by being able to move your feet in the right direction. Like this, up and down."

I showed them the feet movements, and they imitated me. While talking to them now about music, singing, and dancing that went on every evening under the dome tent outside the beach, I was able to shift their thinking. Then, I dropped myself into the water in front of them and just sat there. It was pleasant to sit in the cool water and face both of them, drawing their attention to me.

"I'm thinking about tonight, Ildiko. Instead of just sitting on that bench outside your house, we should go dancing tonight. What do you say? Come closer to me so the whole world wouldn't hear our conversation?" I suggested.

Instead of Ildiko, Laszlo jumped next to me. He had not danced before, and the subject aroused his curiosity, thinking that he would find a girl there tonight. He didn't know as yet that Lisa was coming on the five o'clock train this afternoon.

Ildiko hesitated to join us. In order to see both of them, I turned halfway toward Laszlo and halfway toward Ildiko. I wanted to make sure that she had eye contact with me, for what I did now was the most important step learning to swim—the control of breathing. I repeated the same practice I did with Tony. Laszlo imitated me, but Ildiko hesitated. Then, I said to Laszlo, "I want to show you how my upper body would be floating in the water when I filled my lungs with air."

So I asked Laszlo to push my body underwater after I filled my lungs with air and held my breath. He did it. Each time he did it, my body popped back to the surface. Then, I released all the air. This time my body stayed underwater. I did this several times. They were convinced now that it was the air that held my upper body floating. Without saying anything, Laszlo wanted to try it. He wanted to prove this for himself. And that was good, for self-confidence was the key to overcoming his fear.

So it was now my turn to push Laszlo's body underwater. The outcome proved that he could float his body as well as I could. We went back and forth practicing the same thing till it became a plaything for him.

After this exercise, we just sat there for quite a while, talking about tonight's activity. I didn't do any more training, for learning to overcome fear needed time and patience. Ildiko didn't care to try floating underwater.

"Tomorrow, we'll continue," I hinted.

It was Mama Clare, Ildiko's mother, who broke our conversation, reminding us about picking up Lisa at the railroad station. And that it was time now to pack and go.

What she didn't say, however, was that half the crowd left the beach already, fearing the oncoming storm from the north. Threatening, unbelievably dark clouds were moving fast over the mountains and were heading in our direction.

I knew from past experience that a storm like this could start on Lake Balaton without warning. So fast in fact that smaller boats couldn't escape overturning. Five-foot waves, coupled with the gust of wind, tipped them over in no time. Hail mixed with heavy rain and high wind could reduce the visibility to nothing. The fortunate part of these storms was that they only lasted a few minutes and mostly circled themselves over the Lake.

So we hurried out of the water and ran to our blanket. I asked Laszlo now to pick up the blanket and circle it around me so that I could change to my dry pants. Then, I did the same thing to him and also to Ildiko. There was nothing embarrassing about this as everybody else was doing it. We all respected each other's privacy.

* * *

Because Ildiko had already agreed with her parents that we would go separately to pick up Lisa, they already left the beach to go home. By the time we packed our belongings, the dark clouds had been blown away. There was no rain, no hail, not even wind now. The sun was shining on the rainbow that arched the fringes of the far-flung clouds. It was a breathtaking view of the heavens. In my eagerness to keep viewing the sky, I walked straight into a tree and received a light knock on the side of my head. I ignored it and didn't look back anymore. I rushed instead to reach my friends. Since the railroad station was about a half mile away, we got there ahead of time and waited for the train to arrive.

The train was ten minutes late, which was good timing for a commuter train. It had been ordered to park on a side track as the Oriental Express was coming from the opposite direction, heading to Bucharest this time. It had to pass the station nonstop before anybody was allowed to get on or off the commuter train.

The passing train hardly slowed down, but it blared its horns nonstop. We covered our ears to reduce the deafening sound. It was outright scary to think that it could have easily killed any careless passenger.

To our surprise only ten passengers, in addition to Lisa, departed the commuter train. She was lugging one suitcase, which looked as heavy as her own weight. Otherwise, she would not have dragged it so clumsily. I ran to her to lift it off the platform. "You must be Arpad," she cried loudly enough to reveal her identity to Laszlo. I only smiled at her as I was numbed by the weight of the suitcase. In addition to her clothes, she was carrying gold nuggets.

Her father packed the suitcase with it and instructed her to bury it deep under a walnut tree that stood behind the same house Ildiko's parents were renting. Lisa's parents used to come here every year also. This year, only Lisa could come.

While Lisa ran to meet Ildiko, Laszlo rushed to give me a hand carrying the rickety suitcase.

This luggage was wrapped all around with a quarter-of-an-inch-thick hemp rope. The suitcase was ripped at the seams. It was very cleverly wrapped though. The wrap formed three handles, one on the top and two on the sides as it twirled around the suitcase. Now, we grabbed the side handles to make it easier for us to carry it. This way the weight was evenly shared between the two of us. Ildiko and Lisa walked in front of us, and we followed them.

As yet, only Lisa's and Ildiko's fathers knew the contents of the luggage. The two were brothers, known as the Smith family. As soon as we dropped the luggage on the kitchen floor, Ildiko's father disappeared with it. He anticipated the weight of it because for him it felt like manna just dropped from heaven. He buried it as it was already agreed to between the brothers.

In the next few days, Ildiko told me the truth. The two brothers were Jews, converted to Christianity when they were still young, when the persecution of the Jews in Hungary was still in its infancy. In order to protect themselves, both became members later in the Communist Party, but in name only.

(The best way to stay safe, whether one was Christian or Jew, was to become a Communist Party member and participate in the party in ways that didn't hurt people. By keeping quiet about it, strangers had no idea who was a real Communist.)

* * *

So now, we left Lisa and Ildiko and went home, early enough to do some fast cooking. I sent Laszlo home to let his parents know where we were and what we were doing. I also reminded him to talk to them about tonight. Only a few minutes passed, however, and unexpectedly, he was back at my house.

"Father wants to see you about tonight before he would let me go."

I knew that Laszlo had spit a few words to his father in a split second and expected him to grant him freedom for tonight. Laszlo vented words with a speed of light that required slow repeating to make sense out of it.

So I'm back to Laszlo, not even thinking about tonight. He was now standing before his father watching us talking about Joseph and Mr. Forro. Foremost, I wanted to know whether he knew Mr. Forro—who he was and what he was doing. The only answer I received was that he was an American citizen.

Now, I changed the subject and talked about the good times Laszlo and I had this afternoon in the waters of Lake Balaton. All along I assured him that Laszlo was with me, doing what I did and eating what I ate, mainly the grapes from Joseph's vineyard. Laszlo didn't say anything but watched every word I said. And I said all these things to convince his father to stay calm and realize that Laszlo was safe in my company. Finally, he asked the question I wanted to hear: "What are the two of you planning to do tonight?"

I explained everything to him regarding Lisa and about dancing. And he agreed to let Laszlo come.

We came back now to my house. Since there was nothing cooked to eat, we ate rye bread heavily spread with lard.

As we were slowly munching the crusty bread to satisfy our churning stomachs, Joseph and Matild arrived home from the wheat fields. They were manually harvesting the golden spikes with the help of Joseph's relatives. They saw that my kitchen door was wide open, thinking that gypsies might have broken into the house and left the door open upon escaping.

As soon as Matild saw me, she rushed closer and opened her wide mouth, sputtering her words into my face. Joseph pulled her back as he was convinced that she would knuckle me to the floor.

"I looked all over for you this afternoon. I wanted you to cut the wheat stalks for us. But you ran away. Why?" she demanded to know.

"I didn't know that you were in such pain that you couldn't do it yourself," I replied.

"Pain I don't have, but I have you. A sloth courting a bitch from Budapest. I know all about it. If you don't want me to light a fire under your straw mattress, you better fall in line," she yelled.

"What do you mean, 'fall in line?'"

"Nothing less than work! Work in the stall—cleaning and feeding the cows. Work in the field—harvesting everything that is ready to be stored. Work around the house—cleaning and feeding the animals and bringing firewood from the forest," she demanded.

"Wouldn't you like to have two or three youngsters like me around you?" I yelled back.

Now, I became frazzled over her cruelty and snapped back at her again, "I'll call Iren to straighten you out."

Only one person in the whole world Matild was afraid of. That person was my oldest sister, Iren. Hearing the word *Iren*, she choked, not being able to say another word. She turned around, almost pushed her limping husband over, and went home to her side of the duplex. Joseph stayed behind for a moment or so and said, "I'll have a word or two with her. I'm on your side, Arpad."

He followed Matild now and left the scene. As he was limping away, I called after him, "Don't fight over me, Joseph."

We had no more time left as it was seven o'clock in the evening already. I locked the kitchen door, and off we went to meet the girls without even looking at Matild's kitchen.

Ildiko and Lisa were already walking toward us, for they couldn't sit on the bench in front of their house. The landlord occupied it.

(This landlord was Matild's second cousin. It was she who spread the gossip about me and Ildiko. Her name was Helen, and she lived behind Ildiko's place in a separate building. I don't know a lot about her but remembered from Mother that she didn't return our family Bible she borrowed. I also know that this was the woman who was the mouthpiece of the Communist Party. She roamed the town day in, day out to pick up information about anybody who was against the party. Now, she would see us again as we had to walk by her to go to Lake Balaton. Matild would probably know about it by tomorrow, as gossipers spread news fast as in olden times, on horseback.)

As I met Ildiko again, I kissed her, all the more now that Helen was watching. We paired side by side. I was in the back with Ildiko, while Lazlo with Liza in the front. We talked and laughed about how the day went by so fast on the beach.

We walked by Helen as if we didn't know her. After passing her, I felt that she was eagerly looking at us. She never had the opportunity to do what we did, holding hands through which our hearts sent the message of love to each other. She is still an old maid like Matild used to be. Still feeling that she is feverishly looking, I turned my head back and said, "Matild needs to know that I am in love with Ildiko."

I must have pumped her blood pressure high, for she jumped from her seat and disappeared like a cursed ghost.

* * *

We picked up speed now as we heard the loud music, echoing lovely melodies. The band was playing mostly rock and roll. It was the same type of music I used to listen to and dance to in the evenings when I was home alone. (And I didn't care if anybody saw me.)

There was nothing elaborate about this dancing place. It was under a large dome tent erected wide and high in the grass field that bordered the beach. It was nearby where we spent the afternoon just a few hours ago. The members of the band were amateurish, yet they knew quite well many of the Western songs in fashion now.

Because of the simplicity of the place, most kids came the way they were—barefoot. It was better to dance on the velvety grass barefoot than wearing shoes. And while the grass lasted, all those who wore shoes took them off and threw them on the side, only to fight over them in the dark later. For when the dance was over, they couldn't find the matching pairs they wore before—others wore the same style shoes also.

We have now only one problem: Laszlo doesn't know how to dance. Regardless how much I tried to teach him privately, I wasn't a girl to give him that attraction girls add to motivate a partner to learn.

I was just the opposite from Laszlo. Dancing was not only in my feet but also in my mind; and in that sense, I was dancing in harmony to the tact I heard. So now, I was dancing one rock and roll with Ildiko and one with Lisa. Laszlo danced to the slow-type music only. That way, he could hold onto Lisa and chug left to right and right to left without fanfare. It really didn't matter whether anybody knew how to dance or not; the whole arena was packed with girls and boys from East Germany. The best that anybody could do was to move outside the tent. And that was what I and Ildiko did.

No drinks were served in the immediate area of the tent; but not far, beer, wine, and even hard liquor were available for grown-ups. We had none of this stuff, for we knew that that would have been the end of keeping our company together.

The band took a ten-minute break now. So we decided to go home a little earlier than planned. It was after ten o'clock already. This was a good decision on our part, for Laszlo's father was already on his way looking for his son's whereabouts. We met him halfway home. And when we did, his worry turned to joy. "I'm glad that you have managed your time well. Do the same tomorrow and the day after," he said.

What he had in mind, however, was more futuristic than a compliment for keeping track of time. He knew that keeping track of time in Laszlo's mind was a constant irritant for him. He also knew that I was kind of an expert in telling the time of day, almost as accurately as if I wore a wristwatch.

Yes, Mr. Smith was correct; but I never thought of it that way. Keeping the time was more part of my survival than anything else. I learned it very early in life that keeping track of time was key to keeping my promises to others also on time.

Since Laszlo's father came on bicycle, he turned around and left us. But he didn't pedal homebound. He chose to check out the very area where we were dancing. He was looking for familiar faces to assure himself that there was someone supervising the area—in case of trouble. He wasn't concerned over the combat-ready Germans, but rather the safety of his son, being there at the wrong time. When he saw that three cops dressed in civilian clothes were patrolling the area, he pedaled back and caught up with us. Laszlo and I were still entertaining the girls in front of their house.

"Come on, boys, enough for today!" He yelled from his bicycle and kept pedaling home. The fatherly reminder made Laszlo follow his command, and he left us, saying: "Arpad, hurry to my house as soon as you can."

On the way there, I was wondering what kind of trouble was waiting for him now.

It was, however, the best thing that Laszlo could have asked me to do. For, when I entered the house, his mother had a full meal prepared for us. It was beef stew with mashed potatoes. She knew that we had not eaten anything meaningful before we left the house. Frankly, I didn't have beef stew for the longest time I could remember; and for that reason, my stomach craved far more than I could eat. And without even asking for more, Laszlo's mom put the whole pot in front of me. There wasn't much more left in it; but whatever stew was there, I wiped it out with a slice of rye bread. I had no pretension whatsoever to quell my hunger.

"Go home now and go to sleep," Laszlo's mother said. But I couldn't go home without asking his father whether he would allow me to pick up his son tomorrow and go to the beach again. I did this as a matter of courtesy, rather than assuming Laszlo's previously granted freedom.

"Will that be an everyday thing from now on, Arpad?" he asked.

And I explained myself this way: "Sir, when you were my age, weren't your eyes rolling and your pants shivering to see girls? What did you do?"

"The same thing you do," he answered.

"Well then, we aren't doing anything wrong, are we?"

Laszlo jumped and quickly assumed that what his father did, he could do as well.

But in reality, that wasn't the case. His father wasn't thinking that way at all. He was more like a preacher, *not as I do, but as I say you do.* He was not going to let Laszlo make the same mistakes he did. But that mentality wasn't correct either, for the same mistakes he made took on different versions in Laszlo. The timing, the people, and the events made all the difference.

"I was not allowed to be with girls in the open, and I heard that you had a girl on your hand today, doing just that. Because I defied my father and did foolish things in the open, the old man grounded me from being with girls after that. By tradition, he was supposed to choose a girl for me, whether I agreed to it or not. Don't you think that I should have done the same thing for you, Laszlo?"

"I look at traditions differently, Father. I want to date a girl that I like, and if I fall in love with her, then I would ask your permission to marry her—but only as a matter of courtesy. I think, it is wrong to marry a girl that parents choose for their children, thinking that they will learn to love each other in due time by getting used to each other." Laszlo made his point.

Mr. Smith was only probing his son's mind regarding the orthodox Jewish tradition and the modern *free-will* mentality about dating and marriage. He himself didn't agree with the old Jewish tradition either. When he got married, he chose a girl he loved. And his father never knew about it, never mind getting his approval for it. Of course, they were separated by a thousand miles from each other because the Nazis were already persecuting the Jews in Croatia.

The gist of the matter boiled down to this: Mr. Smith didn't want his son to do anything in secret, regarding dating girls. He only wanted to know about it. Now he confirmed it: "Youngsters are tempted to do a lot more forbidden things in secret than in the open." Then added, "You should have at least told me that you and Arpad were dating girls. Go tomorrow and every day when possible, but tell me about it."

As far as the dating and the marriage dilemma between Laszlo and his father was concerned, I had nothing to worry about. I no longer had parents. Nevertheless, it left one significant impression in me—Jews were guided by the laws of Moses. What will I be guided by when I become an adult? Only God knew that better.

* * *

Now, it was almost midnight when I bowed my head onto my feather-filled pillow. Nothing bothered me, nothing at all. Next day, the glowing morning sun woke me up. And my inner clock reminded me to go to Joseph, for he was waiting for me.

Just as I entered Joseph's front yard, Mr. Forro was leaving it, carrying two sacks in his hands. They looked like short burlap bags with two handles attached to each. They were full of fresh vegetables of all sorts that he just dug from his garden. He was selling them to the eateries close to the beach. The sacks looked heavy to me as his shoulders were sagging low from them. Being about seventy years old, he had difficulty now walking straight. The sacks pulled him from one side to the other as he was moving forward. He appeared to me more like an orthodox rabbi, dressed in black from head to toe and wore a broad-brimmed hat. I was afraid to ask him as to why he was wearing black clothes all the time. But when I did, he said, "That's all I have."

I always admired my strength in the morning. Since I was an early riser, I used to finish all my chores before others usually woke up. The only time I couldn't do it was when I had to wait for others, as in the case of Joseph or Matild. They both loved to sleep late in the morning.

Now, of course, I decided that Joseph would have to wait today a little bit longer, as I volunteered to carry Mr. Forro's sacks all the way to the place he was going with them.

"Aren't you kind, Arpad?" And he handed both bags to me. They were heavy, indeed. Every couple of hundred feet, I had to put them down and rest until the old man caught up to me. The church was only about eight hundred yards away from Joseph's house, and we rested there for about five minutes. The old man needed a break to recover himself as he was rushing after me; all the while I was running with the sacks. He turned toward the church, bowed his head, and made the sign of the cross on himself.

"Why have you bowed to a building?" I asked him.

"In my heart, this is not a building only. This is the house of God. It is a building for those only who don't believe in God. I call them Communists. Do you have a heart for God, Arpad?" Mr. Forro asked.

"How should I know that? I never saw him."

"You don't have to see him. You know, there are only two things in your heart, either the devil or God," he responded and went on saying, "And the way you know which one is in your heart is by judging yourself. Am I doing good deeds to others, or bad things to hurt them?" he explained.

"What about mischief? I do a lot of that. Where would that fall?" I asked him.

"As long as you don't hurt others with it, mischief is only fooling around," he answered.

"I like that. You cheer me up, Mr. Forro. You really cheer me up." I smiled at him, thinking that this man was really a good man. For at his age, this man had real wisdom to know what was bad and what was good. Without saying anything more, I picked up the sacks and went with them all the way to the beach and waited there for him to catch up.

"I thought I would never get here," he said. Then added, "I never thought you would be the one who would help me, for you are always on the run."

156

"I don't run because I fancy it, Mr. Forro. There is always a chore ahead of me, and I run to finish it. Now, I am heading back to Joseph to help him. I hope he is still sleeping."

*   *   *

It was now about seven o'clock in the morning, for the church bells were calling folks to prayer. But as I saw it on my way back, there wasn't a soul around the church. Its doors were shut by the Communists. But I wasn't sure, so I ran to the main entrance door and found it shut. Then, I peeked inside through the railings that covered a small window in the upper part of the door. All I saw was a body prostrated before the altar. Whether he was dead or alive, I couldn't tell. So I left now to see Joseph.

I found Joseph sitting on his bedside. He had a bad dream. He was flying just below calamitous clouds. Hail with rain was pelting his body, and he couldn't escape from it, no matter how hard he tried to fly away. "I wonder who had control over my dreams. This dream I had was so real that I thought it would mean the end of me. I was going to get up earlier, but I couldn't. Anyway, it's now over. Thank God, it's over and I'm alive."

Regardless what Joseph dreamed or said, my attention turned now to Matild.

"Were you able to talk to Matild as you said you would, Joseph? She can't demand that I do all that work she said I had to do."

"Yes, I did talk to her. I even told her that she could end in jail for abusing a minor. She got scared when I said that. Then, she said, 'I won't demand anything from him now on. I would rather ask him instead—if he could help me out—and I would return his help with favors,'" Joseph explained.

A big weight fell off my shoulders after hearing what Joseph said. But I did not believe Matild. I no longer trusted her.

I now stepped outside from the stall and heard the sound of bells ringing, signaling to the cow owners in the village to let their cows out in order to join the herd that was heading to the grass fields to graze. I ran back to the stall and reminded Joseph what was going on. And he replied, "Other times, I let them go grazing. But not now. They have not been milked yet."

It was now almost routine as to what I needed to do: Fork out the manure-soaked straw from under the cows, brush them, wash their udders and milk them. It took me about an hour to finish this task. Joseph didn't have to do anything. I asked him not to do anything. Nothing was more bothersome to me than having him poke the straw around me, picking up a few strands here and there, and limping to the cart with it. I discovered a faster way to do the work. I took a garden rake, pulled all the mess into one pile, and loaded everything onto the flat-bed cart and pushed it out, all at once. And while I was doing that, Joseph stuffed his pipe, lit it, and sat down on the edge of his bed, puffing the smoke into circles, admiring how quickly I moved around and finished the work.

"No wonder Matild wants you to do the many different jobs for her. Your skilled movements and the speed of your hands make me feel depressed for not being able to imitate you. On top of that, you sing along while your work." Joseph giggled.

"This was I, Joseph, and I have no control either over the speed or the skill as I do things. My mother used to say, 'The speed of your hands was pushing your mind to think ahead.'"

* * *

The day was still early, and I had about three more hours left before I would call it quits. It was disheartening to realize how quickly Matild and Joseph could come up with other works once I finished the first load. This was the time I also realized that if I don't control my goodwill nature, they would exploit every shred of my energy for their benefit.

Now, Matild showed up with a hired laborer and asked me to spend a couple of hours with him to harvest the still standing wheat in the field.

"Why do you want me to do this, Matild?" I asked.

"I'm testing your willingness. I figure if you agreed, I would send the guy home and have you do the job alone. We need only one man to cut the stalks."

"That is very shrewd, Matild."

"I thought you had nothing else to do anyway. Why should I give this guy a fried duck, instead of giving it to you? A fried duck is a very expensive bird nowadays. What do you say?"

Matild was manipulating my mind by whetting my appetite, and with it she hid her ruse. She knew how much I loved fried ducks.

"I lost my appetite, Matild, for the food was meant to be given to this man in exchange for his hard work. Now that you promised this man a fried duck, you shall give him a fried duck. If you don't, I'll fry one for him from my ducks that you stole while I was away at Iren's."

This hired man was a beggar. He was begging for food around the eateries on the beach where foreigners gave him their leftovers. I saw him many times before and always had pangs of sorrow for him. I knew that I was not far behind him. The only difference between the two of us was that I was young, gutsy, and daring to work, many times just for a good meal in exchange. How Matild found him, I don't know.

Having outsmarted Matild this time, I ran to the canal to wash myself. I couldn't have been happier, for what I had done began *"the watch out for yourself"* thinking in light of the advantage seekers of my goodwill nature. I cannot tell you how many times I heard my sweet mother say: "Watch out for yourself!" A word of wisdom is the hardest thing to keep when it requires my absolute submission to accept it, at times contrary to my stubborn resolutions.

* * *

Now that I had plenty of time left before I would team with Laszlo and join the girls on the beach, I set my mind on lighter things for an hour, singing along as I was cutting the young shoots off from willow bushes that lined the shores of the canal. One of my hobbies is weaving wicker baskets from the skinned and dried willow shoots. I learned the procedure from my godfather. It was his hobby, too, during the winter days to weave baskets from the already prepared snow-white willow shoots. He had customers lined up for the whole winter days. His work was so nice that some folks collected them as a piece of art for decorating their parlors. Needless to say, I have learned enough from him that now I could do the simple weaving of utility baskets on my own.

After I collected an armful of these three-foot-long, slender shoots, I ripped their leaves off backward from the top down and put the shoots aside. The armful now became a handful, for the leaves took up the space between the shoots. So I went back and cut more and more until I really had an armful. Then, I tied the bundle together with several of the same shoots and carried it home on my shoulder and put it in a cool, moist storage for the winter days.

Next to my potbelly stove, I used to sit and weave utility wicker baskets. I was singing quite aloud, too, or reciting poems of my favorite poet, Sandor Petofi.

* * *

While swimming in the canal and collecting willow shoots in between, Laszlo was home preparing himself and also some food, as we were going together later to the beach. By the time I arrived home with my heavy bundle, it was almost twelve o'clock noon. He was already waiting for me at my kitchen door, playing with my docile hens. They thought he had food in his hands to feed them. When the rooster saw what he was doing, he took flight straight at Laszlo's head in order to protect his hens. That left a minor scratch on the left side of his face. Laszlo was slightly bleeding from the scratch. He ran back home to his mother in order to clean the mess and patch the scratch on his face. Soon he returned and was crying as I arrived. Crying because the tape marred his handsome Jewish face. He explained the incident. As a result, I became really angry at this rooster, the only one Matild had. I rushed to the kitchen, grabbed my slingshot and shot him dead. I left the dead bird on the ground for Matild to dispose of. She would never know what had happened because (stone) slingshots didn't leave open wounds on the carcass. It was the stone concussion against the rooster's head that killed the bird.

"Laszlo, you are a cuckoo! Don't you know that roosters attack to protect their hens?"

"You think I could still go with you?" he asked.

"Laszlo! This is nothing more than a claw scratch. I get it almost daily. Don't worry about it. It will be over as soon as the blood dries."

Just before we arrived to the beach, I ripped off the tape that covered Laszlo's scratch. There wasn't much of anything left visible. The reason as to why I ripped it off, instead of gingerly removing it, was because Laszlo was a crybaby, very sensitive to the slightest pain. By ripping the tape off, he didn't even hiss. He didn't know, however, that when I ripped off the tape, I also ripped off the dark fuzz that was sticking to it. Now the patch mark was more visible than the scratch. Laszlo didn't see that, and I didn't say anything about it. For he would have run back home to check it and might have changed his mind coming to the beach. Good thing that we didn't carry mirrors with us as girls do; for seeing the patch on his face, he might not have wanted to face Lisa with it.

Although Laszlo was initiated into adulthood by the bar mitzvah ceremony, he didn't have the maturity behind it to withstand pain and hardship as part of growing up, especially the type of hardship that I was going through. To me, pain and hardship during my growing years meant education in the making of a real man. It all happened, though, by the whims of destiny.

* * *

Both Ildiko and Lisa weren't looking for us any longer on the beach. They were sure something unexpected happened to us. Since they sat at the same place as yesterday, we knew where to look for them. As we got closer and closer, we saw that they were playing canasta on their blanket. I wanted to sneak up on Ildiko from behind and surprise her, but Lisa noticed me from the opposite direction and smiled. It alerted Ildiko that we were there.

We came empty-handed this time. Even Laszlo's bag we forgot in front of my kitchen door. Ants probably already crawling and feasting inside on the fatty pork sandwiches Laszlo prepared for the two of us. We had no need for the handbag anyway, for we wore the same swimwear we had yesterday. Besides, who cared for the sandwiches now? Two beautiful girls fulfilled everything we needed.

It was undeniably visible to Laszlo and Lisa that Ildiko and I were in love and that they weren't. They greeted each other with fake smiles and wondered how it would be possible to fall in love.

Later, on the way home, Laszlo wanted to know the meaning of love. I couldn't really define it for him. Nevertheless I said, "Love can't be handed over one another, and it can't be copied either, regardless of how much one tried to do it. Real love is a time-honored mystery.

Nobody can see it coming, only can suddenly feel its presence." And Laszlo replied, "I can't wait for that moment."

These words, of course, weren't mine. I put them together from reading the love poems of Sandor Petofi—the most popular Hungarian poet of all time.

Ildiko and I left the blanket, leaving Laszlo and Lisa behind to mind their own. We went to the edge of the water and sat on a huge red stone that slanted toward the water. It was the right time and the right place to talk about how to keep our relationship on fire once she returned to Budapest.

I thought that after she returned to Budapest, I had a better chance to see her than she had to see me. My sister, Iren, lived less than twenty miles from Budapest.

"I could take a fast train every Sunday morning and, less than three hours, could be at the East Station in Budapest waiting for you. We could spend a few hours there together and do whatever we liked. Then on my way back, I could stop at Rackeresztur and visit my sisters, Iren and Ella."

"How would you pay for your tickets?" she asked.

"It's free. My father was a railroad official. Therefore I could travel on any train anytime free of charge until I turned eighteen."

"Wow, that's great! We should go right now to the railroad station here and look at the schedules. I could be waiting for you at the end of the rail tracks on your arrival."

As she finished saying this, we slipped off the slanted stone straight into the water and waded to the ramp to get out. We ran back to the blanket and invited Laszlo and Lisa to come with us to the rail station. As we passed by Ildiko's parents, we stopped and told them where we were going.

"What's the rush, Ildiko?" her father asked.

"It's very interesting, Father, but I want to keep it a secret for now. I'll tell it to you tonight."

It was best for both of us to keep our plans secret for now in order to avoid any embarrassment should things turn out wrong. It was I who insisted on this. I didn't want Laszlo to travel to Budapest every time I went there. Inasmuch as I liked Laszlo, I could not afford sharing all my free time with him. I wanted to devote myself just to Ildiko.

At the railroad station, I asked Ildiko that she go alone to the waiting room and check all the train schedules posted all around the wall for the whole country.

"Pick out a fast train that runs on Sundays with only a few stops. Make sure it stops here, I mean, both directions. Don't worry about my time, just yours," I said.

My two companions were under the impression that Ildiko had to run to the bathroom.

While she was inside, we walked around to see the different flowerbeds surrounded the railroad station. Each bed had a different type of flower planted in it. We were mingling now with foreigners who came to marvel at the same flowers we marveled. Nobody touched any flower, except me. I didn't care to read the postings, for each bed had one. They highlighted the type of flower in different languages; I wasn't about to spend the afternoon reading them. When we reached the rose beds, I just broke off a yellow bud as a child would have and kept on walking. I made up my own rule this time and followed it, thinking that if it meant to express real love, even the gardener would have given it to me, just for the asking. I was so sure about that.

Just as Ildiko returned, I gave her the flower, convinced that she would interpret the same sign I did—the sign that flowers meant to tell.

*   *   *

It was now almost six o'clock in the afternoon, and we had to hurry back to Ildiko's parents. Folks were already streaming from the beach; the parents were among them. While Ildiko and Lisa joined them, I and Laszlo decided to stay behind awhile in order to enjoy the beauty of the lake and just walk around observing the foreign boys and girls—their clothing and their manner. On leaving the girls, I said to Ildiko that we would be coming to meet them again in front of the house around seven o'clock.

Dogs and cats were running on the beach, picking up tidbits of food here and there. We could see hawks too, circling above and eyeing the careless pigeons, doing the same things the dogs and cats did—scavenging for food.

Aimlessly walking and talking, we could see and hear just about anything happening around us. Lots of boys and girls were still huddling and loudly talking. We could hear who were joking and who were serious in their attitude and manner. Their faces cast a million signs to tell it.

"I'm now convinced that learning about how people behave is best observed by being among them. What a great opportunity this is to recognize what I still lack and how to improve myself! Don't you agree, Laszlo?"

"I was so awkward with Lisa. We just sat on that blanket like two dummies, turning and looking whether others were watching us. And I saw you talking and doing things that Ildiko enjoyed."

"You weren't listening to what I just said, Laszlo. Now that you saw what I did around Ildiko, you should have discovered the answers to your awkwardness. Others show us the way how we should change ourselves.

"Next time you see Lisa, move out of your box and keep talking, explaining to her what you know, what you like, and even what you don't know and don't like. Tell her also who you are. Then, she would respond and tell you her life's story. Interaction is what you need to do, Laszlo. That's how even birds find each other.

"But remember, usually, it is not the girl who melts the ice in a cold relationship. My brother told me all this. And I know this to be a fact, for he always had a girl to go with, dance with, talk with, and simply enjoy life with. Sharing was the building block to his romance."

* * *

Now, I turned my head, and in my disbelief, I saw Mr. Forro in the distance coming toward us, weighed down on both sides with the same bags I saw him this morning. This time he was carrying leftovers from the same eateries he sold his vegetables to. He was surprised, too, seeing me again, looking as if I had nothing else to do.

"What brought you here at this hour, Arpad? Shouldn't you be helping Joseph and Matild?"

"Must I be with them all the time? Don't I deserve some liberty of my own?"

"Yes, yes, of course, you do! I don't mean it that way. What I mean is how did you break away from them?"

"I realized how cunning Matild was with me, and I told her so and left her to her miseries. She will be the same tomorrow, but I won't be. I won't put up with her slave-driving anymore. I am too young for that," I answered.

"You have to be clever with those folks, and I see that you are getting smarter day by day. One day, I'll tell you something—how I lived in a foreign country," he said.

"In a foreign country?"

"Now, it is not the right time to talk about that, for it was a long journey," Mr. Forro responded and changed the subject. He asked us to help him carrying his bags.

I took one bag; Laszlo took the other.

"Is there anything good to eat in these bags?" I asked him.

"Yes, plenty. Are you hungry?"

"Terribly."

"Let's go then to the church's yard over there. There are a couple of benches there where we can sit and you can eat your full. I have fried chicken, bread, and fried dough. But they are all sizeable leftovers. Both of you can help yourselves to it."

So we hurried to the benches. They were only a couple hundred feet away. As soon as we got there, he unpacked the leftovers.

I really didn't care that the food was leftover. I was very hungry and ate just like it. And now the church bells rang again. This time it was seven o'clock in the evening.

"Did you hear what had happened here yesterday?" Mr. Forro asked and went on saying, "The Communist agents beat the parish priest and threw his body before the altar. It took the priest all night to recover there. But he is all right now."

I didn't respond. Now I knew what had happened to the man whom I saw this morning lying before the altar. He wasn't just any priest. He was my catechist.

"Mr. Forro, are you a Catholic?" I asked.

"Yes, I am. But I no longer practice it openly. I am scared to practice it. The whole village is scared," he said.

"What are you going to do then?"

"I pray alone. I carry God in my heart. He is in my heart. If he weren't there, I wouldn't be able to find him in this church or in any other church. He knows that. He sees that 'cause he is everywhere, whether I call on him or not. Although I physically don't see him, I don't need to see him—'cause I believe in him. That's how strong my faith is in him," Mr. Forro asserted.

What Mr. Forro said to me meant more than the entire lessons I received during my catechism classes: "I carry God in my heart."

Can anyone love God more? I wanted to ask him, but I changed my mind.

Laszlo was carefully listening to what Mr. Forro said, and as he heard his proclamations, he was convinced that what he was doing by reading and believing the words of Moses, he had God in his heart also.

It was time now to pack and leave. The church stood high on this hill, now an empty place. As we left, I was pondering how many people in this village would dare to say now, "I carry God in my heart."

As we came close to Ildiko's place, I saw that the bench in front was empty. I had no idea what could have happened. So we kept walking to Mr. Forro's place which was diagonally located on the other side of the street. We handed the bags back to him and politely parted company.

Just next to us was Joseph's bench, where we sat and waited now, thinking that the girls had to attend to their *business* before coming out the house. And we were correct in thinking that. But it was only Ildiko who showed up. I waved to her, and she waved back. Then, she ran across the street to us and handed me a piece of paper on which she had written my train schedules for my visiting her after she returned to Budapest. Then, she said, "Lisa is not feeling well. She has her period. She won't come to the beach tomorrow." Then she continued with a message from her, "'Tell Laszlo, come to visit me in the afternoon tomorrow. I'll be sun-tanning in the backyard.'"

"Does this change your schedule also, Ildiko?" I asked her.

"It does. Dad wants to take us on a boat ride tomorrow across Lake Balaton to Badacsony. And he wants you, alone, to come. Will you come?" she asked.

"Let me ask Laszlo first if he could do me a favor. I would need him to attend Joseph's cows. If he would, then, I could go with you."

When I asked Laszlo, he responded with total commitment as good friends would do. "Yes, I would," he said and continued, "I'll go to Joseph in your place tomorrow morning and help him."

(Badacsony is a very well-known tourist attraction. It's a low but a wide mountain with a flat top, perfectly visible from the south side of the lake. Its famous wines and its many wine cellars draw thousands of tourists from all over Europe every year. Mr. Smith, Ildiko's father, comes here every year, for he loves to drink wine. But he doesn't drink wine from Badacsony every day, for he couldn't afford it. So every year when he visits Balaton, he makes a holiday out of it coming here.)

This time, however, I would be in Badacsony with the family, and I'm guessing that many surprises would be waiting for me—maybe even the first of its kind in my young life.

Ildiko left us at the bench as fast as she came, hurrying to join her family having a late supper. Soon after that, Laszlo and I left also. On the way home and even at my house, we discussed the uncertainties of tomorrow—the cows. The closest Laszlo had ever been to cows was the milk bottle. So now he asked, "What am I going to do at Joseph's place?"

"Tell Joseph first why you are there. Then, ask him how you can help him."

When Joseph saw Laszlo and heard what he wanted to do, he decided to do all the clean-up himself. Going close to his cows by a stranger was equivalent to receiving first aid. They kicked the minute a stranger touched them. That was the extent of Laszlo's help at Joseph's. He returned home being sad, not so much for himself, but for my sake.

"Tomorrow, I'll go with Arpad, and I'll make up for today. I'll learn how to tame cows. I swear that I'll learn how to tame cows," he vouched for himself.

Laszlo had plenty of time on his hands now. So he offered his help to his invalid mother, suffering from internal bleeding that doctors couldn't determine where it came from. She knew that the source was internal, for her stool showed it. Occasionally, it was black, and at other times red. She knew in her heart that her days were numbered. Yet she never complained. When Laszlo noticed that she was in pain from lifting and carrying things, he jumped to help her.

Laszlo and Lisa

While he was helping his mother, he couldn't help thinking about the afternoon, his meeting with Lisa. He had to find the way to elicit from his mind all the answers he needed to overcome his tepidness talking to Lisa. He remembered what I told him: "Usually, it's not the girl who breaks the ice in a cold relationship." Thinking about this, Laszlo decided that he would not hesitate to ask questions from Lisa and respond to hers as well. This way he would find out who she was and what her interest in life was. And, then, he would tell her all about himself, too. This way, one thing would lead to another in the process of knowing each other. This was Laszlo's game plan, and he was determined to follow through with it. If nothing else, he could really talk convincingly to Lisa about his Jewish background. After all, she had similar background also.

It was now two o'clock in the afternoon. Laszlo told his mother all about his plans with Lisa and went his way to visit her. He didn't want to go on Main Street this time, for he didn't want to meet, see, or talk to anybody who might have softened his well-thought-out resolve. The backyard where Lisa stayed fronted onto the same street Laszlo chose to walk. On his way, he collected a big bouquet of wild flowers, assuring himself that it would definitely help convince Lisa that he cared for her. As he walked closer and closer, he saw Lisa, sitting on a red blanket and reading a paperback. Lisa noticed him also, and she closed her book and put it on her blanket. Her eyes suddenly became fixed on the bouquet, as she has never seen anybody carrying an armful of wild flowers.

"I don't know whether any boy ever brought you wild flowers, Lisa. So I thought I would surprise you with it," Laszlo said.

"As a matter of fact, you did. No other boy did this to me before. You know, Laszlo, it takes a special person to pick wild flowers. That person reveals something special about himself. Does your heart cry after mine?" she asked. Then, she took the bouquet from him and marveled at the beauty of the various colors of wild poppies propped here and there with daisies.

While Lisa was marveling the beauty of the wild flowers, Laszlo's eyes caught the title of the book Lisa was reading, *Ruth, Judith, Esther*. His feelings surged high from reading these names; they were heroic people from the Bible he also read. He fast responded.

"Yes, my heart is yearning to know you. You know, this book you are reading, I read already. I recognized the names immediately."

"Was it in Hungarian or Hebrew? Mine is in Hebrew."

"What you are really saying is that you have a Jewish heritage. Can you speak the language, too?" Laszlo wanted to know.

"Not as well as I should like to. What about you? Do you have a Jewish heritage also?"

"I sure do. But I don't practice the traditions in the open, and I cannot speak the language either. I'm also converted to Christianity."

"So am I. And I don't practice any of my Jewish traditions in the open either," Lisa responded.

(Needless to say, it was a well-known fact already that the Jews had been, and in some ways even now, being quietly oppressed under the Communist system.)

So the cold relationship between the two instantly melted. Whoever could have foreseen that Laszlo's relationship with Lisa would be continually destined for the better even though the uncertainties were interrupting the path to it? Laszlo's tepidness disappeared, and his hesitation turned to boldness. Laszlo couldn't wait for tomorrow to tell me how good he felt about being able to communicate with Lisa, similarly, as I did with Ildiko.

CHAPTER ELEVEN

Ildiko's Father and I in Badacsony

I didn't want to see Laszlo that morning in case he would change his mind. I didn't want him to come with me to Badacsony. It was also better for him to be alone in order to work out his own problems uninterrupted. These thoughts came to mind as I saw Laszlo walking to Joseph. He couldn't see me, but I could see him through the cracks in my window's shutter.

So I reassured myself now that Laszlo wouldn't run after me and wouldn't come with us to the railroad station, hence to Badacsony.

So we went first to Fonyod by train. This town was another tourist attraction; it was the homeport of several nicely looking ferries. The train ride lasted only fifteen minutes. By the time we arrived, the ferries were already in full swing. One was going, while the other was coming to and from Badacsony.

Being on the ferry now, I watched the mountains ahead, getting bigger and bigger in front of me. Seagulls circled the ferry as the tourist fed them. The ferry was packed, as the summer season was almost over for the children who had to return to school. They all wanted to see Badacsony, if for no other reason, climb the gentle slopes to the top, and look back, viewing the unparalleled beauty of the surroundings. Our purpose was different. Mr. Smith invited me and the family for a fancy dinner halfway up the mountain and then wine tasting on the way down. This time, he didn't want to climb to the restaurant as he did in previous years.

So he hired three horses, one for me and Ildiko, and two for themselves. Ildiko was skilled already in handling horses, while I knew nothing about them. Now, the horses were all saddled and waited for the riders. Ildiko hopped in the saddle on her horse, and I sat in the back of her without a saddle, just holding onto her and pressing my heels against the horse's belly. Right from the beginning I was troubled. My private part was squeezed too much against the v-shaped backbone of this skinny horse. As I was trying to wiggle myself into place, I kicked the horse accidentally with my heels, and that meant the end of my horseback ride. The horse jumped up and down with his rear until I lost my balance. I fell off. This was, of course, *rodeo* for the onlookers nearby. They laughed as I was flying through the air. Ildiko held her own and quieted the animal and prompted him to move on. I yelled, "Go on! I'll walk up."

Uphill we went and arrived at the same time. The owner of the horses waited for us at the other end; and as we arrived, he took them away and gave them to those who were going downhill. Then, we were led by a hostess to a table from where the lake was in full view. The south side of the lake was almost flatland with the exception of a couple of large hills—Boglar and Fonyod.

I had not been in a restaurant before, and for that reason, all the etiquette and eating manners were new to me. And I wasn't at all embarrassed about it. I told Ildiko, "You are my teacher now. Tell me everything I need to know."

"I can't tell you everything, for we wouldn't be eating 'til sundown, but if you watch what we do, you'll be just fine," she said.

Throughout my young life most of what I know up to now, I learned by watching others. That would be the case here also, had it not been for Ildiko, kind enough to tell me a few things.

"First, you pray silently for a second. Just bow your head and thank the Almighty—how grateful you are for this meal. This way, nobody, who may be watching, suspects anything.

(The Communist agents were looking for signs of who prayed, praised, and glorified God. They could have been here, for nobody knew their identity.)

"When you eat, hold your fork in your left hand and the knife in your right hand. Let Mom and Dad help themselves first and keep your talking to a minimum. Don't point with your utensils all over when you talk and don't cross over other people's plate when you help yourself from a common plate, centered on the table. There are other things to know, but you'll pick those up by watching us eating," she concluded.

I said to myself that I would be the last one to eat here, for I couldn't remember all these rules at once. I never held a fork in my left hand. If I do it now, I wouldn't be able to find my mouth.

All these etiquettes seemed to apply this time, as we had a common plate from which we helped ourselves to pick what we liked. This common plate took up the whole center of the table. It was fully packed with fried meats and potatoes and cooked greens. It was quite a frequent practice here to order this smorgasbord dish, for everybody loved sampling from the variety of meats offered on one plate. (But what was not known to the guests was also the most practical way for the restaurant to prepare the next plate for somebody else. The untouched leftovers were scraped over from one tray to the other and served again to the next guests.)

While we were dining, a gypsy band was fiddling the best of folklore music and czardas, boosting our appetite for eating and drinking more. Ildiko and I received only a half glassful of one the best wines grown here in the hills—Keknyelu (Blue Tongue).

Mr. Smith thought for sure that I was a Jewish kid old enough to taste wine. My name said it all. It had a biblical connection. In the second Book of Kings (18:34), "Arpad" was called out, and "Gaal" was a leader of his kinsmen in Shechem (Judges 9:26–41). And, of course, I had no knowledge of these things at all, for I was not a Jew.

We left the restaurant around three o'clock in the afternoon and started walking downhill. About every hundred feet apart, there was a wine cellar on one or the other side of the stone-lined road. We stopped at every one. By the time we reached the bottom, we had stopped at eight cellars. Mr. Smith drank a four-ounce glass of wine, while I drank half of that at every cellar. Toward the bottom of the hill, we were already singing folklore songs one after the other. However, we weren't the only ones who were singing. Young and old, uphill to downhill, were visiting these cellars, drinking, and singing along as well. Since I loved music, I knew a lot of the folklore songs and, on top of that, had a good voice, too. At the last cellar, we lingered longer and drank more wine. Neither of us could walk straight anymore. Ildiko and I were arm in arm already. She supported me in order to stay straight, while Mrs. Smith supported her husband.

To make matters even more enjoyable, Mr. Smith brought along a gallon jug that he filled with Keknyelu at the last cellar. From all this drinking, we weren't plastered, however, but were quite tipsy and in a very good mood for singing. At the dock, several groups were standing in circles, singing and drinking. There was no clarity to any song, however, as there were more foreigners than Hungarians present. Each let out his own melody.

Now, I must admit that this trip was a very special surprise in my youthful life that I will never forget.

If for no other reason, it taught me a lesson: how to do drinking in moderation. Not that I drank more than I wanted, not that I talked silly, and not that I staggered, but that I lost control of my faculties, I concluded. While I had a good time, could I have had just as good a time without drinking? That remains to be seen in later years.

Now, a large ferry docked, and hundreds of passengers poured onto it like ants into a honey jar. By the time we were to board this ferry, the captain closed the entrance gate. The ferry was overloaded. We moved aside and sat on a nearby bench and waited there till the next ferry arrived. Mr. Smith couldn't just sit there and be quiet. The good drinks he had urged him to tell everything he couldn't tell when he was sober.

"I wish I could figure out what's going to happen to me and the nation," he said.

"If you are trying to tell it to me, Mr. Smith, I wouldn't understand it. I saw what went on in my village. Beyond that, I don't know anything," I answered.

"You see, I had a small orthopedic reconstruction business in downtown Budapest. Now, the Communist Party collectivized it. I joined the party so that somehow I could save my business and stay private. My tactic didn't work. Now I work there as an employee only. I wouldn't have any extra money to go on vacation next year. We wouldn't be coming here anymore, Arpad," he explained.

"I'm saddened by that, Mr. Smith, very saddened. I would be separated from Ildiko."

(It became evident now that the main push of the Communist regime was to nationalize, not only farming, but also most other businesses as well, throughout the whole country. What this meant was that all the workers in the collectivized businesses equally would share the work and the profit of the business. Mr. Smith knew that without competition there wouldn't be any initiative that drove the employees to work harder to make more money. And money, of course, was the catalyst that added juice to the brain to go for more of it.

I was thinking of Matild now. It became clear as to why she wanted to collectivize farming in my village. She wouldn't have to work, only just enough to kill the day. She would be like a union steward, a mouthpiece for the socialist movement. But she would be sharing in the crop distribution equally with those who worked hard to keep the farms going.

While the concept may have been very interesting, the reality proved itself to be totally counterproductive, for men would rather become corrupt first before becoming honest. Hence, there wouldn't be the *Ten Commandments*.

Individually, nobody owned anything; therefore nobody cared for anything. Typical bureaucracy became the fact of life. Everybody was waiting for the next guy to do the work. The best opportunity had been created for lying, bribery, embezzlement, cheating, and outright stealing. Even honest people had become part of the corrupt system, for herd mentality only had followers. This is socialism at its worst. *Obamacare comes to mind.*

And similarly, this will be the state of affairs in the United States of America and the beginning of the collapse of the democratic order. While a little more time is still left, 2016 would be the turning point. Oh, people of this great nation, know the facts before you pull the lever! I don't want to be a freedom fighter again against the leftists.)

The next ferry just parked itself at the dock; we rushed to the entrance to board it. We were still in a very good mood although the strength of the wine in us slowly dissipated for the lack of replenishment. Others, of course, went on drinking and singing and propping up each other in this dazzling crowd. It was also an interesting moment to watch as the Germans tried to sing Hungarian with their companions. The crowd was in groups on the top deck of the ferry that was now curiously bobbing back and forth from the lopsided overweight. It was obvious that everybody on board had a fleetingly terrific time, for the moment reminded mostly everyone that drinking wine was just one of the ways to forget the onslaught of Communism.

The Almost Forgotten Honor

Ildiko and her mother were mostly observers on our cruise to Badacsony. On the other hand, I and Mr. Smith were entertaining each other under the influence of one, then two, then three glasses of wine. Ildiko commented later, "How easy it was for both of you to talk foolishly just about anything that came to mind. One thing from the entire cruise I liked the most was that my father treated you as if you were his own son. I think from now on you could expect to be treated as a member of my family."

I accepted Ildiko's comments as a foregone conclusion. Mr. Smith always showed signs that he was interested in knowing more and more about me. But he didn't know how to bridge the age gap between us. This trip to Badacsony did it all. By the time we returned to the south side of the lake, he said to me, "Let's be pals from now on and don't *mister* me to death. Just call me Louis."

For me calling a man or a woman three times my age by their first names was very difficult to accept. I always respected older folks for their knowledge and experience and as the people to look up to for advice. In my mind older folks deserved veneration and utmost courtesy, for they are the ones from whom all good things in life are passed down to us. Exceptions to this, of course, are the evil doers— my aunt Matild and my godfather. And even with these, I had great hope that one day they would change, for the devil couldn't stand love and hate in one body very long. Or could it?

By the time we left the ferry on the south side of Balaton, I was as sober as when I first stepped onto it this morning. "What a foolish thing this was!" I said to myself. "How difficult it is to remember now what I have said, and if I said something inappropriate, how difficult it is to apologize for it." Embarrassment was my problem now.

I couldn't remember whether I said anything inappropriate.

It was, however, in stressful moments as at this instance that I was at my best to think clearly and fast. I turned to Ildiko and her mom and apologized, "I drank too much."

I didn't apologize to Louis, for he was my equal in this foolish behavior, and if anything, I gained something out of it—we became friends.

It was now about seven o'clock in the evening, when we got off the homebound ferry. I was very hungry. I didn't dare to ask Louis for a second treat after Badacsony. I was not alone being hungry, however; everybody else was also. Without anybody's asking about eating, Louis led us straight to the cafeteria located inside the railroad station. There, we ate fried dough loaded with toppings of our choosing. After that, we took the train home.

Close to my house now, I was very careful to avoid Matild seeing me entering the house. I was dead tired from all the events that wore me down during my trip to Badacsony.

CHAPTER TWELVE

The Bible and the Two Jews

While we were on cruise to Badacsony, Laszlo and Lisa spent their afternoon praising and admiring each other for the things they had in common—their Jewish heritage and the stories to back that up.

That they found each other was in itself an uncommon event, for most of the Jews in Hungary were already deported to Nazi Germany before 1945.

Since Laszlo didn't speak Hebrew, they talked Hungarian. Now that both of them were Christians by baptism, they agreed to talk first about the genealogy of Jesus Christ since he was also a Jew (New Testament, Matthew 1:1–16). They spent the better part of the afternoon, however, discussing both the earthly and the heavenly significance of Abraham and Jesus as they related to God the Father. Laszlo had no idea as to what the difference was between worshipping God the Father through Abraham or through Jesus Christ. He asked Lisa, and she responded, "I truly don't know that, Laszlo. But I will try to think it out loud for you. But if I'm wrong, don't hold me to it.

"Abraham was a Hebrew, an *earthly* man. The Jewish race began with him and continued by his son, Isaac, and his descendants. The Hebrews, and therefore the Jews, were God's chosen people through Abraham, the father of all nations (Old Testament, Genesis 17:1–8). On the other hand, Jesus was both *heavenly and earthly* (New Testament, John 1:19–34; John 17:1–26). But he was not yet revealed to the world. He was united in the Spirit and was one with God the Father from the very beginning of creation. The scriptures tell us everything I just said.

"Now, God the Father loved his chosen people, the Jews, and was with them and guided them through Moses who was also an earthly man (Old Testament, Exodus 3:1–12). And God gave Moses a myriad of laws through which he instructed God's chosen people. But they repeatedly disobeyed them. Although God always forgave them, soon after that, they went back disobeying him even more than before.

"What we have to remember, however, is that God also gave us the laws through Moses. And the most important laws are the *Ten Commandments*.

"At last, God the Father gave the Jews one more chance in order to repent and turn back to him. He, himself, came down from heaven to earth through the birth of his beloved son, Jesus Christ. This was how Jesus had both a divine (heavenly) and a human (earthly) nature. He lived among us as man and God. He wanted to save his chosen people from eternal damnation, but they didn't receive him and recognized him. He said this himself when he was in the *temple* in Jerusalem (New Testament, Matthew 23:37–39).

"This much I read from the scriptures. However, none of this answered your question.

"I have one more thing to say, which may give you the answer, or at least guide you to it. But I think you should rephrase your question. Instead of asking 'what is the difference,' you should ask how God the Father liked whether I worshipped him through Abraham or through Jesus Christ or through both? Again, the scriptures tell us what God is looking for in every person when that person turns to him. 'For the Lord sees not as man sees; man looks on the outward appearance, but the Lord looks on the heart' (1 Samuel 16:7)," Lisa said to Laszlo."

So Laszlo became convinced that God was not interested in *lip service* but rather what was in a person's heart for him. From this day on, he never read the scriptures again as he would read a newspaper, but rather as a prayer book. He read the Bible with his heart.

It was time now to wrap up the day, for both of them were exhausted from searching for the truth from their knowledge that they gained from reading the scriptures. It was close to six o'clock in the evening. It was a beautiful daylight, still with a clear sun and sky. Only the birds were chirping in the trees all around them, digging into the fresh and juicy apricots to quench their thirst for the night. And Laszlo thought that if all these birds could sing to God now, it would be a chorus, singing to God and telling him "how much I loved him."

Laszlo and Lisa parted company by rubbing their faces to each other and thanking each other for the great time they had together. Both of their lives were changed just by knowing that they could rely on each other's company in the future to talk about their common traditions. They agreed to meet tomorrow, joining me and Ildiko on the beach.

On the way home, Laszlo's mind was a collection of imaginations. On the one side, the great scriptural stories were like good music to his ears, received with joy; on the other side, it was like an unforgettable message, needed to be told to someone. Laszlo became very anxious to see me that night as I was the only one to whom he could honestly tell that message—*lip service* to God was self-praise and a waste of time.

A Sign of the Cross

The following morning, I arrived at Joseph's place very early and found him still sleeping. It was perfect timing, though, for Mr.

Forro was already in his garden, stuffing his burlap sacks with freshly picked vegetables. I went to him and greeted him as I did a couple of days ago. But he didn't say anything. His greeting was instead a hand blessing with the sign of the cross. In my amazement, I didn't know what to make of it. Nobody up to now did this to me, and what he did made me to ask him, "What was that for, Mr. Forro?"

"That was for thanking God that he brought you here again to help me carry my bags to the same place we went the last time."

"Do you always believe that by throwing crosses on somebody, your wishes would be answered?" I asked.

"No. But it makes me feel good that I could pass on what I feel in my heart, always giving thanks to God for the good things he brings my way," he answered.

"Well, in that case, I'm here to fulfill your wishes. Your prayer has been answered," I said.

On the way we went with the vegetables.

This time, I walked slower so that M. Forro could keep up with me, for the bags weren't as heavy as the last time. This allowed us to talk to each other as well. The sign of the cross stayed in my mind, however, and I couldn't help bugging him for more explanation about it. This was what he said: "You know, the sign of the cross was one of the most important showing of faith and trust in the Lord. Now, if I'm ashamed of it, what do you think, how would he feel about me?"

"Why wasn't everybody doing it then?" I asked him.

"Not everybody had kindness in his heart. Kindness means having others in mind."

"You weren't thinking of me and Ildiko. Were you?" I asked.

"I wasn't. But that would be a very good example for you to understand that kindness was second only to love. In other words, there can't be love without kindness," he said.

"So if I loved the Lord, I had kindness in my heart?"

"Wasn't it from your kindness that you offered to carry my bags? Can you help others without kindness in your heart" (Luke 10:29–37)?

"I can't explain that, Mr. Forro, I really can't. I only know that helping others makes me feel good about myself."

"You don't need to explain that. That was what the Lord asked us to do to one another."

We have stopped talking because we reached the entrance to a small farmers market where more people than usual were coming and going. It was a Saturday morning. I didn't go any farther with him, as we were quite close to the eatery he was heading to; furthermore, I wanted to get back fast to Joseph's stall to clean the cows.

In addition, if I'm allowed to tell the truth, I didn't want to hear or talk anymore about who was kind or unkind, who loved God or who didn't. I was already convinced that I was his child, and he had a lot more to do with me than I had to do with him. He controlled my destiny. He willed that I become an orphan.

The Death of Joseph

Back at the stall, I found Joseph still in his straw bed, and I didn't care, thinking, *Why should I care how long he wanted to sleep, as long as I could do my work?* My work this time was doubled, however, because Joseph didn't do a thorough job yesterday even though Laszlo wanted to help him. So I opened the stall's door and started the usual work I did every morning. Therefore, I did not pay attention to Joseph. In two hours, I finished with everything. Joseph was still sleeping, and I left him alone. Instead, I walked to the vineyard and ate my full with overripe grapes. Then, I ran to the canal and bathed myself in the somewhat turbid water. Here and there, a fish jumped high; and as soon as it did, a seagull plucked it out of the water. Muskrats were busier today than at any other times before, crossing the canal from one side to the other and back again. Since I didn't bother them, they swam quite close to me, being curious as to what I was up to doing during the early morning hours when they, too, enjoyed themselves floating on their backs. I left them alone and returned back to the stall.

The door to the stall was still wide open. I left it that way so that the swallows could fly in and out feeding their young ones. The cows were standing and looking at me as they always did. And Joseph was still lying in the same position as when I left him.

It didn't look right to me that so much peace could overwhelm his body when so much work waited for us. As a joke, I wanted to make him jump out of bed. So I stepped to his bedside, holding a half bucketful of water in my hand and slowly poured it over his head. But he didn't jump. Then, I touched his face and it was cold. I shook his shoulders and felt that his body was stiff. I yelled: "Joseph! Joseph! You aren't dead, are you?" He didn't respond, but I did. "Yes, Joseph, you are dead."

Even though Joseph was dead, I didn't panic over it. After my mother's death, nothing else could have devastated my life deeper. Yet as I was standing by Joseph's body, I said to him, "You know, Joseph, you took part of me with you. Now, you have created the second biggest calamity in my life. I have no one else left whom I could turn to and ask for advice or look for compassion. Oh Lord, give him peace, for he didn't have any while he was still living." And I made the sign of the cross on his forehead and left.

I ran home to look for Matild; she wasn't home. Then, I ran to the town hall, she wasn't there either. I turned around and ran to the house of that woman (Helen) who was known to the good peasants in the village as the *mouthpiece* of the Communist Party. I bolted through her front door as if a whirlwind had suddenly torn it open. I was so sure that Matild would be there. I was right. She was sitting among ten party members, planning the formation of collective farming in the village. I yelled, "Joseph is dead! He's dead!"

Matild stormed out as fast as I had stormed in, and ran straight to the stall. I followed her.

She looked at me with a stern face upon seeing Joseph being dead. I looked back at her, emotionally being very angry. I yelled in her face, "You have killed him by neglecting him. When was the last time you saw him?"

"Two days ago. But he didn't want me around. It seemed like I was always in his way. Well, I won't be anymore."

She had no sorrow or guilty feeling for him.

"I don't want to be part of any burial activities. I don't want to cry, Matild," I declared and added: "I'll see you after the funeral. I will have a lot to talk about then."

Yes, I had a lot to talk about regarding her involvement with the Communist Party.

Looking for a New Mentor

If what I just said to Matild sounded cruel, even sarcastic and revengeful, I didn't mean that at all. I reflected my discomfort only because Joseph was dead. I had no one else to trust now.

Joseph was my mentor, kind and unsophisticated, a downright good-hearted person. I loved him, and now I lost him. I had to find now someone else to replace him. Finding a new mentor had to be a two-way street, I thought, on which strangers meet and unexpectedly become trustworthy friends. It would have to be almost like looking for a new bosom buddy.

Who could be that person I can turn to? Who could tell me from his experience what life, fate, and the future would hold? Not even the brightest star in the vast heavens could now lead me to that source. No one could drop the answers down in front of me beside God himself. I concluded.

Through it all, however, I suddenly realized that nobody had to. The answer was right in front of me, but I couldn't see it. The old truth that I shouldn't look over the fence and dream the impossible when reality was on my side of the fence is as true as ever. It only needed my discovering it. And I did just that at the least expected moment and place, after I almost went crazy, mentally looking for my new mentor.

There he was! Mr. Forro. Unknowingly, he was already my mentor.

And I found him at the least expected place. He was having his siesta now on a bench in the remote corner of the beach where it was shady and cool. His hat was covering his face for one reason only—so that nobody could recognize him. But I did, for he wore the same black attire for days already and his shoe laces were untied as always. As soon as I lifted his hat, he jumped. His surprised face slowly shifted to a broad smile upon recognizing my face.

"I just had a nightmare, Arpad. I saw you praying over Joseph's dead body," he said.

"You must have a connection in heaven or in hell, Mr. Forro!" I exclaimed.

"Don't say that! Say rather that you were thinking about me so much because you wanted to tell me something. What was it that you wanted to tell me?" he asked.

"Now that Joseph is truly dead, I would like to stick around you more often than before. I would like you to become my new mentor."

"You mean Joseph died! That scares me. You know in my old age, I need someone like you to talk to. I'm alone, and you're alone. The two of us could keep life very interesting for each other. I could keep mine joyfully reflecting on the past, and you could keep yours happily dreaming about the future. It's always worthy to hand over ideas from the forgotten past to those who can reshape them anew again."

"Isn't that what mentoring is all about? Although I cannot explain it, I think that every word you just said sounded to me as if you would have answered my own questions."

"Now that Joseph is dead, what's going to happen to you?" Mr. Forro asked.

"I'll be around for quite a while. I have no place else to go to. I hope that you could be around, too. This way we would be able to talk about how you lived your life. On the other hand, I could tell you how miserable my life is without Mother and Father. And you could adjust my thinking to avoid mistakes that happen because of the lack of parental guidance. Most importantly, though, you would keep that just between the two of us."

"I like the way you think, Arpad. You want me to plant some good seeds in your mind that may come handy some day in your future. As for myself, I want to pass on my knowledge to somebody. The trouble is, I have nobody. I have no children of my own to tell them the stories of my life. I would be more than happy to spend time with you from now on. Look me up any time you want to. I live next door to Joseph's stall."

With that said, we parted from each other. Mr. Forro went home, lamenting the death of Joseph as he saw that his body was being taken to the local cemetery's morgue for burial. He noticed that Matild wasn't even present at the time. It was Joseph's brother who lifted the corpse onto a flatbed horse-drawn wagon and afterward covered it with a black tarp.

I also went home, being assured that I had found a new mentor now as unexpectedly as the ocean waves washed ashore of a long-ago sunk treasure chest that was in front of me but I couldn't see it.

CHAPTER THIRTEEN

Believing in Myself is the Key to My Confidence Building

The following day I went to the beach again. Since I knew that Ildiko and Lisa were already there, judging it from the sun's position, I went to look for them at the usual spot. As I looked in that direction, I noticed that Laszlo was already there, restlessly turning his body from left to right and looking at the two girls who were playing cards. Because I was sad, almost at a point of crying for the loss of Joseph, I didn't know how to contain my feelings.

When Laszlo saw me, he jumped from the blanket and ran to me and embraced me. He started crying. But he wasn't crying because of Joseph's death; he was crying because of his mother, who was taken to the hospital by ambulance this morning. He didn't know what would be happening to her. So he came to the beach thinking I was there. Since I wasn't there yet, he lingered on with the girls, knowing that sooner or later I would come there. He didn't look for me at Joseph's place, because Matild already told him what had happened.

We stayed there awhile and were lamenting each other's helplessness; only our tears eased our sorrows. Both girls looked at us, recognizing that something was wrong. I turned to Ildiko, embraced her, and with quivering lips told her what had happened to me. Laszlo, too, while holding Lisa's hand in his hand, tried to tell her what had happened to his mother. But Lisa couldn't fully understand Laszlo's incoherent words. Neither Ildiko nor Lisa could say anything, for the sad moments muted their tongues from being able to utter words. We all knew immediately that our happy togetherness had come to an abrupt change.

It was Ildiko's father now, who also sensed our grief; he rushed over and led all of us to his blanket in order to talk our way out of our predicament.

"I don't really understand the reasons behind your crying, Arpad, but don't lose yourself over it. Contain yourself! Let's leave this place for now. We'll go to have something to eat at the canteen, where we can sit down and discuss the events that brought you here," Louis explained.

This was a clever move by him. By inviting us to change the scene and the place, he also changed our moods with it. It gave us time to quiet down and bring us back to reasoning our way out of our helpless situation. While we ate pizza, we discussed our sadness.

My situation was the most urgent and most troubling as I really didn't know at the moment what to do. Two responsibilities I had that I couldn't change. One was my commitment to myself and the other was to Joseph. Just because he died, that did not alter fulfilling my promise to take care of his animals. They were dirty and hungry and didn't know one way or the other whether Joseph was dead or alive. By evening, they needed my attention to clean and to feed them.

As to my own commitment, I had Ildiko, the dearest and sweetest treasure of my heart with whom I had to find a way to keep our relationship going just as before.

Still, I had another commitment besides the two I mentioned. It was my inseparable bond with Laszlo with whom I shared all my secrets.

As for Matild, I had no commitment at all. Only life's necessities for survival kept us together. Food and work.

When Louis said to me a little while ago "contain yourself!" I interpreted that as "behave like a grown-up should." But I also received it as an advice: Hold your emotions to yourself and privately, for others will laugh at you. From that time on, before I allowed myself again to lose control of my emotions, I remembered the man who said it. He stayed in my mind as a fatherly image.

We stayed at the canteen for about an hour and finished three large pizzas. Louis kept the conversation going by steadily asking questions about my plans for the future. He had lots of questions to ask because by now, he knew from the folks around him in the village that I was an orphan and was exemplary in my maturity to handle it. All the others at the table knew it, too, and were carefully listening to the two of us talking.

"Arpad, being an orphan, how do you keep track of things in your life?" he asked.

"I divided every year into its seasons. Each season had its own impact on my going forward as the time moved on. And as it did, I noticed that the seasons were repeating themselves while I was physically changing, growing up day by day. As I kept track of the passing of each season, I also kept track of my needs for each season. The only thing that wedged itself into my daily life was my aunt Matild. She wanted to screw up the flow of events and direct them toward her selfish benefit. Even now, this is my dilemma. I keep watching," I explained myself to Louis while occasionally looking at the others who were listening.

"Where did you get the idea that life moves on with each season and that you have to plan for it time after time?" he asked.

"I didn't get it from anybody. Kids drift with the passing of time unless their mother or father guided them. I had neither and was forced to take notice of it very quickly. If I didn't raise chickens,

I had no meat. If I didn't sow seeds in the ground, I had no wheat for bread. On and on, I learned that if I wanted to survive, I had to keep track of time in relation to my needs, season after season."

"Arpad, you are simply amazing! What you just said fits into everybody's life and for all seasons. It's not the simplicity of your words, but the wisdom behind them that I shall remember. I'm at a point now, almost afraid to ask any more questions. I still think, though, that you have a Jewish background," Louis concluded.

Then, Ildiko's mother asked in her broken Hungarian, "When will *us* see you again?"

"I'm not going anywhere from this village, not for a while anyway, but you folks were ending your time here. I know that I'm still going to see you in the coming three days, but after that, well, Ildiko and I have already worked out a plan. But we want to keep it secret until after your approval," I explained.

"And what was that plan? Can you tell it now?" Louis asked.

"Sure, I have free train travel allowance all over the country, given to me by the railroad authority. Because of my father's lifelong service, it was given to me freely. I can use it anytime and in any direction at my discretion. Ildiko and I figured that on weekends, it would be a good time to see each other."

"And you come to *us* house, yes?" Ildiko's mother responded.

I corrected her incorrect grammar by saying, "You mean that 'you come to our house.'"

She smiled, and Louis nodded in approval.

What I didn't tell them, though, was how much I loved Ildiko and how frequently I would want to see her. I felt, however, it was not necessary to tell them that, for the way I behaved around her was so obvious that I loved her. Every night I dreamed how our relationship would grow closer and closer.

Laszlo keenly observed every word I said and wondered whether he could come with me to visit Lisa at the same time I would visit Ildiko.

It was time now to go back to the beach and enjoy ourselves for two more hours before we would go home. I did not attempt any longer to teach Ildiko how to swim as that was impossible to do. I was mentally stressed out.

Laszlo and I left the beach earlier than the rest of the folks did, as nothing else was on his mind than the condition of his mother. And nothing else was on mine than Joseph.

* * *

On our way home, I prepared Laszlo regarding the coming death of his mother. I told him how I felt when I finally realized that I don't have my mother around anymore. For a long time after her death, I still asked her questions but ended answering them myself as she would have said them herself. The toughest part to remember was when they lowered her casket to the bowls of the earth. It was then when I bitterly cried and wished that my sorrows would bring her back to me. The moment of my emptiness nobody felt, except God himself, as a river of my tears drenched my mother's casket.

Laszlo knew that his mother would die from her illness. It was just a matter of time.

As I was talking to him, he put himself into my place and thought that he would have to do just about the same thing I did—cry, cry, cry. The only thing that bothered him most, however, was that he didn't trust himself that he would be able to withstand the great suffering he would have to go through after his mother's death. He thought of hanging himself. That way he would end all his pains. To convince him all the more that life was more precious than death, I strengthened him through his faith in God:

"Now, Laszlo, I know that you have a very strong belief in God, for you wouldn't have spent yesterday afternoon with Lisa and talk about God's words from the scriptures. In times like now, you want to believe in yourself also because if you don't believe in yourself, how can you expect help from above to lessen your sorrows? Unite your belief in honest faith in God, and he will hear your cries."

"Was that what you did, Arpad?" Laszlo asked.

"My situation was totally different from yours, for I always believed in myself. I know who I am. I have no trepidation and no hesitation in my mind questioning the outcome of events confronting me. Now, recognize that you have in your bones both the doubt and the fear to confront events that face you. You could overcome both if you believe in yourself as I do that all things are possible if you have the courage to confront them fearlessly. Stop questioning yourself whether you can or can't, should or shouldn't do what you want to do. If you do what I do, you can be sure that you will become a positive thinker, too. The more positive thinker you become, the more faith you will have in yourself and in God and the more he will listen to your cries."

"I know that you have a steadfast mind," Laszlo said. "But I don't know from where you got it. Now, I know that it is that you believe in yourself that gives you the courage overcoming your fears. Could it also be that your faith in God is enflaming your will?"

"It is. But nobody knows that because I don't show it. My relationship with God is mine alone. I lovingly hold his spirit in my heart. And nobody can see that. And in secret I pray to him all the time. That is why I believe in myself. That is why I also have faith in myself," I said.

"Arpad, you probably don't know this because you don't have a Bible, that what you are actually doing is written in the New Testament as to what you can expect to receive in time, if you have faith.

"Jesus said: 'Have faith in God. Truly, I say to you. Whoever says to this mountain, "Be taken up and cast into the sea," and does not doubt in his heart, but believes that what he says will pass, it will be done for him. Therefore I tell you, whatever you ask in prayer, believe that you receive it, and you will'" (Mark 11:23–24).

"Well, don't just read the words from the scriptures, Laszlo. Believe in them."

As we arrived at Laszlo's house, we heard that his father was bitterly crying. Laszlo ran to him and broke down in his father's arms. I couldn't say anything. I didn't need to; for I felt that if I had interrupted their union, I would have torn apart their intimate bond in the sharing of their sorrows, as father and son usually do have an intimate bond.

So I walked home instead and prayed there alone for Laszlo and his mother. She died that afternoon.

Doing One Thing at a Time Set Me Free from Worries

It was now about eight o'clock in the evening. Matild wasn't home yet, and the flock in the yard ran all around me, no matter which end of the yard I went. They were gently picking at me while making all kinds of noises. And they were jumping in front of each other, for they knew that once I opened the shed door, grain would be flying at them like raindrops from the sky. I hated this part of my chores. Every time I showed up in the yard, the same thing would be repeated. They followed me everywhere unless I hurled feed at them. The only good part of this event was that whenever I wanted to grab one of them for a fry or a stew, they were at hand for the taking.

As the days went by, Matild complained more and more, "I can't figure out where my chickens are disappearing. Arpad, do you have anything to do with this?" she asked. I never said yes. I just ignored her.

She seldom fed me but expected that I would do five men's work. I was the one, though, who helped myself reducing the flock one at a time in order to feed myself. I loved to cook and eat chicken stew, spicy hot, spread on top of homemade dumplings. Sometimes I added a pint of sour cream batter to it. That made the stew the crown jewel in Hungarian cuisine, known in English as *creamed chicken paprika.*

(The batter is added to the stew after the stew is almost fully cooked. It is prepared by adding two to three spoonfuls of flour to a pint of sour cream and a cup of water or milk, well stirred together until all clumps disappear. Then the batter is stirred into the stew while the stew is still cooking. After the broth is thickened, the stove is shut off, and the *goody* is ready to be served. *Don't overcook the chicken parts as the meat will fall off the bones.* Forget this warning if you cook the stew from boneless chicken breast.)

It was time now to retire for the day, but not before I ate the just cooked chicken stew. The flame from the stove gave me just enough light that I could wash myself, eat my supper, and go to bed.

But I couldn't go to sleep for hours. I recounted how many events had befallen on my shoulders at once: two deaths within a short time, the works at home and at Joseph's stall, tending to Laszlo's worries, keeping in touch with Mr. Forro, and of course, visiting Ildiko. These were my immediate concerns that bothered me. Then, my long term worries: going back to school in about ten days; harvesting the corn, the beans, and the potatoes; collecting firewood in the forest; and on and on. Even a grown-up would turn pale over this great a task that awaited for me to do. I was sweating in bed from worrying. So I jumped out and walked around in my dark room, cracking my fingers and thinking that with each pop something would happen. It did. I knocked something over.

Then I sat on my bedside and lectured myself: *Listen, Arpad, carefully listen! You, who just gave Laszlo all the faith-boosting talk, now burdening your mind with how to shirk off the inevitable work-load ahead of you? Come on, guy! Don't you believe in yourself?* And I responded. *Oh yes, I do believe that I can overcome all my problems—but only one at a time.* And I went back to sleep believing in myself, in my strength, and in my stubbornness to carry them out—one at a time only.

All this chaotic warm-up in my head turned out to be a very useful exercise in sorting how to stay the course when worries overwhelmed my mind. It is good to remember that I have to find myself in different forms to recognize my strengths and weaknesses.

I woke up the following morning as usual, by admiring the sunshine piercing through my window, shining on everything on the walls as it moved higher in the sky. As it moved from place to place, it also revealed all the spider webs in the corners of my room. These webs were full of live mosquitoes and houseflies buzzing in their captive circles. For a moment, I wished the sky would become dark, for the sight was ugly in my eyes. But, then, I praised heaven to keep the sunshine going until I get rid of every one of them. This was my first joyride for the day—killing all the flies for the bites I suffered during the night.

While being energized from getting rid of the flies, I ran to Joseph's stall and finished all the things I had to do. The last thing, of course, was milking the cows. The best part of it was filling my stomach first. Since I didn't hear or see Matild anywhere, I gave all the leftover milk to Mr. Forro. He was just coming in from his garden and was about to greet me. I surprised him with a large pail of milk. He dropped the sacks from his hands and took the milk inside. When he turned around, he saw me running already far away to the canal. Although he yelled after me, I didn't understand it. I kept running to the canal to clean the manure spills that had splashed on me. The cows suffered from diarrhea.

Bosom Friends Understand Each Other

As I was coming back from the canal, Laszlo was running toward me from the opposite direction. His eyes were cried out and his face looked sad. We hugged each other in brotherly fashion and sat down in the tall grass where nobody could see us. I started talking to him. As usual, I did most of the talking while he did most of the listening.

"You don't have to say anything, Laszlo. I feel your pains and know your state of mind. My state was no different from yours when my mother died. I suffered through them the same way that you are suffering now. While I'm here to support you in any way I can, I had no one to support me when my mother died. Nothing will help you more now than thinking about something else. Look at it with clear thinking and make peace in your heart. After all, there will always be a new beginning after every hardship. We overcome our sorrows by hoping for the better," I said.

"We didn't bury Mother. We cremated her yesterday afternoon. Since we have no relatives in this country, Father decided that crema-tion would be the best course of action to take. This way, no matter where *we had to go*, we could take her with us. So here I am now, almost alone in this world. Please guide me in order that I may grow up having the freedom of mind. Something that you have," Laszlo asked me.

"Laszlo, you are doing one thing very wrong by asking me to guide you. I need guidance myself, too, as I haven't really grown up yet, either. You still have a loving father. You don't want to break his heart. Do you? But I'll be around, just in case you become lonesome and disheartened. A lot of good times are ahead of us still."

Laszlo took my advice as sincerely as I told him. In his yearning to be with me, he had forgotten his father. He wanted to be around me more than around him, for bosom friends didn't reprimand each other. They guided each other only—though sometimes the wrong way.

We walked back to my house and talked instead about the girls.

Laszlo decided not to come with me to the beach, as he was in deep mourning for his mother. He wanted to find consolation by reading this time the Gospel of John in the New Testament. He needed *spiritual* uplifting now more than anything else. Before he left going home, he asked me to tell Lisa that he wanted to see her at least one more time before she returned to Budapest.

A Feigned or True Prayer

Just as Laszlo left, Matild arrived. "Why now!" My monologue went on. "Why do my encounters with people have to happen when I least expect them? Not just now but all the time as far as I can remember. Oh heaven! Give me a break! Will you? I probably couldn't even thread a needle without having you turn somebody's eyes on me."

Matild erupted: "You couldn't even come to say a prayer over your uncle, could you?"

"Must you be looking at his dead body to say a prayer over him, only once? Or can you pray for him all the time somewhere else without physically seeing him, even when it's dark?" I asked Matild.

"Was that what you did? Do you hide yourself when you pray?" she wanted to know.

"Do you want others to see you pray, Matild, or just God? Don't you think the first one is *lip service*, a feigned practice for others to see, while the second one is perfect union with God?"

Matild couldn't figure out the difference, for God was not in her heart. Finally, I said to her: "Both you and Joseph pass through my prayers as I fall asleep looking at the cross on the wall. And to your ears only, I can even see the cross in the dark."

Matild showed signs of fear in my presence and hurriedly left me. But it was the truth what I said. In the back of my mind, I always feel the presence of God, no matter where I am, or what I do. Not even mischief had blotted that out. I never said this to anyone until now and probably never will, for it was nobody's business who was with God or who wasn't. It was enough that he alone knew it. In this area, I was well pleased with myself. For, I understood that prayer didn't have to be a drumbeat for others to hear, a hocus-pocus for others to see. A prayer to me is meant to be a heartbeat, a flash through my mind, or even a split-second admiration of creation for being in union with God. For once, let this be my humble manifestation to you, my grandchildren, to remember that I had already felt many times that the Lord hears *the cries of the poor.*

* * *

(For whatever it's worth, I already knew that Matild was practicing idolatry, a false prayer to a fake god. Her idol is a dried pigtail. Over it, she lights candles and makes fake holy water and even tries to conjure up the dead during her ceremony. When she finishes with her bizarre practice, she hides the pigtail under her pillow. In my hatred for everything that is evil, I decided that I would scare her. I took the pigtail, burnt the hair off of it, and put it back where it was. My trick, however, didn't work. Instead of throwing the stinky bone away, she added a hairy one to it.

As the time passed between the two of us, the chasm that separated our beliefs grew only wider and wider almost to the last minute of her death. At that point, she repented all her evil deeds and died.)

CHAPTER FOURTEEN

The First Hint about America

After Matild rushed back home on hearing that I could even see the cross in the dark, I turned to more interesting matters in order to forget all the things that depressed me about her. I decided to join Ildiko and Lisa on the beach.

This time I chose to run far outside the village, through fields and wild growth that united my freedom with the natural beauty of my surroundings. Had I run through the village, I would have been stopped by my godfather, who was a very inquisitive man regarding my life with Matild. He wanted to adopt me, no matter what.

As I reached the entrance gate to the beach, I noticed that Mr. Forro was just getting up from the same bench on which he had rested every time after finishing his errands for the day. I couldn't pass him, for I considered him now as my mentor. I knew that I liked him and also knew that he liked me. And as far as I was concerned, that meant a very close relationship between the two of us. No deceit, no gainful expectation, and no bad-mouthing had already cemented our friendship. As I reached him, he tapped the bench inviting me to sit there.

"I bet you are hungry," he said and continued, "All I have is fried dough. Care to eat some?"

He unwrapped the stale round pieces and placed them in my lap. While I wasn't hungry this time, I couldn't refuse food from the gracious hands that offered it. I rewrapped them and put them in my pocket, thinking that that will be my supper tonight.

"If you want more later, just stop at my house. I have days-old food in a steady rotation. The not-so-fresh stuff, I give to the pigs. They devour almost anything.

"Now that you don't have Joseph to keep you company, maybe, we could see each other more often. There are a lot of hours in the day when I have nothing to do. But I don't feel like talking just to anybody. You see, long ago I traveled all over the Western European countries, and in America, too. I was then a young and daring fellow in my early twenties.

"During that time, I met a lot of people from all walks of life and learned who was smart and who was boring. I find in this village mostly boring people, so I don't wish to talk to them. I would dry up from doing all the talking, and they would be bored to death because of it. They wouldn't understand what I talked about. When I talk and receive no response, I know that that person doesn't understand what I'm saying. But I want to talk to you about America, the land where even birds celebrate their migration undisturbed. The land where I was able to look up to heaven to thank God for all the great opportunities he granted me—without being threatened by the Communists," he said.

"I wouldn't be much different either from the others in this village, Mr. Forro, for I don't even know where the West is. But maybe because your talk would be new, and maybe you could make it interesting, your words would open my curiosity. Yes, it would, for curiosity is as strong in me as the urge to run, discovering new things along the way. You know, a runner's mind is always ahead of his body. I would prefer though that we talk about your travels some other time when I would have more curiosity. Right now the girls are waiting for me," I responded.

The word *America* sounded to me enigmatic. I never heard it before. But because of it, my curiosity tickled my brains all the more to hear about it.

It was now three o'clock on Mr. Forro's wristwatch. That meant I had about two more hours left to be with the girls on the beach. So I reminded him that I must go now. The time to talk about this other world had to wait a day or two, after the girls returned to Budapest. But he insisted on talking.

Ildiko and Lisa knew that I was with Mr. Forro. They saw me standing by the bench the old man sat and noticed my impatience as my body turned more toward them than toward the old man. By eying the girls now, I gave them the hint to come closer to break us apart. When he noticed that the girls were coming and looking for me, he realized that no matter what, I had to go. So I parted from him, promising to see him tomorrow.

The weather turned cooler today, and for that reason, the girls wore grey jogging pants. For me this was perfect weather. It kept me from sweating like an overworked horse. Sweating had been very much discomforting all my life. That was the main reason as to why I wanted to finish all my work very early in the morning.

As we walked back to Ildiko's blanket, I held her hand in my left hand and Lisa's in my right. Being full of pride, I see that folks around are eying the almost unusual scene. For once, nobody knows how poor I was materially; but I was the richest emotionally. Even for youngsters, it was unusual to walk on the beach holding the hands of two girls as I was now. But I didn't care at this time how others looked at me; for if it wasn't eye-catching, who would care? Besides, who wouldn't feel good when others notice him doing something worthy to emulate, having two beautiful girls on hand at the same time. Good people wouldn't think anything wrong.

The summer was almost over on Lake Balaton. The foreigners slowly filtered away, not only because of the onset of cool weather; but also because their children had to go back to school. Laszlo and I were in the same situation, except that we were locals and the time didn't rush us as much. On the other hand, Ildiko and Lisa were highly spirited to talk about their school and related matters. They had to return to Budapest, too.

The Future was Not Mine to Tell

"Are you girls smart students? I mean, as far as your grades go?" I asked them.

Ildiko responded: "We have A grades. We both want to be either lawyers or medical doctors. When you are a Jew, you have to choose a study that you can take with you no matter where you *must* go. *They* can't take away what's in your brains."

"What about you, Arpad?" Lisa asked.

"I don't know. I don't have plans that go that far. I'm drifting now like a walnut on the crest of waves. Wherever it will land, it will take root, and a new life will begin from it. You know, I have no mother or father who can guide me as you have been guided. But I hear what you were saying, and I also hear and see everything others around me are saying and doing. One day, though, I will have to make up my mind, for I wouldn't want to be like that walnut tree from which one nut fell away but the tree stayed put where it grew up. My life will drift to new places just like that walnut on the crest of waves and will take root somewhere because I won't rest until I attain something big in my life," I said.

The girls were totally puzzled over my dreaming about my future. Frankly, I didn't know what I was prophesying. The words rushed out of my mind as if I saw my future also drifting on the crest of waves. After hearing all this, Ildiko asked me, "What about me? Where is my place in your life?"

"You are already in my life because I love you. That will travel with me no matter where I go. In that sense, I'll take you with me wherever I go. You see, my love for you is not like the draft coming through the window and going out the other. You are in my heart, and there is no escape from there until I die," I answered.

Now Lisa heard everything I said to Ildiko and was wondering, could what I just said to Ildiko be true between herself and Laszlo? She, however, convinced herself that it could not be. Laszlo didn't have what I had, an enflamed heart that flooded my whole being, throbbing faster and faster until becoming exhausted in the fires of love.

But she wasn't sure, because she had not been in love with anyone and only wished to be. Then, she asked me: "When will you see Laszlo again?"

And I said to her, "Laszlo asked me to tell you that he wanted to see you at least one more time before you returned to Budapest."

That had embraced her desire all the more to see him again.

"Please tell him to come to see me, either this evening or, the latest, tomorrow. We are leaving back to Budapest on Saturday morning."

Then, Ildiko added, "We won't be coming to the beach tomorrow, Arpad, because we have to pack our stuff and also clean our rooms. Will you come to see me off on Saturday?"

"Not only Saturday but also tonight and tomorrow night," I stressed my desires.

We talked our time away without realizing that the beach was nearly empty around us. Ildiko's parents had already folded their blanket and were waiting for us to finish our talk.

As I parted from them, I said, "I'll come tonight with Laszlo, but I have to run now because I have a few things to do before I could come to see you again."

These few things meant feeding the cows, feeding the fowl, cooking my supper, and cleaning myself. But before I could do any of that, I had to tell Laszlo to prepare himself to see Lisa tonight. She was anxious to see him.

Ildiko had only two more days left; therefore I yearned to be with her every minute of it. After that, I knew I would be like a soldier in battle, living from day to day with the memories of his loved one left behind.

When I entered Laszlo's house, he was still sitting in the same spot I left him a few hours earlier, still reading John's Gospel. He said to me: "Everybody should read these passages in order to fall in love with God."

"Now that you read so much about love, hope, and expectation, why not come with me this evening and practice it here on earth with Lisa? She is greatly anxious to see you and talk to you about love," I said.

Laszlo now closed the Bible and said, "I should practice it, shouldn't I? If I don't fly out of this house now, I would never see Lisa again… not until you let me go with you to Budapest."

"Get ready then and wait here until I finish my work for the day. You can also come and help me. That way we can go earlier." Laszlo decided to come.

* * *

As I turned my attention to take care of the animals first, I decided that I should talk to Laszlo about them because he didn't have any animals of his own to take care of. He did not know how much he missed by not having pets around he could spend time with during stressful moments, telling them whatever bothered him. It sounded stupid that I would even suggest talking to animals.

(But I tell you, in stressful moments I was doing just that, talking to my animals to free myself from those stresses that related to my disappointments, to my boiling anger, or to my aches and pains coming from failures of being an orphan. Although they didn't understand what I was saying, they were my perfect *listening posts*. They were even curious as the tone of my voice changed. At times, that was all I needed—for nobody heard it, nobody felt it, nobody cried and yelled back, and nobody laughed at me. Since they were nobodies, there was no rebuttal, no argument, and no haughty feelings to exchange.)

"Laszlo, you don't know what you are missing when you don't have animals around you. They don't fight with you. They accept you as you are as long as you feed them. Being without them, you miss them. And that's where just one source of my problem is. I'm attached to them. When it comes time to part with them, I wish God had not created them. I have yet to learn how to dislike them."

"You know, Arpad, I can tell you one thing. If you read the creation stories from the Bible, you would have known already that God created the animals, not for pets, but for food," Laszlo explained.

"You mean to tell me that God didn't like animals?"

"Of course he did. But he placed them under the *dominion* of men. So if you wanted to have them as pets, that was okay with him also as long as you didn't *worship* them" (Genesis 1:26–28), Laszlo said.

"We have a very jealous God, don't we?"

"Yes, we do," he answered.

* * *

All this discussion between the two of us happened while I was feeding the cows at Joseph's place and Laszlo was bucketing the water from the well into the trough for them to drink. After we finished here, we ran home to feed the fowl. We were surprised, however, seeing Matild feeding them already. I asked her right the way, "How do you feel, Matild? Are you happy or sad? I didn't see you in the past three days. Did everything go your way or somebody told you, 'Go to the hell'?"

"Which one you want to hear first?" she asked.

"I don't want to hear any. I just asked so that you wouldn't have the time to ask me any questions. I don't have anything cooked for you, either," I said.

"But I'm so hungry. Do you have any leftovers? I would even eat that now," Matild asked.

I gave her the four round pieces of fried dough that I received today from Mr. Forro. I also told her that I fed the animals every day while she took care of Joseph's funeral.

While she munched on the fried dough, I kept talking to her: "This weekend, Ildiko and her parents will be traveling back to Budapest, and I'll be with them in my free time. But, starting Monday, I want to sit down with you to talk over everything I have planned for the coming weeks. So organize yourself! Stay away from your Communist friends so that we could finish the works waiting for us in the fields. Or if you don't want to, tell me, for I am just about ready to leave you and go for good to my godfather."

Matild became scared after hearing that I would leave her for good. She promised that she would do just about anything to have me stay—of course, anything, for my labor was free.

The truth was, however, I really didn't want to leave her. Not yet, anyway. All I wanted to accomplish was that I wean her away from her Communist friends.

Why should I go anywhere from here? This is my own house and my sweet home. My best memories are rooted here, my best friend lives here, I thought.

So I left Matild in deep thought. Her mind agitated like driftwood caught in between the edges of two stones in a rushing creek. Matild had forgotten that our food supply was at stake here, both for the animals and for us. Everything would have to be harvested and stored before the onset of bad weather.

* * *

So now, I sent Laszlo home in order to prepare himself for the evening, as I had to do the same thing in my privacy. Now, I lit the kindle wood in the stove under a big pot of water. When it was warm enough, I poured some of it into my bathing vat, and in the rest I gently dropped whole eggs and pieces of hotdogs given to me by Mr. Forro from his leftover pile. Then I washed myself while the eggs and hotdogs danced around in the boiling water on the stove.

The food was ready by the time we got back together again. We ate everything as two well-mannered kids would, using forks and knives, practicing how people ate in glamorous places. It must have been close to eight o'clock in the evening because the swallows were flying low already, gathering their last meal for the day. When I looked at the declining sun, I could see half of it still shining. The sky around it was clothed in pale red and in foggy mist as it disappeared. Right above me, the mosquitoes were springing up and down, getting ready to swoop on my half-naked body. I ran inside the house and grabbed my shirt and jacket and yelled to Laszlo, "Let's go!"

On the way we were running to join the two girls from Budapest.

We could not have imagined, however, that our dates with the girls would be interrupted by a bunch of peasant boys from the neighborhood, prancing around the two girls, who were waiting for us in front of their house. These boys were expecting our arrival and knew that we were coming to join the girls. They judged it from the previous evenings. For whatever reason, they were ready to confront us and chase us away. They didn't know, however, that we were ready, too. They didn't know that the power of love in my heart and the power of love in Laszlo's head were more powerful than the loose strength of them all.

Besides, I was always prepared for such an event and other encounters, too. I had my pocketknife and my slingshot in place in my waistline, always ready to be used to defend myself from man or beast. The boys knew it, too, that from my previous confrontations with them, I was a fearless fighter to prevent any type of bullying around. Not just for the fun of it, but also for the revenge for it. But this time, it was more than that; it was also jealousy on my part.

The girls anticipated that a fight would erupt the minute I showed my face. Therefore, they moved behind the house, leaving the boys to their fate.

Before I showed my face, however, I pelted them with round pebbles with my slingshot. The ones I hit ran off crying out loud enough that the others heard it. Within a short time, they scattered after them, except one boy. This boy was the same fellow that I almost drowned in the murky ditch water last year because he bullied me.

As I came closer and closer to him, he was proportionally backing off. And when I pulled my knife, he knew that I was ready to slash his throat this time. He took off, following the other boys while looking back, at times checking whether I was running after him.

Laszlo was nervously standing all this time in my shadow, gaining strength from my boldness.

The whole episode lasted no more than a couple of minutes. All I said to Laszlo: "If you don't have guts to fight for your survival, even the swaying reeds would blow away whatever strength left in you."

Now the girls didn't go inside the house. They walked to the backyard and waited there for the encounter to pass. And it did. Nobody got hurt.

Laszlo commented, "I wouldn't be afraid to go with you anywhere."

The Last Dance for a Season

Laszlo and I went after the girls and caught up with them almost at the end of the backyard, where the village road touched the property line. From there, we went to the shores of Balaton to take part in the closing ceremonies, marking the end of summer.

We were, of course, unknowingly enjoying our last togetherness forever on Balaton. The band was continuously playing heartfelt music, love songs mostly, as if they knew it also that some of us would only have memories left after this day.

We danced and danced and danced again, nonstop for a couple of hours. The love songs from Elvis Presley and others united my heart with Ildiko's to the point of meltdown. I was kissing her in the dark until my brains blanked out for a second or two.

I saw that Laszlo had a real good time also. His head was warmly pressed against Lisa's head; I should think that even a whirlwind could not have separated them apart. Laszlo's evangelical passion had finally turned his emotions down to earthbound reality. This was the moment of truth for Lisa also as her wish finally came true.

We didn't see the girls after this until Sunday morning when they departed from the railroad station, going home to Budapest. It would be in two weeks from now when I would be traveling to Budapest to see Ildiko again.

CHAPTER FIFTEEN

Harvest and Helping the Poor

My plans were already drawn up in my mind as to what I needed to do in the coming weeks. I did this during my past two weeks when I was daydreaming about Ildiko and the world around myself. I couldn't deny that the past two weeks took its toll on me, for truly being in love was much like being on hunger strike; the purpose was clear and the commitment to it unwavering. I lost ten pounds during that time.

Now that I was still in my own prison, Ildiko's departure unlocked the door to it. It freed me from the mental anguish and the physical desire to run to her without regard for the duties that were waiting for me. About one hundred miles separated us now. While love knows no distance, it can't be expressed without being physically in place to do it. As lofty as my desire after her is, the distance between us kept it only that—a lofty desire. Love was as faith was. It needed action to fulfill it. And that had to wait for at least two more weeks before I would be traveling to Budapest.

Now I realized that the freewheeling love affair that I had pursued with Ildiko was the most thoughtless act as yet in my life. I had no responsibility coupled to it.

The drawback was enormous in my judgment, for my own field work came to a complete halt. And now it was pressing that I should talk to Matild about it because she wasn't doing anything either. Agitating the peasants to join collective farming was more important to her than harvesting her own crops for the winter.

Monday came faster than my recalling where I had left my work off the last time. Joseph was no longer living to help me. All I know now was that most of the crops needed harvesting. This included the corn, the potatoes, the sugar beets, and on and on. My big concern was that once the rain began falling in September, all the crops would start rotting in the ground.

Now, as soon as I finished my routine work at the stall, I looked for Matild in order to fulfill my promise to her—nailing down her commitment to work. But I couldn't find her anywhere in the neighborhood. She was somewhere with Helen, the mouthpiece of the Communist Party. They were visiting and agitating the many rich peasants in the village, explaining to them as to how the collectivization of most of the farmland around the village would be done. They were ordered to follow the *one-shoe-fits-all* planning of the county's Communist Central Committee, which was the planning arm of the Communist Party in the district.

From my disappointment of not being able to find Matild, I went home and killed a couple of chickens. I cleaned them, cut them up, and quick-fried them in a large pan. As I was turning the birds in the frying pan, I heard the sound of dirty words and the rattling of forks and shovels. I thought that the ground opened and was swallowing the neighborhood. In the midst of it all, I heard the anguish cry of Matild.

"Hide me. Quickly hide me. They want to kill me."

I yelled back to her, "Jump in the well!"

At the back corner of our house was a dried, shallow well, half-filled with debris, long forgotten that the top was still open. It was surrounded by lilac bushes so that nobody could see it. Matild jumped straight into it. She was pursued by the angry peasants who were fighting against the collectivization of farming. The farmers' anger was directed mostly against Helen; but because the two women were together, the peasants accused her of collaboration. The real culprit, of course, was Helen. She had spied on the peasants and reported her findings to the Central Committee. She reported that they had buried their crops, wine, and other goods underground in order to hide them from being confiscated by the Secret Agents.

The two women ran away in different directions from their pursuers, and I didn't know until the next day what had happened to Helen. But Matild was now squatting in the well, waiting there until her pursuers gave up looking for her. They couldn't find her anywhere and thought that she had disappeared in the cornfields behind the house. She had one big problem though; she couldn't climb back out.

The following day, someone found Helen's body dumped far away in the forest. She was bludgeoned to death by her pursuers.

Nobody pressed charges against the suspected killers, for even the party members hated her. They, too, did the same thing that the peasants did, buried whatever they could from being confiscated. Helen, of course, was spying on them also.

So Matild was in the well now, and I was sitting at the edge of it, keeping her company from a distance of about fifteen feet below and seriously discussing with her the aftermath of her actions.

"You know, Matild, you are bringing shame on me by what you are doing. Don't you think that what had happened should be a good lesson for you to change the course of your actions?"

"I'll think about that once you pulled me out of here," she answered arrogantly.

"I will not pull you out, but I will tell your pursuers that you are here in the well. Let them talk to you so that you realize you are against the will of the people in this village."

I stepped back from the well so that she could no longer see me.

"Arpad! Are you still there? Don't leave me here to die. You know that I have no one else besides you. Please help me out of here," she begged.

"Now that you realize that you don't have anybody else beside me, promise me that you will quit the Communist Party. Then, I'll pull you out."

Laszlo heard my voice just as he arrived to the scene and was wondering why in the world I was talking to the well in which he used to empty dead wood and ashes. He thought that the pit was now my wishing well. And I said to him, "Look down there and see for yourself who is there." When he looked into the well, he became alarmed and said: "Matild, I don't believe you wanted to kill yourself! This well is not deep enough for that. Do you want to die there or want to come out?" Laszlo asked her.

"Don't joke with me, Laszlo! I want to come out of here, right now! Get a rope and pull me out!"

Her eyes were shining like that of a cat in the dark.

"Not so fast, Matild!" I yelled down to her. "Now that Laszlo is here also, promise me that you will quit the Communist Party."

"Let me die here first, then you won't have to worry about me anymore."

I decided not to nag her any longer because I felt that exacting a promise this way would have been cruel. So I went to my shed and brought a thick, long rope and lowered it to Matild. She grabbed it tightly but slipped back for lack of strength. I pulled the rope back and tied a cross piece to the end of it. I lowered it again so that she could now straddle her legs on the cross piece. Now holding the rope tight as she sat on the cross piece, Laszlo and I pulled her out. She was in terrible pain from the fall, so much so that Laszlo and I had to clasp our hands together forming a bridge under her bottom in order to carry her onto her bed.

Suddenly, I became her nurse, her cook, and her companion. It looked unreal to me to see how fast she turned from being belligerent to a fake saint.

No. I didn't believe myself, for in better times, even the devil came to her for advice. And once she would recover, she would be the same person as before as that old saying goes: *Can't make a purse out of the sow's ears.* If at any time a miracle was in real need, it was now. But come what may, I only had compassion for her at this time. She fell asleep from being totally exhausted. Laszlo and I went now to my side of the duplex and ate the fried chickens with boiled potatoes.

Matild's recovery would last more than a week, I figured. This meant that all the harvesting in addition to the other works at home and the stall have fallen on my shoulders. As was always the case when necessity had the upper hand, I had to rethink and readjust my plans in order of priority.

As it was next to impossible to do all that labor intensive work by myself, I decided to form a team with a couple of honest kids from a poor family I met through my gypsy friend, Tony. After Tony went back to Romania with his mother, I still kept the friendship with these kids although not on daily basis. They lived at the outskirts of the village close to the forest from where I gathered my firewood every week. Every time I went by their house, I stopped and talked with them about Tony and also about other things that touched our lives—mainly how to overcome hunger when we had nothing to eat. Their names were Andrew and Paul, and they were twins. They were also my schoolmates. In order to let the boys help me, I had to ask their father first. His name was Frank Strong. But I called him Fred.

Now, these boys were also hard workers, but only when their father ordered them to, and were honest and polite in their demeanor.

In their spare time, they used to help their father take care of the local church's property. In better times, their father was the janitor at the church. Since the church stopped functioning, the maintenance work was also suspended along with it. So now I asked all three of them to come and help me harvest the crops on Joseph's property, which after his death belonged to Matild.

We made a deal, fair and honest. I would give half of everything to them in return for helping me finish harvesting the corn, potatoes, sugar beets, and beans.

Harvesting was the easy part of the job. Hauling the goods home—half of it to Joseph's place, the other half to their place—was the tougher part.

While I had the basic experience in a number of these works, I had only little experience in setting up the cow-drawn wagon needed to do the transportation part of the goods from the fields. This used to be Joseph's job, and I didn't pay serious attention as to how he used to do it. So I asked the boys' father whether he had skills in this area.

"Yes, of course, I know that. I used to do that when I had my own cows. But in this case, I don't know your cows, and they may be fidgety around me," Frank said.

"I know how to make my cows your friend. They will even lick your face if you just show them love," I said.

Frank came early that Tuesday morning, but early meant something different to him than to me. By the time he showed up, I was milking the cows, and he was now watching me doing it. Again, I had a full bucket of milk and, again, didn't know what to do with it. So I invited him for a drink, straight from the bucket. He went at it several times. Soon, Andrew and Paul showed up, and they finished the rest of it.

I was ready now to introduce Frank to the cows. When Joseph was still living, he reminded me of the fact that cows were much like us—they didn't like threatening surprises. So I led the cows to the front of the stall in order that Frank could face them. Then, I fed them shredded sugar beets. After that, I led them back to where they were before. Tomorrow it would be Frank's turn to feed them. We did the same introduction two more times, and the cows accepted Frank without fear after that.

The fact that I offered Frank the sharing of the crops made him anxious to begin working. In order to talk over what we would be doing each day, we took a few minutes and discussed the location of each crop type in the fields that surrounded the village. We agreed to meet every morning at Joseph's place and drink milk first before we would set out to work.

I said to Frank: "I would like you to take charge of the work. You have much more experience than I have. You lead Andrew and Paul to work with you. We will all learn from you because you are much older than us and you have the skills. Of course, I would be working along with you on and off. But I have to do other things as well. I will be cooking our lunch and taking care of my sick aunt. I also would like to ask you that you bring with you every day enough water to drink and the proper tools to work with."

Frank looked at me in disbelief. He admired my simple way of telling what to do. To him, it sounded as if an old man were telling his children what to do. At this time, he looked at his sons, almost bewildered, that they had no planning skills at all and that they needed to be prodded even to tie their shoe laces. He was wondering what was behind my life that made me so neatly organized in ways of doing things. Well, I was an orphan and nobody cuddled me as parents did, hindering their children to think logically.

In the following seven days, we dug all the potatoes, shucked all the corn, picked all the beans, and pulled all the sugar beets. After the first couple of days, we had the cows with us. They followed me as I walked in front of them. They pulled the wagon, whether it was empty or full, wherever I guided them. I didn't have the skill to guide them with the touch of a whip to steer them to the left or to the right. When we arrived at each place of work, I tied them to the wagon and gave them hay or greens. Their heads always turned to my direction, eyeing my movement in the field.

We placed all the harvested potatoes and corn into burlap bags in order to divide them between us equally. The sugar beets we measured by filling the wagon, one for me, one for them. And the beans—heaped in a pile, yet in their sheaths—we split in half on the ground.

I still had other crops—cabbages, carrots, and root celery—that I left in the ground. Since they were not sensitive to frostbite, I left them alone for another time. Right now Joseph's corn granary and his underground root cellar were full.

On the last day, we finished all the planned work by early afternoon. Sitting in a circle under a mulberry tree, we had time now to relax and talk. I was mostly listening as Frank asked questions from his sons as to how they liked working for a living. Paul showed his palms to Peter; then, both showed them to Frank.

"Look, Dad," Paul said. "We have calluses and blood blisters all over. We never felt pain like this before."

"That's because you never really worked before, helping to support the family. Now, if you look at Arpad's hands, I bet you wouldn't see any blisters," Frank commented.

And they looked at my palms and saw that I had no blisters anywhere. That was because I always worked with them and, as a result, had grown thick skin all over my palms, immune now to swelling and blistering.

"How would you like to spend a few more days with Arpad?" Frank asked the kids.

"We wouldn't have blood blisters then, would we?"

"More than likely not. But you would learn something that would last longer than your blisters. You would learn how Arpad planned his work ahead of time, day after day," Frank answered.

"But we don't need to be with Arpad to learn that. You did something like that, too," Paul commented.

"But I wasn't talking about myself. I was talking about the two of you. I don't see in you what I see in Arpad. He has motivation in his whole body. He guides himself step by step to the finish line. He moves around as if his mind is glued to goodness itself," Frank said.

Frank tried to tell his kids that they needed discipline. But he didn't realize that discipline didn't come by itself, least of all for children. Paul and Andrew had to tell their father that he was the problem.

"Of course, you saw how Arpad was doing things. You saw how he worked and planned his work ahead. How could we be like him when you do everything for us?" Andrew asserted.

"Yes, Father, tell us what to do, then come back later to see how we did," Paul agreed with Andrew.

"What the two of you mean is that I should be motivating you, should be guiding you, and should be showing you what's right and what's wrong," Frank responded with a sad face, realizing that he was the problem as to why his kids lacked the motivation and the initiative to follow through with their chores on their own. He took all that away from them through the blindness of love. So the kids stayed undisciplined, and they rightfully blamed their father for it.

* * *

It was very interesting to hear this conversation, for I didn't see in myself what Frank saw. One part of this conversation I didn't understand at all: "He moved around as if his mind was glued to goodness itself." Later, when Frank and I were alone, I asked him, "What did you mean by that?"

"You probably don't even realize that your mind is more on others than on yourself. What drives you to think of others more than you think of yourself? During this whole week, I didn't see in you any sign of greed or selfishness. You shared your crops without ever thinking to give yourself more than you gave me. I was wondering how could that be possible in a young person like you?" Frank asked.

He was telling me what he saw and asking me about what he didn't. And I said to him: "Now, that you noticed that I have this trait of giving and helping more than taking, to which I paid no attention at all, tell me, what's wrong with it?"

"If you do it to everybody, they would think you are crazy. In this world, most people are only for themselves—greedy and selfish. And if you would do it to the same person over and over, he would exploit you all the more. Think about that," Frank said.

"But I don't have much to give. I only have foresight, noticing when others need a kind word or a little help to move things along. I feel very good when I do that. I see the joy in others, accepting it," I said.

"In my case, you did a lot more than a 'little help' to receive my joy. My family would have starved this winter without your help. Arpad, you gave away half of your crops just to feel the joy of giving. I pray that God bless you for it. You have truly inspired me. Inspired me so much so that I will give away part of everything you gave me to those who are starving," Frank concluded.

I never told Matild, and she never asked how I finished the harvest in a hurry with the help of others. Even during her healing that lasted almost ten days, her talking centered on only one subject—she was ready to hand over Joseph's farm property to the state-controlled collective farming.

Matild had plenty of time while bedridden to think about what had happened to her. Why it happened and why her life was at stake if she continued. The murder of Helen scared the hell out of her, thinking that she would be next.

"I'll turn in my membership card to the Communist Party. It is not worth it to be part of this godless gang of thieves, and it is not worth it to oppose it either. I'm so scared for my life now that I don't even want to step out of this place," Matild said while I was washing her stinky feet in a tub of hot water.

"Are you thinking of killing yourself?" I asked.

"Yes, I am. That will put an end to all my miseries," she answered.

"Don't you want to save your soul from hell first?"

"How can I do that, Arpad?"

"Go to every person you have offended and tell them, 'I'm sorry that I offended you. I want to be good to you from now on.'

"And while I am here with you, you should start it first with me, for you had offended me countless times," I said to her.

"I already said all that to God. Why should I bother with the people, even you? I would have to go from one end of the village to the other end," she said.

"You know, Matild, as long as what you did troubled your conscience, God won't forgive you. You have to settle your account here on earth first with all those you had offended" (Matthew 5:22–26).

"Where did you get the idea that I should be doing that?" Matild asked.

"This is not my idea, Matild. All this is written in the Catechism that I had to remember. You probably were taught, too, but you forgot it. You know, when your mind is on bad things all the time, even the good things in you turn to evil. Remember that doing good things happen from person to person. Think of your greed and selfishness, Matild."

"There was nothing to think about that. I was born that way. Don't you eagerly crave for some of the things others' have?" she asked.

"I do, but I turn my feelings off, while you don't. You had no qualms taking my ducks and chickens. Did you?"

Matild couldn't bring herself to eye level with me and apologize, for the ill will in her kept feeding her arrogant mind.

From here on, she didn't participate in any party activities and stayed away from those who did.

By the spring of 1953, all the farmland that surrounded the village was combined into collective farming and was managed by those who became members in it. Those who couldn't be forced to join received a meager crop allocation at the end of harvest. That, too, depended on good harvest.

All of Joseph's land in the fields were confiscated and became part of one giant track, plowed under for wheat or corn production. The small garden plots around the houses in the village and those in the wine-growing hills were left alone. So Matild was left with two garden plots, one close to her house, the other behind Joseph's stall. I was also left with two plots, one in the wine-growing hills, the other far away, close to the forest.

With the collectivization of Joseph's property, I had that much less to do. Only the garden properties remained to worry about.

My Romantic Nature Enkindled My Fortitude

Almost two weeks or so had passed now since Ildiko and Lisa returned to Budapest. Most foreigners also went home. The eateries were no longer open, thereby Mr. Forro's fresh vegetables were no longer needed. Lake Balaton returned to its undisturbed beauty, for there was no one left to pollute the water. The flyway of the migrating birds was clearly marked by the gathering of wild geese and by the group formation of swallows, practicing for their annual departure for the season. They made sure that every one of their kind was on board for the long flight. The weather turned now to the chilly side, signaling to everybody and everything else living that the fall season began to show its wonders and reminders.

The fall and spring seasons are the dearest banquets to my soul. One shows the passing of time, and the other, the beginning of life. As a young boy, almost thirteen now, I would find scenic places where I would fold each season's beauty into my soul, keeping the world at bay and keeping my imagination fit to shed the past or to plan the future. Sometimes this beauty in nature came through my escaping tears.

Romantic is my nature, therefore it adds a positive outlook for the better things to hope for. I discovered that being romantic had a lot to do with my positive thinking to get out of the doldrums of my trivial life.

* * *

I received two letters already from Ildiko but have not yet responded to any. Her beautiful handwriting and the glowing example of grammar sent shockwaves into my hands as I read them over and over again, trying to nudge myself to answer them. The heavy use of my hands working in the fields made my fingers shaky. Funny, my mind saw perfectly shaped letters, but my fingers couldn't follow through with them. The lack of handwriting skills proved how little practice I had. So when I finally answered her letters, my sentences were third grader in style and form—I... I... I... and love you.

In closing, I told her, "Next Saturday, after sunrise, I'll be at the East Station. Bring Lisa."

I also sent a letter to my oldest sister, Iren, telling her that I would be visiting her and Ella on my way back from Budapest.

The main reason for my visit, however, would not be just to see them, but for my dire need for winter clothes and shoes. I asked her to prepare these for me by the time I would be coming from Budapest.

Laszlo didn't hear a word from Lisa since she returned to Budapest. Just the same, I invited him to come with me and be my companion and surprise Lisa at the same time.

Disillusionment in Laszlo

All the years I have known Laszlo, I have not known one thing about him—how much he loved money. What a tight-fisted Jew he had become! He would wear holes through the sole of his shoes before he would buy a new pair. I knew that he had a lot of money in the form of gold and silver coins. All of it was buried under the foundation of his house, accessible only from the inside of his bedroom wall. He had displayed them to me and gloated over them and wished for more. One gold coin was so big that he used it as his mirror, seeing his gloating face being reflected from it.

All this meant nothing to me, for my treasure was in my heart, visible to God alone and shined through by helping those poorer than I, or inviting a beggar (a gypsy) to fill his stomach at my table.

So now the true Laszlo surfaced as it was time to pay for his train ticket to travel with me to Budapest.

"Since you have invited me to come along with you, you should pay for my ticket, too," he said and pulled the inside of his pockets out, showing that he had nothing in them. I didn't believe him.

"You call yourself an honest friend, Laszlo, a bosom buddy, a best friend? Call yourself a hypocrite, an underhanded swindler, instead!" I walked away from him, silently crying my heart out.

While I had a few dollars on me from the pittance Iren and Ella gave me when I left them the last time, it was not enough for the price of a round-trip ticket to and from Budapest. Laszlo knew how little money I had. And it was not the money part that jolted my feelings. It was how he wanted to take away from me even that little I had. With his pale and stern face, he demanded that I pay for his ticket. On top of that, he embarrassed me by pulling his pockets open in front of others who were around us waiting to buy their tickets. When he realized that he just let out a lurking imp from his soul, he ran after me to regain himself. Subconsciously, though, he revealed the truth that was in his heart—money, money, money. I turned around and faced him, filled with emotion, and said: "Go back home and look at yourself in your shining coin and live with it. You're no longer my best friend nor my bosom buddy."

I saw in that moment that the train had just pulled in for boarding. I no longer cared what would happen to Laszlo and left him. I boarded the train without him.

Although we still kept contact after this terrible split between us, we were never the same buddies, never had the trust in each other as before, and never shared our secrets as before. This incident left the deepest unhealed wound in my heart forever. It stayed as a wake-up call—money and true friendship don't exist together for long.

On My Way to Budapest to Visit Ildiko

Additionally, two more persons knew that I was traveling to Budapest for two days, Matild and Mr. Forro. Before I left to go to the railroad station that Saturday morning, I talked to Mr. Forro as he was going to his garden in order to gather his vegetables to supply the eateries for the last time this season.

"I can't help you, Mr. Forro, this morning, 'cause I'm traveling to visit Ildiko. But before you go to your garden, take this bucket of milk as I won't be around for a couple of days."

"Who will take care of the cows while you are away?" he asked.

"I have to talk to Matild about that, but if she won't, maybe you can look after them. If nobody shows up by noon that would be the sign that she doesn't care."

"I'll be looking for that sign. I would give them hay to eat and water to drink. That's all I can do, for I have no strength in me anymore. Hurry back, though, because I need to talk to you about America. I really meant to do that when I said the last time, 'The land where even birds celebrate their freedom undisturbed, where man can freely look up to heaven and say to God: "Thank you for all the great opportunities you have granted me."' That was when you woke me up from my sleep on that bench at the beach. You remember that I said that to you. Don't you?" His long neck stretched as far as it could. He wanted to make sure that I heard every word he said.

"I sure do, Mr. Forro," I replied.

I ran to Matild now to tell her about what I intended to do for the next two days. I didn't elaborate the agreement I made with Mr. Forro.

In her objection to my travel, she told me disgusting remarks about Ildiko, and I felt so deeply insulted that in my reply I said to her, "That could be said about you, when you were an old maid." And I left.

So now, I was on the train already, standing by myself and looking out the window, trying to enjoy the passing scene. I saw nothing, however, for my mind had a different image running before it—the incident between me and Laszlo.

It was a heart-wrenching disappointment. It was like that of a bird just shot out of the sky without being killed, trying to escape the reality of the wound. The true friendship had died in me. How better was that man who never had a true friend? I thought. Then later, after the train pulled away from the lake, I thought to myself, *Stop pitying yourself! This was just the beginning of many other disap-*

pointments you will face in your life. For man falls into these things, not by his thinking, but by his foolish heart, trusting in vain.

Then, I sat down and fell asleep.

I slept for three hours uninterrupted. The conductor woke me up at the East Station in Budapest.

"Young man! Someone is looking for you, right there!"

He pointed at Ildiko without really knowing that she was the one awaiting my arrival. I looked toward the pointed direction and saw that Ildiko was really there, trying to gain a glimpse of me in the crowd. I pulled down the window and alerted her that I was still inside the train. In a real hurry, I rubbed my eyes to remove all signs of drowsiness and combed my hair with my fingers. Then, I jumped out of the train straight in front of her.

We greeted each other as if a year had gone by already. It was only three weeks ago since we saw each other the last time. That tight hug I gave her revealed the inseparable bond between us. Then, I lifted a small notebook from my shirt's pocket and gave it to her. On each page, she saw a small dried wild flower with a note under it: "I'm looking at you with love."

At the time I collected each flower, I truly imagined her looking at me through each flower. That was the only gift I gave her, for I had no money to buy a bunch of roses from the paddlers.

Then, we walked and sat on a bench in front of the station. I told her everything about Laszlo, and she told me everything about Lisa.

"Lisa found a new boyfriend because 'Laszlo was boring to look at, hearing him talking and seeing him being tepid and awkward in his demeanor to me.' Lisa said this yesterday. For that reason, she didn't come here with me," Ildiko explained.

"I knew that they weren't for each other. He feigned himself, and Lisa noticed it. In a different way, he did the same thing with me. While he knew I had no money, he still insisted that I buy his ticket to come here. That was when I thought, *Go to the hell, you tight-fisted Jew.* But said instead, 'You're no longer my true friend.'"

"It's good that they aren't here. We don't need interrupters. What should we do now? Where would you like to go?" Ildiko asked.

"I leave that up to you. I have never been here and don't know a thing about Budapest," I replied.

Then, we kissed each other. The same thought, the same yearning for each other pulled us together to do so. We didn't care who was looking at us or what they were thinking of. Love had only one meaning for us—sharing it.

From there, we took the subway and went to Heroes' Square. Nothing resembled here what I left behind in the village. I gazed at the architectural creations with the curiosity that nosy kids have. I wanted to ask questions from Ildiko, but I couldn't match the questions to the reality I saw. So I waited for Ildiko to read my mind and answer them. As she did, she explained much more than I cared to grasp. Historical facts didn't interest me as the details drowned the highlights. Anyway, I was more mindful of her rather than what she said.

Being my leader now, Ildiko stopped in the center of the square. I became a good listener as she highlighted what we saw: "That's the Museum of Fine Arts on the left and that's the Museum of History on the right. Both are built in Gothic designs. Connecting these two creations in a semicircle are the numerous columns, the tops of which are tied together with Gothic-style caps. Within each column you see the statue of one famous Hungarian patriot. In total, they immortalize the venture-filled history of Hungary. In front of these heroes stand, in high elevation, the statue of Arpad on horseback. He was the leader of the seven tribes who founded the nation of Hungary in the ninth century."

Unfittingly in the center of the square stood the enormous statue of Joseph Stalin, standing higher than all the other monuments and facing toward the nicest boulevard of the city, Andrassy Street—with a heroic gesture of his right hand raised high, asking perhaps, "Give me honor and glory, for I liberated your nation from the Nazis."

As we wandered around for hours from one museum to the other and from statue to statue, Ildiko explained briefly the meaning behind each exhibit. After a while, I became so tired, physically and mentally, that I asked her to stop talking, for I forgot most of the words she already said. I have not been accustomed to hearing so much history being told at once. Nevertheless, I praised her for the time and the patience that she could do this for me as naturally as if she had been practicing it on others. And that was true. She told me later that she is now a tour guide in her spare time for student groups.

It was now two o'clock in the afternoon, and my train was leaving the station heading toward Martonvasar at 4 p.m. With this in mind, we returned to the East Station and sat inside the station's cafeteria to have a light lunch. In between spooning the spicy fish chowder, I asked Ildiko as to what had happened with her in the past three weeks.

"Quite a lot, Arpad. My father's business is collectivized. Therefore, I have to work to earn the extra money to cover my expenses. I figured that I would become a tour guide since I know a lot about world history, especially national history tied to world events. Then, because of my excellent grades, I got promoted to the eighth grade from the sixth grade. What about you?" she asked.

"The usual stuff—work, work, and more work. I broke up with Laszlo. I argued with Matild over her nasty and careless attitude. I missed three days of school and now have makeup assignments to do. The negatives are piling on me as if God waited to dump them all at once.

"I also heard that all the school books were rewritten. Everything about the West is replaced with Communist ideology. I wasn't good at understanding that stuff anyway. Now, I hate studying history even more. That's why I stopped you talking about it before."

"You can't hate history, Arpad. That is one subject from all the others, I love the most. History is my guide to the future—how to avoid making the same mistakes again, how to improve my life by weighing the past in order to change the future. You see, if you don't keep track of history, it could repeat itself and destroy you. Look at what the Nazi's did to us Jews," she commented.

(By this time I heard from Mr. Forro that so many Jews were deported from Hungary to the concentration camps that the government had to recount the population in order to figure out the number. For a few moments I commiserated with Ildiko about this tragic event. Then, I changed the subject, for both of us were crying. Nearly a million Jews had been exterminated just from Hungary alone.)

"Ildiko, do you remember when you came to me to that bench on the beach where that old man was talking to me?"

"Of course, I do."

"Well, we have become real good friends since. Just before I came here, he said to me, 'Hurry back, though, because I need to talk to you about America.' What can you tell me about that country? I'd like to know some things about it so I wouldn't look so stupid in his eyes when I talk to him again."

"Ohhh! America! The land of opportunity! The most hated country in the minds of the Communists. But it was the most beloved country to those who wanted to be rich, who wanted freedom, who wanted opportunity.

"My father wanted to go there, but since he couldn't speak English, he changed his mind. The country is rather far from here, but still a lot of Hungarians left this country to go there. The constitution of America grants liberty and justice to all. There will never be another nation like America where you can be whatever you want to be if you have the will and the courage to work for it.

"Arpad, you want to be very careful in school not to talk about these things, because your teachers could nail you for sabotaging their teaching the new ideology. You see, this was just one reason why you should know history," Ildiko explained.

In the meantime, I was watching the clock on the wall opposite my seat. Ildiko didn't notice that I was doing it. She was captivated by America and could have talked about it all day. She even mentioned that one day she wanted to go there.

All the money I had in my pocket, I left it on the table to pay for the chowder as my train pulled onto track three for boarding. We hurriedly left the cafeteria. Ildiko came with me onto the train's platform, and we spent the last few moments hugging and kissing each other as there were no passengers around. Now, the conductor whistled, and Ildiko stepped down from the train. We didn't set a new date for my next coming but promised each other to write once a week.

Learning Discipline from My Oldest Sister

My commuter train left Budapest and headed toward Martonvasar. From there I took the bus to Rackeresztur. In two hours, I was at my sister's house, hugging the eight members of the family. One out of this group of people is my sister Ella, who is more cheerful than all the others combined. I whispered to her: "Are you well treated? Did you miss me?"

"I'll tell you later, when we're alone," she responded. Her eyes were moist which implied that things went not that well with her.

Then, my oldest sister, Iren, called all of us to eat supper. I was already acquainted with the ceremonial moves before I touched the food—wash hands, orderly sitting, praying, and keeping quiet during eating. For me this was an ordeal as I was on the run most of the time eating my food that way.

After supper, the boys went with their father, taking care of feeding all the animals; the girls went to wash the dishes. I and Iren went to a different room in order to talk about my turbulent situation with Matild. There was nothing she could do at this time to help me other than give me some money and provide a few of the material things I needed—shoes and winter clothing. She had her hands full with her own family, and besides, she knew how stubbornly independent-minded I was to accept orders from her.

I didn't tell Iren anything about Ildiko, for I already knew the answers she would have thrown at me: "No. No. No. That is one thing you must not do at your age—falling in love with a *city girl*."

Everybody around me had a bad impression about this *city girl* I loved so much. None of them knew, except me, how well mannered, how smart, and most of all, how beautiful she was. Nobody understood that I was craving to differ from the manners and the attitudes of the peasants with whom I was surrounded in my village. Ildiko was the only one with whom I could express the manner and the attitude I was craving for to express in my extraordinary life.

When Iren received my letter a few days before I arrived here, she traveled right of way to Budapest and traversed the city in order to find the stores that were selling secondhand clothes and shoes. She came back with such a bundle of clothes and shoes that a less-aggressive woman would have suffered a hernia carrying it.

The day after I arrived, the bundle was still unopened. She not only bought things for me, however, but also for her children as well. Because I needed clothes more than her sons, she gave me the opportunity to open the bundle first and pick and choose what I liked. But I refused to do it.

I told her, "When you picked out the stuff for me, you knew what I needed. Now give me only those things that you intended to give me. And I'll be satisfied."

She insisted that I go through the bundle and try the ones that best fit my size, for she bought various sizes of each type, thinking that in time I would grow into them. I think she bought the clothes by the pound, rather than the style and quality I dreamed to have.

While I was in Budapest with Ildiko, I saw how kids of my age were dressed, and I wanted to look similar to that.

I found very little in the bundle that perfectly fitted me since I had a muscle-bound body that featured sporty-looking arms, chest, and legs, developed from all that hard farm work. Her sons, when stood next me, looked like half the size of my body although they were about my age. Hard physical work was not part of their life.

My fitting room was Iren's large pantry. I had the privacy here and had enough space to move about. Plus I had enough nails already driven all over in the walls and the sides of the shelves to hang all the clothes for having a better view of the sizes and the colors.

At this time I wore a T-shirt and short pants. I wore no briefs. I couldn't afford it. And, besides, I hated briefs, for they rubbed rashes on my testicles. So I was half naked now in the pantry, trying to figure out what went with what before I tried it. I wasted a good part of my late afternoon and early evening inside the pantry only to come out almost empty-handed.

In trying to find something that would fit me, I tried every coat and pants. As long as they hugged my body without bagginess, I could shorten the legs and the arms without any problem, I thought. So I ended up with two sport coats and three pairs of pants. All were woven out of wool that would last me until I outgrow them. The coats had extra-long sleeves and the pants extra-long legs.

(As soon as I arrived home, I shortened and folded them and hand-stitched the ends, just as a tailor would have done. Then, I ironed them. Now, I would look in them just like a city boy would, I imagined. Everything I did, regarding my clothes, I had Ildiko in mind. Her taste was my self-critic. The only real problem I had was holding the needle during stitching. It kept falling out of my fingers, for they were stiff from being overworked.)

As far as the shoes were concerned, I found nothing that I liked. They all had tapered heels and pointy noses. While they were in fashion, I still objected to wearing shoes like that. Girls wore similar styles, and I didn't want to dress half-and-half—mannish in clothes, girlish in shoes.

I left all the clothes hanging on the nails, for my two nephews came after me to try their chances, finding something that would fit them. Hurriedly, I dressed up, unlocked the pantry door, and shoved it open with my hip, slamming it into Ella's face. She wanted to talk to me through the pantry door.

Instead of leaving now, I invited her to come inside. I locked the door again, and we sat side by side on the top of a big sauerkraut barrel. As she looked at the clothes, which had different colors and shapes, hanging on nails all over the place, she chuckled over my elaborate dress rehearsal, thinking that something was wrong with me. When she saw how I had sorted that large bundle of pastel-colored clothes (that otherwise looked like a heap of autumn leaves tossed on a burlap spread to be junked somewhere), I said to her that I had become finicky about my clothes on account of Ildiko.

Iren had carried that large bundle of clothes on the top of her head from the bus stop. It took two men to lift it up there.

"This is not funny, Ella. I get two coats and tree pairs of pants out of this bazaar. But forget now this whole thing and tell me quickly how things are going with you. Say it very quietly, as Iren might be eavesdropping on the other side of the door. I don't want you to be in trouble," I whispered.

"When will you come and take me back home?" she asked.

I expected that she would tell me anything but "take me back home."

"I can't do that now. Things are not going well back home. Joseph died, and Matild was almost murdered. I don't have chickens or ducks left anymore to have eggs and meat. Matild killed them all, for she thought that I wouldn't return back home. Then, there is a big problem in the village. The Communists have become community organizers in order to brainwash the peasants to join farm collectives. Thereby they would give up their ownership rights.

"Then in school, there is this Communist-inspired idealism about how promising *socialism* is for those students who take it to heart to follow the proletarian cult already formed and coerced on the people in the Soviet Union. In line with this, all our schoolbooks have been rewritten, and on almost every page, this totalitarian idealism is interwoven with the text in the pages," I explained.

"We were taught the same thing here in our school. Iren told me that they were lies. I didn't understand it anyway. I just listened to the teachers and fell asleep. It made no sense to me," Ella replied.

"What I want to ask you, though, since everything is so uncertain back home, is that you stay here for a few more months. I want you to know that I have plans already that sometime next spring I would come for you. We would then settle in our house and stay away from everybody. We would be on our own, and we would not let anybody from the relatives to bother us. So be in a good spirit and try to get along with everybody here in this family in the meantime. I'll come for you, I promise."

Ella was happy upon hearing my promise; she knew that it was as solid as gold that wouldn't tarnish with time.

* * *

The following morning, I was up early. The sun was not up yet and the air was cool and breezy. So I went outside to do my routine exercise. I enjoyed being outside in the cool breeze. It dried my sweat off. The only noise that disturbed my peace was the countless chickens, ducks, and geese flapping and grooming themselves and looking at me from the other side of the fence that separated us. They were begging for food in their own language.

Iren is up, too, and is preparing breakfast in the kitchen. She looked at me through the open window and yelled, "Peasants don't exercise, They work."

"What else do they do—pry in the life of others?" I retorted.

"How else would they know what's going on!" she snapped back.

The next second, I jumped inside the kitchen to tell her my reasons for exercising.

"I have taken lessons from your animals out there in the yard and wondered why in the world they were flapping their wings and grooming themselves. Well, they did what I did. They tuned their muscles to stay fit for the day. What is wrong with that?"

Iren paid no attention to me, for her mind was on cooking. Yet she knew what I was doing. In her mind, however, exercise meant to be done through hard work.

"Here, ten pounds of potatoes, peel them. That will practice your fingers, too. Then, go and grab five chickens, chop their heads off, and scald them. Throw their heads to the cats. They will gladly chew on them.

"After you clean all the feathers off—I mean all the feathers—split them into individual pieces. Throw their guts where the manure pile is and watch how the crows fly away with them. Then, wash the parts again and bring them to me. I'll deep-fry some parts and cook a stew from the rest. We'll have chicken stew with mashed potatoes for lunch. The fried pieces I'll pack for you for the road. Now, that is what I meant when I said, 'Peasants don't exercise. They work,'" Iren concluded.

I took no offense whatsoever as my sister ordered me around. In fact, I enjoyed her instructions. Instead of telling me what to do step by step, she only highlighted the process. In this manner, I was left alone to figure out the details myself.

When she saw, however, what I did with the chickens, her face turned red. She looked at me sternly and raised her voice: "Now that I let you make your own mistakes, I'll tell you what you did wrong. You allowed these chickens to stay in the hot water too long. As a result, you cooked their skin, and now the meat looks naked and has lost most of its flavor. Then, you cut them as if a fox had mangled them apart, a chunk here, a chunk there. Now they are unrecognizable pieces. I feel like throwing them away, but I can't afford to do that. So I'm forced now to cook them as they are. You'll have to tell my husband what he is eating. Do you see what you did wrong?" Iren asked.

"How can I not see it since you pointed it out in detail? From now on I'll cut up a chicken the way nature created that chicken, in recognizable pieces—legs, wings, breast, etc.," I replied.

It was in this manner that I learned to become aware of my mistakes. Doing something wrong did not appear to be wrong until somebody pointed it out that it was wrong. One thing I was sure of, the wrong didn't stop me from trying to do something else, for it was through my mistakes that I became knowledgeable to improve myself. The more mistakes I made, the more common sense I gained. But it was the price also I paid for being stubborn. It lasted until I realized that by asking and by heeding the advice of wiser people, I could become prudent enough to avoid the same mistakes again.

Now the whole family ate lunch, and John, Iren's husband, didn't question from where the mangled chicken parts came from.

Within that hour, I left Rackeresztur and traveled by train to Balatonkeresztur. All along, I kept my eyes on my backpack, not so much because it was big and new, but because it was made out of expensive deerskin and, also, my money was in it. This was the money Iren gave me in order to buy my shoes with it. My dear brother-in-law gave me the new backpack, as he was embarrassed seeing me lugging my stuff around in a burlap bag.

Animals Know Who Love Them

Before even going home, my first stop would have been at Joseph's stall to check on the condition of the cows. But as I reached the church at the intersection, I saw that the usual herd of cows were coming in from the grazing fields and were turning, each heading to his home in the village. Joseph's cows, however, separated themselves from the herd and ran straight to me. They stopped and looked at me, pushing their noses against my face, showing how much they missed me. I embraced them and kissed them individually, for I missed them too. So now I led them home by walking in front of them. (Would anybody dare to say that animals can't show affection toward those who love them?)

As I reached Joseph's stall, Mr. Forro was already waiting for the cows. He didn't think I would be leading them home.

"You come just the right time, Arpad. I am totally exhausted. Matild never showed up, and I ended doing all the work by myself. I didn't milk the cows, though, because I don't know how. You think the milk in them would still be good?" he asked.

"The milk will be still good, but the amount will be less than before. I see that the udders are smaller now than before I left. That is not a good sign. They have reversed milk production for lack of regular milking. A similar thing would happen when a calf is weaned. Unless somebody kept up the milking, that cow would slow down milk production. Joseph explained this to me long before he died. For as long as the milk is emptied from the cow's udder, her body wouldn't know the difference who did it.

240

"Within a few weeks I wouldn't have to milk the cows anymore. That would be the good thing. The bad thing would be that I wouldn't have milk for my breakfast any longer," I explained.

So now, before I did anything else, I milked the cows, drank some of it, and gave the rest to Mr. Forro.

"I'll be back early tomorrow morning. I hope that you come, too. I didn't forget what you told me the other day: 'Hurry back, though, because I need to talk to you about America.' You didn't forget that, did you?'" he nodded and smiled as I left him.

CHAPTER SIXTEEN

Communistic Fervor and the Opposition to It

As I left Mr. Forro, I was wondering about Matild, whether she changed her mind about joining collective farming. As I entered her kitchen, I found her in bed, groaning as if she were dying. I lifted her and gave her water. She then started talking: "You should not have left me alone. Those angry kulaks (rich peasants), who wanted to kill me before I jumped into the well, came back last night and beat the hell out of me. I'm bruised all over. They said that if I don't stop clamoring about collectivization, they would hang my skin on the town hall's gate."

"That tells me, you were in the village again pumping somebody's nerves against you. Weren't you?" I asked.

"Not exactly happened that way. Soon after you left, one of those fast moving tractors pulled up here in front of the house and a bunch of party guys came in here and asked me to join them. And I did. Then, we sat in the open trailer and held up red flags as the tractor rolled through every street in this village and two other villages. I think my flag was the highest. It fluttered like a towel on a close line in high wind. I enjoyed every minute of it." Matild regained her spirit.

"You know that that the red flag is the symbol of Communism. Now that you held it high, whoever saw you knew it that you were a Communist, or at least a sympathizer. No wonder the *kulaks* came after you and gave you a hint what could happen to you."

"I really didn't think that this would happen to me. How many sides this movement had, anyway, Arpad?" Matild asked.

"You know as well as I do how many sides they have, but you don't want to admit it because you sympathize with them. The Communist government wants to rule the whole country just like it is done in Russia. Since they couldn't force everybody at once to join their ideology, they decided to do it little by little, inveigling at first certain segments of the population. Where that didn't work, they used force.

"They started first with the church by locking up the cardinal, and later, either locked up the priests or took them away to hard labor. Then, they pressed the intellectuals. Some went to prison, some to labor camps. At the same time, they nationalized all the big industries and collectivized the small ones. Now, they reached the villages. They want to collectivize all the farmland, even if they have to persecute the rich peasants or take them away somewhere. Are you surprised then that some of them want to get even by beating those who supported them? You know, Matild, I'm surprised that you are still living!"

"How come you know all this? What else do they teach you in school?" she asked.

"I think, Matild, you know what is happening. You are just ignoring it. You won't give up pursuing the Communist cause unless they kill you. You may be even looking for it—to make yourself a Communist hero.

"All our teachers are either party members or sympathizers. They don't persecute schoolchildren. They indoctrinate them. They know that the children are bendable if they lie to them long enough and treat them with favors.

"This year, the authorities revised all the schoolbooks and filled them with Communist propaganda and illustrated the pages with pictures of those who were the forerunners of Communism, especially in Hungary. Right now, most kids are confused, for the old books emphasized freedom, religion, respect for parents, and a lot of historical truths. But they are now huddling and asking, 'Who is right?' I don't ask anybody. I know it in my heart who is right. So I keep low. I know that those who deny the existence of God are wrong. I'm done!'"

Having said all I wanted to say to Matild, I picked my backpack and went next door to my house. I went straight to bed with all my clothes on and slept until sunrise the following morning. I was extremely tired from the day's tumultuous activities.

Once I woke up the following morning, I couldn't stay in bed any longer. I went outside and did my usual exercise while watching the rising sun and the noisy animals. I heard also that Matild was still snoring. Today is a Monday, and while exercising, I recounted my commitments for the day. It wasn't long, however, before the chickens and the ducks surrounded me and begged for food. They probably had not been fed since I left last Saturday. Since I couldn't exercise any longer for they were picking at me, I ran to the shed and brought out a pale of barley and spread it all over the yard.

This was an unforgettable scene as to what followed. The sparrows, the crows, the pigeons, and God only knows the rest descended the yard and picked all the grain before the fowl had a chance to get it. I was foolish. Instead of putting the grain into their feed trays, I strew it all over the yard. I couldn't give the fowl any more grain now, for that was their daily allowance.

As I rushed back to my kitchen to get ready to go to take care of the cows, I said to myself, "These birds from the sky are in many ways just like the Communist are—*freeloaders.*"

Within a short time, I was already inside Joseph's stall, taking care of the cows. Since I did this a hundred times before, I knew every step of the job. I finished the clean-up and brushed the cows and did the milking within an hour.

Then, I left the milk bucket, now full of milk, outside Mr. Forro's kitchen door in order that he would see it once he stepped outside. After that, I ran to the canal where I washed myself and swam around a couple of times in the chilly water. I hurried back to the stall, thinking for sure that Mr. Forro would be waiting for me there already. But he wasn't there. Neither the milk in the bucket. The cats and dogs from the neighborhood finished it all. I couldn't believe myself as to how screwy things could happen to me on certain days. I was prepared now for more trouble coming for the rest of the day, as when trouble starts coming, it comes like an avalanche, takes everything with it all the way to the bottom of the hill.

So I left the scene and went home. It was about eight o'clock in the morning, and it was now time to prepare myself in a hurry to go to school. I was late already but couldn't allow myself to skip another day. My teachers would have reprimanded me. Since I was an orphan, they were instructed by higher authorities to keep an eye on me, for if needed, they could recommend that I be taken to boarding school. That threat alone was good enough for me to be on good terms with my teachers. That didn't mean, however, that I liked them.

Before I left the house, I brought plenty of food to Matild because she ate nothing since yesterday. I noticed that she was getting better and was able to sit up in her bed already. She guessed that I was going to school as she saw me wearing nice clothes and was groomed as if I was going to visit somebody important—like the school's headmaster.

"On your way back, find out if anybody was talking about me." she wanted to know.

I acted as if I didn't hear anything and left her in a hurry to go to school.

Denial of the Past

My school was located just across from the church. It was formerly a parochial school. Only the local highway separated it from the parish, where the priest and the nuns resided before the state confiscated both. The school's structure looked much like a large manor house. The inside, however, contained only three rooms. The two big ones accommodated the seventh- and eighth-grade students, and the smaller one in the center served as the administrative office. While the front of the structure faced the church, the back of it joined a vast open field that served both as playground and as exercise field for parades and physical training. The playground area was shaded by huge chestnut trees, smartly planted to beautify the area. It was here where I finished my elementary school.

I had five teachers, three males, two females. Four of them were locals so they knew everybody and everything as far as village matters were concerned. All four were party members, but in name only. The fifth one, a woman, was an outsider who had moved to town from far away, only two years ago. She was the headmaster, and her name was Edith Marish. She was a die-hard Communist and was the propagandist for the group and could talk for hours nonstop, praising the Communist ideology and glorifying its leaders. It was she who was responsible for brainwashing everybody else, teachers and students alike. Hence, there developed a heated friction between her and the other teachers regarding teaching methods and how to teach the *truth* to the students who were taught before by a priest and two nuns. She kept her office out of fear not in the school building but in the old parish hall.

When I stepped on the school grounds, I saw that there was recess and all the kids were playing, talking, and chasing each other in the playground. I didn't stop, although I knew every one of them. They didn't stop either. So I kept walking straight to the office, tapped the door several times before I heard, "Come in." I was very self-assured and politely presented myself and told the truth as to why I had missed three days of school. Edith Marish was in the middle of brainwashing the teachers and said to me: "Wait a few minutes, Arpad, I'll be finishing shortly."

So I sat at the conference table next to my grammar teacher and patiently waited, listening to what Ms. Marish had to say:

"You must not shed light on the past as you are explaining the contents of the new books. And the best way to do that is have the students read loudly all the contents and comments given on the pages. You will not go into details, explaining in your own words any critical analysis about past history, religion, or even God. None of that stuff was true anyway in light of the proletariat ideology. The Capitalists from the West distorted the truth in order to fatten their pockets through slave-driving the workers from sunrise to sunset. I will continue tomorrow at the same time. Thank you."

The teachers were now looking at me, wanting to know my impression about Edith Marish's harangue.

"It was very amusing. I would have to be born again to understand it. Looks to me that I wouldn't have to study much at all. I wonder if she knew what she was talking about."

My remarks provoked the teachers into deep thought. Their eyes frozen in their sockets and were wondering whether they, too, understood what Edith Marish said.

The essence of it all boiled down to one critical topic: how to *deny the past.*

My physical education teacher looked at me and said, "It's good to see you here and nicely listening to Edith talking to us. You know, she was talking to you also."

"She was? I would like to know why," I asked.

"Since you are the strongest kid among the others and also level-headed, we want you to become a member of the Communist Youth Organization. It would be good for you to gain knowledge of the future. Maybe even promoting the new *thinking*," he said.

His name was Robert Fish, a good-looking, young teacher, still single. He had a well-formed body, perfectly suited for physical training others. Furthermore, he was dating an equally young and beautiful girl teacher on whom my eyes rested more often than needed to. Her name was Iren Block. She was teaching grammar, literature, and history. The other two male teachers were much older, probably in their fifties, and were teaching mathematics and related fields like geometry and physics. All four were party members but in name only. They all agreed that I should be helping Robert Fish, who headed the Communist Youth Organization in addition to teaching physical education, and through it, he promoted the *denial of the past* to my schoolmates.

The reasoning behind their thinking was that I was the best candidate—knowing the least about past history and had no parents teaching me about it—to promote the *denial of the past* to the other students. What they didn't know however was that I knew more about past history and the underhanded tactics of the Communist Party organizers than most students did. I traveled a lot, listened a lot, and saw a lot.

From all this, I recognized very early that the past is always interwoven with the present; and that there is no future without the knowledge of the past. For, everybody and everything came from somewhere. The only thing I didn't do a lot, moreover, was talking about it. But I was a very good listener and realized therefore that the people are the ones who had everything to do with the past, the present, and the future. And from listening, I reflected my own past and brought forth my dreams for the future. For these reasons, I decided that I shall not be a promoter of the *denial of the past* to the student body within the Communist Youth Organization, to which I was now forced to belong.

So I responded to my teachers: "I'm not a good student to lead others. The past meant to me that I wouldn't have revived what's dead to life to tell me what I'm doing wrong. But I'll listen to others to lead me, if I agree with them."

For the first time in my young life, I was faking myself.

I didn't say that I would follow others. I just said that I would listen. The teachers missed my point. They were satisfied that I wouldn't be saying anything about the *denial of the past* that Ms. Edith Marish had pounded into their heads. I would be just drifting along in silence.

* * *

This new way of teaching—the denial of the past—slowly ushered in the formation of three separate groups in society.

The first layer of society was the old guard, who believed in God and practiced it now underground. They held the core values of Christianity—faith, truth, liberty, and justice. The middle layer of society became the mixed breed, hanging on to the old values while feigning the new in practice. The third layer of society was the diehard Communists—godless, brutal, senseless.

This last group held the seat of power, hence the advantage over the others. Corruption, favoritism, and backstabbing moved the gears of the regime forward. Where these tactics failed, threats, torture, and imprisonment followed. The Secret Service Agents assured steady progress in all areas to install the Soviet-style socialism. These agents were inventors of brutality. They were the ultimate defenders of Communism; therefore, they were the watchdogs. They were installed at all levels within state institutions and the population at large. They operated in disguise, trusted no one, and carefully monitored suspects. They fearlessly acted the minute suspicion surfaced. Everybody lived in fear.

* * *

Now the recess was over and all the students returned to class. I was the last one to enter after the teachers, for I was wheeling in the new books on a flatbed cart. It was customary to show respect to the teachers by standing up when they entered the class. Now both the teachers and the students were still standing as I pushed the cartful of books to the open space between the teacher's desk and the students. I held my head high and pushed that cart as if it had candy bars stacked on it. The students didn't know that their new schoolbooks were stacked there so neatly.

I stopped and looked at everybody as if I was taking a picture of them. Then, I said: "Here are our new schoolbooks. I am entrusted to tell you that the books will teach us everything we need to know about the future. These books are written for the young pioneers (the young Communists). They are full of new instructions and pictures from the *old pioneers* (previously locked-up Communists) who promoted socialistic ideology in the past. Ms. Marish just explained to our teachers in the conference room how we should use them. One thing she didn't say though, that if we are in doubt, we may correct ourselves from our old books. Come now, one by one, starting from the right and get them. I'll hand them to you."

So I handed the books to every student in the class, smiling and saying "hallo" to each of them. I knew that they were wondering what kind of an assignment I had now to have earned this privilege, telling about the general contents of the books as if I had already read them.

Had they known the truth that I had never seen these books before and didn't care if I ever would, they would have thrown them back at me. The truth was, however, that now I had become the handyman to my teachers to do the things they didn't want to do or were embarrassing for them to do. When I finished handing out the books, I went to the last seat in the row and waited there while my teachers dismissed the class on account of holding another conference among themselves.

I was now ready to justify my words that *we may correct ourselves from our old books.* I noticed that the words caught the teacher's attention. So they went to conference to discuss how to overcome that problem. They couldn't agree, for they themselves knew that it was impossible to erase the past, even from their own memories. Besides, the church kept volumes of it. But still, lies gained the upper hand, for they sounded better to gullible people.

* * *

So it was that I spent most of my time during class hours doing all kinds of house or yard work, or even field work for my teachers in exchange for letting me stay away from class. I never took tests and final examinations in my seventh and eighth grades, yet I still passed both grades even though I barely studied. It was in this way that I had out-maneuvered the useless and idiotic brainwashing tactics my classmates had to endure about the *denial of the past.*

While I stayed way behind the academic gains from schooling, I gained the benefits of independent thinking by avoiding this mind-alteration maneuver practiced on the other students.

Since I was able to read and write quite well already, (thanks to practicing writing and memorizing the poems of Sandor Petofi), I cared more to do and to learn the practical things—the things everybody had to learn and do in life, sooner or later. As often as it was the case, these practical things grew on me, not so much by my willingly running into them, but rather by the whims of exploiters (Matild, Godfather), as well as my teachers from school who either didn't have the time or hated to do them.

It was in this manner that I learned farming, masonry, whitewashing houses, gardening, pruning threes, caring for bees, distilling moonshine, harvesting and pressing grapes to make wine, and even smoking hams and sausages. So by the time I was fifteen years old, I had more knowledge and experience as to how simple folks lived than a lot of people would learn in a lifetime. Was I ever bored? Never!

Listening to My Mentor Mr. Forro

Now that we were dismissed from school for the day, I went to visit Mr. Forro, who was so anxious to talk to me about America. I caught up with him in his garden, pulling the stems of dried beans and planting cloves of garlic in their place. While he was busy doing that, I gleaned Joseph's vineyard just behind his garden for the last clusters of grapes that the starlings missed. Although these grapes were already wrinkled, they were the sweetest and tastiest fruits that I had ever eaten as a kid. The frostbite turned all the juices in them to sugar. When I told Mr. Forro how aromatic and sweet these wrinkled grapes were, he told me that the secret in making real good wine resulted from such wrinkled grapes.

The most famous wine of this kind is the Tokaji Aszu which contains several vatfuls of juice compressed from wrinkled grapes. Each bottle has a number printed on its label, stating how many vatfuls of this stuff was mixed into the bulk. I learned something new again. Then, the old man opened his treasured American know-how:

"If you want to discover something really new, something really amazing, Arpad, you have to go to America. There, you can be what you want to be, go wherever you want to go, and do whatever you want to do. Only one thing is needed—guts to go for it. And if you have that, you could work anywhere and make plenty of money to support your dreams. I was there once and I know it."

"How far is that place from here? Everything looks to me so close on the map."

"Very far," he said, "it is almost like looking up to the moon and trying to figure out the distance. But you should never think of distance when you look for adventures. In itself, distance could be the greatest adventure for a young person like you."

"Why do you think that America is so good and you live here in misery? Why did you come back, if it was so good there?"

"Well, my heart wasn't in it. My body was there, but my heart was here. I became aware when I got there that everything I wanted to live for was here in this country—my parents, my friends, and most of all, my girlfriend," Mr. Forro said.

"Why did you go there then?" I asked.

"Money!" he exclaimed and continued, "Money then as money now and in the future will drive all to go where it's available. Then, once you have it, you may be destined to lose it. This entire socialistic movement that is going on now is nothing more than resetting bank accounts. Take away from those who have and give to those who don't. And to make it happen, one may have to kill the other," he said.

"Gee, Mr. Forro, you put me on the spot to think about myself more and more. I never thought that it was money that made man juggle his mind and go for it, even to the end of the world. Is there anything man can do without money?"

"Yes, steal. That's what those without money do. Know, my son, that a man who steals today is a lazy man looking to the Communists for handout. What he should be doing instead is right in front of him. Only that he would have to work for it."

"But I am not one of those who does that," I told him. "I never look for a handout. I look to the stars to thank God for his blessing that he cared for me today. He always grants me the *will* to grab my hammer and beat the iron while it is still hot. This is my belief, and I know it in my heart that as long as I have the *will*, I can overcome any hardship that would otherwise drag me down. Work means money to me of a different kind, rather than a handout. I earn it."

"Then, you should definitely go to America the first chance you get. There, a man with your *will* can become rich and independent. You wouldn't have to worry about losing your liberty as in this country," Mr. Forro concluded.

It was very interesting to hear again someone else talking about the same country that I didn't even know where it was. Ildiko told me already that it existed. Since I had now more than enough problems of my own in this country, I decided to ignore whatever I heard from Mr. Forro about America.

To get away from him for the time being, I went to milk the cows, the second time today, as I promised I would do. As soon as I finished it, I handed him the bucket of milk so that no animals could lick it empty again. Then, I disappeared from the scene.

CHAPTER SEVENTEEN

Don't Expect Rewards for Good Deeds

On my way home now, the mailwoman stopped me. She was already looking for me over an hour. She had a registered letter that needed my signature to receive it.

"I have been looking for you all over to deliver this mail. Matild told me that she was anxiously waiting for you also. She is moving around her kitchen, trying to dab her wounds on her face with some kind a tea she brewed from herbs," she said.

"It was there, where you looked for me for an hour, right?" I asked her.

"I was only listening and couldn't get away from her. She didn't know what to do with herself, and I couldn't give her any advice because I am a mailwoman. But I know she was nervously waiting for you," she replied.

I knew that that mailwoman was lying to me because I was not her ordinary customer who would patiently listen to her idle talk. This woman could, in proper moments, spew fifty words in a wink's time without having her vocal cords stop. She had one good thing going for her, though; she mostly sided with the talker, thereby holding back criticisms of others while she was on duty. All that changed, however, the minute she was off duty. At times, it took her hours to reach her home from the post office which was no more than a thousand feet away. Whichever direction I ran to do my chores, I could see her gabbing with somebody.

"Anyway," she said, "here is your mail. Please sign for it. You are my last customer."

As soon as she jumped on her bicycle, I looked at my mail and saw that it came from Romania. My name was misspelled, and my address was wrong. There were at least ten *Kereszturs* in the country, and this mail went to every one of them. Had *Balaton* been prefixed to *Keresztur*, I would have received it in a few days, instead of two months. The letter came from my dear gypsy friend, Tony. He was on his way back to Hungary but had not yet arrived. For a moment, I recalled the good times I had with him. Then, I jammed the letter in my pocket and rushed home to see Matild.

Matild was waiting for me already just as the mailwoman said. At this time, she was already outside her kitchen, leaning on the half wall of her veranda. She was surrounded by the hungry chickens wanting grain, but she couldn't get to the shed for it. I knew that she was up to something on account of what she heard from the mailwoman. An hour was a boringly long time to listen to somebody gabbing without having the listener add her share to the gossip. The mailwoman told Matild that I gave half her crop to Frank.

As soon as Matild recognized my coming, a blood clot from her throat jumped out in her anger as she forced her words, yelling: "You gave away my food! You gave away my milk! You gave away my money—my profit. I'll make you starve for it all winter!"

"You didn't work for it, did you, Matild? Did the mailwoman tell you something?" I hollered back.

The moment I came close enough to her, she grabbed the broomstick that she used aiding her walking, and she pounded my shoulders with it. I didn't grab it out of her hand, knowing that if I did, one whack with it would have probably killed her. Her strength compared to mine was like that of an ant biting at the foot of an elephant. Besides, what would have I gained from it? Only pain in my heart, for I would have overpowered a woman, the easiest thing to do for a strong man.

As she was beating me, I stood still in front of her with tears rippling from my eyes, for I didn't do anything wrong. I only gave away half the potatoes, corn, and beans to the poor. I felt it was the excess from her bounty, the excess that I reaped from Joseph's abundant harvest. Isn't that what every man should do from his plenty? My feelings had rushed together with my tears, asking forgiveness and blessing from the Almighty—the first one on Matild, the second one on me. I was hurt, not from the beatings, but from her cruelness that drove her greed to selfishness and anger.

When she saw that I wouldn't even lift my finger against her, she recoiled and said: "Cursed is my hand that lifted this broomstick against you!"

And she threw the broomstick away, turned around, and limped back to her kitchen.

"I'll be back when you are starving and want to take food from my hands again. That would be the only time you would realize that hunger had stripped your selfishness from your cruel heart," I hollered after her.

When it clicked in her mind what I have just said, she immediately turned around and said, "Forgive me, I have nothing to eat, and I'm hungry now. Will you feed me again?"

"No. I won't feed you because you are faking yourself. Think about what you just did to me. When I see tears in your eyes, as big as mine, and lots of it, I'll know then that you have repented. I'll feed you then," I replied.

As I now left her and went back to Joseph's stall to feed the cows, it dawned on me that Matild could have been very hungry after all. The last time I gave her a piece of fried meat was this morning, just before I left to go to school, and now, it was early evening already. But, instead of returning, I went ahead and fulfilled my promise to Mr. Forro, to milk the cows the second time. It was almost evening now.

Farewell to Mr. Forro

The next day as I was arriving close to the stall again, I saw that Mr. Forro was sitting on a stool, leaning with his back against the wall of the stall and was waiting there for me. Something was in his hands that blinded me from clearly seeing him. The rising sun reflected its brightness back. Facing him, I asked, "What's that in your hands that blinded me from seeing you? Did you do that on purpose?"

"This is my rosary, and what you saw were the gold beads shining in your eyes. I was rolling them while praying."

"I never heard of such a thing to do. I never saw gold like that. Where did you get it?"

"When I was in America, I followed hundreds of others who were rushing to a place called California, searching for gold. There, I sifted the sand in a riverbank for it. After weeks of sifting, I gathered enough gold that my leather pouch was full with it. I thought that in order to bring the gold back home one day, it would be best to have a goldsmith form the odd pieces into beads. Then string them like a rosary which I would hang around my neck and bring it back home with me. And here it is in my hands now, telling you something about America, doesn't it?"

He lifted the chain and was enticing me to go to America.

"If you mean that the shine or your rolling of it would impress me to go to America, they don't. It just surprised me because I have not seen anything like that before."

"I'll give it to you free, if you promise me that if you have to *run* from this country, you would choose America to go to."

"I won't. I have no need for something that would pull my body to the ground. Why should I run? Nobody is chasing me, and I didn't kill anybody. But if I ever have to run, it would only be in search for my freedom which I have less and less of," I responded with subdued indignation, for the word *run* sounded to me more as a premonition than as a perception.

"How about if I tell you that it would brighten your mind knowing the value of it?"

"The gold or the rolling? I suppose you want to climb to heaven with it, don't you? You need a true heart and a clean mind to do that. The rosary alone won't do it."

The old man became flabbergasted upon hearing my words; he stopped altogether rolling the beads, moving his lips, or even marveling the shine of his gold chain.

"You know anybody who wanted to buy gold?" he asked.

He acted as if an angel had told him, "Get rid of it!" He threw the chain of gold a few feet away from his body.

"Yes, my neighbor Laszlo. Being a Jew at heart, he is under the impression too, that the shine of gold connects him to heaven. He would buy it from you, if your price is right."

"Here, take it and sell it to him and give the money to that legless man who used to beg at the church's entrance. Then, come back to me, and we will set our hearts and minds up high and think about what's up there," he said.

As I accepted the gold beads from him, he closed his eyes while at the same time turned his head high as if he were already seeing heaven.

I sold the gold to Laszlo for a pocketful of change which I gave to the legless man who was now begging at the entrance to the village store, instead. Then, I returned to the old man about an hour later and found him still in the same position I left him.

He died, I thought, the minute I handed the money over to the beggar. But I wasn't sure, and I nudged him only to find that he was in deep sleep as old folks often are.

"You are back already, my boy! How did you do? I'm so relieved not having that heavy chain pulling my hands down. I was always afraid that somebody would steal it from me. Now, I have no more worries," he said.

"I bet you were thinking about taking it down to the grave with you," I commented.

"I was. But even then, I would have been worried that on my way down somebody would have lifted it from me. What a terrible greed I had, leaving this life with the idea that even in the grave I would be a rich man."

"Now you will because you gave *all you had* to the poor."

While all this went on between the two of us, the cows were mooing as never before, wanting to eat. So I helped the old man get up, and together we went to feed the beasts. He, of course, couldn't do anything except looking at my movements as I was forking the hay and the sugar beets from the barn to the feed bay.

This was the last memorable event we shared together. The following morning, I let the cows join the other cows headed to the grazing fields. There, they were rounded and trucked away by the *Secret Police* to a collective farm twenty miles away. After that, I never went back to Joseph's stall, for even looking in that direction, sorrows drowned my heart after my beloved pets. I never saw Mr. Forro either. He died a few days after I lost my pets. I lamented him from the top of an apple tree nearby the cemetery, as his body was lowered into the arms of destiny. After it was all over, I climbed down and visited his grave, promising that I would keep *America* in mind for as long as I lived.

It would have been impossible for me to be near his coffin, as I didn't want anybody to see me sobbing after him. This was all that I could promise him now for the love and kindness he always had for me. He was really a good man who had inspired me to look *high* in times when I was troubled and couldn't do anything about it.

CHAPTER EIGHTEEN

Collective Enterprises Become a Fact of Life

After the funeral, it was time now to go home and find out what Matild had done regarding her joining the collective farming. Even though her attempts to convince the rich peasants to join had failed, her wish eventually was fulfilled—collective farming became a reality by force. It was decreed by the Communist government that all farmlands in the whole nation must to be collectivized, except garden plots located near houses and in selected areas.

Since Matild had inherited all the farmland Joseph had, she was now more than willing to let the authorities take them in order to combine all the small tracks of land into one vast property that surrounded the village. All landowners had been given the opportunity to join collective farming, even those who were deadly against it.

As it was time now to plow under all the individually owned tracks of land into one vast field, all the property markers were removed. The collective farm received from the state confiscated farm equipment that nobody knew to whom it had previously belonged. It was only this way that the farmlands could be plowed under to become one vast farming area.

Matild joined the work brigade the following spring. I had nothing to do with any of the undergoing hassle as I lost no land due to confiscation. The two half-acre garden plots remained in my possession. One was close to the forest in the outlying areas of the village; the other was in the hill country where small vineyards were planted almost side by side.

* * *

After I told Matild that I stored the winter crops from Joseph's properties in his cold cellar, she asked me, "What are you going to do with your crops?"

"I'll use them as I need them since you said that you'll starve me to death because I gave half of yours away."

"Is there anyone who could starve you, Arpad? It may happen that I'll starve to death myself instead."

"If you don't speculate all the time how to take away what others have, someone would probably offer you a slice of bread. That someone would more than likely be I, for you have no one else."

By the end of December, what I have just said to her came true. Her pantry was empty. She did something that her greed drove her to do. She sold all the crops I gathered for her in Joseph's cellar with the intention of grabbing mine later. She wanted to take advantage of me again as so often had happened before. But this time, I stood my ground.

"You know, Matild, you deserve your lot. You are actually driving others to hate you, to run away from you. I have now the biggest surprise in your life coming. I'm running away from you, too.

"Tomorrow, I'm locking up my side of the house and moving away. I'm moving to my godfather. I'll come back sometime later but only to check how you have pilfered my crops. Be careful though because after that you'll have to earn your own living by working on the collective farms," I remarked.

Foretaste of What is to Come

I wished so often that Matild would have been kindhearted, and if I could have, I would have done anything to change her over to be one. Finally I accepted the fact that innate habits only God can change.

Come to think of it, and as long as I have known Matild, she had never kissed me. As I was growing up, I really missed the hugs and kisses that loving parents showered on their children. When I saw it happen, I yearned to receive an occasional hug myself from somebody. This was just one of the many reasons why I loved and cherished every minute with Joseph and with Mr. Forro. They treated me as their own son. They fulfilled my wish as they were the only ones who showered me with love hugs every time I helped them. In return, I hugged them, too. Not just helped them, but helped them out of love for they were old and weakened by the cruelties of life itself.

After Mr. Forro died, I gave deep thought to the meaning of life itself. Fast recounted the three truly major events that happened so far in my life. Yet I was only thirteen years old. Within the last two years, three people died—my mother, Joseph, and Mr. Forro. I was thinking who would be next in line that would be taken away from me. Could life be that cruel to me? It seemed that the hands of the Almighty might had something to do with it, as by now I noticed he didn't treat everybody alike.

In times like this, when I saw myself facing all kinds of problems to support myself, I received incredibly short but strong messages racing through my mind, *stay by me*. Not knowing the reason, not understanding the meaning, I ignored it.

While I still had living relatives, I didn't consider them helpful. They all knew that I needed help in the worst of times, when they themselves also needed help, for the Communists swept their attics clean, too. Because most of them didn't even come to say *hallo*, I have forgotten them. So now, I had my two sisters and Matild left. While Matild was the nearest relative lived close to me, she really didn't love me. I could tell that by her selfish nature. But I could also tell that sometimes she cared for me. She would not have thrown that broomstick away and cursed herself while she did it if she didn't care for me, if she didn't have a repentant heart for me. On the other hand, I knew that my sisters loved me, but they were quite far away to offer me a helping hand to aid me doing my daily chores or worry about my food supply.

In the midst of my recounting what had happened to me since I lost my loved ones, I realized that my life moved on just the same. And moved on because I had faith in myself to let go of the past. Whatever would happen in the future, it was not within my grasp to decide who's going to live or die, or whether my endeavors would succeed or fail. I thought.

Should I recoil or recharge myself? I settled the answer as fast as I conceived the question. My *will* to survive shall overpower all my doubts and all my fears.

There was always the temptation to lie, to cheat, to steal, and to connive. I saw it happen all over in people in the village. I also saw it from my teachers and from Matild. By this time I knew the Ten Commandments so well that even in my sleep I would be able say it had the devil tempted me to do wrong.

In my desperate situations these evil temptations always moved to the forefront, if for no other reason just to confuse me. For the opposite involved a definite struggle with the truth. And if I would have taken up any one of these temptations, I would have ushered in the beginning of corruption itself. That, I would never have allowed myself to fall into even though it would have been so easy to do the bad things in life first. Matild, my aunt, could lie, cheat, steal, and connive without even knowing it. For after doing it so often, she couldn't tell the difference anymore. I had plenty of examples from her now to know the difference.

Plus, I could tell, I could feel it, and I could see it that an honest person was peaceful, while an evil person was restless. I had the spirit of Joseph and Mr. Forro in my conscience guiding me to know the difference.

* * *

Nothing convinced me better about who lied than hearing the headmaster at my school brainwash my teachers how to *deny the past* in order to promote the Communist ideology. She was so nervous and restless as she told the lies that I thought her neck had a twitching problem. Every other second as she was emphasizing how to *deny the past*, she looked out the window to check whether a gang of peasants weren't coming her way to lynch her. The other teachers listening to her nonstop *homily* had a problem holding their heads up from passing out. They understood that to promote the truth, they cannot forget the past; for what was true in the past must also be true in the future, unless proven otherwise. They learned quickly, however, that lies could only be promoted with more lies until the last lie totally contradicted all other lies.

(This is the operational scheme for promoting socialism. President Obama stupefies me in this respect. His ulterior motives have not yet been fully realized. And when it will be, it will be rather late to reverse it. "Mark my word!" My sister is reminding me.)

So what was that Ms. Marish tried to convince my teachers that they didn't already know?

She was trying to convince them that in order to teach the totalitarian ideology to the children, they would have to be taught by denying the past. The more the lie was repeated, the more the children would think that it was the truth. Repetition formed their habits; repetition altered their thinking to believe that what they were doing was the right thing to do. And that was the way gullible people practiced the totalitarian cult.

This was the vision that drove all the die-hard Communists to lie, cheat, and steal—emaciate the wealth of the rich and distribute it among the lazy in order that they would be converted to believe that it was the right thing to do in order to promote socialism. Conversely, the lazy believed that by relying on handouts, they could forever glorify the socialistic movement for the rest of their lives. But as the vault became empty, there was nothing left from which to freeload. My country became bankrupt, both morally and economically.

No attention was given, however, as to what would happen when there would be no more rich people left. There would be nothing left to confiscate and to distribute. To whom to lie now? From whom to steal now? So these die-hard Communists began to lie, cheat, and steal among themselves. They set the example for others to follow, and within the course of couple years, even those who were party members in name only joined in to follow the same practice. After all, in a totalitarian state everything was owned *by the people, for the people, and of the people.* So help yourselves, for "*What's yours is mine*" became the slogan. The evil nature of men divided the *house of evil* and set one against the other—lying to each other, cheating and stealing from each other.

So the Communists had succeeded in dividing the nation; they held the *seat of power* through the strength of the *Secret Police.*

The Final Split from Matild

When I said to Matild, "I have now the biggest surprise in your life coming," I meant every word of it. Within a few days, I locked my side of the duplex and moved away to my godfather, half a mile uptown and only two houses away from the church.

I had many reasons and many problems piled up. Next to food, the biggest push for my going away was the fact that Matild and I couldn't get along with each other. The character differences between the two of us played out in earnest as time went by, and it eventually impacted our relationship to be even near to each other. She didn't believe in God; I did. She couldn't tell the truth; I could. She was greedy; I was compassionate. She was a gossiper; I wasn't.

A lot more could be added to the list. I don't want to throw up from the rotten memories I have about her, so I shall not go on mentioning them. As bad memories only clouded my thinking, the faster I forgot them, the better I felt about myself. The fact of the matter is, however, that bad memories only moved to the background and reappeared again whenever I faced similar incidents that associated themselves with them. The devil made sure of that.

From this respect, my growing under Matild's mentoring would have become nothing less than she was. But it didn't happen that way. My stubborn nature, coupled with my intuition, always recognized the differences between us faster than any similarities we may have had with each other. So for these reasons, one rotten apple didn't become two rotten apples. Besides, I had two of the most important drivers in my soul strengthening me—faith and will—vigilantly steering each other toward decency. Being an orphan, I had two choices—either sink in my miseries or swim out of them with the strength of my faith and will. My stubbornness quelled my doubts and endured all the more as I wanted to be a better man today than I was yesterday.

* * *

Everything material becomes valueless in the absence of food to eat. Being young, healthy, and energetic, my foremost concern had always been where to get it. Singularly, this had become my foremost preoccupation day in day out. It had determined what I did and where I went to keep my stomach full. Hunger had tortured my mind to become my own slave to be the *jack-of-all-trades* in cooking, farming, domestics, and husbandry. Far from being perfect in any, but as long as it satisfied my needs, I really didn't care for opinions. My mother used to say, "Perfection and beauty are only in the eyes of the beholder." And being so young, perfection was a very lopsided imagination to me to worry about.

It was hunger that moved my mind and body to learn cooking. It was the same thing that chased me to work in the fields and to raise animals and to maintain the logistics to it—the orderly planning to succeed in each.

Orderly planning, of course, meant that if I wanted to cook, I had to work the fields, had to grow my vegetables, had to raise my own chickens, ducks, and rabbits. I needed to follow the natural evolution, for everything depended on the availability of something else.

Patience, of course, was not my second nature. If it were, I would not have been young and foolhardy. Only the passing of time and countless mistakes along the way ensured that I would learn the values of patience one day. That time was coming, but not before I was suckered into another person's empty promises.

CHAPTER NINETEEN

Moving to My Godfather, Gary Ludvig

Inasmuch as I and Matild couldn't get along with each other, my leaving her for good was not as easily done as I thought it would be. As the anger and the heated quarrels subsided, my sanity returned; and whatever goodwill I had, it took control of the moment.

Matild begged me to stay, promising to amend what she cheated me out of and promising to love me from now on. When I heard this coming out of her quivering mouth, I embraced her and told her: "I will look after you, but only from a distance. I'll forgive all the wrong you did to me, but I will not stay. For whatever you did was not a temporary misdeed but a habitual selfishness and greed that you think you can fast change now through your crocodile tears."

I had great difficulty overcoming my compassionate nature as I saw Matild crying; and it was for that reason, I embraced her. But more and more I was using my brains instead of my feelings. I realized that I had been a hired horse merely in her service. I remembered what Frank, the janitor from the church, told me: "You probably don't even realize that your mind is more on others than on yourself. What drives you to think of others more than you think of yourself? During this whole week, I didn't see in you any sign of greed or selfishness toward me as you gave half of your crops to me, and I was wondering, how can that be possible in a young person like you?

"If you do it to everybody, they would think you are crazy. In this world, most people are for themselves only—greedy and selfish. And if you would do it to the same person, over and over again, he would exploit you all the more. Think about that."

Well, I did. That person was Matild, who exploited me all the more. She probably thought that I was crazy.

I gently released her from my arms now and tried to lift her spirits by explaining how fortunate she was to be still alive. I consoled her even though I wouldn't be around her as I used to be. Because my real home was still here next door to her, I said, "I would be coming back sometimes to check on things, and at that time, we could even get together and talk things over again."

Of course, talking things over again suggested that I would return to my old ways. No, no way! For my bad memories of her instantly averted that I would feel good about helping her again.

"Can I still rely on you to put stones on my eyelids after I died?" she asked.

"That is foolish to say, Matild. It is harder for you to die naturally than to live with a crooked mind. I'm sure you know what I mean. I think you are trying to melt my heart. That won't work this time. I'll be leaving tomorrow and going over to my godfather. Although I don't know what is waiting for me there, but I'm going—going into the unknown," I said.

Matild had more questions on her mind, but I stopped her, as my house cleaning and packing the few things I wanted to take with me weren't done yet. I told her that she could start amending her wrong doings by giving me a hug before I left—a hug that she never gave me, not even now.

I walked slowly away from her without showing the slightest regret about what I had just said to her. I went back to my house, and instead of cleaning and packing up, I stopped. Hesitation came over me about moving to my godfather.

Since I would be under the control of a totally strange person from now on and who I only knew from hearsay, I was now questioning and answering myself. As I did it, I stayed on the positive side thinking about my future: "So far I did pretty good," I said to myself. "From now on, I'll try to do even better. I have nothing to lose, only to gain. I'm young, I'm daring, and I'm honest. I can always come back here to my sweet home and do what I did before."

So I vented my pep talk. By giving myself this kind of encouragement, I was able to overpower my fears and hurried to pursue my next adventure in my life, moving to Gary.

* * *

It was now my godfather, Gary Ludvig, who kept the unwanted contacts with me, luring me with plenty of food to eat, plenty of freedom, plenty of fatherly love, and the eventual inheritance of everything he owned. But only if I would become his friend, and later his adopted son. And I said to him: "Your goodness would be beyond my dreams. I am now at a point to choose between joining either the Communist Youth Organization or moving back to my oldest sister, Iren. But before I would commit myself to accept your kind offer, allow me to do just one thing: follow my mother's advice.

"On one occasion, when a nail pierced through the sole of my worn-out sneakers and it pricked my toe, she said to me, 'Go and buy yourself a pair of new sneakers but make sure they fit.' You know what I mean, don't you?'" I asked him and wondered whether he really understood what I meant.

(The *new sneakers* meant a new place and the *make sure they fit* was to be the suitable place to live.)

Odd was my comparison about what I wanted to convey to Gary, but I used it anyway. I didn't know any better how to tell my doubts about him.

"Well, if they don't fit, don't buy them," he replied. He didn't understand what I was getting at.

"Could it also mean that I'll look for another pair? Maybe even a better pair than the first one was?" I asked.

"What does all this shoe buying have to do with your becoming my adopted son?" he asked.

"If the shoes fit me nicely, I would wear them nicely, I should say. But if they don't fit me exactly, I should reject them, shouldn't I?" The man became irritable the minute I phrased the truth.

"Are you trying to compare me to a pair of shoes, or tempting me to fit you into one?" he revolted.

I realized this moment that he didn't understand my saying. I thought all along that he would grasp the symbolic meaning of the adage.

"As a matter of fact, I have both in mind, but I don't know how to come out with it. But now that you said 'tempting me to fit you into one,' I have to ask you something.

"Gizella, whom you adopted as your daughter a few years ago and who died in your house, why did she die? Your brother, John, said to me just yesterday that you had so overworked her that she died from exhaustion.'"

"John didn't tell you the truth. Gizella actually hung herself in the barn because he chased her away and didn't allow her to return. Gizella told me, 'How much I love him and want to return back home, but he does not want me back.' That was when I accepted her. But after a few months, she said to me again, 'I would rather die than be separated from my real father.' The following day, I found her hanging from the cross beam in the barn,'" Gary replied.

"What about this gossip I'm told by my classmates that you forced her to do her homework in the middle of the night while she only had four-five-hour of sleep between work and school? You don't have anything like that in mind for me, do you?" I asked.

"I have not even adopted you, and you already telling me what others told you. It was Gizella's idea to study at night. She chose to do that," he replied.

Gary didn't realize that the reason as to why Gizella had to study at night was because she had to work in the fields during the day.

My godfather never went through formal schooling, and his reading and writing skills were at best second-grade level. Probably for this reason, he didn't understand the meaning of the adage I said to him.

And he never had his own child to know how to raise Gizella. He thought that by overworking her, she would mature faster. It would be now my turn to take her place. Gizella was twelve years old when she hung herself.

Then, I said to Gary: "I told you what others told me and wanted you to know before you take me in that I am not Gizella. I have my own mind already and could see through feigned truth."

What I didn't tell him, though, was I needed his support more than he needed my helping him to do his all-around work, the kind of which I already was accustomed to. I didn't tell him that I needed a warm home and plenty to eat. I knew that he had both. And I also felt in my gut that whatever work he would demand from me to do, it wouldn't be as hard as what I had to endure under Matild. One big difference between the two of them was that Gary was organized, while Matild wasn't at all. Under her disorganized conditions, I needed twice as much time to finish any of the many works she already started but never finished.

When my godfather saw my straightforwardness and common sense thinking, he envisioned that I would be good enough for him, if I would just relieve him some of the repetitive work that robbed his time from being able to philander with women, besides his wife. When he saw how bold and daring I was in telling him that I was no pussycat to play with, he said to me: "I understand your needs, but you must understand my needs also. I will treat you as you treat me. I will talk things over with you, and the two of us will decide what's best.

"Besides everything else, what I need most is your friendship. You see, I never had another friend after the Russians killed your father. And now, I see your father in you. You think you could be my son?" Gary asked.

This was the last thing I expected Gary to say. I was dumb-struck, scared, and perplexed, all at once. All of a sudden, I was searching for answers that would give me some understanding as to what was behind Gary's motivation to turn my thinking and feeling toward him to accept him as a friend, a companion, and a partner. These nouns had one inkling in common. They needed time to prove their worthiness between the two of us before they could truly match their meanings, individually as well as together. What would make our relationship all the more tenuous now was that he was fifty years older than I was. His life was waning, while mine just began to flourish.

I already experienced friendly relationships with Joseph and Mr. Forro. The time I spent with these two loving men revealed their inner values to me: the moral fibers that bonded our mutual respect and love. And by the understanding of our strengths and weaknesses, our cries and laughs, we consoled each other. Nothing of this sort existed as yet between Gary and me.

I had nothing but doubts about Gary at this time. So I ventured to say to him: "Don't go through the legal steps to adopt me as your son. I don't know you, and you don't know me enough to make such a serious decision. Rather, give me the chance to prove my worthiness. And at the same time, I would also learn to know you better."

This sounded like *holy water* both of us could take a dip in—to receive blessing on the just or curse on the evil.

We went from here forward with good intensions. I left Matild with a hearty hug and received Gary's likewise.

* * *

Within a short time, however, Gary's wife, Anna, came between us. She was always unsure of Gary's intentions. Thus, suspicion consumed her mind. Therefore, she was always searching for proof by which she could prove Gary's wrong.

Not long after I settled down, Anna found Gary's *last will and testament* which he had hidden inside his horse's saddle pocket. When she read the contents, she discovered that Gary had given all his earthly possessions to his adopted son, whom he has not yet named in the document. Since I was already living with them, Anna took it for granted that I was his adopted son. Although she never said anything about it to Gary, she confronted me with it in a rather kindly fashion. As I was sitting at the kitchen table, she served me lunch and watched for the proper moment when I would be looking at her to say something. She didn't know as yet that I wasn't a gabber and seldom listened to one. Once I started eating, I never looked up. So I didn't look up this time either. But she was terribly itching to tell me something.

"I can't wait to tell you a big secret," she said.

How long could a gossiping woman keep a big secret without having that secret jump out of her skin to tell it to somebody? The occasion offered the perfect timing. Anna edged herself closer and closer to my ears to whisper me the secret. I was still sitting and spooning soup. She was now in a stooping position just behind my ears and began to reveal the big secret. I hated having anybody so close to me. So I turned toward her and loudly said: "Don't shout in my ears, Anna! You are bursting your saliva into my soup. Stand up and say what you want ten feet away. Nobody else is here listening."

"You'll be my landlord when Gary dies!" she softly enounced every word.

"How could you even imagine such a thing?" I replied, anxiously waiting for the rest of her remarks.

"It's here in my hand—the *last will* of Gary. I'll have nothing. You'll have everything! That's why you are here, aren't you?"

She cried out loudly and was confused. I then asked her to give the *last will* to me so that I could see what that one-page *document* from a notebook contained.

I saw five handwritten short lines scribbled with a pencil: "I give what I own to my foster son. Nothing to Anna. Nothing to relatives. Nothing to friends. Nothing to anybody else." It was undersigned with an "X." It contained no date and no witnesses. I noticed that *daughter* was erased and *son* was written over it. This piece of paper must have been old as there were housefly drops all over it. I looked to Anna and said: "Give me a pencil. I want to write a few words on it to make it clear to Gary that I want no part of his possessions. Anyway, this piece of paper is only a rough draft and has no legal standing. Furthermore, don't worry yourself to death over it.'"

So I wrote *000000* all over it and *means nothing to me* on the bottom and signed it. Then I said to Anna, "Now, you can either put it back where you found it or burn it, for all I care."

"Better if I burn it and deny it should he ever ask me about it," Anna decided.

The last thing on my mind was to inherit something from Gary when he died. Waiting for his death so as to get land and other possessions, first of all, was as uncertain as a dog's supper. Second of all, it would have meant that I would have to give up my dreams about

Ildiko and my future. Furthermore, I would fester in this village from where even dogs escaped to find new friends. Questions about what had happened about that *last will* never came up for discussion. Anna was thrilled about burning it. I didn't give a damn about it, and Gary thought he misplaced it somewhere.

CHAPTER TWENTY

Gary's Background was His Moral Value

It was November 1953 when I moved away from Matild to Gary Ludvig. I didn't say anything about it to my sister Iren, who was my legal guardian. She knew Gary very well from the time Father was still living and before I was born. She knew that Father and Gary were buddy-buddies and the biggest poachers within seven villages in any direction. Wine was used instead of water for drinking, and wild game of all sorts was hanging on nails all over the house. They bartered wild game for wine and kept their guns hidden in different locations inside the private wine cellars of those with whom they could make a deal. They had at least thirty cellar keys at any one time at their disposal to freely move around from place to place. They kept their guns there. Nobody ever knew where they were as they moved about at night to stay hidden from the world. The game wardens were their friends, for they loved free wine and a free boar now and then. All this took place long before I was born, when the land and forest were still in the hands of the nobility.

My father, being a railroad official, was transferred from Balatonkeresztur to Ercsi in 1938, and the great poaching adventure that the two pursued ended. Now it was only Gary who kept his limited poaching activity going until 1945, at which time the Russians *liberated* Hungary from German occupation.

It was my sister Iren who gave me this information after my mother died in 1950.

Because Gary didn't even come to Mother's funeral, Iren couldn't say one good word about him. She told me then that she hated him. May be it was for that reason as to why he didn't come to the funeral. Among few other things, Iren labeled him as a notorious poacher, a crook, and a first-class thief as well. I was troubled hearing such harsh accusations about my godfather, and I asked her: "Do you have any proof to prove your point, Iren?"

"No, I don't have anything now. Nobody ever caught him actually doing the things they said about him. I can tell you one sure thing, though. He had guns—all types of guns—hidden all over the places, some in trees, some in attics. Most of them were hidden inside of empty oak barrels in the wine cellars of those who hobnobbed with him. At a couple of times he and our father brought home a bunch of those guns to clean them and alter them with silencers. I saw them but didn't pay any attention to it, for I was a young girl then, seriously considering marrying John, your brother-in-law.

"Every time they went hunting, they brought home something, mostly rabbits or pheasants, and occasionally a deer, or even a boar. We ate so much of the stuff that I got sick of it. Mother didn't know what to do with the carcasses anymore, so she buried them. Pretty soon, she ran out of burial grounds. She was scared to death to give the stuff away to anybody she couldn't trust in case they would turn them in. On top of this, they brought home wine, enough to fill a well with it. Now, if this is not a sign of wrongdoing, then I don't know what is," Iren explained.

"How come I didn't know anything about these things before?" I asked her.

"How could you? You weren't even born yet. I got married to John, your brother-in-law, in 1938 and you were born in 1939. Father was transferred to Ercsi the same year I married John, and we lived in Rackeresztur while you and the family lived in Ercsi, a mere three miles away," Iren said.

Although Iren wanted to tell me other things about Gary, she couldn't find the time for it because of the urgency she faced burying Mother. The lack of money for a coffin and other problems she faced regarding the burial prevented her to spend any more time with me to talk about him.

* * *

Now two years passed since Mother died. The information Iren gave me about Gary I kept in mind for future reference. At this time, I wasn't convinced enough to hold it against him, for I had no proof of it. Bygone was bygone, and now a new chapter began in my relationship with him on the day I moved to him.

It was about mid-November when Gary had more and more time to spend with me. The outside work on his three separate gardens was winding down. Now, he turned his attention to line up the inside work he used to do during the winter months. He was a workaholic, and of course, Anna, his wife, and now I also, had to pay attention to him and give him this or that in a hurry to satisfy his demands. Once he sat down to work, the only thing he reached for more was his wine bottle. He was sipping it from sunrise to sunset, yet he got never really drunk. I watched him move around working like a beaver, finishing whatever he started with the zeal and speed of a thief. In the meantime, I was waiting when the time would come for him to ask me to follow him doing what he was doing. This was my first month with him.

* * *

Attached to his manor-style house were three separate rooms joined to each other in a row with solid doors to provide entrance to each. The first room next to the kitchen was used for his all-around hobby work. Therefore, it was bigger than the kitchen. Half of it was devoted to woodworking and the other half to blacksmith works. Between the kitchen and the hobby room wall there was a huge chimney built in order to pull out the gasses from the open-pit fire. This chimney, when there was no blacksmith work done, was converted to smoke hams, bacon, and sausage. The third room, behind the hobby room, was used to dress slaughtered animals. Separated from the house and about a hundred feet away toward the back was another building, used as his cow and horse stall. To that a huge barn was attached.

In my first days, Gary led me around and showed me his workshops, explaining what he did in each, when and why he did it, what was or wasn't important. He was sipping wine as the tour progressed and offered me his bottle to sip along with him. I refused by telling him that it was not my time to start drinking.

Everything I saw or touched or heard as we moved from shop to shop was new to me. As Gary was explaining things, I was listening only, for I didn't know what to say or ask. Every tool he used had a storage place. Every equipment utilized to accomplish his work was clean and oiled for the next job. The walking areas were swept clean from all the loose debris. I was immensely surprised to see neatness and order all around. But I was also perplexed about what will happen to me in this totally new environment.

As far as I could tell, what I learned from Joseph and Mr. Forro was nothing compared to what I had seen here. Nobody said anything to me about this side of Gary; for few, if any, knew the good side of this man. So I was now wondering as to how I would come to terms with myself when the good side of this man contradicted his bad side and I happened to be in the middle of it. I settled this matter rather quickly. I decided that I would hold onto my moral values, no matter what, and keep only the useful parts of my new experience.

Now we moved to the last shop. There, next to a large area for dressing the already killed animals, was an eight-by-twelve-foot-long pantry. It was added to the back wall of this spacious room in order to store spices, dried goods, and most importantly, smoked meat. Overhead were all the smoked goods hanging, and below were shelves butting the walls all around.

Gary told me, "Anytime you are hungry, come in here and eat whatever you feel like."

We had spent more time here than the combined time inside the other rooms. There was no end to the goods that were stored here, and there was no end to my curiosity either.

I would never go hungry, I thought to myself. The pleasant smell of smoked hams, sausages, and slab bacon invited me to come back here real soon to taste everything. But I would come only when I would be alone, as I would be embarrassed should anyone see me gorging the goods like a starving bear.

* * *

Since Gary was a skilled carpenter, wood carver, and coach builder, besides his other talents—all of it acquired by show and tell from his father—he was more than capable of building shelves in the pantry with all types of hidden compartments, where he would hide the hard-to-find things held dear to his heart, his gun collection. He couldn't use any of them now as that would have meant treason under Communism. So, toward the end of our tour, he opened these hidden shelf pockets and allowed me to see and handle any one of his guns. I looked at them with the curiosity of a child who wished to see and touch real guns. I didn't realize at the moment that these guns were really functioning weapons. My curiosity didn't rest until I asked Gary questions about them:

"Can I hold one in my hands—but before I do, show me how—as I never had a gun in my hands before?"

"Of course you can after I tell you a couple of handling rules. I'll hand them to you one after the other. Rule one, never have the barrel pointed at yourself or at others. Two, never store a gun loaded and triggered, or even untriggered."

It took us at least half an hour before the show and tell was over in the pantry. Gary explained far more information about the handling and usage of these weapons than I needed to know. I wished that I had written them down, for I have forgotten most of them, except the two handling and storing rules. When later he allowed me to target practice with the one that had a silencer on it, I had to ask him all over again the same rules he already explained the first time. It was at that time, during a short pause, that I asked him one more question that was on my mind ever since he showed me his gun collection.

"Gary, where did you get all these guns? If someday I want to buy one, where could I get it?"

"Not today, Arpad. The only way you might get it if you steal it. The Communists don't trust anybody with guns. If there was a person armed, there was another person watching him."

"Was that the way you got yours also, by stealing them?"

"That is a long story how I lifted these guns from the armory of the old duke, who lived locally in the same castle you attended school in your first, second, and third grades. After the war, the Communists deported him to Austria, where his family lived. Never saw him or heard from him since."

"Tell me, how were you able to *lift* these guns from the duke's armory?"

"One of the duke's favorite hobbies was hunting. Almost every other day, he went hunting with his two rangers. These two rangers were my patsies. We used to drink together and shared lots of lifted goods, too, from the duke's granary. They were also my informers about the duke's hunting areas. I knew from them which day and which direction they went hunting. They took care of the armory and were in charge of his gun inventory and their upkeep. They also maintained his three horses, two for the rangers and one for the duke, and had free access to the granary. The rangers were rounding up the wild game and chased them in front of the duke so he could shoot them.

"Now these rangers knew that I was a big-time poacher but had only one shotgun with which I couldn't shoot long rage. The duke never gave them caught games, even after they begged him for them, for he needed them for his household.

"They gave me the key to the armory, which key I duplicated for myself, then I returned the original. So now, whenever they went hunting in one area, I went hunting in the opposite area. Since the armory was in a grove, I simply unlocked it in the dark and took a rifle at a time and went hunting. I always caught enough rabbits, boars, and even deer to share them with the rangers.

"Within a year, I had ten rifles. The last five I gave to your father, who was hunting with me most of the time. This is the short version of my great adventures in poaching. The others I'll tell you later, when we work together on my projects."

He casually ended talking to me and we moved to see the rest of his possessions.

After hearing what Gary said, I knew more about him in a few minutes than Iren could have told me in a lifetime. I was confused. I pieced together what I heard from him and what I heard from Iren in order to shed light on the truth about him. I didn't ask him any more questions, thinking that he would talk himself to death. He wanted to tell me everything he did in his lifetime—so that I could follow his footsteps one day. After all, I was now his *son* and had almost a vested right to everything, including his gun collection. In due time I secretly target practiced with blind shells with each gun inside the pantry. Nobody knew that I became so knowledgeable about guns that I would be able to give instructions to others—how to use them.

Gary was in the same situation as Mr. Forro was. He didn't have his own son to whom he could hand over his knowledge, experience, and possessions in order to remember him. I faced a real problem here, which side of him to remember. Seriously, I supposed that all sides of him would have been fine. But for my own satisfaction, I could only accept the moral side of him. Otherwise, accepting his immoral side would have been just another lousy memory, holding back temptations to do likewise. I decided, therefore, I would go through it all, whatever he wanted to tell me and teach me, if for no other reason than to know the differences between good and evil. After all, an orphan, as I am, would face more desperate moments in life to attempt to do the sinful things first in order to survive, rather than the rightful things and stay hungry.

Now we moved to the last building in the yard. This structure had three sections. The central area was the stable that housed Gary's white horse and his brown cow. Her calf was lose and was now sucking milk nonstop, giving her mother that occasional nudge for more of it.

There, on the left was a shed-roof attachment where Gary kept his horse-drawn wagon stored. On the right was the barn with a higher pitched roof than the stable was.

Inside as well as outside the structure, rabbits hopped around with unlimited freedom, and it just happened that the mare kicked one to death as I patted her. Her name was Lucy and was somewhat nervous as I approached her.

Gary didn't say anything as I was looking around and was gently rubbing Lucy's head. She knew instantly that I loved her. She poked my back in wanting more patting.

Gary was a fast mover; he picked up the dead rabbit, hammered a nail through each of its rear foot, then hammered the same nails six inches apart into one of the center posts that supported the ceiling of the stable. Now the rabbit was hanging upside down, and there in that position, he flayed it by pulling its jacket off in less than a minute. "My horse is a real kicker. I don't have to kill rabbits. She does them for me," he said.

After he degutted the thing, he handed it to me by its still furry rear paws. "Give it to Anna. She'll know what to do with it," he said.

She certainly did. She chopped the rabbit into many small pieces and scattered them all over the front yard to the cats. They were already sitting on every fence post waiting for the treat. Gary never knew what had happened to the rabbit because Anna had two others in the cold cellar, marinating to be cooked for supper.

It was now mid-afternoon as we bicycled away to Gary's small vineyard located about three miles from home and about a thousand feet from the shores of Lake Balaton. Gary yelled back to Anna from his bicycle, "Feed the animals. We're going to the *Cellar*."

Cellar was the name Gary gave to his vineyard. It was located in the gardening section of Lake Balaton; therefore it was not collectivized by the Communists.

The structure had a thatched roof, and it looked more abandoned than maintained. There was a good reason for that. It camouflaged the real activities that went on inside. It was Gary's habitat in which and from which he pursued a number of lawless activities— like distilling fermented plum and apricot slurry for brandy, or trapping fish in Lake Balaton or entertaining the wife of another man. This man did so many things here. I often wondered, could there be the souls of others in him?

The minute we arrived, he grabbed his siphoning tube and filled a quart-size bottle with chardonnay and gulped a third of it down. Then, he refilled the bottle and gave it to me.

"This is my new vintage, still settling, but I couldn't wait to taste its flavor. Have some. It's still as sweet as honey, but it is already turning (fermenting) and has a slight kick to it."

This time I didn't hesitate and had a few gulps of the *must* myself straight from the bottle. But I drank too much of it, and in less than ten minutes, I had a war going on in my belly. Good thing that the outside toilet was built just behind the wine cellar so I could run to it quickly. Others were probably glad, too.

I didn't return to Gary after my urgent gassing, thinking that I may have to revisit the pit again. Instead, I wandered around the property and checked the fruit trees that had been planted all around the borders of this one acre vineyard. Just as I reached the border fence at the roadside of the property, I noticed that two women were bicycling toward me, one behind the other, on this dirt road that was used mostly to accommodate horse-pulled wagons. They pedaled by me and didn't even look up. If they had, they would have lost control staying in the trenches that the wagon wheels deepened every time they rolled in it. They looked like mother and daughter. My eyes followed them because the last one was young and very pretty. They turned at the entrance to Gary's wine cellar, dropped the bicycles as if they weren't needed anymore, and rushed inside.

I couldn't deny how I felt seeing this beautiful daughter. Any healthy boy in his thirteenth year would have felt the same way as I had felt, for the beginning of manhood defined my feeling. For a moment, I had forgotten that I belonged to Ildiko. But anyway, looking and seeing another beautiful girl stirred my blood all the more to hurry to see Ildiko again. There was nothing wrong feeling that I had extraordinary life in me.

I rushed after them and introduced myself with a smiling face, bursting with joy and showing that I could be a very good company with those who returned my smiles. The young girl was looking at me as her mother embraced me and said: "You must be Arpad. I heard so much about you from Gary. He was eagerly waiting to have you around him."

I took that complement with a grain of salt as I didn't know who Gary really was—fatherly, priestly, or just a double-faced monster.

The woman's name was Lili and her daughter's Lidy. And I said to Lili, "You must have known Gary for a long time, since you heard him talking about me so much."

"A very long time. It looks almost as if we grew old together," she said.

Then, I looked at Lidy and asked her to come outside so as leave the grown-ups to themselves. We stayed inside the fenced-in area and began to know each other.

"Do you have a boyfriend, Lidy?" I asked.

"Just friends. I have a lot of friends, but they all live in Budapest," she answered.

"How come you are here visiting Gary?"

"Oh, we own a villa located just behind the railroad station. We used to stay there all summer, but now we came for the weekend only. The Communists confiscated the place, and we'll have to abandon it within days. That's why we are here to ask Gary to help us move our belongings to another place, to the very shores of Lake Balaton," Lidy explained.

"Was that the place behind the rail station that looked like a miniature castle?" I asked.

"I don't know if I would compare it to a castle. I tell you, though, it is big inside. We had a formal dinner there once. My grandfather, who was the admiral of the Hungarian Royal Navy, invited his officers with their wives there once and I still had room to play around with their kids. He still owns the place even though he disappeared a couple of years ago. I think the Communists killed him.

"Now *they* are after his possessions also. It is terrible how much persecution we have to go through because of him. My father, with two doctoral degrees, is now pushing a wheelbarrow, building roads somewhere. We don't know where he is either. And now it's I and my mother, the only ones left from the whole family. If it wasn't for mom's profession as a neurological specialist, we would have been starved to death," Lidy explained.

(Now I knew from two reliable sources, Ildiko's father and Lidy, that the Communistic movement engulfed the whole nation. What had happened locally in my village was nothing to compare to what had happened in Budapest. It was only a different phase of it. But the main thrust of the movement remained the same: take away everything from the rich—their lands, their businesses, their professions—and put the Communists in charge in the formation of the new socialistic order. The model of this socialistic order was already coerced on the people in the Soviet Union under Stalin's dictatorship. Millions died. The ones that opposed the movement were the enemies of the Communist state, enemies of the *progressive movement*. The less knowledgeable the people were, the easier it was to brainwash them in the *denial of the past.*)

I asked Lidy, "Are you starving now?"

"I can't say that I have a full stomach. I didn't eat anything since morning," she said.

"Let's go to the cellar then, and I'll fix you something. There is plenty of stuff there hanging from the ceiling beams."

Sure enough, plenty of smoked kielbasa was wound on six-foot-long poles, hanging from the ceiling beam. Elsewhere, similar poles supported clusters of grapes tied together with strings and were neatly hanging side by side for winter keep. With similar setup, red peppers were strung by their stems, hundreds of them, hanging and dehydrating to be crushed later to become paprika powder. They were still unwrinkled and edible.

So while the grown-ups were in the front room, deciding when to do Lili's relocation, we were busy in the backroom, unwinding the kielbasa from its hanging position, stripping clusters of grapes, and ripping the healthier-looking red peppers into a wicker basket. We carried it outside and set it on a makeshift bench nailed to the trunk of a dead cherry tree.

"Help yourself, Lidy!"

"Aren't you going to eat?" she asked.

"Of course I will. But I'm waiting that you eat all you want first, and if need be, I'll get more," I replied.

Lidy was extremely hungry. I enjoyed the way she ripped the stuff apart and hurled the chunks into her mouth.

"I was afraid, Lidy, that you would be looking for a fork and a knife and neatly folded napkins on a shiny plate before you would even touch the food."

"When you are really hungry, those things would only hold you back from reaching your mouth. Are you kidding me! There is nothing like feeding myself naturally. I remember how I used to knock the spoon out of the hand of my nanny. I had a lot of fun with that, chuckling like crazy as I saw her jumping around to get it back to me. Now I know she was only playing with me. Well, we don't have those silver spoons anymore. The Russian generals are probably eating with them now," she remarked.

It was now about a half an hour after sunset. And in the opposite direction, the full moon was brightly rising, giving us the light needed to see each other's youthful face. We were looking at each other and were waiting which one of us would impart a hopeful smile that would set us free from our momentary numbness about our past.

"Let's forget the past, Lidy. Let's talk about tomorrow. Young kids like you and me should think of the past as if it were only an old playground from where we moved our toys to a new playground. As far as I'm concerned, I'm looking at myself every day as a renewed toy, the same cast in a new setting—hopefully thinking to play better than I did on the last playground. How about you?" I asked her.

"Could that be true in my case as well?" she asked.

"Of course, it could, but you probably weren't raised to think that way. You had your mom and dad to think for you. I didn't. I lost both of them, and now I'm all alone."

"So what should I do now?" Lidy asked.

"Sooner or later you'll ask yourself, 'What will I be when I grow up?' Why not answer that question now? Your mom wouldn't be around forever, you know! You may want to think about that 'same cast in a new setting.' That is how I leave behind the sad part of my life,'" I answered.

We ate all the food I brought out from the cellar without ever thinking whether there was anything wrong eating with bare hands or washing the food we ate or washing our hands and teeth after we ate. These routines would have been fine had we lived in a castle-like environment. But not here and now. We were happy to find something, anything, to eat in order to kill our hunger pains. Anyway, I think a little dirt is good for me to eat as I'm still growing. My body has to learn how to purge impurities out of my system.

Although there was a dug well on the property, I couldn't get the water up from it. The bucket had so many leaking spots that by the time I reeled it up, all the water leaked out. So we ended up drinking the sweet must in order to quench our thirst.

It was time now to check the grown-ups and nudge them to finish the conversation about moving.

I don't think that they had spent more than a minute talking about moving. But I would bet my life that they spent most of their time on the carousal side of the moment, eating the same stuff Lidy and I ate, but instead of must, drinking true wine.

Both Lili and Gary drank so much of it that they had to prop each other on the way out the cellar. Without saying anything, I wheeled the two bicycles inside the cellar, locked the door, and declared: "We are walking home. Lidy, you take care of your mother! Gary, I'll take care of you. Let's go!"

So we went home in different directions, staggering all over the place like the devils in hell, trying to escape to a cooler place. Gary could still talk, especially about his past.

I urged him, pressed him along, and pressured him to tell the truth about his past relationship with my mother and father.

It was the first time ever that I saw anybody taking more steps backward than forward, the first time anybody swore more ugly words than I could imagine existed, and the first time I held anybody up by his waist belt to guide him home. I should have knocked him out and carried him home on my shoulders. But I didn't know where that exact spot was, on his head or on his neck. So I was staggering along with him during the course of two hours in order to cover a three-mile stretch from the *Cellar* to his house.

* * *

This was also the right time to move Gary's heart and soul to tell me the truth about his relationship with my mother. All the good and the bad came out his mouth, for the wine was a powerful stuff that eased his mind to talk about all the aches and pains, and the hopes and sorrows he kept secret for at least twenty years.

Thinking also about Lili, I didn't know and really didn't care to know how she landed on her threshold, face up or face down.

This event had left an ugly image in my mind as to how quickly Gary's personality revealed itself through the power of wine. The lessons I learned made me recognize the strength of wine, the strength and weakness of mind and body, and the utter loss of self-control and dignity under the influence of booze. It shall be a stark reminder that I should never have more than a couple of glasses of it.

For Gary this was not an occasional event, for he found in it the illusory happiness that alcohol brought on and had given him a temporary escape from reality: that he couldn't have a true son of his own from a woman he loved for that woman never loved him, never kissed him, and never had sex with him. That woman was my mother.

Anna, he never loved. Their marriage was arranged between their fathers for the sake of hoarding wealth. And besides, she was barren.

But Lili, on the other hand, craved Gary very much, for her husband couldn't satisfy her. But Gary didn't love her either.

The only one Gary passionately loved was my mother. He loved her alive; and now, he loved her in death even more. So I have become the only pulse in his heart that connected and held onto that love.

(Gary's friendship with my father had been for one reason only, that he could be close to my mother. But my mother abhorred Gary because he had influenced my father to excessive drinking and to do the things he would otherwise have never done—breaking into every wine cellar within seven towns in order to have wine flowing at home like water from a broken tap. Gary wanted to destroy my father—not with one big bang, but slowly—so that he could have access to mother's company for a longer time. The final break in their *friendship* happened when in 1938, Mother succeeded to have Father transferred to Ercsi, a good hundred miles away. With that everything ended between my family and Gary.)

Although Garry slowly regained control over his steps, he was still wobbling in mind and body. He was much relieved to tell the truth to the one who most importantly needed to know it. And I was greatly relieved to hear it and finally put an end to the persistent rumor about the relationship between my mother and Gary—that I was his true son.

I couldn't wait now to travel to Rackeresztur and tell the truth to Iren. This time it wouldn't be hearsay. This time it would be straight from the *horse's mouth*.

* * *

After this incident, I lost my eagerness to know anything more about Gary or his companions or his knowledge. Since this man wanted to destroy my father in order to attain a sinful end, what else was still left in him that he would try to do to change my personality to be more like his? It was this thought that had pushed all other thoughts aside and evoked my vigilance for every move that he planned for me to do with him.

Since Gary's background was his moral value, I had plenty to think about as to how I would now identify those values from the past that moved him forward in his daily activities. It wasn't very long before I realized that Gary had a hardened habit. He was a kleptomaniac—the past was his future and the future was his past.

So I asked myself, what is the difference between what the Communists do versus what Gary did? I couldn't find the answer that would have given me peace of mind, for I thought both were wrong. Both actions were sinful. But to what extent? My youthful mind couldn't determine it. Here again, I remembered my mother's words: "One thing leads to another thing," she said. Also, "whatever you really need, ask for it. If you don't receive it, work for it. But never steal it. Stealing contained the urge to cheat and lie for it. You could even end up killing for it. Keep in front of you the story between Judas and Jesus Christ."

While physically I don't think that Gary could have forced me to do anything. However, the frequent stealing he did, even as I lived in his house, could have infested my mind to get used to it. And in time, I, too, would have ended not knowing the difference, whether stealing was moral or immoral. The last thing I ever wanted was stealing something from somebody for which he had honestly worked. So for the next five months I still stayed in Gary's house. I was, however, very selective in what I would be willing to do together with him. To that effect, I said to him without the slightest hesitation: "Gary, I want to know every week what kind of work you want me to do for you, for anything that involves stealing, I wouldn't do. And if you force me to do something like that, I will run away from you."

Living with Gary and eyeing his movements in order to decide which way he was turning was a harrowing thing to do, as at my age, figuring out motives, I lacked the human experience to do it.

I also reminded him as to what he promised me to do before I moved in with him that "I will talk things over with you, and the two of us will decide what's best."

When he didn't do what he promised, I reminded him again of his own words. He answered, "It would be next to impossible for me to talk over with you every little thing I wanted to do, for I wouldn't be doing anything else but talking."

"Well then, don't tell me what you want to do and don't expect me to follow you to do the things I don't understand and would turn out to be sinful to do. Let me just do the things that I already understand. You know, Gary, I can do just about anything you do around the house, and that would be plenty beside my schoolwork."

"That would be fine with me. Why don't we try it your way? But I would still ask you to help me now and then in areas that I think you should learn, like woodworking or weaving wicker baskets or distilling brandy," Gary said.

So Gary agreed and allowed me to follow my way of thinking. These other works that I haven't learned as yet, I considered good practice for more knowledge, for that was a very important part of my growing up. My desire to learn new things kept me looking forward since I never knew when I would be using them to earn my living.

When Gary said, "I would still ask you to help me now and then," I didn't know that he had other ideas behind it, namely, to burden me with his work while he would be gallivanting to do his adventures—fooling around with Lili or *lifting* things that didn't belong to him.

So from this day forward, my relationship with Gary followed a more routine course than before. I accepted the repetitive works, the everyday chores—cleaning and feeding the animals and the related stuff. Realizing that I have become as much of a slave as Gizella was, I looked forward to spring when I would escape Gary's household. My reasoning to stay until that time was based on the necessities of my current needs, having a warm house and plenty to eat. That which I would not have been able to provide for myself had I moved back now to my own house next to Matild.

The winter months were fast coming, and I was glad to stay mostly indoors where I could do my homework or work with Gary in one of his shops. But I was allowed to work there with him only after I finished all my other chores.

Our relationship became almost frigid, for we have realized that we lost the trust in each other. And the lack of it harbored suspicion in everything we wanted to talk about or do together regarding the future between *father and son*.

In due time, I realized that the plenty of everything Gary had was partly the stolen goods added to his pantry or to his granary, or used up in other ways to make something else out of them. In this regard, I benefited from all the things he had stolen from others, and

I became sick over it, sick in mind and body. The worst part of it was that I didn't know what to do about it—who to talk to, who to go to, who to cry to. Anything I would have done would have labeled me as partaker of ill-gotten goods.

I was now inside Gary's *Cellar* when I realized that there was no earthly power that could deliver me from this evil man. It was the first time ever that I fell on my knees reciting Our Father. Whether I remembered the words correctly or not, I didn't care. My spirit was united with God.

Now being alone in Gary's wine cellar distilling the fermented slurry in order to turn it into brandy, I had plenty of time between reloading the stove to think that even here that I am not alone. Oh yes, I am not alone!

Then, I went outside and prayed more there on my knees under that huge cherry tree in front of the wine cellar. All of a sudden, the slurry container exploded due to overheating. The fire escaped from the stove, and in no time the thatched roof was in flames. The whole wine cellar burnt down. Only the clay walls were left and were gaping wholly open to the sky. It was midnight. I ran over to Lili to seek help, but she said, "What's gone is gone. The good times had come to a quick end. Sleep here tonight."

I had no regrets over this incident whatsoever, for the whole place was a collection of ill-gotten goods and the source of evil pleasures. And now, the beginning of my *delivery from evil* had begun.

While the wine cellar was burning, Gary was deeply involved killing a couple of pigs with one of his silencer-equipped guns. He wanted to steal the pigs from a collective farm that belonged to a neighboring village. He and his partner were caught in the act and were arrested right there on the spot. Both of them were kept in jail until a county judge sentenced a stiff penalty for the crime committed,—two years in prison for Gary, one year for his partner.

(In Hungary's justice system, one was guilty before proven guilty for the crime committed even if found innocent later. So that person was kept in jail without bail.)

It was January 1953 when the wine cellar burned out to the bare walls. People who heard about it were glad that it did, for they knew or at least suspected what Gary was doing there. They were also glad that Gary was in jail now. But animosity erupted among Ann's relatives, harboring ill will that now I was in charge of his household. When I heard all this talk, I quickly called on Anna to clear up the matter; for she was under the impression also that I had orders from Gary to be in charge of everything in case something had happened to him. We were in the kitchen, just having supper, and I started the conversation with her:

"Anna, don't even think for a moment that I am now in charge of Gary's responsibilities. I'll tell you something that will shock you. I am not his real son. Gary himself had explained his entire relationship with my mother and father. He said he loved mother, but Mother hated him. He tried and tried again to gain her friendship, but it was no use. The other day, when Gary was truly drunk, he mumbled the whole truth to me about his relationship with my mother. In between his slurred words, he was crying. He also said that he just wanted me to be around him to lessen the pain he still suffered over the fact that he could not get a son from the woman he loved most. So now, you also know the truth and need not worry about where I stand.

"His time in jail will be good for him, will be good for you, and will be good for me." For him, it will be purification for wrongdoings; for you, it will be freedom from bossing you around; and for me, it will be the end of my relationship with him," I said.

"Will you tell me what's on your mind when you say, 'the end of my relationship with him'?" Anna wanted to know.

"Anna, you knew Gary long, long before I did. You knew that he was stealing goods. You knew that he had other women. You knew that he was lying and cheating. You still stood by him. Now that I also know these things, I wouldn't want to stay by him even if he were my real father. I hate those who steal. That is the main reason I hate Matild, and that is also the main reason why I hate Communism.

"It isn't merely what Gary did that bothers me. It is much deeper. He hurt other people by doing it. That's what really bothers me.

"So now, it finally caught up with him, and he shall stay in jail for two years. This will give you the time to readjust your life and stay honest about everything that would touch it. If you can promise me that you would, I would stay with you a few more months and help you with all the chores befallen you."

"And where would you go from here? Wherever you go, I want to be in contact with you, for you were honest with me right from the beginning. It is almost painful to hear about honesty nowadays, and hearing about it from a young person like you draws tears in my eyes," she said.

"You know, Anna, I really don't know the meaning of the word *honesty*, but when I see an innocent person hurt by the actions of evil men, I feel that it is very much wrong.

"And now to answer your question 'where would I go,' largely, that depends on you. You can throw me out now or can keep me with you. But not later than April.'"

(My promise to Ella was an unbreakable promise that I would come back for her during spring.)

"You stay here as long as you want to. I will not even ask you what to do because I know from your behavior that you would not be able to have peace in your soul until you returned the kindness you received. And I have a lot more for you than just kindness," Anna replied.

So it happened that I stayed with Anna until mid-April. These past three months went by rather quickly. I had unhindered freedom to pick and choose whatever I felt was important to set Anna on her way to manage what Gary used to do around the house and in the gardens. I was satisfied and happy and knew that Anna was also satisfied and happy.

When the time came to part from each other, we were crying and couldn't stop thanking each other for everything. Then, finally Anna said to me: "Take anything you need from my pantry to sustain yourself. Come back anytime you want to. I will have room for you in my heart and also in my house as long as I live."

She reminded me of Joseph and Mr. Forro. They, too, had just as good a heart as Anna had.

Anna allowed me to take anything I liked from her pantry that would tie me over until I was able to support myself. Her last words were "Come back for more food when you hungry. Come back when you need my help. Also come back when Gary is out, so that he could hear your words—words that only a child can say."

* * *

Now, I moved back to my own house and discovered the unexpected disaster that Matild caused. My kitchen became a chicken coop and my yard a junkyard. The fence that separated the two halves of the property disappeared, and the shed was filled with broken furniture and odds and ends. My yard was full of broken branches for kindle wood. The only thing she didn't dare to do was break into my bedroom.

Seeing the mess everywhere, I almost became violent and said, "I'm traveling tomorrow to Iren. She will come here to straighten you out, for you really don't understand how to respect what belongs to others."

Nothing could have changed my mind now becoming my own master. For once, I had the guts and the mind to pursue my own life without orders from others. I also gave up one of my many weaknesses—looking out to helping others at the expense of my receiving nothing in return. After all, there had to be such a thing as fairness. That didn't mean at all, however, that I lost any of my kindness where kindness was due in return. Or where compassion played a role in protecting the innocent. With this mindset, I resolved that from now on Ella and I would live together in our own house, free from the interference of Iren and Matild. I was thirteen years, six months old. So I set out to go to Rackeresztur to bring Ella back home, knowing full well that we would face the world on our own. We would have to take care of ourselves; we would have to plan our future and work for our keep. That would be the cost of my liberty.

Section Two

PART TWO

CHAPTER TWENTY-ONE

The Beginning of My Independence

My oldest sister, Iren, was our official guardian. She already knew about our plan, for she overheard my talking to Ella about it last night. We thought everybody was sleeping; yes, everybody else was but her. By the time we got up the next morning, she already had settled in her mind that she would help us to go away from her own family.

Then came the unexpected surprise that we didn't know anything about. As our official guardian, she was receiving from the government monthly benefits on our behalf for the past two years already. She kept all that separately for us in a postal savings account. It didn't mean anything to me, as I didn't know the value of money. The sum was about fifty dollars a month. I learned how much the value of this money was when she took us to Budapest in order to shop for us used clothes and shoes, plus a few other things we needed to begin our new life. Truly, we needed everything. The next day, we traveled to Budapest.

Budapest is the capital of Hungary. I had already seen one percent of it with Ildiko. Now, I would see the center of it, the pulse of the city, where people do the same things as in the village, looking at each other and asking what's new. Here, of course, a lot more of it.

The streetcar we traveled by broke down at the Buda side of the William Tierney Clark–designed Chain Bridge that was built over the Danube River. It connected the two halves of the city, Buda with Pest; hence it became Budapest. In itself this bridge was a monument, an engineering marvel at the time it was built. It opened in 1849 and connected the West to the East in Europe. It is called *Chain Bridge* because the suspension part consists of one-foot-thick cast-iron chain links, interconnecting each other to form the entire upper span between the high towers and the base at each end of the bridge. The linear center span is 663 feet long. There are only two of its kind in existence today. The other one is over the Thames River in London, England. Both bridges were designed by William Tierney Clark.

Walking across this Chain Bridge afforded me the most spectacular and beautiful views of either side of the two cities. We had to walk a half mile now to catch another streetcar on the Pest side of the city, carrying our bags on our backs. My eyes rolled like that of an eagle above taking in everything to feed my curious mind. I asked Iren to stop and rest awhile because my bag was heavy. The truth was, however, I wanted to have a closer look at both sides of the Danube River.

On the Buda side I saw the king's castle, appearing majestically high on the Buda Hills from the awesome Danube. The traffic on this river was always heavy, for there were all sorts of boats carrying tourists and trade up and down. They looked as if someone was pulling them with a rope to avoid collision.

On the Pest side there was the Parliament Building with its unmatched beauty and style. It had three hundred plus towers and is built in Gothic Revival elegance. The glimpse of the beauty on both side of the Danube lifted my spirit to believe that I would be coming back here for a closer look at everything. Now, Iren stepped closer to me and nudged me back to reality. "Let's move on! The day is wearing short," she said.

Our last stop before heading home was at the biggest farmers market in Budapest, after a quick fact-check, we found the English name of the market to be the Great Market Hall. Here, one could buy just about anything to feed the body and satisfy the mind. I begged my sister for two dollars to buy myself a double-banded slingshot. Before parting with the money, she wanted to know what that thing was. "Sister! That thing is a toy with which I would shoot pebbles at targets."

I, of course, would use it for hunting pheasants and rabbits. Besides my slingshot, I also bought a small stick of hard salami and a loaf of crusty wheat bread.

We moved to the outside of the building to eat. I ripped the loaf of bread into five pieces and stuffed salami in between each piece. Two of these sandwiches I gave to the poor who were nearby. Eye contact with them revealed that they were very hungry also. I felt that I was one of them. After eating, we picked up our bags, stuffed with used clothes and shoes, and took a streetcar again to go to one of the three railroad stations. We boarded a train heading toward home. The train stopped at Martonvasar, and from there we took a bus to Rackeresztur as there was no other transportation available to this muddy village.

Walking from the bus stop to my sister's house was in itself an exercise in disaster control. Potholes everywhere interconnected the mud-filled tracts that horse-pulled wagons deepened. Dogs were barking at us from every house, distracting our attention to watch our steps from slipping into the side ditches of this muddy, winding road. It was springtime and raining.

Ella and I wanted to stay at our older sister for a few more days packing and debating our future. My oldest sister, Iren, was highly confused about how we would take care ourselves without somebody guiding us. Finally, I couldn't stand the barrage of advice from her any longer and spoke to her loudly and pointedly.

"Sister, for the past two years I was a slave, following the orders of our aunt and then my godfather's. At the same time, I also attended to my own needs, although secretly and quietly. I washed my clothes in the canal, while covered my front with skunk cabbage leaves tied on with creeping ivy. I fed myself mostly from what the opportunity provided. I tilled the soil, sowed the wheat and corn, and manually helped harvest everything from grapes to potatoes. I cleaned and fed the cows, horses, chickens, and rabbits, and I even killed the chickens and rabbits and cooked them for myself. Sometimes, I even sun-fried eggs to quell my hunger. Now, tell me, Sister, do you still think I need any more advice how to take care of myself?"

She was shocked and in crying anger against our aunt and my godfather. Then, she said, looking at me: "I can't tell my feelings for these two. Maybe when I see them, I'll curse them. I can only think it meant this way for you. Surely, you will need now every bit of the experience you gained during your suffering. And maybe your—oh yes, your slingshot, too."

"Forget about my suffering, Sister! My mind is miles ahead of my body. Work is hard only when it is in my mind rather than in my hands. I don't think of work, but I do think what to get out of it. Like food. Lots of it. Someday I'll leap over all my hardships and have lots of it," I replied.

We ended talking suddenly as my brother-in-law stepped inside the kitchen, coming home from work.

He was a burly, tall man who seldom smiled. He looked fearfully commending when he spoke. Otherwise, he was a loving soul and gracious provider. He kissed the eight of us and asked, "Why is everybody so quiet?"

Iren promptly replied, "We are talking about the upcoming travel to Balatonkeresztur, and we are facing problems as to what we should bring with us."

"After supper, we'll talk about it," John replied.

Iren promptly ordered all of us to the kitchen. "It's time to have supper."

The kitchen table looked more like a picnic bench. Sitting eight persons around it didn't leave much wiggle room. I hated that because I had sizable arms and liked to stretch them wide around my food so that nobody would encroach on my dish. So I thought I was going to eat alone in the corner. We were standing now in silence as my brother-in-law circled his eyes saying, "How about thanking the provider?"

Everybody looked at him, silently praying. I did not understand what he meant as I have never eaten together with this family before. So I looked instead at the crucifix hanging on the opposite side of the wall. John noticed what I did and said, "From now on when I say 'thank the provider,' everybody should look at the crucifix instead of me. You don't have to say anything. He knows that it's your heart doing the talking.'" He pointed to the crucifix hanging on the wall. "There, he is the Provider."

We ate a thick potato and meat mix, simmered together with carrots, celery, green peppers, tomatoes, and onions, and all sorts of spices like paprika, ground black pepper, and thyme. Up to this time, I didn't eat any such a savory concoction. It fully satisfied me.

(Much later I learned that this dish was one of the most famous Hungarian dishes, called *gulyas*. I also learned the reasons for it. During the 1848 war between the Hapsburg Empire and Hungary, the soldiers were fed *gulyas,* as that was the most nutritious food in one bowl that supplied daily what their bodies needed. Today, every better European restaurant serves it. And of course, I do it, too. My dog, a vizsla, rears to my shoulders every time he smells it. He knows a big bowl of it will be his.)

After supper, my brother-in-law invited me to go outside with him. He wanted to talk to me privately. Since it was the second time I met this man, I was fidgety, for he didn't say anything except "come." Being now outside and standing under a huge walnut tree, he put both of his heavy hands on my shoulders. My knees almost caved in. He was at least a foot above my height and four times my waistline. He stared at my face and said: "I'm in amazement ever since you stared at that crucifix hanging on the wall. What were you thinking?"

"Not much. I had to look somewhere since I didn't understand what you were saying. That crucifix on that empty wall stared at me, and I stared at it back."

"I stared at it, too, and when I did, I almost fainted. I became a different man from that moment. I lost my cockiness. My overzealous pride emptied. Suddenly, I realized that it is God, not me, who is the real Provider."

"Why are you telling me these things, John? I'm too young for these deep sayings."

While he was still talking, I stepped back a few feet to release his big hands from my shoulders.

"I received that crucifix from my father before he died in the war and hung it up on the wall without really paying attention to it ever since. You now made me realize the meaning of it," John said.

"That's good. What else you want to tell me?" I asked as if nothing had happened, for I had a crucifix just like that also, hanging on my bedroom wall for my noticing it.

"My wife told me about your intentions that you are planning to live on your own in your house in Balatonkeresztur. Don't you think you are rather young for that?"

"John, you are looking at my age and not my willingness. I'm trying to better myself through the things I already learned from slavery at my aunt and at my godfather. I am going with Ella from here, no matter what, even if we have to escape," I responded.

"I don't think you need to do that, Arpad. My wife and I talked about both of you last night. We decided that we will help you along and set you up in order that you can begin life on your own," he said.

"Tell me, John, how do you mean that? You know I'm determined. I'm not afraid to squarely face what's ahead of me. Only one thing I don't want: that you would be checking on me every other week. I don't like prying eyes behind me. If I make mistakes, they will be my own mistakes. They will make me smarter in the long run."

"Here is what my wife thought we should be doing. But we wanted to find out first what you thought about it. Be free to say what's on your mind if you disagree. We want to give you lots of foodstuff from our own storage, and we want to give you livestock as well. We thought we would ask a friend of mine who owns a high-speed tractor to take the stuff to your house. You and I would be traveling together in the back wagon of the tractor," John explained.

My mind swirled from the kindness that these folks were planning to give us. In a hurry, I realized that we actually needed everything they offered us, as now we had nothing beside wishful thinking. I also realized they knew it better. They were grown-ups with a large family, knowing how a household should be managed from scratch. I liked the arrangement, too, to travel with the goods home.

"John, you are so gracious to do this for us. I have no idea where to even begin after we have left here. And I wouldn't dare ask. You know, asking for something was always so hard for me to do even though my mother taught me when to ask and when not to ask people for their help. My inside is humbled now because of your kindness. Nobody ever gave me anything freely before. I had to sweat for it."

"Cheer up, my boy! You will have it better from now on. I had it tough myself when I was young. I was adopted into a cruel family.

Manners and kindness I learned from a friend of mine who later became a monk."

John tipped his head forward in honoring his friend and turned away. I didn't know whether he was crying or just wanted to walk with me to the garden, where a couple of gypsies were planting corn and vegetable seeds. I now realized that he wanted to send them home, as the sun was declining while the half-moon was appearing on the other side in the sky. It was calm. It was a late April evening.

John led me around the backyard. It was fenced off from the garden. He showed me the many animals Iren raised to keep meat on the table. Chickens, ducks, and geese were jumping now in all directions as his frenzied white poodle pranced around chasing them. John quieted him by lifting his arm. The dog immediately understood the meaning of it.

On the left were four coops, housing the fowl; on the opposite side were two sheds with large structural canopies, providing shade for the pigs. Around the trunk of a tall walnut tree, under which we were standing before, were built the many rabbit cages. Each containing different colors and sizes of rabbits.

I was dumbfounded by the scene, by the noise, and by the reek, leading me to entertain my expectations that I would get something good out of this. Something good, indeed. John looked at me and said: "You can choose from these animals, and we'll take them with us. What do you say?"

"I don't mind that at all, but how are we going to transport them?"

"I have wooden cages piled on the top of the pig's pen. We could use those for the transportation. We could place them in the back of the tractor's trailer. Arpad, you will help me to do that, all right?" John explained.

"I'm ready whenever you say so," I replied, and we stepped inside the kitchen to join the rest of the family.

While we were outside looking around and talking, Iren was chatting with Ella inside. She said the following just as we stepped inside: "I thought that before we all travel back to Balatonkeresztur, you and I should go there first in order to clean up the place and properly arrange things inside as well as outside. This way, we wouldn't be surprised when we got there. I suspect calamity would be waiting for us if we didn't go there first. I know from the past how Matild is operating. She is very quick to take advantage of anything that suits her fancy, especially of things that weren't hers," Iren explained. Ella, of course, agreed.

John and I heard this last part of the conversation. We agreed, too, that it would be better to have the girls go first and clean up the place.

I know, of course, how things were back home, and above all else, my aunt needed to be straightened out. But I didn't say anything about it to Iren. She knew it better than I did. It was for this reason I padlocked my bedroom door before I came here.

The next day my sisters and Maria, Iren's first daughter, left, going to Balatonkeresztur on a fast train from Martonvasar in order to clean up the place.

(Worth to mention, Martonvasar is not just any town in the country. It features the famous Beethoven gardens. Beethoven himself used to live here in a small, beautiful castle. He composed a number of his well-known pieces here. Ever since he died, there is now an annual festival held in his honor every August.)

* * *

While my sisters were gone, John and I kept busy preparing the wooden crates that would contain the fowl and the rabbits during transportation. I wasn't sure how many I should take. So I asked

John. Instead of just pointing out the animals, he gave me a short advisement in husbandry.

"You should look at it this way," he said. "Take six pullets, six hens, and a rooster. The pullets you should kill, one a week. The hens you should keep for eggs and the rooster to mate with them in case you want hatchlings. You should also take seven rabbits and four ducks. From the rabbits, I'll choose six females and one male. Keep the male rabbit separate until you want to mate him with the females. Rabbits are prolific breeders. From the six females you could have fifty or even sixty rabbits within weeks. So you may want to eat four of the females soon. Keep in mind though that these animals need to be fed every day. I'm going to load some grain also for you that will last a few weeks.

"Who's going to cook for you, Arpad?" he asked.

"I'm a good cook, John, if there is something to cook from—my way, of course. After Mother died, I was forced to dabble fixing food for myself. Since I was always close to her and seeing her kneading pastas and bread, preparing the ingredients for soups and stews, making pancakes and all sorts of things from potatoes, I gained some knowledge about cooking. It wasn't easy at the beginning as I didn't know what came first, the fork or the knife, but I didn't give up and ultimately developed the right combinations.

"I ate everything I cooked, even if it didn't taste good. And while I was eating it, I was developing the improvement steps for the next try. After two years of practice, I don't dilly-dally with cooking any longer, so long as I have the stuff at hand to cook from."

John was puzzled over my cooking experience and could not find the fitting words to match his doubts. So he said in a subdued voice: "I don't know how to cook, and now my wife is away with Ella and my oldest daughter. We aren't going to have any cooked food tonight, unless… unless you volunteer to show me your skills, now that you went on exciting me about it."

"Would you like to eat rabbit stew? How about a couple of these rabbits, John? They are fast to clean and cook." I looked at him with a suggestive smile.

"Why not! Let's have rabbits tonight." He smiled back.

We stopped talking. Now, like two men practicing teamwork, John pulled two, four- month-old rabbits from their cage. He handed me one while he held onto the other by its hind feet. Now the rabbit was hanging upside down, and John exerted one strong whack with the edge of his palm behind the rabbit's ears. The strike rendered the animal instantly dead. I did the same thing to the other rabbit. Then, we ripped down their coats, cleaned their guts and washed them in a plastic bowl. Next, I chopped them to neat pieces for stew. The whole thing took ten minutes.

John was watching me to see whether I showed hesitation butchering the rabbit. After the meat was in the bowl already, he said, "I thought you would be crying over it."

"John, I'm an orphan. I'm left alone to endure the pains of it since my mother died. Do you think I'm going to cry over a rabbit when no one ever cried over me? Don't worry, I am already tempered. I see nothing else in it, except meat for my stomach. I feel the same way with any other animal that's good to eat. Can we go inside now, and I'll start cooking?"

"Oh... yes," he said. "Let's go." John was in awe over my self-assured remarks.

Inside the kitchen, I was unfamiliar where the needed things were for cooking the rabbits. So I opened every cabinet door and took out what I needed. I saw that everything had its own place inside the cabinets and everything was handily organized.

John was sitting and watching me from the kitchen table, waiting already to be served.

First, I took a wide pan with its lid, big enough for the two rabbit parts. Then, I scooped a quarter cup of lard into the pan and lit the gas stove. Now, I chopped two large onions directly into the pan and waited until it sizzled. Quickly now, I added two tablespoonfuls of paprika over the sizzling onions, stirred it, and added the meat into the pan and stirred it again. Next, I added a teaspoonful of black pepper and the same amount of thyme and two teaspoonfuls of salt and stirred that also into the stew. Then, I diced a whole tomato and a green pepper to it and added a tablespoonful of sugar. And, then, I added a cup of red wine to it. Now, I covered the pan and turned the heat low. In a few minutes, the kitchen was full of the mouth-watering aroma from the simmering stew. John's dog was sitting on the threshold, oozing saliva and steadily looking at me instead of his owner. The stew was fully cooked in one hour. Then in a separate dish, I mixed two tablespoonfuls of white flour into a pint of sour cream and stirred the two together into a smooth batter and mixed it into the simmering stew. For extra flavor, I added one bay leaf and shut the stove off as soon as the stew started boiling again. (This is my wild-game stew recipe from domesticated rabbits.)

It was now five o'clock in the afternoon. John's children, four of them, were noisily outrunning each other toward the house and only slowed down when they saw their father standing in front of the kitchen door. They were running home from school. They embraced and kissed their father. I was inside the kitchen and saw the warm greetings. A pang jolted my heart, for I didn't have parents to hug me anymore. Now, they moved inside and sat around the kitchen table. John sat down also and explained to the children what was going on. They didn't ask any questions but stood up and one by one washed their hands and sat back to the table again. Then, they silently looked on the crucifix that was hanging on the same wall where it always was. *Thank you* was done rather quickly while I carried the pot of stew to the table.

Then, I sat down next to John and fast wanted to fork the meat onto my plate. John suddenly pressed my right hand down, for I didn't thank the Provider as the others did. I instantly obliged. Now, everybody took more stew than they could eat with slices of crusty bread. Nobody looked at each other and nobody talked. It was their custom not to talk while eating.

Supper ended with cheerful thanks. John remarked that I should learn to be a chef, and asked that I should repeat the cooking tomorrow as well, except with chickens this time. I acknowledged him and took the nearly empty pot outside for the dog to lick it. Afterward, he also licked my face as well. I supposed he was thanking me for it.

(Cooking is more of an instinct in me than the monotonous following of cookbooks to learn it. The best way to call it: concoction. And that was because most of the time I didn't have all the ingredients needed for flavorings or complementing my stews with side dishes like potatoes and vegetables.

Bread I always had because I learned from Mother how to knead the dough. So I baked four large crusty rye loafs every month.

I saw the whole process from scraping the leftover sour dough from the vat after it was dried, saving it as yeast for the next batch. Mother always reminded me that the texture of the dough and the punch-back of it during the leavening process were the most important steps in good bread making. The dough had to be as supple as a fat sow's underbelly.

Nothing I hated more from the entire process than the waiting time between the dough rising intervals. So Mother decided to put me to work in between. I was now in charge of cutting the wood, including the kindle wood, preparing the wood stack inside the brick oven which was built outside, and finally lighting it. The wood had to be dry to prevent smoldering or else the brick oven would have remained only lukewarm. Then, when the wood burned down and the oven was hot, I shoveled out the still glowing ambers and ashes. After that, I mopped clean the remaining ashes inside the oven and closed its door.

Now, the oven was ready to receive the nicely formed bread dough. The last thing Mother did with a pointed knife was to make small crosses in the top skin of the dough. This was done to release the gasses from the additional fermentation during baking.

My final task was bucketing water from the neighbor's well in order to extinguish every bit of the still flickering ash on the ground. I said to Mother afterward that I didn't want to eat bread anymore. But, then, when the bread was finally baked, I was the first one to cut the ends off. I tell you, that nothing tastes better than a fresh slice of crusty rye bread smeared all over with a thick layer of home-churned butter.)

* * *

John and Iren had five children, two boys and three girls. The first born was a girl, named Maria. Then came a boy, named John after his father. Then came another boy, named Laszlo, and then came two other girls, named Iren and Zsuzsanna. A little more than a year separated them from each other.

Now, Maria went to Balatonkeresztur with her mother and Ella. The others stayed with John and I here in Rackeresztur.

Iren was sixteen years younger than John, my brother-in-law. Therefore she always addressed her husband formally by his last name. That was customary at that time in Hungary in order to show respect toward the older person.

Now I was thirteen and a half years old, but I looked more like eighteen. Working physically every day, I looked as if I were training myself to be a specimen for body builders. On the contrary and unknowingly, the good Lord was preparing me for something else— the pending work that I would be doing. I was ready to face my new life with a surer outlook and stronger body than at any time before.

It would only be a few more days now that John would be moving us home to Balatonkeresztur. Therefore, I was waiting for him to tell me when to pack the things that he and Iren agreed to give us.

John was thinking about the same thing I was. But he didn't want to say anything until his wife returned. Consequently, however, I saw him doing things that suggested he was preparing for the journey. Burlap sacks—full of corn, potatoes, and other grains—he piled already side by side inside his granary.

Now Iren and the two girls were back home at Balatonkeresztur. They are doing many things there that were not planned initially. The animals were still kept inside the kitchen at night, as when I left home to come here. Iren became almost crazy over this and grabbed Matild by her clothes and pulled her inside the kitchen.

"I'm going to lock you inside here for an hour, so as to breathe the stink you created and never forget what you did to these orphans." Then, she told her, "Scrub the floor and disinfect everything with lye solution."

The second episode came right after the first. Matild removed the fence boards and pulled the posts that Mother erected to separate her side of the yard, and thereby keep her privacy. Now, while Matild was locked inside the kitchen, cleaning it, Iren and the girls gathered all the fence parts and repositioned them.

Suddenly, Matild was banging the kitchen door. She wanted to come out. Iren heard the bangs but didn't respond. Not until the banging became nonstop, accompanied by loud cries, Iren responded. Matild was suffocating from the reek. At this time Iren dropped her hammer and the girls dropped their shovels. All of them ran to the kitchen door to remove the barricade Iren erected to hold the kitchen door tightly shut so that Matild couldn't escape. When they finally opened the kitchen door, Matild was on her knees at the door, begging forgiveness. Iren let her out. After Matild and Iren made peace, they finished the cleaning together. It was now noon.

(The church bell was solemnly peeling again, honoring the defeat of the Turks at Belgrade by the famous Hungarian warrior and general Janos Hunyadi since the 1456 victory. This was a monumental defeat of the Turks in European history. For, after this defeat, the Turks didn't try again to invade Hungary and Europe for seventy years. This is really why the Catholic churches' bells are ringing at noon worldwide to this day. The Pope at that time so proclaimed it.)

This is the first part of the day Iren and the girls did at Balatonkeresztur. The second part of the day was spent on settling grievances.

Iren declared to Matild: "I want you to know that I am the legal guardian of Arpad and Ella. You have absolutely nothing to do with them legally.

"If you intend to hurt them or cause hardship for them, I'll come after you with the police and put you in jail. Is that clear to you, Matild?"

Iren waited for Matild's answer, but she said nothing for a while. Then, she began: "I thought that I am Arpad's guardian. But now you say that you are his guardian. I don't understand. After their mother died, you took both kids with you. While Arpad quickly returned, you kept Ella with you. But I have not seen you coming back to visit Arpad ever since. I'm the one who cared for him most of the time, although he was coming and going between me and his godfather. How can you say that you are his guardian?" she said.

Iren responded, "The court didn't separate them even though they lived separately at times. I was appointed to be their guardian, just the same. Now, of course, they are coming back to live here for good. This is their home, and they want no interference in their lives from you. I'm back here now to make sure that their place is clean and the yard is separated and kept that way from now on. You understand?"

"Is this what they want also, or you are imposing it on them?" Matild inquired.

"This is what they want. This, of course, is not what I wanted. But John and I could not persuade them otherwise. They said, 'If you don't let us go, we'll escape.' And we thought that the best thing for them is to come back to their home. Also, we have five children of our own, and they don't get along well with Arpad. So John and I decided we would supply them chickens, ducks, and rabbits, along with the grains to feed them and come back here in a few days. But you must stay away from them," Iren warned again.

"They would need a lot more than just the yard animals. Are you going to supply them also with cooking oils, potatoes, flour, spices, and other things they need?" Matild inquired.

"Yes, all that is in the plan. We would also bring some wood and clothes," Iren said.

Matild was now out of her mind and couldn't find words to express it. Then, she stepped outside the kitchen and looked at the separated yard, being convinced that Iren really put her foot down this time. Now she turned her eyes to the shed and said, "Inside of that shed is full of my junk. Will I have to clean them out?"

"The sooner the better, like tomorrow," Iren demanded.

On the second day, Iren and the girls set out to visit our properties. One was a half-acre empty field in the meadows, the other a half-acre garden plot in the hills of the village.

Iren already had plans for both properties. The meadows would have corn and potatoes planted this year, while the hills would have vegetables. This way, both the animals and the kids would have plenty to eat. She also had plans to turn the soil over before she would be heading back to Rackeresztur. Then, later in the spring the kids would do all the plantation.

Along the way, they met old friends coming and going to and from the meadows. Some walked; others rode on horse-drawn wagons. The two girls were busy picking wild flowers on the roadside or chasing swallow-tailed butterflies, though they closely followed Iren. Here and there partridges crossed the road, taking cover in the small acacia bushes along the roadside. And up in the sky, larks circled at different heights, gliding up and down as the gentle breeze fanned them. They were singing to each other their love songs, only they understood. It was now noon again, and the church bell was peeling as it always had at this time since 1456.

Iren and the girls finally reached the property. Iren cried out, "The devil must have been here just to disappoint me."

The entire plot was already plowed under. Half of it was planted with corn and the other half with potatoes. The seedlings were just poking through the ground.

"This witch of a woman must be a mind reader or some other quack. I will find it out in a hurry," Iren turned around and rushed back home together with the girls.

At home there is no sign of Matild. The neighbor, that is, Laszlo, told Iren that she went to the Hills to press beans into the ground next to each of the already sprouted corn. They grew together well as two crops in one hill. Every gardener did that for lack of space.

Now, Iren and the girls grabbed bread and slices of slab bacon to eat on the way, hurrying to the hills, thinking to find Matild there. She was there, all right, on her own property. Our property was already made into her own garden.

Iren moved to Matild who was sitting on the footing of a small monument on her property that the Turks erected centuries ago. She invited Iren to sit next to her. Iren, not being aware, sat on part of her pleated, baggy skirt. Now, Matild couldn't stand up nor move away. She thought it was a threat that Iren would now manhandle her. No harm was meant, however; it just happened that way. Now, Iren was talking:

"Matild, I want to say to you quietly that I have a lot to tell to you. How are you going to explain to the judge who appointed me the legal guardian of Arpad and Ella that you have appropriated their land and are using it for your own selfish gain?"

Matild now explained how the whole thing happened.

"There is no guilt on my part, Iren. You probably don't know this: I had to plant the grounds at both places because if I didn't, somebody else would have. The state does not allow bare land anywhere uncultivated.

"So now that Arpad and Ella are coming back, we shall cultivate both properties together. We shall split both the labor and the harvest in half. Or else, you decide what you want, but do it before you return home," Matild explained.

The year was 1953, just about when the Communist government enforced collective farming and nationalization of private property. Small tracks were exempted but had to be cultivated. Our properties fitted the small-track definition.

Iren now is facing an unusual dilemma. How to get along with Matild without having Arpad and Ella exploited. She knew from past experience that Matild was exceptionally greedy. In her book greedy people were synonymous with cheaters and liars.

Iren, therefore, decided to split each property insofar as cultivation and harvesting was concerned, but only for the current season. This was, of course, her split-second decision. So she turned to Matild and said: "I don't agree with you, for I see trouble ahead. I want to divide the properties in half and let Arpad and Ella cultivate their own half alone. This would be the honest way to do it."

Matild agreed and even offered help fertilizing the growing plants. Then, they got up and went to stake out the properties. The two girls, Ella and Maria, who accompanied Iren, heard everything being said and were now the eyewitnesses.

After they staked out the properties, they walked home together. The feud ended peacefully.

* * *

As they walked, Iren explained to Matild what would happen in the coming days regarding the return of Ella back home.

(Ella was now fifteen years old. During the past two years, she was with Iren and John at Rackeresztur and was part of their family. Iren had her constantly under training regarding house cleaning, clothes washing, cooking, and most importantly, manners between boys and girls. She was thinking that one day Ella would get married. Might as well prepare her for it.

Ella was a beautiful girl, five feet, eight inches tall, a bit on the chubby side, but otherwise, a fully developed young lady. With her dark-brown hair and beady black eyes she had the attraction that boys from left and right immediately noticed. She was, however, quite strictly trained by Iren: "Never, never fascinate your mind with boys, for that leads to temptations and foul play.")

Back at Rackeresztur, John and I had already loaded the tractor trailer with everything that was given and were anxiously waiting for Iren and the girls' return from Balatonkeresztur.

"That has to happen tomorrow," John said, "or the animals would be dying."

Soon after Iren and Matild parted company last night, Ella asked Iren to let her stay with Matild for the two days, between now and the time John and I arrived with the tractor. Iren agreed to Ella's wishes on strict conditions:

"You will be her guest only for two days, and as a guest, you return here to your own house anytime should Matild want you to do her own work. Keep her out from your house as much as possible, for sooner or later, she would interfere with whatever you are doing.

You will clean out the shed with Matild's help tomorrow, but if she doesn't want to, you clean it out alone and throw her belongings on her side of the fence. Know how to take care of yourself from now on as I have taught you. Within two days Arpad will arrive, and after that the two of you will be on your own. I'll be back in a few weeks to check how well you were doing.

"One more thing, every month I will send you some money from your postal saving account. Spend this money only on the bare necessities. But always keep a little put away, just in case you need it in an emergency. Remember, there was no one else who would give you money. Nobody throws money around to those who couldn't repay it."

For Ella, this was a lot more than just the permission she asked for. It was a farewell speech with definite overtones about her relationship with Matild.

Now, Maria, Iren's daughter, heard everything as she was sitting next to Ella on the edge of the bed and was contemplating on the meaning of her mother's stressful words. She understood that very soon, maybe tomorrow, Iren would be traveling home with her and she would never see Ella again.

The two girls were of the same age. During the last two years, they had grown close to each other. They shared all their secrets, went to school together, and promised eternal friendship to each other.

Both girls were under the same disciplinary training from Iren and often shared crying and laughing together over Iren's motherly attention. All this now would suddenly end. From now on, nobody could replace Ella, for true friends can never be replaced by anyone else.

Maria went to bed early but could not fall asleep for long hours. It was painful for her to accept this reality.

The next morning, while the girls were still sleeping, Iren went to Matild and said to her what she hasn't yet said. She was blunt and rather straightforward:

"What Ella is doing shall not be your business. She shall be on her own from now on. I will occasionally check back to make sure that you were not interfering in her life."

With that said, Iren waited for Matild's reply, but Matild did not reply to Iren's declaration. Instead, she asked her: "When are you leaving back to your home?"

"I bet you are anxious to see me go. Don't worry, I'll back sooner than you think. For that matter, I'm leaving right now," Iren answered and left Matild with that veiled threat. "Back sooner than you think."

Now Ella and Maria were already dressed and were reflecting on the past and promising each other to write letters in those secret codes they invented last year for themselves.

Iren returned from Matild. She already had packed the few things she brought with her from home. Now it was time to leave to the train station. They had only one more hour left before departure back to Rackeresztur. Ella went along with them to say that last *good-bye* to Maria. It was now exactly 8 a.m., the last Wednesday in April 1953.

The steam-driven locomotive with its ten wagons arrived on time at 9 a.m. and was full of passengers. Therefore, Iren and Maria had to run to the front wagon where the first-class compartments were still empty. And that was good because it afforded only seconds for the hugs and kisses for the girls that would have been otherwise a stretched, emotional pain to bear for both of them.

* * *

After the locomotive pulled the wagons from the station, Ella walked to the shores of Balaton and sat on the rocks that lined the edge of the water. She was reflecting on the seriousness of the responsibilities facing her. The most serious was her moving back to me. She would be facing new circumstances requiring tough choices, some of which would require tough decisions. But her consolation was that I would be with her. And that would make everything so much easier to bear. After all, I would be the *man of the house.*

As Ella prepared to leave the shore, a good-looking boy about eighteen years old showed up in front of her. He carried two tin pails and a fish-scooping net with a long handle. He recognized Ella right of way because he saw her yesterday with Iren and Maria coming home from the meadows. His name was Steve Fodor, and he called my sister by her first name. Since they didn't know each other that well, it became difficult for them to start a conversation beyond a mere *hallo.* Iren taught Ella that girls don't start conversations with strangers without good reasons. So it was Steve who asked her: "What are you doing here alone, Ella?"

Ella told him that this spot was her favorite swimming area during the summer. The water was clean, shallow, and warm here. She didn't divulge any of the events that were to happen to her in the coming days. She was curious, though, about the tin pails and the fishing net.

"What are you going to do here with those things in your hands?"

"These things are my fishing gear. The net is my scoop and the pails are my fish holders. This time of the year, I come here because the minnows are out by the millions, spawning around the rocks. I'll show you, just watch," he alerted Ella.

Sure enough, Steve wasn't kidding. He grabbed the long handle of his scooping net, dunked it into the water right in front of Ella, and quickly pulled it back. The weight of the shiners almost broke the handle. Ella jumped as the minnows wiggled themselves and landed on her feet. She had never seen so many small fish in one place.

"What are you going to do with so much fish, Steve?" Ella asked.

"When these pails are full, I'll take them to my big barrel I have there on my pushcart."

Steve pointed to the barrel and went on, "Then, I'm going to push my cart from house to house and sell the fish, pound by pound, to the villagers. They will prepare from them pickled herrings, sardines, or the well-peppered and baked fish cakes. It will only be for the next ten days or so that I could do this. Would you like to help me? I would split the profit with you," Steve suggested.

"I cannot stay, Steve. Maybe next time, after my brother arrives. Now, my aunt is waiting for me to help her with a cumbersome job," Ella explained.

"Can I give you some fish to take to your aunt? I'm sure, she would love it." Steve made the offer. Then, he pulled a small linen sack from his pocket and filled it with shiners.

"Give it to your aunt and tell her it was from Steve."

Ella hesitated to take it because the fish were still wiggling in the sack. So Steve tied the sack's mouth. That way Ella accepted the offer and left Steve, hurrying home to help Matild to clean out the shed.

After Ella gave Matild the sack of fish and told her that it was from Steve, it became evident who Steve really was. He lived on the same street Ella and I would be living, just five houses away. Steve and I were always good buddies, regardless of the differences in our age. Ella did not know that.

Now the train on which Iren and Maria were traveling back home left Siofok, the biggest resort center on Lake Balaton. From there, it picked up speed as it was changed from local traffic to non-stop express. It only stopped at two or three places before reaching Budapest. One of those stops was Martonvasar (Beethoven's place).

In about a half an hour later they boarded a connecting bus that took them to Rackeresztur. The bus ride, while it was only a half an hour long, was only interesting to those who loved to see farms and pastures. For the others, it was flatland. After Rackeresztur, the bus went to the next town, Ercsi.

(Ercsi was my birthplace [1939]. Since my dad was a railroad employee, he was transferred here in 1938. We stayed here until 1943. Then my father was transferred again, this time to Polgardi. It was here where the invading Russians captured him and deported him to Siberia. I was then six years old. And from there on, I vividly remember the later part of the war and the beginning of the desperate times that followed the war and followed my life's journey as well.)

Now, John, my brother-in-law, saw that only Iren and Maria were coming. He and I were tending the animals behind the tractor trailer when they appeared, coming around the corner of the house. John ran to the front gate to open it. I was not far behind but saw no urgency to run to meet them.

All of us now went to the kitchen, sat at the table, and listened to Iren telling us about the bizarre events that went on between her and Matild. Iren became exhausted from talking and John became exhausted from listening, so the two went to take a nap.

I had the life of a falcon now, as I felt that my freedom is coming tomorrow. My independence would start the minute Iren would shut the front gate behind her.

Back home at Balatonkeresztur, Ella was exhausted from worrying about how we would be able to provide everything we needed, living independently from everybody else. She didn't know as yet that John and I would be bringing with us the mini contents of a household.

When napping was over, Iren had a lot to tell me:

"I did all this because of the two of you. From now on, Matild will know what's hers and you will know what's yours. When you arrive there tomorrow, you'll enter on your side of the yard, and you'll store all that's yours on your side of the property. You will keep Matild on her side of the fence from now on. Or else, I'll have to step in again, but this time through legal action. I'm your legal guardian, and you'll have to listen to me until you grow up. Understand!"

I really didn't understand her and didn't know what to say or do at the moment. What did *legal guardian* mean? I was probing my mind. I let the time solve Iren's ailment as I thought she was angry. So I turned to John and asked him, "How early you think we should leave tomorrow morning?"

"I figure that we should leave four o'clock in the morning. That way we would avoid the heavy traffic and the heat. It will take us about three hours to get there. I'll contact the driver later today. You and I will sit in the back of the trailer. We'll need a couple of extra blankets to hold the wind chill down," John concluded.

Now, Iren went to do the inventory of the already loaded stuff in the uncovered trailer. She had a checklist made while she was on the train coming home. As she was about half way through, she called me to review the checklist with me. She showed me what was already packed and what was still missing. She alone knew exactly what we needed as she alone understood the household business. I didn't know half the stuff she was explaining to me. So I thought it would be better to keep quiet about it, for I had plenty of time to discover later as to what everything was for.

Then, she disappeared inside the house and gathered the things she wanted to give us in addition to what we already packed. I saw her coming out with the additional goods. I noticed the handles on the pots and pans. All the pots had smaller things loaded in them. She was telling herself aloud that I had a good look what they had and I know that they needed these things also. The last thing she loaded was two five-gallon ceramic pot, one filled with lard for cooking, the other with deep-fried duck parts, covered with its own fat to preserve it. As she loaded the ceramic pots she said, "You will eat this next winter with boiled potatoes and rye bread when you won't have anything else." She then packed hay around each pot to protect it from breaking, as the trailer would be bouncing around from the million potholes that covered the single-lane highway to Balatonkeresztur.

John left to inform the driver about the early morning departure.

Iren now sat with me under the walnut tree and began talking.

"Well, my youngest brother, you are going to step into the wild world. Few kids of your age would even dream of doing such a thing. Many nights I have been wondering, what was in you that moved you to take this daring step?"

"Sister, last year I met a man who went to America. His name is Joseph Forro. You probably knew this man, too. After about ten years living and working in America, he returned back to Hungary and lived in the middle part of that house where Joseph Magyar had his farm. I was there for many months tending Joseph's cows. In the evening hours as we sat around, this man told me a lot about his life and his regrets. I was mostly listening and trying to relate his comments to my life. Here are the sayings I most remembered:

"The first thing is you have to know yourself and know the facts about yourself. When you know both, you can change the wrong in you accordingly. The second is all the mistakes you make come from your not knowing what you can or cannot do. And the third is have the courage to change direction."

Then, I added my own convictions.

"Now, Sister, I have taken these sayings and compared them to what I have been doing and found that most of the things I did were wrong. But now, I know for sure that working for others for nothing was the worst thing I ever did. The more I did it, the more I was exploited. That is why I want to be on my own. From now on I will aim my life for the best of things, for I could always turn back to the bottom."

My sister thought that an angel was talking out of me. She was totally speechless. She got up from the wooden bench and went to the dug well nearby to fetch water for the animals as she noticed they were already panting. I myself also got up to mind the fire under a huge kettle filled with water. I would be bathing myself for the last time in Rackeresztur.

John had already returned from the tractor driver and now joined Iren in order to make sure that we didn't forget something important for the road. My sister that evening prepared and packed enough food, not only for the road, but also for Ella, plus extra for a few more days after that. The only thing was still missing was fresh water for the road.

* * *

Being overexcited to travel, I couldn't sleep well last night. There was nothing that really bothered me, still, the unknown ahead of me kept me exceptionally excited. The unknown was always mystifying to me. For that reason, I already learned to put a positive spin on it. Turn it in my direction so that I would always have a positive outlook forward. I did the same thing this time. Everything would turn out to be just fine, I had reassured myself. Now, I heard the rooster's crow the first time. That meant it was three o'clock in the morning. It was almost time to get dressed and wait for the others. But I lingered.

Because I slept in the hallway, I had the disadvantage of hearing everybody walking by me, and the biggest bother of all was the awakening when somebody accidentally kicked my bed. This last time, though, it was all anticipation as to who would be coming first kicking my bed.

Iren was the first who kicked the edge of my bed as she probed her way in the dark through the hallway. There was no electricity available in this area as yet, and walking in the dark without bumping into something was not uncommon without a flashlight. Iren knew, of course, that I was there. She whispered, "Are you up?"

I whispered back, "Yes, I'm up, all right. I'm coming out to the kitchen after you."

Both of us were habitually early risers. We talked and laughed about it in the kitchen.

"How lucky are those who can count the stars in the sky early morning. They are the ones who can finish a day's work before noon and watch the others sweat all afternoon." (Even today some sixty years later, I'm mindful of her saying.)

Now she lit the kindle wood in the stove, getting it ready to cook grits with smoked ham for breakfast for the four of us—for John, for the driver of the tractor, for myself, and for herself. The time must have been around four o'clock in the morning as the sky had a slight reddish appearance indicating a clear sunrise.

As Iren was doing her thing in the kitchen, she also kept talking to me. This time, the subject was money. She gave me Hungarian money for the road. She also told me that she gave the same amount to Ella. Furthermore, every month she would send us more in order to keep us going. I put the money in my pocket and said to her: "After we settle down, the first thing I and Ella will be doing is to get familiar with the value of money. We would be going from store to store, figuring out the cost of things we need and comparing that against the money we have. This way we would be able to do budgeting. I don't want to run out of money, Sister, because of my ignorance of it."

"If you learn how to do that, you would never run out of it. Make sure you do that!"

Just as we finished talking, John and the tractor driver stepped inside the kitchen. The grits and the ham were already dished out for eating. The breakfast was actually gobbled up as it was already way after four o'clock. I was the first one to finish. Oh yes! When it came to food, I ate as fast as I worked.

Now, the tractor was idling with the trailer hooked up to it and was ready and waiting to get going. The trailer had an open top but the sides were closed about four feet high. This was good, for we needed to be protected from the wind shear and the draft, as John and I would be sitting on the floor. John put a straw mattress under us, and Iren provided a couple of thick wool blankets to cover ourselves. These were the type of blankets that people threw on horses. The time was now about five o'clock in the morning. The sun started to show its face on the horizon. All the animals, whether they were in the coops or free roaming, indicated that it was morning now. They chirped, cried, crowed, and fought with each other. They were hungry.

It was time now to say *good-bye* to Iren. I was the last one to hop on the trailer because I had to run back to fetch my slingshot from under my bed. The tractor pulled out the yard rather swiftly. My sister was waving till I could no longer see her hands. I knew she was crying. She lost her young, vagabond brother.

* * *

The distance from Rackeresztur to Balatonkeresztur was about eighty miles, roughly three hours' drive. John had planned to make the round-trip the same day. Both, the driver and John, had to get back to work the following day.

The highway on which we traveled was the only route that meanders from Budapest to Zagreb, Yugoslavia (Croatia today). It was a single lane highway and a dangerous one. On horse-pulled wagons and on bicycles, people were traveling in both directions with the faster vehicles. Those who wanted to pass the slower drivers had to move like a snake in order to prevent a collision which was rather common. This was the main reason as to why John wanted to start early in the morning so as to avoid the heavy traffic.

As soon as the sun rose high enough, I leaned onto the side of the trailer and stood there most of the time. Because I had never been on this highway before, I wanted to see everything that was worthy of noticing. "Who knows one day I may have to walk to Budapest or back from it" sprang through my mind. For about twenty miles, I didn't see much more than villages and meadows in between. The high marks were the enormous nests of storks built on the top of the equally enormous chimneys. A stork was standing in its nest on one leg. I thought that that was a cute scene.

Then, we passed through a big city, Szekesfehervar. It took us half an hour to zigzag through it. As I looked about, practically every building was damaged from the war. Bullet holes pepper the houses as if there was nowhere else to shoot. I couldn't wait long enough to leave the city. I didn't want to see any more destruction. So I sat till we left the city.

Now, between this city and the east side of Lake Balaton, I saw many other villages and meadows. They looked very similar to each other. The houses had the same roof styles, narrow but long, covered porches, and those broad chimneys looked as if everybody wanted a stork's nest on them.

The meadows were mostly grazing land, featured a variety of flowers and colors that only appeared in the springtime. It looked like a flowering hillside. The storks were here and not on the chimneys, gracefully measuring their steps as they plucked the frogs from the dew-drenched grass. Here and there I saw cows munching the dark-green grass as if their heads were glued to the ground. This was the pastoral life I frequently saw repeated as we were slowly progressing on this narrow highway.

Aggravation after aggravation drowned the driver's patience because flocks of geese, ducks, and chickens often stopped him from being able to move forward till they crossed the road.

Lake Balaton was roughly fifty miles long, and the area around it was quite populated, especially the south side of the lake. There were lots of stores located here, and there was a farmers market that opened at six o'clock in the morning. The first wave of traffic jam was caused by the farmers, bringing the produce from the surrounding villages. Then, the shoppers and the vacationing foreigners, disregarding the highway traffic, jaywalked as the animals did. This is the most populated town on this side of the Lake. It is Siofok.

I wanted to stop here just to look around. I was always interested in browsing around to look at things. John thought that that was useless for him to do. But on my part, seeing people work and hearing them talk would be an experience itself, gathering the common sense of others. John turned me down.

In less than an hour, we arrived at our house. The tractor parked right in front of the yard as there was no gate in the fence big enough to move inside. It was now ten o'clock in the morning. It appeared that the whole town knew we are coming. I hated that. I hated seeing the lips of people moving and their bodies huddling, for that meant gossip had agitated their curiosity.

As we arrived, I hugged and kissed my sister Ella. Matild was there also looking at us from the other side of the fence. I smiled at her and yelled, "Here we are!" She turned around and went to her kitchen. She must have thought, *The troublemaker is here again.*

John and the tractor driver went straight to the shed to look around in order to start taking off the animal cages. I joined them and pointed where I would prefer to locate the cages. Luckily, these animals suffered no shocks to the point of death. I let the ducks and chickens from their cages to free-roam inside our small yard. Every one of them flapped its wings as if it wanted to fly back home. Ella looked with pleasant surprise, for she didn't expect to see this kind of gift from Iren and John. She went to John right of way and thanked him for it. I interrupted, "Wait until you see the rabbits and the other things we received."

So we now unloaded everything. Some of the things loaded inside the house, some inside the shed, and some we left outside. The unloading was done rather hurriedly, and therefore, not everything ended where it should have been. I could tell on John's behavior that he was more anxious to return to Rackeresztur than to mind neat unloading. I accepted that without saying anything as time was on my side. Tomorrow, I would put everything where it belonged, I thought.

John rubbed his hands and quietly said, "Arpad, there isn't much left to tell you anymore beyond what I already explained regarding your independence. Live responsibly. Always honor your commitments to yourself and to others as well. That is how people know how steady you are. Promise little to others but keep what you promised. Always keep what you had promised, for your promise is part of your dignity."

John gave me a very tight hug. I noticed tears in his eyes. I had to turn away from him for I couldn't hold my tears back either. I couldn't describe how great I felt that somebody gave me a real love hug at last, a love hug that I often missed in my growing years. Both the driver and he now left the premises and headed back to their homes at Rackeresztur.

Section Three

CHAPTER TWENTY-TWO

Independence Has Its Price to Pay

But I was only kidding myself, for I didn't know as yet that man was not allowed to see his future within his independence—only his plans. And independence I have more now than ever before. Suddenly, I wasn't dreaming anymore, for reality opened my eyes to put all my plans into attainable order. I was no longer following orders from others; I gave them to myself and Ella. Therefore, I placed them in priority to ensure first our survival, then our freedom. In truth, everything revolved around food. Food for ourselves, food for the animals. One complemented the other. I had now all the basic skills in mind and body to fulfill my plans. God had been exceptionally good to me. He made sure that I toiled for everything, for that was the only way I appreciated everything received, including now my independence.

Iren trained Ella how to maintain domestics. She had prepared her to be a good wife one day for a good man. Ella didn't have the slightest clue that that wasn't meant to be so—not right now, anyway.

On the other hand, I was trained by two devils and two angels. Matild and Gary were the devils; Joseph and Mr. Forro were the angels. The first two were in combat with God; the last two were in spirit with God. And I was placed between the two groups to sort out for myself the good from the evil. If it wasn't for the chastisement of that Augustinian priest who whacked me so often to remember the moral values written in the catechism, I would not have been able to recognize one from the other. I was no different in attitude from any other kid in the whole world, inclined first to do the forbidden. So by the time I broke away from everybody and moved back home with Ella, I experienced both the presence of the holy and the presence of the folly. The moral teachings remembered from catechism now set me free from deluding myself.

Now to face the world, however, and survive in it, I was required to know what I wanted from it and then pursue it with united mind and spirit. For one without the other, lacked the *will* to stand up and tell the world: You are nothing more than what I make out of you and not the other way around. For, if the two weren't united, I would not have had the will to combat my ignorance—which I also had plenty of. One thing was certain that I already gained, both the knowledge and the experience to have a clear vision of what I wanted at last—my independence.

Few things needed more attention now than to understand the value of money. Neither I nor Ella understood the value of it. We didn't have a lot of it, but the little we had, had to be enough to buy sugar, salt, and spices. Cooking without them would have been monastic food. Not that anything was wrong with that, but I got accustomed to something else. I got used to eating spicy food, sweet noodles, and salty meats.

Although these ingredients might have been poisonous to my body, I couldn't eat even the very basic foods like bread, meat, and potatoes without them. And now we had none in the house, and none was available in the village stores in the surrounding towns. I knew of two individuals, however, who definitely had plenty of sugar, salt, and spices, for they were hoarders of these things. They understood that under Communism shortages of these basic necessities were as common as a cloudy sky in the morning. Hence hoarding was a habit with two of these cunning individuals, Iren and Matild.

Since Matild and Iren had faced shortages before of these basic commodities needed for cooking, they stashed away enough of them that would have lasted perhaps until the collapse of Communism. The problem we had, though, was that Iren had totally forgotten to give us any of it and Matild denied that she had any to give away to anybody.

In about two weeks, we finished the food Iren packed for us. The time came now to prepare our own food. But no tasty cooking could be done without salt, no baking done without sugar, and no flavorings added to stews without spices. So I wanted to send Ella back to Iren in order to bring enough of the stuff that would last until the shortage was over. But she was scared to go alone on account of the many gypsies who were roaming around Rackeresztur. It was for that reason, I went and she stayed, tending the animals.

It turned out that Iren's supply of these ingredients is now dwindled to a pinch.

"Let's go to Budapest right now! You'll help me carry the stuff home. We'll make the trip in a few hours," she said.

"You think there is no shortage there?" I asked.

"If there is shortage of these things in Budapest, the top Communist whose name is Rakosy would be fleeing for his life to Moscow. *Mark my word!*" she replied.

We now quickly got ourselves together and left for Budapest and went straight to the Great Gallery (giant supermarket), where even enormous walnut shells could be bought as cups for baking special brownies in them. Iren led me straight to the grocery section, and sure enough, there was more supply of everything available that would have lasted our lifetime had we bought it all.

While being there, I got the idea that we should go back home separately. "Why in the world should I carry sixty pounds of sugar and salt in my backpack to Rackeresztur when I could go straight home with it," I said to Iren.

"Well, in that case, I would only buy a few pounds for myself, as I can't carry more than that. My hernia would completely rupture in my belly lining, if I did more."

So I carried the sixty-pound bulk on my shoulders because the straps on my backpack had already been severed from the weight. In a separate handbag, I carried the spices. Iren couldn't believe that I was able to do that. I said to her, "I'm carrying merely soul food, Sister, and it had no weight for its necessity."

She didn't understand what I said. We then boarded separate trains and left Budapest. What I really meant was that my will to do it was stronger than the weight of sugar and salt. It was all *mind over matter*.

So I made the round trip the same day. I left Balatonkeresztur at five in the morning and returned the same day at nine in the evening. It was almost dark already, and I met no one on the way home. When Ella opened the kitchen door to let me in, I fell on the floor, being exhausted. Matter was over mind this time. As I lay there, Ella sat next to me and said, "While you were away, I went to the attic and found in Mother's canisters as much sugar, salt, and spices as you just brought home on your shoulders."

I concluded that there was a third cunning person in the family—Mother.

This time I was shaken. I couldn't figure out why I didn't go to the attic first before I threw up my hands and abruptly left to go to Iren.

Was there a message for me revealed by this incident? I was wondering. No answer surfaced, but weeks later, it did.

When I threw up my hands again in frustration, I realized that I lost direction to reasoning. My frustration being an orphan had at times erupted, for my future looked bleak more than ever. But as always, I recovered, for in bleak moments my inner world opened my eyes to ignore the past and look beyond my nothingness. Yet at the same time, I also realized that frustration had its own merits to ponder. Out of it came the hope that from every disappointment in the past a lesson was given that I had ignored to learn. And that lesson was that I am impatient with myself when it comes to momentary helplessness. I wanted too much at once, thinking that all things were successes for those who had the will over the secrets of reasoning.

Impatience and ignorance were my biggest enemies. Who in the world didn't possess both at the same time? All of us or just St. Peter? I wished now that I could ask that Augustinian priest for the answer.

The following morning I went to the attic early. I was waiting there for the sunlight to pierce through the cracks of the roofing tiles (clay tiles) so I could see. I lifted the tightly sealed bags from mother's canister in order to check whether the sugar, the salt, and the spices were still useable for cooking. Everything smelled as fresh as when Mother put them there. The tight seal of the canister lid kept everything unspoiled. So my unrevealed motive was now answered. Every bit of the stuff that I brought from Budapest, I will sell to the villagers at three times the money of its original cost. This shall teach me one aspect of the value of money—profit. I remembered that I learned something good from my Jewish friend Laszlo. *Profit* he had on his mind when he wanted me to buy his ticket to Budapest.

Since there was a shortage of these ingredients in all the surrounding stores, I could have sold everything for a lot more money than that, but I allowed the buyers to name their prices. Five well-to-do peasants bought my whole supply. They lived close to each other and colluded to bring the price down. I accepted the offer. I still tripled my original price.

This act of doing business with strangers had enlightened me to the fact that it was money that controlled the interaction among these peasants more than their compassionate feelings toward me. At the same time, it sent shockwaves through me that money was also a source of sin that urged people to cheat, to lie, and to steal for it. And to behave dishonestly the first chance they have. Collusion meant exactly that, I thought.

Matild stood in front, tall, in this example. Then Gary, my godfather, far exceeded even that of Matild. In short, I quickly learned that money had to be handled with no less responsibility as I handled my own behavior, for it had the persuasive power to convince me to do the wrong thing with it and for it.

Ella couldn't believe at first that I sold every bit of the stuff I brought home from Budapest.

"But why did you do that?" she asked.

"I wanted to know how to sell things, how to haggle with buyers, and how to hold my ground in face of those who called me crazy before because I was doing things for others for nothing. Some were even saying that I was selling the stuff from Matild's pantry. Don't worry, Sister, I defended myself with unusual fearlessness. You want to know something, Sister? They didn't believe me. So I picked up my backpack with the stuff in it and left. The peasants stepped after me and held me back. Now, they believed me, shaking the money in my face to buy all I had."

"What are you going to do with all that money, Brother?" Ella was curiously asking. She had no idea either about the value of money.

"We'll save it for the *rainy days*. Why shouldn't we follow Mother's example?" I asked and reminded her that that was the best thing to do until we learned the cost of things in relation to the money we had.

* * *

In a few days, we went to the closest city, Keszthely, in order to become familiar with the prices of clothes, shoes, garden tools, and whatever was on display in the windows. We went through one side of Main Street and back on the other side. Halfway back, there was this flower shop displaying all kinds of flowers in vases and pots, the beauty of which I have not seen before. I stood there gazing at their beautiful colors and shapes. As I was doing it, I imagined that these flowers were covering my mother's grave. I became very sad, realizing that Mother was buried in this city and I had not seen her grave in three years. Remembered also that when she was still living, I used to bring her wild flowers when I disobeyed her.

Since we were walking side by side, we were also talking about what we saw. Ella was also gazing at the same flowers.

"Ella, do you see anything in these flowers?" I asked her.

"Yes, I see them all on Mother's grave. Why don't we take them there?"

So we went inside the shop and asked the attendant about the price of the whole ensemble that was on display in the window.

"They are not for sale. They are fake flowers on display in order to invite people to come inside and shop for these real flowers."

She stretched her left arm in a sweeping motion over the flowers she had in the store.

"And how much do they cost?" I asked her.

"They are individually priced. These white roses cost a dollar a piece. These tulips in the pots cost five dollars. And these purple lilies from China cost ten dollars a pot. Which one you want?"

She looked at us with suspicious animation and asked again, "Which one you want?" thinking that we might be gypsies, ready to grab a pot and run out with it.

When I explained that we were orphans and our mother was buried here in the local cemetery and that we were really penniless compared to the prices of these flowers, she said: "I'm an orphan too. My mother and father are also buried here. And I'm wondering now… that that grave next to my parents… wasn't the grave of your mother. It looked to me that nobody took care of it. It was full of weeds all the time. It looked awful next to my parents' grave site which looks like a small flower garden. So I decided I would take care of it. So now that grave, too, looks like a flower garden. Go and check it out, and if I'm right, come back and thank me for it. You won't have to buy flowers then," she said.

I didn't say anything after that. I felt certain that it was my mother's grave.

We then left the flower shop and walked to the cemetery to find Mother's grave site somewhere in that vast place. Row after row of graves we went searching without being able to locate it. I had long forgotten where her grave site was. It wasn't her grave site I kept remembering. It was her love and kindness that engulfed my mind after she died.

This cemetery looked to me more like a showcase of miniature monuments. Black, white, and gray marble headstones, statues of big and small sculptures, all shapes and sizes of grave covers enhanced the beauty of this cemetery. Then the mausoleums of the rich and famous we couldn't miss even if we wanted to. They looked like works of art. I thought for a moment that the souls of the dead were living in them.

It was already mid-afternoon, and I noticed that we spent more time admiring the beauty of this cemetery than looking for my mother's grave site. After about four hours of looking, we only covered less than half the area and gave up the search. I said to Ella, "You know, Sister, we made a mistake. We should have asked somebody. Let's find the cemetery's office and ask the caretakers."

After the registrar asked two questions—namely, the year of death and the name of the dead—he led us to the layout map of the cemetery and pointed out Mother's grave site. It was that simple. My dumbfounded face glowed with anger over my stupidity. I had not yet learned that *if you don't ask, you don't get answers.*

It took us two minutes now to find Mother's grave site, and it was not the grave site that the flower shop attendant said it might be.

I didn't want anybody to see us now. I was embarrassed to the point of shamefulness. This was my mother's grave I had ignored and neglected! For all the love and care she did for me, was this my return for it? Remorse consumed my soul, and I fell on my knees in the tall weeds on the grave site, crying the same way as I did on that solemn day when she was buried here. Ella also fell on her knees and cried as I did. We have watered the weeds with our tears.

It became evident in a few minutes what we needed to do. Still on our knees, we pulled every single weed and threw it in a pile a few feet away from the grave. It was the first week in June 1953. The weeds were still tenderly green and wanted to grow more. They covered the entire grave site as if someone had intentionally seeded them there. Here and there a few already grew tall flowers of blue, yellow, and pink colors. These I broke off and handed to Ella to hold in her arms. Then, we walked to the edge of the cemetery, and I broke off a thousand similar flowers and filled Ella's arms with them, then mine, too. Now, we decorated Mother's grave site with them. The ones with the thicker stems, I pushed into the ground, wishing that they would grow roots, but if not, may live longer after the others have wilted. After, we went back to the edge of the cemetery again, and this time I filled Ella's apron with red and white wild poppy petals and decorated with that the edges and sides of the grave site. Now, Mother's grave looked like an altar, worthy to pray before it. And we did, thinking that she might hear her two orphans praying.

* * *

Ella and I quickly learned that our household required a lot more attention than usually kids would worry about—let the parents worry about that. What parents normally did, however, became now our own responsibility, individually and collectively. It became now ours to divide, to share, or to ignore. Instead, we ordered each other around to do this or that. We bickered with each other as a result. We didn't really know as yet each other's personality differences that surfaced more now because of our common duties. What we really needed at this time was mutual planning in order to set priorities and assign responsibilities accordingly—no longer kid's stuff.

So I said to Ella, "Let's just sit down for a couple of hours and talk about what we should be doing. And plan it as if we have hired someone else and told that person what to do, how to do it, and when to do it. That way we don't bias our thinking."

Ella responded, "You identify what's needed to be done. You practically ran this household here before by yourself. So I think you know it better than I do, who never organized a household."

"But I was alone and my needs are different from yours. Whatever I did here had to be second only to the demands of others. Now we should identify our chores for ourselves, for we would have to do things this time for ourselves and not for others," I said.

"I had pretty much the same situation at Iren. But my work was more inside the house, not like yours, outside the house," Ella rebutted.

"So you know more of the housework than the farm work. You see, I had it the other way around. What would you say if I identify what I need to do in the field and you identify what you need to do in the house? Then, tomorrow we'll sit down again and compare and decide how we could help each other in order to find the common ground."

"That would be nice. But I may end up showing you what I used to do at Iren instead of writing it down," she said.

While I was finishing the seventh grade now, Ella already dropped out of school after the fifth grade. Writing something was more of a punishment for her than a necessary part of life. Writing was more of a mind-controlled matter, a thought arrangement that made no sense to her on paper and that she loathed with utter escape.

So the following morning, Ella became a totally different individual from yesterday, realizing that what she did at Iren's house was no different than what awaited her at our house.

The difference, however, was that at Iren she was ordered around to do things; while here, she had to find her own initiative to establish her own schedule. And that was the problem. She didn't know where to start. She lacked the organizational steps, and in that, where the beginning was.

So, for instance, when she started cooking a chicken stew, she already burned the onion in the pot, yet, the chicken was still on its legs, running around the yard. Or she wanted to make a fire in the potbelly stove without first starting it with kindle wood. Or she was washing dirty clothes without soaking them first. The flow of her work lacked the logical arrangement as to where the beginning was.

In my case, I had no problem at all. I was gifted and had the knack as to how my work trend evolved right from the beginning to the end. I had a complete view of the whole project. My problem was a different kind—speed. I was mostly in hurry to do things which resulted in skipping a step or two, and when I realized it, I had to go back to correct myself. So we both had shortcomings that lacked the *time-honored* experience. And there was nothing we could have done about it, for experience couldn't be copied from books which only taught guidance. It had to be acquired through practice by doing our chores and along the way learning from our mistakes.

We didn't have to sit down the second time, as she, without my saying another word, became her own boss and in some ways mine also. So we accepted each other's mistakes and learned from them as we worked side by side in order to finish the works that related to our household and to our garden.

There was, however, one inescapable truth—we had to eat if we wanted to live. For that reason alone, we had to plan as to how to get food for now, for tomorrow, and for the months that followed. So planning became a necessary part of our life, forced on us by hunger.

Then I said to Ella, "What if we thought about our daily work requirement based on feeding our stomach? You know, our eating needs depended on a timetable. What comes after what—daily, weekly, and monthly. What I mean is that if we don't weed the garden, the weeds would choke the growth of the plants and vegetables. Or if we don't raise chickens, ducks, and rabbits, we wouldn't have meat to eat in the coming months. Or if we don't harvest our crops in the field when they are ready, they would rot away."

It was in this manner that we organized ourselves, set up our work schedules, and carried out our works day in, day out. We survived the first few months on cornmeal, beans, and potatoes. And occasionally wild pigeons, sparrows, and even crows that I killed with my double-banded slingshot.

Nineteen fifty-three (1953) was our most difficult year, for it was the beginning of everything, so to say. It was the realization that we had to work for everything we needed and everything we wanted. That was the price we paid for our independence.

* * *

Within a few weeks, we had exhausted most of the supplies that Iren provided us after we left her. So now we scraped whatever we still had left in the attic from mother's storage: flour, cornmeal, dried beans, and nuts.

So I was in charge of creating the menu, gathering the ingredients, cooking them, and serving them. I never had it so easy to do it, yet never so hard to figure out what to cook from the meager supply. We rationed everything we had in order to make sure that it lasted until we grew our own.

Ella was in charge of cleaning the house, the dishes, and the clothes. The field work we did mostly together.

This was the way we held fast to our plans. This was the way we did the planting, weeding, hoeing, and timely harvesting. This was the way we acted as grown-ups but with the mindset of kids.

With all the house animals, we had one thing in common. They also needed to eat. They needed constant attention and care for their well-being; otherwise they relentlessly made noises, telling us that it was time to pay attention to them.

It was basically my job to take care of them. All I saw in them *now* was the meat that I always craved to eat. To keep them living and growing, I fed them leftovers and plenty of weed clippings from the roadside.

I didn't allow myself anymore to love farm animals as pets. I already learned my lessons before, as my heart broke too many times from knowing that I killed a pet because I was craving to eat meat. Once and for all I resolved: I closed my eyes, stiffened my mind, and gave my pets to the first gypsy who came by. A new era began with my independence. I had no more pets. All the animals we received from John and Iren, we had *dominion* over them, just as God intended them for us—food.

* * *

I thought that in our plan we laid out everything we wanted to do. But then after a short while, we realized that we didn't allow free time for fun. What we were doing now was nothing more or less than what the other peasants did—work in the fields and tend to the animals. And in between, talk about the affairs of neighbors and enemies. So we set aside three hours every evening after work to let ourselves do whatever we wanted, except work.

Since it was summer now, the real entertainment took place not in the fields but rather on the shores of Lake Balaton. Many foreigners and those with money returned and spent their vacations here, enjoying the tepid waters, the good home cooking, and the worry-free days next to a bottle of wine from Badacsony. The musicians and the entertainers from Budapest and elsewhere were also here to keep the minds and bodies of the young and the old fit for the occasion. In calm evenings we could hear the music and the singing as we walked around in the yard finishing the last things for the day. As we heard the evening entertainment going nonstop, we wanted to be part of it. So we spent our free time now on the shores of Lake Balaton—dancing, singing, and frolicking around as others did. After we released the nerve-wrecking stresses of the day, we started the next day with refreshed mind and body.

* * *

The most painful part of this summer is that Ildiko couldn't be with me. The confiscation of her father's business by the Communists made her family poor and made it impossible for them to have vacations. I understood that because I saw the well-to-do peasants in my village become poor overnight.

The Secret Police knew one thing very well, how to carry out orders from Rakosy (the top Communist), robbing the wealth from the rich and distributing it to those who clamored the most in supporting the socialist movement. They thought that eventually everybody would fall in line. How wrong they were is presented in the last chapter.

Once you had your hard-earned-money taken away, you become the best politician in the world. You wait and prepare for the first opportunity to take it back.

For all the evils these agents committed in the name of Communism, Ella and I were left relatively undisturbed. They were instructed to leave the youth, the *poor*, and *needy* alone; they were the only ones left now that comprised the bulk of the proletariat. They professed the socialistic ideology of Stalin and Rakosy—the masses that relied on the Communist regime for handout. We didn't belong to this group.

Ella and I received none of this handout. And we would not have accepted any, for there was a hidden *payback* to it, touting the ideology and banging the tables in fervent support of the socialistic movement.

More importantly, I always believed that the only thing was mine for which I worked; the only thing that nurtured my self-esteem and uncompromising integrity was what I received from others in return for my sweat. What made me exceptionally happy was that Ella supported me and followed my freedom-loving mentality in all the years we stayed together.

(Now, look at the affairs that are gripping this great nation today [2015]. I'm talking about the United States of America. Doesn't it look like a Communistic socialist movement? In fact, it is. I can tell you that, for I already lived through one. Watch out, for your *neighbor* will rob you blind. He thinks that your wealth rightfully belongs to him because he helped you build it. Watch out! Your *leaders* are chameleons, especially the president of the United States of America. Surreptitiously he follows Saul Alinsky's dogmatic, socialistic, and Communistic theories. Make sure you pull the correct lever next time you vote.)

* * *

My life had gone through many changes since last summer. These changes left their marks, some sadly and some happily. Which one to remember and which one to forget would depend on the events that would impact my unpredictable future. My beloved mentors, Joseph and Mr. Forro, were dead, but my devil-possessed bigots, Matild and Gary, were still living. Fast I wanted to forget these last two, but for some reason, they were a curse on me. They were like wild ivy in my garden; even though I pulled them out, they resurfaced later. This reminds me that there is such a thing as evil that never really disappears, only waits for the next opportunity to return.

Being keenly aware of my past, I never complained to Ella, nor I ever talked about it to others. But in the final analysis of my life on earth, it is worth to put the life story of my youth on paper so that my grandchildren can stimulate their vision from it and know that their future shall be only as promising as what they have learned from the past. And to that they should add their own imaginations to become better leaders in a society that is steadily turning away from God, turning away from democratic values in support of Communistic socialism.

CHAPTER TWENTY-THREE

The Unforgettable Christmas

The pigs were now big and fat, ready to be slaughtered at this appropriate time as Christmas was just around the corner. I heard almost every dawn the relentless squeaking of pigs as they were being quickly knifed to death through their hearts. So I would join the traditional event myself. I would ask my friend Steve Fodor, the fish scooper, to come and help slaughter one of the two pigs we had, now that Christmas was only a few days away.

Steve was already a skilled pig dresser. He learned the skill as he went from house to house to do it. So, on the day he is free to help, he will come and take care the bigger pig first. The smaller one, we were keeping for a while longer, as we didn't know yet whether to sell it or slaughter it.

So he came five days before Christmas and killed the pig. Quick as skilled folks are, he delegated some of the works to me with no less speed. The only things he allowed me to do was of course the mundane works: burning the pig's hair off, washing and scrubbing it clean, and holding it in place while he carved the carcass into neat pieces for further dressing. It took Ella and I days to finish the rest of the work, preserving the meat in brine, then in three weeks smoking it, and carefully storing it so that it wouldn't spoil.

I couldn't believe how fast Steve sliced that pig up, swinging his butcher knife to the exact spot he wanted to do the carving. In less than fifteen minutes, the whole pig disappeared from the top of the kitchen table without the slightest scratch to the wood. He carved out the rear legs first, then the front legs. I barely had time to move my hands around holding onto the carcass here and there. I was worried that he might cut into me. He swung his knife around as if he wanted to impress me. In fact, he not only impressed me but also dazzled me to the point that I have forgotten where the beginning was.

Standing next to him after he finished, I asked him, "Why the hurry, Steve?"

"It merely looked to you that way. That's the difference between knowing and learning.

"Don't you think that I deserve the best part of the pig for breakfast? Now that I did such a great job?"

"Which part is that?" I asked.

"Take the tenderloin that I already cut into slices and quick-fry them for me and maybe for you, but don't kill its taste by over-frying it," Steve explained.

I had no idea which part of the pig Steve was talking about; but since he already sliced the two loins to ten round pieces each, I took them and rolled them into flour and quick-fried them in hot lard.

I know that I was a big meat eater, but when I saw Steve eating the medium-fried pieces as quickly as I could serve them, I said to him: "Hold your mouth! The next batch is mine, Steve, if you don't mind."

"Make it half yours and half mine and let's talk about Christmas," he said.

So I did as he told me to do. But I let him do the talking while I was jamming the soft and juicy pieces down without stop. When he saw me eating nonstop, he threw his leftover pieces on my plate and said, "I'll wait until you finish. Do you know that you eat like a dog?" Steve remarked.

"Do you know that I was thinking the same thing about you? That's why I said, 'The next batch is mine,'" I countered.

"Looks like hard workers eat fast, don't they?" he commented.

After this, we talked about the sobering days of this Christmas and the meaning of it to us. This was one of the two holidays of the year that had the most symbolic traditions remembered and celebrated. The other was Easter. Everybody had something to remember about something shared from previous Christmases. And in that frame of mind, they wished to make the next one even better.

Up to now, I only understood the meaning of the birth of Jesus from the catechism—as the greatest gift of God. Since my parents died, my Christmas days passed as any other day, for I was poor and had nothing to give, nothing to share.

But this Christmas would be different because I wanted to make it different. I firmly believed that my angel had wiped out the thought of misery from my memory. The birth of Jesus Christ took away the memories about my past miseries. He opened my mind to see what I had and not what I didn't.

"Notice your freedom, notice that you have all the basics to survive!" My angel poured the thought into my mind and continued, "Granted that nobody else cared for you except God. Nobody else cared whether you lived or died."

This time, Christmas meant to be a thanksgiving day for me and my sister. And it is for a very good reason to say a few words to Jesus. Even to shed a few humble tears as we would honor the greatest gift of all, the memory of his birth. I know it in my heart that he was around, for I called on his name for the first time in my life. I was fourteen years old now.

"Jesus, I want a Christmas tree!"

I asked for something that only God himself could deliver, for Christmas was no longer celebrated, no longer honored as the birth date of Jesus. The Communists were making sure of that.

Nothing else would symbolize now for us the memory of this miracle more than having our own Christmas tree.

So I said to Steve, "I want this Christmas to be a very special day for my sister and me. Come and help me celebrate already the beginning of it."

"I just killed a pig for you, isn't that enough?" Steve reminded me.

"I don't have meat in mind this time, Steve. That feeds only my stomach. I want something else that nobody else has at this time. Something else that feeds my soul."

"And what's that, Arpad?" he asked.

"I want a Christmas tree. Would you come with me to get it?"

"Christmas trees don't grow around here. You would have to go to the other side of Lake Balaton to the hill country to get it, and that's more than thirty miles away," Steve explained.

"But we could get Christmas trees right here five miles away on the south side of the forest, where the gypsy camp is. I know that for sure because I went there many times before with my gypsy friend, Tony. We went there to watch the dear grazing and raising their fawns in the luscious grass around the pine trees. I'm surprised that you don't know that."

"Well then, I'll go with you. I'll bring back a tree for myself, too. But I think, we should go there first just to scout around and become familiar with the area. It's easy to get lost in the woods, you know," Steve recommended.

It was now four days before Christmas. About three inches of snow covered the grounds already, and I didn't care if it were a ten-foot pack. I had committed myself.

"Who in his right mind would want to trample the snow five miles one way to get a Christmas tree, Arpad?" Steve's remarks showed that he was hesitant to come.

"Well, in that case, I'll go alone. As they say, 'follow your heart,'" I responded. "And in my heart there is nothing more important now than having a Christmas tree."

"But, then, why shouldn't I go with you? If for no other reason, I want to show you that I am a good friend of yours. I won't let you go alone. It would be nice, though, if Ella could come with us also. She could be on the lookout for the rangers," he said.

The way Steve behaved, however, suggested to me that it was not really Christmas that occupied his mind. From the moment he came to take care of the pig, right up to this moment, his eyes furtively followed Ella's movements.

"I don't think that I would let Ella get involved in this, Steve. She doesn't have snow boots, and she couldn't run just in case. Besides, she is a scaredy-cat in strange places," I said.

With this said, Steve gave up trying to win over Ella's attention. She didn't even notice that Steve was eyeing her all this time.

* * *

So we set out late afternoon the following day in order to accomplish the seemingly scary adventure, getting a Christmas tree from the middle of nowhere. Along the way, I guided Steve toward the gypsy camp. When we came close, I said to him, "Let's stop here, for I want to talk to the chief from whom I once bought two big wooden vats we now use for brining the hams and the bacon. I'm sure that he knows the area better than anybody. You wait here, Steve, until I return."

There were about twenty clay-covered huts scattered all over on this ten-acre territory, and I have to find the chief somewhere

here. Each hut had a stove pipe stuck through the pitched roof and was smoking. A light wind was blowing the smoke in the southern direction, and crows were circling above. It was cloudy, but no new snow was falling. There was no sign other than the dancing smoke and the flying crows that indicated life. One set of footprints showed that somebody left the camp.

I gave up and turned around, knowing from previous times that this place was not just any place one would freely move around.

Tony's place was burned to the ground a couple of years ago because he was not a clan member. Being scared as well, I headed back to Steve. My head turned from hut to hut in case someone showed his face. Nobody did. As I left the last hut, I looked toward Steve and noticed that he was talking to a man. Drawing closer and closer, I recognized him. He was the son of the chief, who a couple of years ago was with his father when I bought the wooden vats from them. Since I didn't know his name, I introduced myself first, and he recognized me. But he didn't say his name. So I started talking to him while Steve was jumping up and down, warming his feet as it was freezing. He wore sneakers.

"You remember when I bought those vats from your father a couple of years ago? I want to see him now and ask him a question or two about those pine trees at the end of the woods, yonder." I pointed in that direction and waited for his reply. He looked in that direction also and shook his head.

"You don't want to go near that place now."

"Why not?" I asked.

"Don't you know that it is close to Christmas now and a lot of folks from the neighboring villages want pine trees? Previous years, we used to bring them to the villagers, but now everybody is scared. There are two rangers circling the area, and I think they are looking out for us, gypsies, that we wouldn't go there and cut the trees for the villagers this year. I just came from there and watched them from behind the laurel bushes."

"And what did you see?"

"They are patrolling the area at each end of the property. They have a campfire going. While one is patrolling, the other is warming himself," he said.

"Did they ever take a break?" I asked.

"Yes, they did. Right around midnight, they put out the campfire and disappeared. I have been watching them for several nights now, and they did the same thing every night."

"And where did they go, you know?" Steve finally opened his mouth.

"I think they went home. What tells me that they went home is the fact that not the same guys showed up every night. You see, the place belongs to the town of Kethely, and I think the members of the cooperative there are taking turns to watch the place."

"Did you try to take down a treetop after midnight?" I asked him.

"Not yet. I can't climb, and these trees are quite slim and tall. Can you climb, Arpad?"

I didn't tell the gypsy that I could climb like a monkey and could sway a three top until it would practically touch the other tree. So I said to the gypsy instead, "We want to take home a couple of treetops. If you join us, we would give you one."

"But you can't go there now. It is only five a clock. Why don't you come to my place and keep yourselves warm until after midnight? Then, I go there with you."

So it happened that both of us slumbered inside the gypsy hut for about seven hours while the gypsy tended the fire. The space inside was no bigger than eight feet in diameter. He was now the new chief and owned the first hut at the very entrance to the camp.

The offensive smell inside the hut kept me up because the gypsy was broiling the hind leg of a boar on the open pit. He wanted to serve it to us after midnight. Since I couldn't sleep, I decided to watch him; and within a short while, I joined him holding and turning the other end of the stick which held the leg. This way, the whole piece broiled through and through. While we did this, I asked him how come that he was the new chief of the clan now.

"I buried my father two years ago and was in line to be the next chief, as I'm the firstborn male. I have seven brothers and eight sisters. They all live here in the various huts behind me," he explained.

I suddenly remembered that it was about two years ago when I watched the end of his father's burial ceremony with Tony from the top of the hill across the gypsy camp. I wasn't sure then that it was his father who was buried. Now I know that it was he.

Two years in my life was a very long time, the incident at the time was only a passing moment. I watched the ceremony more from curiosity than from attachment to keep such a thing in mind. But the memory of this event brought back thinking about the good times I spent with Tony in this area. And for that reason, I wanted to ask the gypsy whether he knew Tony. But, then, I changed my mind, for I didn't want him to know that it was I and Tony who invaded their privacy so often by threading the creek up and down next to his camp, looking for brook trout. I didn't want him to turn his feelings against me now and chase us out in revenge for our intrusion.

But the gypsy saw my face as I was rerunning past memories. He saw my face perfectly clear as I was sitting next to the fire opposite him. Then he asked, "What went on in your mind that you stopped talking?"

"I was figuring out how we should go about cutting the treetops without being caught doing it." I didn't tell him anything about Tony.

"I'll tell you how," the gypsy said. "I'm thinking about the same plan you were thinking of. Here it is what I'm thinking. After we eat, the three of us would go to my lookout spot and check if the fire was still burning. If it wasn't, it would mean the watchmen went home. It is from my end of the grove they would be going home. This end is the high point of the hill, and if the moon is out, I would see them walking downhill almost to the edge of Kethely, the village they come from. On the other hand, if the fire is still burning, we could either wait or go to my camp and come back later."

"Sounds great!" I replied.

Even though the boar's leg was fully broiled, it still had the smell of spoiled meat, and I wouldn't eat any of it. Two things I'm finicky about even to this day—the smell and the taste of food. Steve didn't feel that way, so I didn't say anything to him. And the gypsy was already tearing and eating his share with such gusto that the grease was flowing down his arms onto the still flickering amber. The smoke from it filled the space to the point of choking me to death. I ran out and waited outside until the others rolled out, one holding the shank part, the other the butt part of the leg. While they were eating, I couldn't go near them. Because the fume had drenched their clothing and the smell of it made me want to throw up, I kept my distance farther. But our next move required us to stay close together. So I closed the gap with them and led the pack even though I didn't know where I was going. The gypsy behind me tapped my left or my right with the shank to signal which way to turn. In a few minutes fresh air returned, for the gypsy threw the foul-smelling shank away. Then, I switched places with him as we were coming closer and closer to the laurel bushes. The sky cleared, and the moon brightened the horizon to almost unreal clarity. The air was cold and still.

The last few hundred feet, we tiptoed to the place in order to silence the crackling sound of dried twigs breaking apart under our feet. As we arrived to the place, the gypsy pointed in the direction the watchmen were already threading their way in the snow heading home.

"Let's wait here a few more minutes in case there is another group that has already replaced the old guard," I whispered.

"That would be true if the fire was still burning," the gypsy whispered.

What added reassurance that there were no other people patrolling the area was the appearance of deer at the edges of the pine trees, already scraping the snow to get to the grass below it. They would not have been there had a person been present nearby.

"How long would it take you to climb three trees and cut their tops, Arpad?" The gypsy asked.

"I'll climb one tree only and swing over to the others. That way, I would cut the tops off in no time.

"And while I do it, Steve, you stand near the trees and take the dropped tops and tie them individually in a neat bundle. You, my friend (the gypsy), keep your eyes rolling in all directions, and if you notice someone's coming, hiss like an angry deer and run back to your camp."

That was the command I gave to each of them.

While I gave the orders, I had already picked out the trees that were very close to each other and made myself ready for the climb. By the time I uttered the last word, I had pulled my boots off and climbed the first tree just like a monkey would from branch to branch. Being close to the top, I took my pocket knife and as quickly as I could slit the skin around the stem of the tree in line with my chin. The six-foot-long stem, being solidly frozen, broke away like an icicle cone from a gutter as I struck it with my hand.

Then, I held onto the trunk with both hands and swung it back and forth a few times until I was able to grab the next and then the next tree. In this manner, I fell the treetops in about ten minutes. When I climbed down the last tree, I saw that Steve was still confused, trying to figure out how to wrap the treetops in a neat bundle. The gypsy, on the other hand, was in utter delirium. He expected my falling and killing myself on the spot.

Now, I slipped my boots on, danced in place for a minute or so in order to bring life back to my toes. We left the place as fast as we entered it.

Then, on parting from the gypsy at the camp, I gave him the last treetop and wished him a *merry Christmas.*

Steve and I chose a different path coming home, threading the snow covered field diagonally in order to shorten the distance. Thereby, we avoided those who might have had similar thoughts. Halfway in the meadows, we stopped for a short break and prided each other over the dreadful job we successfully accomplished in the spirit of Christmas. It was three o'clock in the morning when we arrived home and parted company. In my joy, I thought the way to heaven was just beginning to open.

So I tried and succeeded. How good it was dreaming of a merry Christmas becoming a reality! How good it would be to share the joy with my sister who was anxiously waiting to see the silvery shine of a Christmas tree through the light of a faintly flickering candle! How good it would be to share that one apple that would be hanging on the tree as the only present we could offer to each other—split in half and slowly eaten, and being thankful even for that. Christmas became a reality, and we celebrated it just as I thought we would be. The Lord heard my cry after all.

Going through hardship to survive, I had suddenly forgotten it during this fleeting moment of joy during this Christmas. All the more joyfully we celebrated this Christmas, for we knew that it was forbidden to honor the undeniable truth—the rebirth of Christ in the hearts of those who loved him.

Other Christmases came and went with memories repeated. But this Christmas left an indelible image that reflected the birth of the Child Christ who came into the world with nothing other than the love of his mother and father. I don't have that love now, but I have a Christmas tree that reminds me of that love, of that first Christmas I remembered celebrating with my mother and father. I was then five years old.

CHAPTER TWENTY-FOUR

My Stubborn Nature

Now I was fifteen years old and finished my eighth-grade elementary school with only passing grades. That didn't bother me at all, for book-learning was not my style of education. I figured that book-learning was good for those who had little to no life experience and didn't need to face survival without parents. I could have been an excellent student had my teachers not forced *denial of the past* on me to the extent they did. All grades and promotions were based on who could excel better in declaring the socialist movement. And there were many who did, for their future depended on it. They could express themselves in terms of the new learning methods which highlighted and professed the socialistic study materials recently written by acclaimed Communist authors. Most of them were recently freed from prisons by the hated Soviet Army.

At the end of May 1954 my school year ended, and by that time, we finished planting everything in the fields.

Leaving Balatonkeresztur became now the main point of discussion with Ella, but she didn't want to hear again any of my future planning. Up to now, she only guessed the reason as to why I traveled to Budapest every month. I finally broke the news to her that I was in love with Ildiko and now wanted to move closer to her.

I said to Ella, "Come along with me. I want to look for work in Budapest. Don't you want to visit Iren? I would pick you up on my way back in a couple of days."

"What about the animals?" she asked.

"They won't die for two days. I will give them enough food and water that will last even for five days. They aren't clock watchers, you know. All they care for is food and water."

"You don't care much about their well-being, do you?"

"Whose well-being is more important, the chickens' or mine?"

The next day we traveled without letting anybody know about it. It would not have mattered anyway whether anybody knew it or not. As I said earlier that my place was where my heart is. I belonged to Ildiko, and she belonged to me.

* * *

The train's steady *clacking* over the rails' joints lulled Ella to sleep. Nothing else to do, I picked up a newspaper someone left behind on the seat and started reading. I had the habit of reading newspapers beginning with the back page first. I thought the front page was always full of drama which excited me no more than gossip that I always hated. Right now, I was only interested in the *employment* section, thinking that if I wanted to live in Budapest, I would have to look for a job there.

I was now both fascinated and dumbfounded as I realized that each job offer required skills and experience. I had experience, all right, but in farming and caring for domestic animals. That was not something people pursued in Budapest. That was demeaning to them, to say the least. Then, I started analyzing and questioning myself.

What did I have that would make employers interested in me?

Well, I was good-looking, full of life with eagerness to face any challenge. I had good manners and astounding faith in myself, and I had a persuasive personality to prove it. I couldn't deny any of these even if I wanted to because my behavior with others would have rather quickly revealed that I had overwhelming control of myself.

Could it be that positive attitude I had in myself that would be the first sign of interest that employers looked for in a person? I think that I was overpromoting myself as I was feeding my ego, I concluded.

So I decided that I wouldn't brag about myself at all, not even to myself, for what I had to offer most was the willingness to work and learn along the way. My other qualities would surface anyway as I would be mingling with people. These thoughts numbed my mind and tired me out. The newspaper fell out of my hand, and I fell asleep, dropping my head on Ella's left shoulder.

My nap would have lasted probably till my arrival at Szekesfehervar if it wasn't for a terrible dream. A drowning feeling came over me in my dream. I was swimming upward from the bottom of a huge waterfall and kept falling back just as I almost reached the top. Trying and trying to overcome this exasperating feeling, my hands and feet were swimming in the air. Everybody watched me doing it and laughed.

Finally, a middle-aged woman jumped on me from the opposite bench in the same compartment and shook me back to reality. She fell on me as if she wanted to rescue me from drowning. She recognized that I had a nightmare and that only a sudden wake-up could stop it. As I woke up, I didn't know what to say or do. I was in shock over the incident. Imitating the herd mentality of others, I laughed as loud as I could with everybody else. Ella nudged me. "Stop faking yourself."

"This sort of thing could happen to anybody," the woman said, "especially when one is troubled over something."

The train reached Szekesfehervar shortly after my nightmare, and everybody had to depart to reach the connecting trains. Ella had to take a different train than I. My train would be the Budapest Express; hers would be a local, commuter train. Mine didn't stop at Martonvasar, while hers did.

As the people rushed to reach their connecting trains, they moved in all directions like bees in and out of their hive. Ella and I did the same thing. The only thing that delayed the rush was that people were pulling their baggage behind them or were carrying them in their hands, bumping into each other without thinking that they might break the wine jugs or the free-rolling eggs others carried. These minor accidents made the rushing travelers yell nasty words at each other, and the push and shove at times ended in fistfights, doing more damage to the already damaged goods. While I took notice of these incidents, I pranced around everybody like a lost dog looking for his owner in the crowd.

My backpack was the only thing I carried. I dangled it in my hands in order to avoid the pickpockets who frequented this crowded area, looking for tight spots so as their moves might not be noticed. They once sliced already the outer pocket of my backpack and lifted the cash I had stashed there. This time I was smarter; I dangled it, thinking I could even swing it against the head of a thief should I see one in the act of stealing. My backpack was light, as I only had a pair of clean underwear and a fried rabbit in it.

This senseless rush at this railroad station was unavoidable since this place was the largest rail connecting hub for all the trains in the western part of Hungary. Train delays were frequent, and sometimes the connecting train didn't wait for the passengers. Therefore, the rush was on day and night in order to reach that interconnecting train which may have been parked on the thirtieth track. Mine was on the fifth track, but I still had to go through the underground passageway in order to reach it. Since I didn't know when my train would be leaving, I was rushing to it, too, as if free dinner were served in its eloquent dining hall on the first-come–first-served basis.

* * *

Along the way to my connecting train, I bumped into the same woman who shook the hell out of my nightmare a few minutes ago. My loud and quick apology sounded odd to her in this busy place where pushovers were as natural as the noise was in the crowd. Yet she gazed at me in her surprise.

"It's you again! Come, we'll sit together in the dining room, and I'll interpret your dream."

"Are you for real or what? Nobody can interpret dreams," I replied.

"I can come pretty close to it. Come and find out," she insisted.

We ended sitting together in the train's dining hall all the way to Budapest. Since it was close to noon now, it was time to order cooked food. As the waitress rushed by, carrying the spicy stews and garlic bread, the strong odor juiced up my companion's appetite all the more. She was a fat lady. Meanwhile, the train slowly left the station.

There was only one menu on the table, and it was already in the hands of my companion. So I changed my seat and went to her side of the table. I didn't do this from curiosity to look over her shoulders to read the menu, but rather from my eagerness to introduce myself and at the same time find out her name. I was troubled about not knowing how to call her, for she looked to me exceptionally direct and open-minded to talk about anything. In ways, she resembled my own attitude dealing with people—be direct, if you want attention.

So I interrupted her.

"It would please me to know how to call you, madam. My name is Arpad."

She dropped the menu flat on the table and turned to me. She was curiously surprised hearing this uncanny village boy calling on her with the courage of a salesman, wanting to know her name.

"My name is Sara but I hate that name, so call me Zsizsi instead. What are you going to do in Budapest?" she asked.

"I'm coming to stretch my imagination. I don't know what I want to do with myself. Since I could travel free, I thought that I come to Budapest, thereby running into somebody who might clear my mind and tell me where to look for work. I don't know whether I want to choose a trade school, a dancing school, or just being a helper doing anything people wanted me to do," I replied.

"Are you going to order something to eat or hold me up from ordering my lunch? You talk too much. I'll clear your mind after I eat. Don't you see the waitress is waiting to take my orders?"

"Go ahead, madam, and order your meal. I have mine in my backpack."

"You can't eat from your backpack here. You do that at a curb where you can throw the bones to the dogs. Order something, and I'll pay for it!" she stressed the words.

After Zsizsi ordered something that sounded like a smorgasbord platter, I ordered a bottle of wine, thinking that that would be the best thing for her to wash all that food down with it. I didn't order anything for myself, for I had no money and, besides, was not hungry for food that was handled by the bare hands of others. I was always mindful of dirty hands touching my clothes or food. Yet I couldn't explain why I was like that.

"I can tell you, Arpad, you are coming from a vineyard, ordering wine for lunch."

"I ordered it for you, Zsizsi. But I would like to have a sip with you so that you may know that I'm not embarrassed by what you just said. I'm not coming from a vineyard; I'm coming from a village where I live with my sister. My folks are dead. We are orphans and do everything on our own."

This stout lady wore a colorful, baggy dress, apparently to hide her weight more than to highlight her aggressive looking, beautiful face. She turned her body as she looked at me and tried to interpret the secrets of my soul. She steadied her eyes for a moment on my forehead, then switched them to look at my hands. I moved back now where I sat before and listened to her like a patient wanting to hear everything the doctor said.

"You have a sizeable forehead with several furrows across it. You will be a world traveler. And your hands, big as if you were already a boxer. You will need them as you will be handling tools and machines."

"Are you a palm reader, Zsizsi? Or a customs agent?" I asked.

"I'm neither, but I had already explored the faces and hands of thousands of people as I hired them for my company. And you are just one of those I see being hired to work for me. Time will tell whether what I just said will happen or not. Keep in mind, though, what I just said. After I eat, I'll tell you what I have in mind for you," she concluded.

Since she was the personnel manager of a giant company, she hired hundreds if not thousands of individuals who were seeking work. So she hired people by reading their personalities through listening to their talking and studying their body features. And I was just one of those individuals with one exception. I was fifteen years old.

Now the food platter was placed in the middle of the table, and a bottle of wine was in the hands of the waitress. It was already uncorked for Zsizsi to taste it. After tasting it, she nodded as a sign of acceptance. I sat there and watched the entire event taking place without any of them looking at me or saying anything to me. My eyes were fixed on the food platter on which the various meat slices and vegetables were neatly and tastefully placed that indicated the chef's skills. I already eyed the pieces I would take if only I were to be invited to share the meal. After Zsizsi tasted the wine, she lifted her glass to the bottle, wanting a refill. One refill after another, she finished the whole bottle of wine herself at once.

Then, she ordered the waitress to take the platter and individually wrap everything and bring the whole thing back to her. The waitress hesitated, but Zsizsi prompted her, "Go on, follow what I said!" My eyes never left the platter until this beautiful, young waitress disappeared with it. My taste buds were teased for nothing. I was hungrier now far more than I had been before. And yet, I had a fried rabbit in my backpack that I was not allowed to eat in this fancy place.

Then, Zsizsi turned and looked at me again.

"I am looking forward to going with you to the company I represent."

With her ebullient face and jolly mood, she rolled her eyes to commend me to follow her.

"Time is running out now to leisurely enjoy feasting. We are almost in Budapest. I hope you would come with me to my office and we would eat the food there and also would talk things over. I could even take you on a tour of my company so that you would have some idea as to what I'm doing. And along the way, you could churn your mind and see whether you liked something you might want to do for me.

"I'm doing this just for you because as I was growing up on the streets in Budapest, a rich Jewish family took me in and raised me up with their own kids. They treated me as if I was their own kind. Part of me collapsed when they were taken away by the Nazis. I never heard from them since. When you mentioned that you are an orphan, I said to myself, 'This would be my first chance to return a little bit of the kindness and goodness I received from this Jewish family.'"

When I heard all this from Zsizsi, I knew the reasons immediately as to why she was so outpouring with her almost motherly caring.

God, forbid me to stop her now! "I'm in dire need of a job to support myself" erupted in my mind the same way as she poured out her willingness to help me to find a job in Budapest.

We took a tramcar from the railroad station to the company where Zsizsi worked and also had her office. When I saw the size and the number of buildings this company occupied right on the shores of the Danube River, I thought that I just reached hell, a place of no return. Everything was in disrepair. Machine parts, iron beams, wire rods, and who knows what else were in disarray and scattered all over the yard of this vast place.

There were more loafers, walking around pointing to this or to that than workers who would tidy up the place instead. We passed everything and everybody. Those who recognized Zsizsi raised their hands waving at her or yelling "hallo" from as far back as the water's edge. I was wondering now as to how the inside of this place looked like, judging everything from the chaotic scene on the outside. But I didn't say anything. I just followed Zsizsi as she paced her steps like a fat duck, looking all over and shifting her weight from one side to the other in order that she wouldn't trip over the coiled wires or the loose machine parts.

"I'm leading you through the back end of this place. This way you would be able to see later how these loose parts were used inside the shops in order to make useful things out of them," she explained.

I kept my impressions to myself and said nothing. I was worried over one thing only, that by any misstep I would drop the wrapped platter, as I was carrying it in one hand and my backpack in the other. I was hopping around with them after her. I wanted nothing more now than to eat those pieces that I had already so keenly eyed for myself on the platter in the train's dining hall. Hunger had suddenly replaced my job hunting adventures for now.

What I had seen all around so far didn't convince me that anything good would come out of this collection of junks scattered all over even to the banks of the gently whirling waters of the Danube River.

Finally, we entered a building from the front. Nothing that was behind it was visible here. Even if I wanted to, I couldn't tell what was going on inside. We now walked through a large room that looked to me much like the classroom I used to attend in my school days. Four rows of student chairs lined in front of a rickety bench behind which the pictures of Lenin, Rakosy, and Stalin were prominently displayed. I placed the still wrapped platter on this desk and politely waited.

"This area is the conference hall," Zsizsi said and continued. "Once in a while we gather here to listen to lectures by party officials. Other times, I call the trainees here, together with their bosses, to excite them about their jobs and their attitudes toward their jobs. Call this more like a screening room, where the trainees are also evaluated on their progress, on their performance, and on their attitudes toward teamwork. Those who fail to meet the *basic requirements* are let go.

"You can be part of this group if you want to and learn one of the skills in the metal's forming field. You could become a locksmith, a tool maker, a blacksmith, or even a machine repair expert. It is a two-year program with pay. When I looked at your hands, I thought you possessed the strength and skill to do this type of work. Part of my job is to oversee the management of this trade school. I would probably see you every day if you stayed. Think about it for a while," she said.

Zsizsi had turned my head into a conveyer belt that carried all the individual pieces from the back to specific individuals who were training people in one of the trades. I felt that I was riding now on this conveyer only to be dropped off any place where I would be worked over by a wise guy to become a metal bender or shaper and maker of something useful. The thought of these things scared the heck out of me, for I knew nothing about these things. Nothing at all.

Then, as quickly as these thoughts left my mind, reality spoke for itself.

"Don't worry about your imagination. It's beyond reality. Worry about what you see. Very few things in your life were foretold, except this one now—a job with pay." The thought encouraged me to follow Zsizsi.

Now, we left the room which I thought was used more for brainwashing than for anything else. What else would be the reason if not brainwashing as to why those pictures were hanging on the wall? A look at them was enough for me to spit on them, for the tyranny they committed in the name of Communism was now repeated in Hungary. They hoodwinked the brains of those who followed them.

"Let's go through one more building, Arpad, before we settle for lunch. Bring the platter, will you?" Zsizsi ordered.

The inside of this other building looked to me more unusual than anything I had ever seen or even dreamed about seeing. It was full of machines, full of people, and full of smoke. The noise alone made Zsizsi to point at things instead of talking about them. It made no difference to me whether she did or not. I didn't understand anything anyway. But I saw that some people were operating machines; others were beating glowing metal pieces and forming them into plow sheers for the collective farms' equipment. And still others were busy on workbenches. They were hacksawing, hammering, and filing chunks of metal pieces that would be formed into things only they knew.

"This is the workshop," Zsizsi yelled in my ears on account of the noise. "The stuff that looked like junk in the backyard is used here to make all types of tools, machine parts and more. Very creative work is happening here. Look at your hands and think that you might be doing the same works here."

And as I looked at my hands, I realized that manual work was dirty work wherever it was done. I remembered cleaning the stalls and the animals at Joseph's and at my godfather's. Also remembered the field works and washing my dirty clothes. All of them soiled my hands up to my elbows and at times beyond. So what difference would it make now if I would dirty my hands and face with soot and rust and oil? I would have it a million times better here than back home. I wouldn't have to worry about anything, for everything would be provided in exchange for eight hours of work *with pay*. This would turn out to be the least expected luck in my life. "I should go for it" peppered my imagination. As the lightning rushed through the sky, so fast I was convinced about staying here. I became interested in being part of this noisy, smoky, and dirty place at once.

My imagination for a better future was the greatest joyride of my mind now. I couldn't wait for Zsizsi to finish showing the rest of the shop. I already imagined myself to be part of it. But not only part of this place, I would be part of Budapest, the cultural center of the country. I would also be minutes away from Ildiko.

The only thing left now to do was eating lunch and working out the details. This would also fulfill Zsizsi's wish—returning the kindness and goodness that that Jewish family had given her in her growing years.

"The best part of the day is coming up, Arpad. Food, food, and more food! Food for the belly and food for the mind!" Zsizsi exploded.

"What do you mean by 'food for the mind'?'"

"I fed your mind all this time in the shops in order to convince you of one thing—choosing a career."

"I was only helping you to swim to the top of that waterfall that you were trying to reach in your nightmare. Remember, I told you that I would interpret your nightmare? The fear you had was all about not being able to find a job in Budapest. Well, I'll offer you one now. While we eat, you make a decision and tell me whether you would accept or turn down my advice."

"Zsizsi, I called you a palm reader and a customs agent before. I would like to take all that back. I realize now that you are a very smart guidance counselor. You took the place of my mother and father. You know at my age my youthful mind is more on dreams than on reality. Tell me, Zsizsi, do you really think that I should take this job?"

"Look at it this way, Arpad. Parents look at their children, and they look to see if they could recognize very early what they liked or disliked the most. For what the kids liked the most, they would want to do that the most. Accordingly, the parents would guide their children to be successful in life. I was trying to guide you, especially in your desperate situation as you are in now. So I honestly think you should take this opportunity to become a toolmaker."

"What do toolmakers do, Zsizsi?"

"A toolmaker is an all-around creator or repairer of anything made out of metal. He operates metal cutting machines and uses all types of hand tools in order to complete his work. He reads blueprints and works with those who imagined them. He can even recommend better ways to rethink and improve their basic ideas. It is a very interesting trade in which there is never a boring moment, for a toolmaker has to read the minds of others and reduce their ideas to become the real thing with sound quality and function."

"Well, in some ways that is something I always did. I planned to make things better for myself. Mine, of course, was more earthbound because I was closer to the ground, closer probably than most toolmakers would ever want to be."

"You already proved to yourself that you could use your mind, not just your hands to plan things and follow them to the end. Peasants do that very well. Just look around in the farmers market. All the nice fruits and vegetables that you see there come from the smart plantings that peasants do. They plan their work, too. They plant the seeds at the right time and harvest the goods just before they are fully ripened. Then, they bring them to Budapest. So planning is a necessary step to do for every smart person. Even a child shows signs of thinking to outsmart his parents, especially when it comes to bedtime. In your case, you would be working together with many other individuals, and you would be sharing your planning with theirs. That is, if you heed my advice. It would be a give-and-take situation," Zsizsi explained.

"That would mean that I would have to give up my own way of doing things. It would mean a lot of listening and following orders. Would it not be?" I asked.

"Arpad, when it comes to learning something new, we all have to listen to different voices beside our own. That is the way we let go our stubborn nature—that we know everything better than others do."

What Zsizsi said to me was enough to realize that from now on I would have to give up part or all of my stubbornness.

As often as it happened before, I questioned myself again whether I should accept or reject what she said. It is hardly possible to give up my stubborn past. But at last, I convinced myself to listen to her, for I was no better from anybody else when it came to learning—give up the beaten track and opt for improvement. I was now convinced that I had to outgrow my bad habits along with my stubbornness for the sake of improvement.

Learning for the sake of getting ahead, I was more certain now than ever before. The good that I saw coming my way made everything even better through Zsizsi's eyes. With that I punctuated my decision.

"I hear your voice, Zsizsi. Your way is the better way to learn new things than sticking to my stubborn ways and proving myself wrong later. Better to improve myself through learning from others. I'll accept your advice and take the job. Apparently, the zesty food I just ate gave me the needed energy to sort out my doubts about this job and to see my future through your discretion rather than mine," I replied.

"I feel much elated about that, Arpad. Both of us did something praiseworthy," she said.

Having said that, she took a piece a paper from the shelf next to her and said, "Let's make this thing binding. In case I drop dead, you still would have a job here."

She filled out the application for employment, and we signed it.

Within two weeks, I would become an apprentice, working and learning to become a toolmaker *with pay*.

* * *

Now, I traveled to Rackeresztur to pick up Ella. On my way there, I summed up what I had accomplished so far today. I couldn't believe that things had happened the way they did. I came to the conclusion that it was God who laid down my path, either to hell or to heaven. It looked, though, that I would be heading to heaven through hell first.

In one day, Zsizsi impacted my life similarly as that of the death of my mother. But, unlike my mother's death that threw me into the hands of vultures, Zsizsi's actions ushered in the promise of a better future. That better future was within my grasp now, and I wouldn't let it go for anything else. I had a job with pay.

It was time now to arrange all my activities so that I could orderly and peacefully make the transition from Balatonkeresztur to Budapest. It was time now to break the news to my sisters, for their life would also be greatly impacted by my sound decision.

* * *

I was happy that I was lucky and that I met someone who thought that I was lost in the untamed world and that she recognized it and acted on her impulses to guide me out of it. I could never repay that to her, for I think it was inspirationally given to her, returning the kindness of that Jewish family who raised her. On my part I can only shower her with many thanks and occasionally give her red roses to show that I have not forgotten her kindness.

Now I turned my attention to the overwhelming task of figuring out how to give up my home in Balatonkeresztur for which Ella and I had tirelessly worked to make it a happy place. It was sweet enough to call it my home. It was the fruition of our hard work which would now be sacred in our memories, as the place where we appreciated even the smallest things in life—like that one apple on our Christmas tree.

My sisters had no idea about my lucky day in Budapest. Judging them from the past, they would probably doubt that there was such a thing in my life as a lucky day.

Having left Budapest in such excitement, I completely forgot to visit Ildiko. As my train stopped at several places before reaching Martonvasar, I had time on hand now to write her a short letter, explaining my reasons without any excuses. Since I was not good at inventing excuses, my letter was rather short and blunt: "I'm moving to Budapest. I found a job there. I have a lot to tell you. Will see you in about two weeks."

Since now I missed the bus to Rackeresztur on account of my train coming late from Budapest, I walked the three-mile distance. As I walked, I was fascinated seeing the sunflower fields in full bloom on both sides of the road; but I was in pain as I could not describe the beauty of it. Words didn't come to my pen as quickly and clearly as what my eyes wanted to say.

It was late evening, not yet dark. The evening twilight with its disappearing beauty kept my mind fully occupied, noticing everything that moved on the ground, everything that appeared in the sky and on the horizon. And now, of course, men and beasts were all heading home from the fields and grazing lands. I was going in the opposite direction and didn't know who to talk to or who to ignore. Because I walked on this road so many times before, I believed that every passerby knew me and could even recognize me by my footprints. I hoped that darkness would blanket the scene fast so that I wouldn't have to recognize anybody anymore. So I hid myself behind a large milestone and fell asleep there. I was awakened by a lovely kitten, sitting and purring in my lap.

Soon enough after that, I reached Iren's house and saw that the whole family was sitting outside in the center of the front yard. The cool evening breeze invited them outside, for inside the house, it was unbearably hot at times like this. The scorching sun heated the mud walls so warm that even the houseflies hurried outside through the open door. They only flew, though, as far as the relatives were, for they could smell human bodies equally well outside as inside.

Nobody expected me to show up at ten o'clock in the evening. They should have, for I was exceptionally fit to do the unexpected.

In order to surprise my relatives, who were now busily fanning the air and enjoying the cool breeze, I didn't show up at the front gate; rather, I snuck by the outside of the wire fence, all the way to the back end of the garden. There, I threw my backpack over the fence and hurled myself over it also by gripping the fence post. As I shuffled through the weeds to reach them, my nose caught the smell of ripening peaches and that was all I needed to do the unexpected. I filled the inside of my shirt with peaches, and as soon as I reached the folks, I pulled my shirt open and the peaches rolled on top of the bench before everybody.

"A thief was in your garden, Iren, and I caught him in the act and took the peaches away."

"How did you get in there, and how did the thief get in there?" she asked, being dumbfounded over the incident.

Iren's children grabbed the peaches as fast as they rolled in front of them. They were forbidden to go near any peach tree with ripening fruit on it, for their mother canned or made jam from everything, even from the half-rotten fruit that already fell to the ground.

"I was the thief, Iren. I wanted to surprise you. I jumped the fence, and I picked the peaches," I declared.

"I should have expected anything from you, the daredevil in my life. Besides grabbing my peaches, did you do anything else crooked today?" she asked.

"I never really do anything crooked, Sister. If I do, it is to teach a lesson. This time, I was thinking that instead of berating your children not to go near your ripening peaches, you should have sent them there to guard them from thieves who are most active right after dark. The kids would have caught me in the act of stripping your peaches, thinking that I was a gypsy. But upon recognizing me, I would have told them, 'Eat all you want, for another opportunity like this, you might never have.' Then, I would have added, 'Fill your baggy shirts and bring peaches to the others, for they were also forbidden to go near the trees.' I would have done this to you to teach you a lesson. You see, Sister, the greedier you are about your peaches, the more you will regret it later. For your children are children only once in your lifetime," I replied.

And I was glad that I said what I said because the following morning when Iren went to her garden, she saw that someone stole all her peaches. The gypsies had cut the wire fence open and had stolen them.

When Iren saw me at the entrance to her garden, she hollered to me from the peach trees.

"You are not only the daredevil in my life, but you are also my doomsayer. No more peaches, no more jam!"

"Don't worry, Sister. It won't be long before I wouldn't be around to warn you. You not only lost your peaches, but you also lost me. I am moving to Budapest in two weeks. Ella shall stay here with you after that," I responded.

"Sounds like another crazy idea just flushed out of your head so early in the morning. I have to sit down now before I faint."

So we sat down on the same bench the family sat last night, for I wanted to explain everything to her that happened yesterday between me and Zsizsi.

She quickly interrupted: "So you would give up everything at home, just like that? One day in heaven, the next day in hell! What will you do in Budapest? Begging the streets for scraps? Then, come back to me hungry as a beast. Should I pity you then?"

She exhorted me without allowing me to say another word about my good luck yesterday. She didn't believe that I would be an apprentice to become a toolmaker and, with it, have a job lined up to support myself. But that was not the end of it.

"What's going to happen with everything that you and Ella worked for? You gained your freedom from me and told the whole world, 'Go to hell.'"

She was breaking down both in mind and body from the sudden impact I caused. Her eyes were wet from the emotion. But in the next minute, she regained herself as she realized that I was unbendable about moving to Budapest.

"I knew it but didn't say anything about it the last time you were here. I knew it, and I felt it then from your roaming nature that this would happen. You couldn't sit on your ass for a moment without setting new goals for yourself with that girl from Budapest."

Now, it was my turn to compliment myself. Finally I gained the courage to defend myself.

"Aren't you glad that you have a young brother gifted enough to think about his future? Would you be happier if I rotted away in the same village, around the same folks, doing the same sweat work and watching and feeding the same animals all the time? Or wouldn't you rather be much happier to call me one day a young hero who made it on his own from nothing?

"Come on, Sister! Be yourself and recognize the good in me. Don't exhort me anymore about my freedom-loving nature, about my adventurous desires, and about my daring attitude. Don't exhort me anymore for being able to overcome my hardships that destiny hauled my way. Say instead: 'Good luck! heaven and earth bless you and succeed.'"

"So be it!" she said. "Make a man out of yourself. Some say you are already one."

* * *

That same morning Ella and I traveled back to Balatonkeresztur. At home everything was quiet; only the chickens and the ducks were restless and noisy, sensing our homecoming. Before I even went inside the house, I let them out. In fact, they practically pushed the shed door open as I moved the stone that held it tightly in place. These animals encircled me, jumped, and cried enough to let me know how happy they were. I would not have believed, had I not seen it, that animals could express joy, too.

In the coming two weeks we prepared ourselves to give up the animals, the field work, and the coming yield from the fall harvest. We would keep the house and its contents. We would also store dried foods in canisters in the attic.

"You never really know the whims of men. In case another jolt comes in our life, we would be prepared for it. We wouldn't starve for a while," I said to Ella.

I had only one problem in getting rid of the animals. I lost the ambition to kill eleven ducks and fifteen chickens, all at once. Some of them were so close to me that they even jumped onto my lap as I used to seat in front of their shed, watching sunset on the one side of the sky and the moonrise on the other side. So when the time came to get rid of them, I called on Frank, the caretaker of the church's yard, to come and help me manage this part of my preparation. He was glad to do it. He was glad to do anything for me to return my kindness for the crops that I gave him from Joseph's fields a couple years earlier.

"Why in the world would you want to kill all these animals at once?" he asked.

"One reason only, Frank. It's time 'to make a man out of myself' somewhere else.'"

He scratched his head to give himself time to think about how to say his next words, for he didn't understand what I said.

"Isn't that a big and uncertain leap to do for a young kid like you?" he asked.

"Frank, this young kid is only young in his body but his mind has wandered far beyond the borders of this village. If I don't keep up with it, my soul will pop out of my body for not wanting to pray somewhere else. I would snap from boredom in this village. I don't want to stay here any longer," I said.

"What should I say, Arpad? But I know one thing about you. Your mind never rests with sunset as mine does. You are always planning the next step for tomorrow. You gave examples of that to my boys. Both of them are planning now for tomorrow. They want to leave this village as soon as they become mature enough to found jobs in the city. They are bored here from tilling the ground without seeing anything in front of them but the ground.

"I know that you will be just fine wherever you go, for the sun is rising for you on the other side in the sky and you will be there already watching it."

Within a week I received a confirmation letter from Zsizsi. It was very short, unmistakably to the point: "Your job and your accommodation is waiting for you. Be sure to let me know the exact time of your coming. I'll pick you up at the East Station in Budapest."

I didn't understand what *accommodation* meant. And I didn't want to ask anybody who might have known the answer. Most of all, I didn't want anybody to know that I was skipping town for good. So I said to Ella, "What the heck, it would only take a day to find out what Zsizsi meant by *accommodation*."

The next morning I traveled back to Budapest in order to find it out.

I caught up with Zsizsi in the conference room. She was in the middle of brainwashing twenty apprentices about the *totalitarian system*. I snuck through the door with the late comers and sat in the last row and listened. She didn't see me, for I was hiding behind a fat man and was motionless. She didn't care to notice any particular individual, for on her mind was not the students, but to promote the totalitarian ideology of Stalin to them. The words burst out of her mouth like recorded music that some liked, some hated. For her, this was routine stuff and, like anything routine, became boring after a while. For me too, her speech was boring. I already heard similar propaganda back in school. But this time, I wanted to act interested, for my job depended on it.

"You are now part of a special group of people, working together to build a better social order in this company and in this country. Indeed, you are part of the totalitarian community, where everyone works for the benefit of everyone else. You are the ones who own this place and in time would own this country and conceivably the whole world. The future belongs to you. Therefore, you must take it to heart that whatever you do, you do it for one reason only: Defeat the Capitalist mentality that 'money controls the world.'"

The fat man in front of me stood up and asked Zsizsi, "Who controls the money in the totalitarian system?"

"Well"—Zsizsi choked on that question and turned around and pointed to the pictures of Stalin, Lenin, and Rakosy hanging on the wall behind her—"they were the ones who knew best what to do with the money."

The fat man quickly retorted, "They probably paid themselves first and as much as they wanted. Were they not in disguise? Were they not the Capitalist villains in the totalitarian system?"

The entire student body roared in laughter. Zsizsi abruptly cancelled the session.

(The fat man was the watchman of the company. He had worked there for over thirty years, long before the Communist confiscated the place. He knew everybody and well understood the political situation. He kept himself informed by listening to Radio Free Europe. He lost his job, however, over the remarks he made, and I never saw him again.)

As the crowd rushed out, the fat man disappeared with them and thereby exposed me to the full view of Zsizsi. She was in pain from the embarrassment the fat man caused her, and when she noticed me, her face turned as red as petals of poppies on the roadside.

I rushed to her and said, "Zsizsi, ignore the fat man, for he lacked the vision of the future. He didn't know what he was saying. He was repeating what he heard on Radio Free Europe. Who would listen to that *misinformation*, anyway?" I said.

Of course, I was faking myself in order to look good in Zsizsi's eyes, for I didn't know as yet that she was also faking herself.

"I, too, listen to Radio Free Europe! How do you think I would know the difference between Capitalism and Communism?" Zsizsi responded.

"Which one tells the truth, Zsizsi?" I asked.

"That depends on how much money you have. Anyway, what are you doing here unexpectedly?" she asked.

"I came to see you because I don't understand the word *accommodation* from your letter and didn't want to ask anybody else, except you. I don't trust anybody else."

"That's nice of you to say that outright. Now, I know for sure that you trusted me. What I mean by *accommodation* is your room and board. You would be living here in our workers' housing and eating in our own cafeteria. All free of charge. But that isn't all that I want to tell you. Now, that I know for sure that I can trust you, I can tell you a few things about myself without fearing that others would know about them also," she said.

"Don't tell me anything now, Zsizsi. Wait until I come here and spend more time with you. That way, I could be part of your fear because I think fear is less of a fear when shared between trusted friends. Now, I have to rush back home and get myself ready to move here," I explained.

Having said that, I left her. I went to the railroad station and took the next train back to Balatonkeresztur.

* * *

Nothing mattered now. I had only one thing on my mind—coming to Budapest and adjusting myself to the new working and living environment. I would be working and learning at the same time. I would be doing the most important thing in my life, acquiring a trade that nobody could take away from me no matter where I went. And the rest of my activities as far as the *ideology* was concerned meant nothing to me.

My train was once again rolling on the southern side of Lake Balaton while this time I had been weighing both the advantages and the disadvantages of the day's events. I was heading home to tell Ella the positive side of my *accommodation*.

My fear about the change that was coming was much less, however, than the courage I had to overcome it. And my answer to it tipped the scale in my favor. Just as city boys became sophisticated as they mingled with one another, so would I.

The hassle of the day completely tired me out. I didn't care anymore what had happened all day or what will happen tomorrow. One thing was sure, though, that I was moving forward to a new beginning, the beginning that would open my eyes wider than I ever had before, to see the different faces of Communism.

I arrived home and found Ella sleeping already. So I quietly fell on my bed, not knowing how I blanked out before I landed on it.

* * *

I woke up the following morning, finding myself in the same spot my body dropped last night. Any dreams I might have had, I didn't remember. My deep sleep escaped the world as if I had passed out from a potent drink.

But I felt now as refreshed as my ducks which were outside already in the downpour of a fast moving shower. They were dunking and ducking themselves in the puddle in the front yard. I watched them through my window. It was my habit to check the weather through my window and set my work schedule accordingly. That didn't mean anything this time whether it was rain or sunshine, hot or cold. Nothing could have influenced what I needed to do in order to leave this town for good.

The scary lightning, followed by a death-defying thunder, scared Ella to jump out of bed. She jumped next to me to the window and watched with me the heavy downpour rushing through the sky. The wind twisted every tree almost to the point of snapping. The ducks ran for cover to their shed. We curiously watched the fast-moving, gloomy-looking clouds sweeping across the sky toward the west, leaving behind a clear sky in the east.

At the edges of the clouds, three bands of rainbows appeared, telling us that the downpour ended. The amazing scene in the sky, sunrise on one side and dark clouds on the other, invited us to go outside and marvel at the seldom seen beauty being displayed for those curious enough to look at it. It was a scene that displayed my entire life in one picture—the rainbow, the sign of hope for better things to come.

* * *

"How was it in Budapest? Tell me, Brother, so I could figure out where I stand," Ella asked.

"I left yesterday, confused about Zsizsi's letter and came back late last night with clear answers about my *accommodation* there. All I need now is your support to make it happen," I answered.

"Tell me the details. You didn't tell me anything yet."

She said this with all the curiosity she could gather from her confused mind.

So we went inside the house because I noticed that Matild was watching us through the raggedy curtains on her kitchen window. I didn't want her to hear or see how we would talk about our problems in the front yard, where it was so quiet now that even the clear sky had ears to hear everything we would have said.

"Sister, you already know that you are staying with Iren, and she knows that, too. It is only I who don't really know what will happen once I moved to Budapest. Although Zsizsi cleared my mind about *accommodation*, I have a lot of other things on my mind.

"The main thing now is that I have returned to you. I have a job in Budapest, and I have to go there. Let's talk about our next moves," I said.

Since we already stored all the food we wanted to save in case we had to come back home to start all over again, we had to take care of one more thing. We had to find somebody who would maintain the still growing crops on our land and harvest them in the fall. Ella came up with the answer.

"Let's turn the whole thing over to Frank. He is a good man."

"What do you think? Should we give him all the crops or what?" I asked Ella.

"Give him the whole thing. I feel that we will never come back here again, except for a day or two. The way I already figured you out, you are on a mission for your own interests without me," she concluded.

It was not easy for me to swallow this truth. Ella felt that the end of our togetherness had come. I would be on my own, and she would be with Iren's family. Ella was correct in her judgment.

So we left the land and the growing crops to go to Frank with the understanding that if we had to come back, he would return half the crop to us. We also agreed that on coming back home once in a while, he would give us enough goods from the harvest so that we wouldn't have to buy them from others. This was our verbal agreement. Nothing signed. There was no reason for doubting our relationship. We already knew each other long enough that a man's word is as good as the man who said it. But there was one problem: Frank couldn't keep his mouth shut.

* * *

So came that Sunday morning, the day of our departure. It was six o'clock in the morning as I guessed the time by the rising sun. I looked out my window again, not because I wanted to, but because that was my habit to do so every morning. Whom did I see walking back and forth in the front yard, having an old shovel handle in her hand with which she was propping herself to support her ailing back? It was Matild. She knew our top secret, that we would be leaving the place without anybody knowing it. I made a mistake when I told Frank what we were up to. I quickly realized that a secret was no longer a secret when two people knew about it. Frank told Matild the day and the hour of our leaving town. And now, Matild was restlessly waiting outside to say good-bye to us.

That *good-bye* was a lot more than a farewell. It turned out to be a half-hour meltdown on her part, realizing that now she had nobody else left to whom she could turn to in time of need.

She had a guilty feeling about the past, I thought—by not giving me that motherly love and care that I needed most after Mother died. She must have recounted the days when she didn't give me food, when I resorted to pressing milk from the cow's udder straight into my mouth.

At times I was so hungry that I even snatched eggs from under her hens and fried them through a flashlight's lens on hot sunny days. So it must have been that and a lot more that I was tired of recalling now. But these must have painfully haunted her. And deeply haunted her because she knew that her actions were willfully imposed on me. So I reflected on these things, too, as I stood silently before her and let her weep and say all she wanted to say about the past. My senses didn't recoil this time because they were artificially driving my sorrows for her.

Nevertheless, I hugged her so tightly that the shovel handle fell to the ground. I couldn't change the true compassion innately resided in my soul. I was only hiding it. So we parted on good terms, the way I always wanted to part from people; for leaving sour relationship behind only created sorrowful moments later when life so chanced that I would have to face that person again.

After we regained ourselves, Matild handed me a farewell letter and said, "There is something in it that will keep me in your thoughts forever."

My last words to Matild were "You had exemplified for me how not to behave, how not to treat others, and how not to believe in a false god. By seeing you being greedy to the point of harming others, I learned that it was just the opposite I should practice in my life. I'm so glad that I didn't have to realize these things now through my own mistakes."

Then, I hugged her again and kissed her and peacefully left her. Ella did the same thing. Both of us ran through the village now as we were late already, dangling our sacks, containing our meager belongings. We were rushing to the rail station so as not to miss our train.

(I didn't dare to open Matild's farewell letter until years later, for I was afraid to find in it the pigtail hair she secretly worshipped all the time I was with her. When I finally opened it, I found in it her last will and testament, giving me her entire earthly possessions. She was already long dead by then. I had assigned everything over to my sister Ella because she cared for her in her old age. I was by that time on the west side of the globe, happily enjoying my true Liberty in the gracious bosom of the United States of America.)

* * *

But Ella missed the train, while I was able to jump on it. When I saw the last wagon pulling forward, I ran a lot faster than before to catch up to it. From the back of the train, I yelled to her, "I'll see you in a week. Take the next train."

The date was June 22, 1954, seven o'clock in the morning. This date was important because it marks the beginning of my opening to a world of culture and to crafty people who were sophisticated in everything that city life demanded. Part of my survival now depended on it. I would have to learn new ways to look at myself and the world. "And I'm on my way now to face it" rang through my mind as the train picked up speed.

My mind couldn't escape thinking about the coming events and the scare of the unknown that would follow. Anything I imagined now wasn't centered on hopes and dreams for the better that I used to be so good at before, but rather, on losing my independence, losing my freedom. I wouldn't be home anymore, where I alone used to set my schedule as I pleased. This time others would do it for me.

Then, I asked myself, how long would this last before I could be on my own again?

Mother had the answer. Before she was taken to the hospital, she embraced me and sat me on her right knee, saying, "For you to grow up, you will have to do things you don't feel like doing. These will be part of your growing up. You will have to listen to others first to learn the necessities of life before you can be your own man. Obedience, obedience, and more obedience to wear out that stubbornness from your mind and body will be your greatest challenge. It was mine also, and you inherited that trait from me. I may not return from the hospital and wouldn't be around to tame you."

I didn't understand what she was saying and why she was saying it. Much later, when I recognized my shortcomings, I realized that she knew me better than I cared to think about the meaning of obedience.

My train had a destination, so did I. I gave up spinning my mind as to what would happen to me now with all this unknown I'm facing. I accepted my mother's words. She knew what life was all about. I accepted the fact that I would be learning to become a tool-and-die maker. And my teacher would know better than I how to teach obedience and perfection in attitude to subdue my stubborn mind.

The beginning of it started as soon as I saw Zsizsi feverishly eyeing the departing crowd from my train, holding her head high to find me. I did the same thing to find her.

"It was good that you held your head high. I spotted your curly hair as soon as you stepped down from the platform, but I couldn't run to you because of the crowd," Zsizsi said.

"The first thing I would like you to do for me is to cut my curly, long hair, so I wouldn't be sticking out from the crowd like a rooster's head in the flock."

"But your curly hair is part of your personality. It also means that you are hiding something under it," she said.

"I am—my stubbornness, my cockiness –but no more. From now on, I will submit myself under your guidance. And I want that to start with my haircut," I demanded.

"That's a great idea. There is a barber shop right here in the train station. Let's both of us have a haircut there, okay?" So we both had a haircut.

As my curly locks rolled to the floor, I was thinking of Ildiko. She would be disappointed. She wouldn't be able to run her fingers through my curly locks anymore to keep me relaxed and to keep herself feel good about it. But, then, they will grow back and nothing would change again. I will tell her that I had to cut my long hair on account of safety. I couldn't have a long hair around my new job, if I wanted to keep my head in place.

How this haircut business had gotten in the way of my real goal, I couldn't tell. That's the way my life was. The unexplainable *incidentals* filled the void whenever I worried about events I couldn't control.

On the way to Zsizsi's home, I asked her, "Zsizsi, do you know why we didn't go straight to your house instead of doing this spur-of-the-moment grooming stuff?"

"If I could tell you that, Arpad, I would be an angel, doing the works of the devil, or I would be an angel, doing the works of God. Which one controlled that spur-of-the-moment thinking, I do not know. These are the least expected things in our lives. They interrupt our way of thinking and doing things. But I'm sure there is a reason for everything we do or don't do. The Greeks called that *causality*. I call it stupidity. Why do things happen the way they happen is *mystery* to me. And don't ask me what that means," Zsizsi answered.

I didn't understand anything Zsizsi said. But it became evident to me when we arrived inside her house that she was a very smart woman. Both sides of the hallway leading to her living room were lined with books. The only thing I was afraid now that they would crush me if they fell down. The books were stacked on top of loose boards, row at a time, all the way to the ceiling and could have collapsed anytime one had been accidentally removed. I didn't dare ask her questions. I didn't even know, suddenly, what to ask. I got scared from seeing all these books, never mind reading them. Gathering useless knowledge could have been Zsizsi's most important hobby, I thought. Book knowledge was something I had little of. Now, if I would ask her a question, she would probably ask me which book to pull from the stacks in order to explain it. And if I did that without thinking, all the books would fall on me. I was happy just to keep quiet and follow her straight to her living room.

There, too, books upon books lined the floor of the living room at every wall, giving me the impression that she must know everything about everything in the whole world. Acting upon my impression, I asked her, "Zsizsi, is there anything you don't know?"

"Yes, there is. I don't know anything. The sum of knowledge contained in these books told me how much more there is that I don't know. Now that I know that, after reading them all, I want to burn them all. Too much knowledge is an overpowering thing. It makes me want to know everything. As a result, I have forgotten how ordinary people lived and how they struggled without freedom to earn their living. The pursuit of knowledge removed my intellect far from the ground. There was a time when I thought that theories answered every problem anybody had. Well, they don't put food in my stomach. They don't change the appetite of my fat body, and most certainly, they killed my faith in God.

"As I realized all this, I joined the Communist Party, the center of gravity of the misled masses. But I want you to know that I am not a Communist. I am only a member in it, for without a job I wouldn't have money. So the knowledge I gained from these books don't mean much anymore. I can't use it for my own benefit—like setting up my own consulting business and running it without having the Communists take it away.

"And now, I realize that the Communists are not different from the czars of Russia or the kings of Prussia or Hitler or Stalin were. Besides killing millions, they all had one thing in common: enslaving those still living, enslaving their minds, and shackling their freedom. That way, they would lose their will to liberate themselves and seek the one thing that every man yearned for—freedom," Zsizsi explained.

(Think about this last paragraph. Sixty years had passed since Zsizsi and I had this dialogue about dictators, their mind-altering tactics, and their hideous practices. I am seeing the same thing in various forms being repeated under the current administration again [2014]. The social welfare system pushed by the Left is ushering in the dissolution of democracy in the United States of America. The *denial of the past* is being rampantly pursued in public schools. The distribution of wealth is spread to those who are lazy to work to support themselves. These actions are nothing less than the surreptitious push toward *Communistic socialism.* Eventually, it will destroy your individual liberty. It will destroy your faith in God. Don't let it happen! There is no other place on earth where you can run to find your independence. It was for this very reason I came to America, for at that time, In God We Trust was believed and practiced.)

Section Four

CHAPTER TWENTY-FIVE

"Kill the Bastards"

Since Zsizsi lived all her life in Budapest, she was not aware of the atrocities of the Secret Police being committed in the villages. News about these events was suppressed and only by word of mouth they spread. When I explained to her what I saw, she was searching for words to contradict my eyewitness account. As she heard the bad side of the *totalitarian system*, I could see that she was visibly shaken by it and said: "In secret, men talk about the truth, because they would be scared to death to say it in public. The Secret Police would eliminate them as rodents."

"That wasn't I, Zsizsi! What I told you, I would tell the world. *Action had spoken the truth.* Had you seen the brutalities I saw the Communist agents did to the peasants—sweeping their attics, rounding up their livestock, maiming their bodies, and even deporting them (to the Gulags)—you wouldn't have nerves left in you to say anything good about Communism. Yet I heard you preach to the workers about the totalitarian ideology as if it were the greatest and best thing on earth, the final judgment on truth itself. I think the great knowledge you have makes you a hypocrite," I responded.

"Well, Arpad, for you and for you alone, I'll tell you that I was a hypocrite. And I'm still a hypocrite. Not for very long though.

"A different kind of brutality is taking place here in Budapest that you don't know about. The intellectuals are persecuted, for very few of them support the Communists' shifty methods of running the country. The only way I was able to save my skin was by becoming a party member. I was already looking for ways to get out from being a propagandist for the party. But I couldn't, for I would have lost my job. So I stayed being the personnel manager of this bridge-building company and also its propagandist.

"You will be working for this company also. But now that you and I oppose the Communists, we will join the underground movement secretly. I know who they are. They are the students at Budapest University, where I'm a part-time professor lecturing in sociology, physics, and literature. In each of these disciplines, I hold a doctoral degree. Pretty much, I know everybody." Zsizsi revealed herself.

"How can you have two faces, Zsizsi?" I asked her.

"Sophistication, Arpad! While you hide one, you show the other. You haven't grown up yet to know the difference. When you do, you'll be able to finesse one from the other. You will be, for I noticed from your background that you are able to take on just about any challenge and come out of it a winner. Survivors have the guts and the charisma to face the odds with undaunted courage. You are just beginning to show that. You see, ignorance of politics dupes people to believe that the wrong is right. And that is where the mentality of this *proletarian society* stood right now. But as you said yourself, 'action had spoken the truth.' The whole atrocities that the Communists are doing in the country would soon come to a boiling point, and at that moment, the masses would realize that they were duped in believing the wrong. Their anger would be like a swollen river, like an erupting volcano. It would swiftly and relentlessly, maybe even brutally reorder what's right. It would destroy everything in its path that is wrong and would give birth to a new life. Nobody can stop the revolting power of angry masses, for that power is the will of the people." Zsizsi was prophesizing what was to come.

Zsizsi was pounding her desk in her living room—maybe to keep me from falling asleep. That was how I could keep my eyes open. I was sure though that she was a tactful propagandist.

"Your revolutionary fervor is like a floodgate, Zsizsi, almost ready to burst open. It looks to me that I would be helping you to crank it open. You remind me of my favorite poet, Sandor Petofi, when he wrote one of his most famous revolutionary poems in 1848. 'Onto your feet, men of Hungary (Talpra Magyar)!'" I commented.

"Not yet! We have other things to do right now. You have to start working tomorrow, and I have to continue working as I have been. Even though we are best of friends now, we shouldn't show that in the open. This way, we wouldn't let anybody know what we are doing behind the scenes. Call that hypocrisy too, but it would be for a noble cause—yours and mine... and the country's," Zsizsi concluded.

From here on, we became best friends and best cohorts in secret. Although I knew very little of politics, I knew one thing for sure—when the Communists destroyed the hope and faith of the people in my village, the people became equally brutal in return, fighting off the Communist agents. I was even more certain now after hearing what Zsizsi said that the hope and faith of the people were the common cause that united them. No matter whether one was rich or poor, peasant or intellectual, denying the past was equal to denying the future. Now, I think that hope and faith had no beginning and no ending in the hearts of believing people, in the hearts of persecuted people.

When Zsizsi and I had finished pouring out the secrets we held deeply hidden until now, she said: "Let's move on. I want to show you the place where you will be staying, eating, and cleaning yourself. All these will surprise you because they are shared by everybody who are apprentices at this company. You will be like a dog with his new owner. Doesn't know what's going on or what to expect coming on. Just follow what everybody else is doing, and soon enough, you will feel like that dog with his new owner—better get used to it for the sake of your survival.

"Life is all about getting used to changes, getting used to hoping for the better even though it didn't look like it. I shall be close to you, and you can cry your heart out on my shoulders. For you to grow up, you need to know the whims and habits of other people around you so you could adjust yourself to them," Zsizsi said.

"I think you are over imagining my weakness in my adjusting to a new environment. You forgot where I'm coming from. You forget that I had been hounded by people before. It was for that reason I chose to change the course of my life. I expect not the best things to happen to me as a result of my decision. Anyway, I would be learning something new from everybody. Good and bad usually follow each other. But this last one seems to come more now that I have accepted losing my personal freedom. And I should think that a lot of that would come now because changes do bring unexpected surprises. Even then, don't expect me to be a crybaby on your shoulders, Zsizsi," I responded.

Having said enough discouraging words to each other, we set out walking to the places where all the things said would happen to me in the next two years. Zsizsi lived about a mile away from the places I would work, sleep, and eat and shower. Only a hundred feet or so separated the clustered buildings from each other, where I would be doing one or the other thing. All the buildings looked to me as temporary setups—here today, gone tomorrow. The surroundings reminded me of Tony's gypsy camp. Nobody cared where garbage fell on the ground, and nobody cared who would pick it up. I remarked to Zsizsi, "You know, I think that the minds of these people here were as disorderly as their surroundings were."

"I'm glad you noticed that. To take notice of such a thing, it needed only one person reversing it, just as it took only one person neglecting it. That's the way human beings are. They follow each other. You can open the eyes of others by doing your things neatly in an organized manner, for you are different. You are forced to do things in an organized manner because you are an orphan. Things in your life, just as it was in mine, needed that step-by-step planning to get ahead. You started first within yourself, correcting your own faults. I did the same thing. You saw the world ahead of you through your soul and changed. Folks call that a *leap of faith*. You didn't see the world through the eyes of others. If you did, you would be like the boys here—careless and neglectful. You know, Arpad, a person who can plan ahead for himself has all the signs of becoming a leader. Let's start shaping up things around here by your disciplined attitude and others will follow you," Zsizsi encouraged me.

A few days earlier, Zsizsi summoned all the supervisors and explained to them that I would be coming to join the other apprentices. She told them a little bit of my background but warned them about my inquisitive and persistent nature, about my willingness to keep my surroundings neat and organized, so that the following day would start from a neat and clean work area. In a sense, she emphasized that I was a firm believer that organized surroundings fostered the mind to think clearly, to plan the orderly flow of next day's work assignments, uninterrupted by having all sort of things thrown all over the place. And at times, I would even be stubborn enough to help others clean up their surroundings after work, every day.

Zsizsi led me now to my sleeping quarters; there, I found on my bed two pairs of my formal uniform, two pairs of my work overalls, two pairs of shoes, and two pairs of underwear. I carefully looked at everything with thoughtful questions in mind. Are they new or used? Are they my size and without oily fingerprints by those who handled them?

Then, I asked Zsizsi, "Where is my hat, my handkerchiefs, my socks, my shirts and… soap and towels?"

"That's what I meant," she said. "No common sense around here! Every person needs another person to think and act for him. This is the hallmarks of *socialism*. So get used to it on your first day— one holds the broom, the other the dustpan, and the third tells what to do. Do you get it?"

"And you expect me to get used to that? What if I did all of that by myself?" I laughed.

"That would be fine, too. The socialist mentality is let the other guy do the work," she said.

It was now Sunday evening. Zsizsi went back to her house and left me alone in my sleeping quarters, which I would be sharing with four other boys, who were now out in the city doing what boys usually do—dating or looking for one. I decided to do the same thing.

I took all my belongings and packed them in my locker and walked the one mile distance to Ildiko.

Although Ildiko knew that I left Balatonkeresztur for good, she didn't know, however, the exact time when. And now I wanted to surprise her. But instead, the surprise became mine. I was barely halfway to her house; I saw that she and Lisa were coming toward me, followed by five boys on the same side of the street. Nothing seemed out of the ordinary until the five boys hopped, one after the other, in front of them. Then, they turned around and walked backward facing the girls. The boys were trying to engage the girls to start a conversation. Although Ildiko saw that someone was walking toward her some distance away, she didn't recognize that it was I. She couldn't; I had a haircut. It wasn't until one of the boys shoved me to the side so that I couldn't come between them and the girls. I had the boy's neck already in my grips and was shaking him.

"Arpad!" she cried out.

I released my grip instantly, and the boy ran away. The four other boys turned around and walked toward the Danube River. They realized that Ildiko belonged to me. Now I held the girls' hands, and we walked together to the place where I would be lodging.

As we walked closer and closer to my place, it became clear that the four boys were heading to the same place we were heading. I really didn't care who they were or what they had on their minds. My mind was on Ildiko, and if I had to confront them again, so be it. My strength was bigger than the four's combined. I was in love and had, therefore, the inner strength to move a mountain on account of her, if I had to.

I said to Ildiko, "It looks like those boys are my roommates. One by one, they entered the barracks."

"Let's walk back to my house," Ildiko said. "I don't want to see you fist-fighting with them. The boy you almost chocked is my classmate at the Budapest University. Since he ran off, you have four more to worry about. But I never saw these others before," Ildiko remarked.

So I did what Ildiko wanted. I escorted them back home. It was strange that we hardly have said anything to each other as we walked back.

My mind was on the four strangers who would now become my roommates. How to greet them on my return. Ildiko's mind was on the boy who ran off—how to explain to him that I was her boyfriend. They were now close friends, almost to the point of dating. His name was Attila. He had one thing in common with me. He wanted to see Ildiko every day.

On my way back to my sleeping quarters, the thought about Attila troubled me more than the four I was about to meet. Jealousy took hold of me as I fought off Attila, who came close to Ildiko. I realized that I had become a dangerous person in this regard, both to myself and to my opponent. Coming to terms with it, however, could only happen if I died, for hate was almost as powerful in me now as love was. The passing of time would only deepen both. Nothing I could do about this now, I thought, until the next time.

It was time now to meet my roommates. Upon entering my quarters, one of the boys yelled from his bed: "What a character you were!"

Another one yelled, "I loved the way you kissed her."

The third one said, "I was glad I wasn't in Attila's shoes."

The fourth one said, "How come we didn't know about your coming here?"

I didn't know which one to answer first. Instead, I decided not to answer any. In a bold move, I stepped between the stacked bunk beds on which the four were now resting. I introduced myself.

"I am good enough to tell you that my name is Arpad. Are you good enough to tell me yours?" My voice was invitational because I was smiling.

Each one jumped off his bed and lined up behind each other before me. They were my age, give or take a few months, and were surprised about my temerity and directness. I had nothing to hide and nothing to fear, as I had already faced similar events before and gained the courage to look straight in the eyes of people who posed a confrontation of sorts.

"My name is Eric."

"My name is Steve."

"My name is Sylvester."

"My name is Miklos."

They introduced themselves one by one.

They had no hesitation in their manner, and I had none in mine either. Each had given me a very strong handshake that revealed to me that each had a strong personality. And I liked that, knowing it right off that I was dealing with courageous kids.

"Let's talk things over before we act foolishly with each other," I said.

"Let's do that," Miklos answered. He was appointed by Zsizsi to be the room's overseer.

So we sat now at a round table in the middle of the room and were eyeing each other for a tactful opening—which one of us would be bold enough to start a conversation.

It was midnight already. The room was hot, and the boys were chain-smoking. Each of us was eager to hear what the other had to say about himself.

Since I was the newcomer, I was more anxious than the others were to tell the highlights of my life. I wasn't shy at all bragging about my revolutionary fervor, primed into my head by my hero, the great poet Sandor Petofi. He hated the Hapsburgs as much as I hated the Communists. My tactic was to find out whether any or all had the same feeling as I had listening to propaganda—how to *deny the past* and embrace the fabricated lies of Stalin's socialism.

Facing the four boys, I asked two questions only: "Were you the other day in that group of laughing kids listening to Zsizsi's lecturing about the totalitarian community? And did you hear the fat man asking, 'Who controlled the money in a totalitarian system?'"

Miklos answered with one voice for them all. "We laughed the loudest because we agreed with the fat man that the Communists were the villains in the totalitarian system. Were you there also?"

"I was sitting behind that fat man and heard everything. The reason I asked this question is to find out whether I could be part of your team, challenging these lies that by *denying the past* we could have a great future in the totalitarian system," I responded.

"Why not!" said Miklos. "Tomorrow we'll go to work together as if we have known each other from the cradle, as if we have been chained together, as if we have been schooled together to believe that the lessons in life were understood from the lessons we learned from the past."

"Miklos, is that your own belief, or you are just faking it to please me?" I asked.

"Arpad, we already know you. Zsizsi told us a lot about you days ago," Miklos said.

After hearing this, I felt more at ease in a group of people than ever before. I also realized that Zsizsi had handpicked those around herself who could be trusted to keep a top secret—the underground movement against Communism.

* * *

The following morning Zsizsi was waiting in order to introduce me to my supervisor and to the group of other apprentices with whom I would be working. She saw through her office window, however, that I was already huddling with my roommates who she thought would give me a rough time accepting me into their circle. She decided, therefore, that she wouldn't waste time going through a formal introduction and a boring speech in order to ease my way to join a group of new people. She thought now that since I was so likable with my friendly smile that I even melted away the four boys' combative nature, I could do the same thing with the rest of the workers in the shop, who held their own distance from new people. So she sent all the students she had invited back to their work stations, except my would-be supervisor, Peter Bohn.

Now, the four boys walked straight to their workbenches in the shop, passing Zsizsi's office, while I walked straight to her. Seeing Zsizsi and Peter Bohn sitting together on a corner sofa and casually talking about my work assignments, I heard Zsizsi's last words: "He will get used to it."

I ignored what I heard and walked to her and kissed her as if she was my mother. For me doing this was not at all unusual, for any woman who was kind to me I kissed twice, once on meeting her and once on parting from her. After I kissed Zsizsi, I turned to Peter and gave him a handshake he probably would never forget. In honoring a newcomer, a man didn't shake hands from a sitting position. So as I was holding his hand, I pulled him up from his seat and gave him a firm handshake and said, "I could get used to just about anything, if I was told with a smile." But Peter wasn't a smiling-type person. He accepted my casual behavior with a forced smile instead and said, "Zsizsi won't be around you all the time, you know."

"Why! You thought that I believed she would? I didn't come here to look for favors. I came here to learn a trade," I remarked, still smiling.

Peter didn't know what to make of it and said, "That you will, I guarantee it, and without a smile at times, Arpad."

So we left Zsizsi in her office and walked to the workshop, where I was initiated in the first assignments of an apprentice—learning the rules and regulations, the disciplines and conduct, and the rigid schedules that would now dismantle every bit of stubbornness I still had lingering in me from the thoughtless work attitude I had developed in my village.

In my first six months as a beginner, I did little more than use eight different types of metal files in order to learn how to shape different alloys into forms that precisely matched the models I was given to follow. At the end, Peter Bohn told me, "I have driven in you the humility of work ethics: Practice makes a man develop perfection, practice makes a man recognize his qualities, and practice makes him hold his mind steady to the task he has chosen to finish."

Peter was an old-timer at the company and was a skilled supervisor in every sense of the word. He was polite but firm, experienced in the skills of using all types of metal cutting tools and respected even the machines to which these tools were attached. He stayed away from politics. In his mind, polemics in learning the skills of a trade didn't add anything to gaining the experience of the trade. Show and tell was his mode of operation, for the quality of one's work revealed the knowledge, experience, and qualification of that person. He practically held the hands of every apprentice and guided them in the moves that yielded quality work. "Do it right the first time" was written in bold letters on every instructional booklet.

Peter Bohn had German parents who settled in Hungary on the invitation of one of the Hungarian kings. Being a German, he was a disciplinarian by nature, and as such, his mind was more on teaching it to me than accepting nonsense that I had plenty of, being young and inexperienced.

I wasn't smiling anymore as often as I used to be. Learning how to conform to the rules and regulations of the workplace squeezed the humor out of me, for filing metals for six months made me to curse even myself for accepting this job. It also squeezed every bit of my ambition as well to become a tool-and-die maker.

I told Peter, "I would rather sweep the floor than learn a trade. I have a problem with repetitive work."

And he replied, "You think that sweeping floors isn't repetitive? Your problem is repetitive, too. Learn to love it, for to gain perfection in anything you want to be good at requires endless repetition. Otherwise, you would become a *jack-of-all-trades*, starting everything but never finishing anything to perfection. Sweeping the floors is just like that. Never finished to perfection, because while one side of the floor is clean, the other side becomes dirty again. Which one you want to be, Arpad?"

I replied, "Thank you," and went back to do more metal filing. The words of wisdom finally sank in. It wasn't the endless practice the problem. It was my youth, impatient to accept it.

Learning to be a highly skilled tool-and-die maker, Peter taught me one of the most important lessons an apprentice required to have: listening to those who know the pitfalls of the trade better—how to prevent accidental injury to myself and to others. Fully understanding every detailed step of my work assignment was the other. Each of these required a *think-ahead* attitude development. Without knowing these precautions I could have lost sight of the consequential impact they would have caused when others were involved finishing my work. By neglecting to carefully observe these lessons, I could have set the occasion to injure others or could have had others add their mistakes to mine, for the problems I ignored to correct, I would have passed onto others to bear.

Peter often complained, "This is the ever-present problem with today's mentality, the socialistic mentality. Nobody cares whether the other guy is hurt or not as long as he profits from his own actions. Put simply, these motives, I would hope, Arpad, that you don't take over, for at the end nobody would have any compassion for anybody."

"Well, Peter, believe it or not, I am waiting for that time to come. So was Zsizsi and probably you, too. For when that happens, the whole country would rise up against this socialistic nonsense. The whole country would celebrate by holding hands, and maybe even guns, for the return of individual freedom. Liberty would be at hand but only when everybody unites and fights for it."

I learned from Zsizsi how to prophesize.

Peter looked at me, and for the first time, I saw him truly smiling.

Toward the end of my apprenticeship, Peter demanded that I should prove to him that I was skilled in every aspect of my trade before he would give me my diploma. To prove that, I had to fabricate a medium-size vise grip from sketches I drew.

"Let me review and approve your sketches first, for in the details lay the figments of your mind," he said and continued: "Choose for

417

every part the raw materials needed from the junkyard in the back of the building. You may use any machine we have here to fabricate the detail parts of the vise grip. Then, assemble it and bring it to me for approval. But don't bring it to me unless you are satisfied with it. Know for sure that if you aren't satisfied with it, nobody else will be.

"That will be a sign to me of your self-confidence and of your belief in yourself. I will know that your work attitude is firm and steady, for only then will you have the guts to complete a project to the satisfaction of others," Peter Bohn emphasized.

I thought Peter would go on and on until I had forgotten every word he said to me.

As was the case, I had to ask him to write these things down so that I wouldn't miss any part of his demands. And I didn't.

It took me three months to fully complete this project. At the end, I liked what I did and was pleased to operate the vise grip back and forth as if I had now my entire knowledge and skill exemplified by it.

When I presented it to him, I saw him smiling at me the second time, saying: "I am as proud as you are now, for I, too, did a good job and that's all that matters. That is the way others will respect us and hold us commendable."

*　*　*

Two years had passed now, and I was almost seventeen years old. During that time, I had my eyes and ears opened to realize that I was becoming a mature person. I learned the work discipline and the attitude to respect it, almost uncommon qualities in a young person. That I learned a trade brought me face to face with one very important reality. I would always have a job no matter where life drifted me far away from home. The skills of my trade were always in need from Budapest to New York. Since nothing lasted forever, I would always have a job to repair a broken machine, a broken tool, or whatever failed. There was always a metal part in every gadget that eventually broke down from use or abuse, and I would be there to fix it. Come good times or bad, I would always have bread on my table. Nothing sounded better than this confirmation: I would always have bread on my table.

CHAPTER TWENTY-SIX

Rage and Retribution

Because I was learning a trade, politics and socialistic ideology had very little to do with me. Anyway, I hated both. It was enough that I saw the atrocities done by the Secret Police in my village and heard the brainwashing tactics wherever the Communists gathered. More of it at this time would have turned me into the hands of the enemy, for I would have been openly fighting them as the peasants did in my village. What is left now is forced silence for the time being until I could join forces with other students and be part of the underground movement against Communism.

This movement started with a small group of students at the University of Budapest and eventually grew into a countrywide uprising that nothing could stop, except death itself—to liberate the country from eight years of terror that the Secret Police carried out, increasingly with more and more vengeance, supported by Stalin and his point man, Matyas Rakosy. They had already pillaged the country of Hungary.

Zsizsi had the connection with those few students at the Budapest University who started to read the minds and hearts of other students whose parents had lost their freedom and dignity through the atrocities of the Secret Police. These students came from the countryside and were also eyewitnesses to similar atrocities I had been. Those who lived in Budapest saw how the business owners and many of the degreed professionals were now digging ditches or doing manual labor or even collecting garbage because they stood their grounds opposing Communism.

So, at the beginning, the sons and daughters of simple folks started the underground movement. This movement, of course, was one of many throughout the country that was already quietly taking place. But because it began in Budapest, it was significant. Anything that happened here spread to the countryside like the voices on the airwaves from Radio Free Europe, fermenting uprising. People everywhere were eager to hear fresh news, foremost the kind that carried anti-Communist sentiments. They were talking and secretly joining forces against Communism. They understood, better than I did, the true meaning of persecution and terror. They were waiting now for the right moment to get even. The Secret Police (AVH) had no idea what would be coming to them.

The right moment came for me also to join the small group of students from the university. Zsizsi was their professor, teaching them sociology, specifically what happens when societal order breaks down in a country. She gave an example: Poland. This country was in uprising now against Communism (1956).

Zsizsi had a clever idea how to introduce me to these students so that I would become knowledgeable, not only about their underground activities, but also about their city culture that I still had only so-so knowledge.

Since Zsizsi and I were close friends, although mostly secretly, during the two years I spent in Budapest, I saw her at least once a week at her house. She knew almost everything about me, especially my feelings against the totalitarian ideology. And she also knew her students' feelings about it. She decided, therefore, it was time now to bring together the few trusted friends from the student body and also the few trusted friends from the workplace in order that I meet them and socialize. On her mind, of course, was something else, very special.

All those invited came to the party. From the group, I knew my roommates only. The others, I never saw. My roommates knew them, however, and the gathering would be therefore just another occasion to talk about girls and dating. So they thought.

This was how Zsizsi introduced me: "Meet my young hero, Arpad. He opened my eyes and ears so that I could hear and perceive the revulsion of the village folks against Communism." And she went on, "But, more importantly, he will be with us on October 23. We will join others, a much bigger group of students from the Petofi Circle, for demonstration and proclamation of our fifteen-point demand. We will show solidarity with the Polish uprising by peacefully demonstrating at the statue of General Bem, the Polish general who fought along with Lajos Kossuth in the 1848 Hungarian Revolution against the Hapsburgs. It will be at three o'clock in the afternoon. Be there! All of you!" And she dismissed everybody except me.

(Kossuth was the second foreign dignitary who addressed the United States Congress about the meaning of freedom and liberty in Hungary and the world at large. At the same time, he was seeking, not only moral, but also material support in order to further the Hungarian cause, independence from the Hapsburgs. His request was not honored. Nevertheless, his eloquent and dramatic speech was so convincing that even after two hundred years J. F. Kennedy was quoting it in his address to the nation, just before the Cuban Missile Crisis. Streets are named after him in many cities, and statues are honoring at many places this never-fallen hero.)

Just as fast as the gathering started, it was over. Nobody in the neighborhood saw anything as it was dark already, inside as well as outside. Everybody filtered out one by one and went home. I was the only one who stayed behind. So I asked Zsizsi: "Who else will be at this demonstration?"

"I asked Radio Free Europe to tell the whole world to join us and demonstrate in solidarity with the Polish people against the unbearable deprivation of freedom and justice taking place in Poland at this time," she replied.

"Aren't you afraid for your life now? This is no longer a secret," I said to her.

"Arpad, I'll no longer be a hypocrite. For eight years, I toed the line, telling falsehood and lies, while inside of me was something else. The pain and agony of those who suffered under the hands of the Secret Police now roars within me like an erupting volcano. Either I kill myself or I kill the bastards. This time, I will not be alone however. I may die, but you shall know that I am doing this for the sake of freedom." Zsizsi proclaimed.

"That will make two of us. I feel that others will follow us. Liberty means freedom of mind, body, and country. That was on my mind the minute I became an orphan. Even a mouse wants that," I remarked and added, "Come what may, I'll be with you, Zsizsi."

I couldn't wait for October 23 to come fast enough as I had never seen a demonstration before and had never heard of a proclamation. I didn't even know the meaning of the words never mind understanding the power of the people behind it. I had no idea that a mass movement could come so quickly together that I would not even be able to come close to the statue of General Bem and hear that proclamation. Radio Free Europe had incited all those who were listening; and as a result, they rushed to the statue before I could even join Zsizsi to go there. They heard that the proclamation demanded from the Communist government of Hungary, the very same thing the Polish people demanded from their own government: the freedom of speech, the freedom of worship, the freedom of movement, the freedom of... and on and on. No wonder all this was stirring music to all the people who gathered now at the statue. All around me, I heard, "Let's make it big. Let's announce it to the whole world."

Zsizsi and I were part of this crowd. She knew exactly what the proclamation was and what it meant once it was loudly recited to the crowd gathered here. It meant rebellion. So many people, about two hundred feet deep, gathered all around the statue. Surely, it was amazing to me to see what people can do when they are united for a common cause. The Secret Police stayed away, awaiting the outcome of the demonstration. I was too. Everything was peaceful for a while. Then, the crowd yelled with one voice, "To the radio station. To the radio station. Announce the proclamation to the world."

That radio station was the Kossuth Radio, the propaganda radio station for the Communist Party. It is located in the greater center of Budapest and guarded by a battalion of Secret Police.

The crowd now broke up. Some headed to the Radio Station, others to Heroes' Square to the statue of Stalin, about a mile from the radio station. I was sure that hell would break out at both places, for I saw that seething anger has taken over the crowd.

People were out on the streets everywhere like ants before rain. The street cars and subways were still moving around, although at a snail's pace, were completely overloaded, fully packed like pickles in a jar. The people were heading to Heroes' Square to Stalin's statue. Zsizsi and I decided to walk the couple of miles to the radio station instead. Along the way, we caught up with my roommates. They were going however to the statue of Stalin. We then changed our minds, decided to go with them there also, suddenly fearing the Secret Police at the radio station.

When we arrived, we saw that steel ropes were already tied around Stalin's neck in order to yank him down. It didn't even budge. Suddenly, a large crane arrived from somewhere and also had a heavy-duty welding equipment with it. It edged itself closer and closer to the giant statue. Now, as the crane was methodically pulling on the steel ropes, a group of welders were melting Stalin's right leg off just below the knee line. Within two to three minutes, the statue hit the ground from its high pedestal. The uproar of about fifty thousand people filled the air. As soon as the pole of a large Hungarian flag was stuck inside the hollow leg of Stalin, still in place on the pedestal, the crowd went totally silent. As if God himself was now the conductor, we sang the national anthem (Isten Ald Meg a Magyart) It rang out with one voice, one feeling and one hope, "God bless the Hungarians." But I couldn't sing it. My lips were quivering as I was totally overtaken by the resounding voices, seeing all these people standing strait as a totem pole and loudly singing the Anthem with utmost pride and solemnity. I, too, straightened my body as if someone just stuck a pin in my rear. Finally, the meaning of all this became clear. *Uprising! Uprising!* I kept thinking.

"What's next?" I asked Zsizsi.

"Follow the crowd," she answered.

Suddenly, I heard the sound of heavy gunfire coming far away from the direction of the radio station. It was 10 p.m., a windless, cloudless evening. My four roommates, Zsizsi, and myself were still standing shoulder to shoulder. They heard the gunfire, too.

Zsizsi suddenly cried out, "Let's go there! They need our help!"

The crowd split up, almost as fast as they came together to witness this heroic event. But some stayed behind and rushed as close as possible to Stalin's fallen statue. They went there to vent their anger: Beating it, spitting on it, and hammering the devil out of it. "No keepsake from this dirty bastard." The voice echoed in my ears. Others from the crowd, including us, rushed to the radio station.

As we came closer and closer, we heard the gunfire becoming louder and louder. It wasn't sporadic anymore. People were returning the shots with increasing momentum. We couldn't figure it out. Was it the army or the regular police who were firing back at the Secret Police, now heavily guarding the entrance to the radio station? The

Secret Police held the crowd back at any cost from having the people take over the station. For if that would have happened, it would have meant the announcement of the fifteen-point declaration to the country, indeed, to the whole world at large.

Then, as we came still closer to the radio station, we saw that guns and ammunition were already handed out by the hundreds to the demonstrators. The Hungarian army, sided with the crowd on orders from Pal Maleter, the Hungarian general and defense minister, ordered the delivery of weapons and bullets to the people by the truckloads from the nearby barracks. I saw several of these trucks lined the street, leading to the radio station. Young and old, men and women, and kids like me—we all grabbed these weapons to soothe the seething anger we all had. We also wanted to fire back at the Secret Police. This would no longer be just to return the fire. It would be killing the bastards.

Now, using a rifle to kill a person is not a simple matter. But at this time, by far, it was the break point between life and death. "Either I or the enemy" was my straightforward answer.

Each of my roommates grabbed single-shot rifles and filled their pockets with live bullets. I grabbed a submachine gun and filled my backpack with ammo magazines. Zsizsi didn't get anything, for she was scared to death to handle weapons. So I put her in charge of carrying my backpack and said, "Stick by me and hand these ammo magazines to me quickly for reloading as I need them."

I was the only one in our group who had some experience with guns, dating back to the days with my grandfather. My roommates had none. Quickly, I took the gun Miklos had and showed him how to use it, saying: "Keep the trigger always locked. Unlock it only when you were ready to fire. Aim at clear targets only. Otherwise you hit what's in between." The three others were watching me and imitating what I did. Zsizsi watched the whole thing also and changed her mind. "I want to try it, too. 'In case'... " Now, she grabbed a rifle and live bullets also. Her pants' pockets bulged from the bullets, like stuffing in a turkey's breast.

There were now more people touting guns than I could count. But because of the crowd in front of us blocking a clear view to the target areas, we couldn't fire a single shot. Only those who were up front had the advantage of taking on the Secret Police at the entrance and at the first floor windows of the radio station. As soon as those in front dropped dead, the next group took their places and fired. Both sides had a lot of casualties. But at the end, the radio station was taken over sometime in the early morning hours.

We left the area after that and moved close to the Parliament Building. We hid ourselves in the basements of close-by buildings. We did this because we heard from people listening to Radio Free Europe that there would be a peaceful demonstration there as big as the world had ever seen. The whole people of Budapest would be there, demonstrating against the atrocities that the Secret Police did at the radio station.

These basements were accessible both from the inside as well as from the outside. They served as bunkers in times of war and as storage places in times of peace. A lot of the freedom fighters hid themselves here and waited. The reason for our move was to secretly back up the masses that would be peacefully demonstrating at the Parliament Building close by, just in case. It was now October 24. For sure, we all anticipated trouble but didn't know how big it would be. It was by ham radio that we, the freedom fighters, communicated with the outside world. Hearing now that ten thousand Russian soldiers, backed by scores of tanks, were heading to the Parliament Building to *defend* it, we were certain that they weren't coming for a picnic.

At this time, fearing a full-blown revolution, the Communist boss, Erno Gero, called on the Russian army to move against the swelling crowd. But it wasn't the Russians who fired the first bullets against the crowd. It was the Secret Police. The massacre resulted close to a thousand casualties within minutes.

At the opposite end of the tanks and behind the hundred thousand demonstrators, the Hungarian army had just unloaded guns and ammunitions and handed them to the furious crowd in order to fight back against the Secret Police. After a while, they turned onto the Russians also. A lot more casualties resulted. In this fight, all the freedom fighters moved out from the basements—including myself, Zsizsi, and my four roommates—and took part in the fighting. We spread out to different locations. While I was hitting the tanks, the four were aiming at individual targets. Who killed who was irrelevant now, so long as the enemy was hit.

I lost track of the four because I had to relocate in a hurry behind the buildings. Zsizsi ran with me, carrying the four magazines still left in my backpack and her rifle. Two tanks turned their turrets in my direction and hit the building we were behind, lying on the ground. We weren't wounded, so we ran deeper behind another building and then to its basement, hoping that the four would find us there when they ran out of bullets.

In about an hour, the guns went silent for a while. The dead bodies were strewn all around Parliament Square like trees after a twister. Hundreds were looking for their loved ones, crying and cursing the enemy. They were yelling, "Rusky, go home." Toward evening, Zsizsi and I ventured out from the basement, looking for the four who had not returned. Before ducking from the basement, I wanted to give my gun and ammunition to a kid who looked about my age. He was so eager to run out with it and fire it that I had second thoughts turning it over to him. I asked him, "You know how to use this thing?"

"No. But I learn it as I use it," he said.

(So it was with most of us kids who dared to pick up arms against the enemy; we didn't know how to use them. Whatever luck had to do with our courage to fight, we always had a Hungarian soldier to help us out. They were on our side and had joined the patriotic fighters shortly after the mass killings at Parliament Square. After all, they were the sons of the suffering masses who were persecuted and maltreated during the eight years of terror the Secret Police unleashed on the country.)

Finally I gave this kid my gun and said to him, "Identify the enemy first before you shoot. Don't just run out of here and be killed before even firing a shot."

We now left the basement unarmed and looked as any other civilian, worried, and hurried to find our four comrades in the midst of others who were looking for their loved ones. I had no hope finding them alive after seeing all the dead bodies everywhere and no fighters anywhere. I also had a hopeful second thought and said to Zsizsi, "They may have jumped into the Danube to escape the firing line." (The Parliament Building is directly facing the Danube River.)

"That would have been the smartest thing to do. Let's get out of here before we become dead, too." Then, she added, "The innocent, as always, paid the price for freedom with their blood. All the dead here are witnesses to that."

We left the scene.

I cannot describe the depth of pain, the grip of sorrow, and the revulsion that tortured my being now. I cannot describe either how others felt, for in times of sorrow no one can truly feel the pain of others, only see it. One thing was certain, though, that all this mutiny brought the whole nation together to fight a million times harder in order to cut down every sign, every symbol, and every person who were beastly connected to Communism.

The whole city of Budapest became now a battleground. Indeed, the whole nation instantly revolted as if everybody heard at the same time the last words of the dying, pleading at Parliament Square— fight now or never, your liberty is the prize.

* * *

The massacre sent shockwaves to the Kremlin in Moscow. Within hours, Erno Gero fell from power. He was replaced by a moderate Communist, Imre Nagy. Although both of these men were trained by the equally brutal KGB (Russian Secret Police), Nagy had patriotic blood flowing in him. During the massacre, both of them were probably watching the unfolding events from the upper windows of the Parliament Building. While Gero was a cold-blooded Communist, he, more than likely, enjoyed seeing the brutality carried out below by the Secret Police. Nagy, on the other hand, must have been in complete anguish and not being able to do anything about it. But he must have heard the tumultuous cry of the people below, "Rusky Go Home!" (Russians Go Home)

The shift in power ordered by the Kremlin suddenly made Nagy the new Premier of Hungary. Now, it was his turn to do something. On October 25, he asked the Russians to leave Budapest and soon after that Hungary as well. His demand carried some weight as he was backed by Pal Maleter, the minister of defense, who threatened to bomb the Russian tanks, unless they left Budapest. Nothing of the sort had happened right of way however. The Russians needed more pressure from the freedom fighters in order to convince themselves how much everybody hated them.

So they hesitated and, instead of moving out, the tank brigade spread out to strategic locations throughout Budapest. Probably somebody from Moscow had ordered them to do that. As they moved from street to street, they encountered their greatest enemy ever unleashed on them.

Zsizsi and I had already moved to the center of the city and hid ourselves with others in basements. As many as twenty of us, kids and grown-ups together, we were now filling up quart bottles with gasoline and corking them with wicks that dangled from the bottles. Now, we were waiting for the tanks to pass by. As the tanks moved, we, the kids, ran close to them and hurled these lit bottles against them. As the gasoline burst into fireballs, it enveloped the whole tank, which then either exploded or burnt out. Those inside the tanks scurried from the heat to climb out, only to be gunned down by the freedom fighters, who were eyeing them above from the windows of the apartments on both sides of the street. At least half of the Russian tanks, we and others throughout the city destroyed in this manner; other *kids* from other locations did the same thing we did.

(The word *Molotov cocktail* became known throughout the world as the weapon of choice against the tanks in city fighting. We were the pioneers of it.)

Downtown Budapest was littered with burned-out tanks which reminded every onlooker of the heroic acts of children. Finding no way to defend themselves, some of the Russians moved to the outskirts of Budapest, but some gave up the fight altogether and left their tanks having white sheets fluttering on their tops. It was in this manner that the freedom fighters gained possession of these tanks and moved them now to the most important battleground yet to take place at the headquarters of the hated Secret Police located on 60 Andrassy Street, Budapest.

Zsizsi and I were looking at these tanks creeping toward the headquarters. We really didn't know who they were or whom they wanted to bombard. We were now out on the street, cautiously looking at the confused crowd to observe how many carried rifles and in which direction they were heading. I was confused also, and on top of that, I was wondering, will I live for another day to see the end of this furious rebellion against Communism?

There was still heavy fighting going on throughout the city, but here, a few hundred feet around the Secret Police headquarters, there was rather quiet for the moment. Zsizsi suddenly remarked, "Let's follow the tanks. They are heading to the Headquarters. If they are our people, we would be lucky. If they aren't, we would have to run for cover. Either way, a massacre is coming."

This enormous building was the hub of the Secret Police who terrorized the whole country, who tortured the people and enforced vigilance on friend and foe alike. Here was the seat of power that protected, at all cost, the Communist regime of Hungary. With the force of seventy thousand agents, they spread out to even the smallest village in the country in order to *bend* individuals to become inform-ers. Under the leadership of General Peter Gabor who received his training also from the KGB in Russia, he made certain that brutality and terror awaited all those who didn't fall in line.

So now, it was already October 30. The entire city of Budapest in sympathy with the freedom fighters unleashed their anger on everything and everybody in order to get even at last for their suf-fering under the unforgivable tyranny of the Secret Police. Every red star, every Communist-related office was destroyed. The streets in the center of the city looked like tornado-swept, devastated battle-ground. The only place that was still relatively intact was the Secret Police headquarters. But now, the tanks were heading there, and the freedom fighters were following them behind.

We followed the tanks in a hide-and-seek fashion. Those with guns were moving closer and closer to the tanks. Since the tanks weren't firing at us, we were convinced that they were on our side.

I asked Zsizsi, "How are we to fight? We don't have guns now."

"Don't you worry about that, Arpad. The minute the fight erupts, there will be rifles next to each dead body. We'll grab them and fight on," she emphasized.

By the time the drivers of the tanks turned the turrets onto the building, there was already heavy fighting between the Secret Police from the inside of the building and the freedom fighters outside on the street and from the inside of the opposite buildings across the headquarters. Yes, casualties were numerous now on the street, and guns were lying on the ground next to the many dead bodies. Not only I, but also others picked up these rifles and bullets. I grabbed two rifles with bullets and ran inside the building opposite the headquarters. Zsizsi was right behind me. We ran to the second floor for a better vantage point and from there fired on anybody who showed his face through the windows of the headquarters. The police returned the fire with submachine guns.

Suddenly, Zsizsi dropped on me, and her two-hundred-pound weight knocked me flat to the floor. I dragged her below the window as she was already motionless and her chest area fully drenched in blood. Staring at me she puffed, "God...," and she died. I bitterly cried in my helplessness, agonizing over her death. "God! Hold my hand. I want to kill the bastard who killed her," I roared. Now, I moved to the third floor to get yet a better view to the entrance of the headquarters.

Whether I killed him or not, I don't know. But I, together with the others, kept firing until the police ran out of bullets inside the headquarters. That was the moment every freedom fighter on the street was waiting for. The two to three minutes of silence that followed allowed the frontline fighters now to rush inside the building, pointing their guns forward, ready to fire and kill on the spot those resisting arrest or the command to get out and face the crowd. I was ready also, being now on the third floor, pointing my rifle directly to the entrance of the headquarters. Others on the street and from other buildings did the same thing, anxiously waiting for the right second to kill the traitors as they lined up in front of the entrance, facing the crowd. "No mercy! No mercy!" the people cried. In the next second, the first traitors instantly dropped dead from the many bullets we all fired at them at the same time. Then, one by one, as the others came out with their hands now stretched high above their heads, were instantly killed. Those who tried to escape through the back door were caught by the people there. They were waiting for the traitors with hatchets and knifes to slice them into unrecognizable pieces. One of them was hung on a tree upside down, having his body lacerated all over.

A lot of the people who witnessed this event went crazy from jubilation and soon left the place in order to get even with their own enemies back home. In the coming hours, the whole nation rose up and searched every nook in every Communist building to finally get even and make sure they wouldn't return again to repeat what they did before—persecuting, terrorizing, and even deporting people to labor camps in Russia.

Within hours, the western parts of the country were in the hands of the freedom fighters.

I was still sitting on the third floor and was hearing the news through the wall from the adjacent apartment—the glorious freedom fighters had liberated the country from… Radio Free Europe repeatedly aired the news. And I believed it because the fight ended at the headquarters.

* * *

Sitting alone with my back against the wall, I was still in contemplative shock: What was I going to do now? There was no one to fight against at the moment. Zsizsi was dead. What was I going to do with my suddenly gained freedom?

Occasionally, I peeked out the window, assuring myself that I could go down now and go wherever I felt like. I was terribly hungry and unbearably smelly. The last few days I roamed from place to place, fighting the enemy, fighting against hunger, and all the while, walloping in my own dirt. All this had sapped my energy. But I was still curious as a spy would be. At the same time, I couldn't wait to get out of this bullet-ridden room. Suddenly, the back door to my room opened and out came an old man, almost as disheveled as I was.

"I knew that somebody was hiding here. I heard the bullets flying in and out from this room. I didn't dare to move out of my closet, fearing that I would be killed. Now, it is all over. I wanted to look out my window and see what was going on below. But I didn't expect to find you here."

"I was the one firing from this room. I'm a freedom fighter and desperate for food and clean water now. Do you have any?" I asked.

"Young man, I'll give you the world, for you had done something so marvelous that none of us thought ever possible. You are my true patriot, my hero. You put your life on the line along with the rest of the students and fought without fear to defeat Communism in the land. Now get up and come inside my apartment. I'll give you food and water and everything else you want. I love you beyond measure for you have saved my life from further terror."

This old man was an Orthodox Jew, looked about ninety years old. Cardinal Mindszenty hid him from the Nazis who were rounding up all the Jews in Hungary before WWII and deporting them to the concentration camps in Germany. He was the one who found Zsizsi in the slums of Budapest and raised her until he and his wife were captured.

As the train that was carrying them from the country stopped to pick up more Jews along the way, he escaped. Unfortunately his wife couldn't. Then, as he walked back to Budapest during night hours, he met other Jews who told him that they were going to the cathedral in Budapest. The Cardinal would hide them somewhere there on the church's compound. And it happened that way that he survived. All the while, Zsizsi didn't know that her foster father was still alive. He lived alone now, quietly and almost secretly in his old apartment, located on the other side of the headquarters of the Secret Police.

The old man told me his life story and prayed to Yahweh (God) to take him fast, for he had nobody left to care for him. I was terribly shocked hearing him telling me all about himself and Zsizsi. I didn't know now how to tell him that Zsizsi was dead and was lying on the floor just below. I decided not to tell him anything. I didn't want him to die before my eyes.

"Here, Papa, is my rifle. I won't need it anymore. Guard it and protect yourself in case. I have to move on."

"You will not go anywhere, not until I feed you and give you fresh clothes," he said.

(So I ate matzos and leftover chicken gizzards. For many years after that meal, I cooked for myself chicken gizzards. The good taste of it at Papa's table never really left my taste buds. And the old man never really left my mind either.)

While I was shoving the gizzards down, the old man fast scanned my body features and moved away hurriedly, thinking what clothes he could find for me quickly. I noticed that the real reason for his quick getting away from me was that he couldn't stand my body smell anymore. It had now filled his tiny kitchen. As his fingers were squeezing his nostrils together, he shuffled away quickly from me saying, "Keep eating while I search my closets for clean clothes for you, but hurry up and take a bath."

"I know, I know, Papa, that I stink. But I got already used to it. Forgive me, but you can't fight a revolution from a bathtub, you know," I quipped.

I didn't leave the table until I finished all the gizzards. Quieting my hunger had priority over my body smell. Besides, I didn't know when I would be eating gizzards again. It was that good.

While I was taking a quick bath, I realized that the scum on my body wasn't coming off. The water was cold as there was no electricity at the moment to heat it, and I couldn't find soap around to soften up the week-old dirt on my body. So I used a grainy laundry detergent instead. The coarse powder not only took off the dirt but also some of my skin with it. It was stinging like disinfectant on an open wound. But I didn't care. I wanted to remove all the oily patches from my body, thinking, who knows when I could take another bath in my privacy again.

All the while, as I took my time cleaning myself, Papa had cleared out his closets in search for clean underwear, shirt, pants, and coat. He found everything that he thought I needed. Now, he threw all the clothes inside the bathroom, commenting, "I just made a new man out of you!"

The underwear was a perfect fit. So was the shirt. Both were snow white and were wrinkled like a dishcloth. I didn't mind, for I wasn't going to church, where every person would have noticed it. The long coat, however, covered it all as the last button on it touched my chin. The smell of mothballs twisted my nose until I threw them out. The suit was pure black and neatly pressed. It was made out of pure wool, the finest that could be found only in a synagogue's wardrobe. I tried it and it fit me as if it was tailor-made just for me. But I couldn't look at myself, for there wasn't a mirror in the bathroom. So I came out with the suit on and showed myself to Papa and waited for his remarks.

"Now, everybody will look at you, for you look like a handsome seminarian. Nobody would ever think that you are a freedom fighter."

"That sounds good to me, Papa. On my mind there is nothing else now except escaping the war zone without being picked up by the withdrawing Russians."

"When you get home, send the suit back to me. That's my burial garment. Promise that to me!"

I did. Now I hugged him and pulled a bit his ten-inch-long beard and said, "Papa, I'll hold you dear in my heart forever."

I never told him anything about Zsizsi, for it would have killed him. At age ninety, even a falling leaf would have taken him to eternity had I told him that Zsizsi was dead.

* * *

On the street below, relatives were gathering the bodies of their loved ones. Those that were left behind were collected on a flat-bed truck and were taken to a morgue to be kept there in case somebody would come to claim them. Humbly and tearfully I approached the driver and revealed him who I was in disguise. I explained what had happened and asked him to pick up Zsizsi's body and bury her for me with the other unknown bodies in the Kerepesi Cemetery in Budapest. She had no relatives I knew of, whom I could have notified. The driver understood that I am now escaping for a very good reason. He had tears in his eyes also as he nodded. Soon he went for Zsizsi to honor my wish. It took four men to carry her. When I looked back from a good distance and saw how honorably they carried her, I wished that I would have died with her. I wouldn't have to mourn her for the rest of my life.

Although freedom was declared in Budapest, nobody really knew, or could even guess, what the Russians were up to. They moved to the outskirts of the city and waited there for further instruction. In my escape I would have to pass through them in a little while. They lined both sides of the highway that led to Zagreb. White flags were fluttering from the top of each tank. Passersby told me they surrendered fighting.

It was now mid-afternoon and cloudy. People were out on the streets everywhere. Hunger and curiosity brought them out. Most of the display windows were shattered, but no one touched anything inside. The shattered glass and anything that fell from the bombardment covered every inch of the cobbled streets. Yet the people were able to find their way out of the downtown areas and reach the caravans that were bringing fresh supplies of bread, milk, meat, and just about anything the peasants could scrape together in the outlying villages, near and far from the city. The outpouring of goodwill took on a most noble cause toward those who fought in this revolution. It was in this manner that I, too, mingled with the crowd and left the city, witnessing every part of the action that brought the people together to celebrate the successful liberation. Nobody knew, however, that I had a good part in it. For that matter, I don't think anybody cared, seeing my outfit, thinking that I could be anybody but a freedom fighter.

As it turned out, somebody did care. It happened as I was still in the downtown area of the city that a real priest, though in civilian clothes, walked up to me and said, "You look obviously a fake, very young to be a seminarian. Here is my overcoat that will cover your outfit and my beret that will cover your head. You are escaping, aren't you? Kids of your age were throwing Molotov cocktails at the tanks and you were one of them."

"You didn't see me, did you?" I asked.

"Yes, I did. I was doing the same thing from the next building where you were. But I can't escape now. I have to do God's work, keeping the faith in those still living. Go now, and God be with you," he said and blessed me.

I was almost bewildered from feeling a tremor in my bones passing through me and was wondering what had happened. Was there a Holy Spirit in that priest's hand that blessed me? I felt the tremor only. Time will tell if there was. Now, I parted from him.

Soon, fear engulfed my mind because I was approaching the tanks, parked now on both sides of the highway. Their turrets were turned backward, and their occupiers were leisurely standing through the port holes and were looking at me as I walked in between them. I kept walking without giving any hint that I was just about ready to wet my pants, front and back, from the fear that they would blow me apart with their machine guns. I heard that they were talking to each other in Russian, the language I had to learn in school for five years.

"I admire these young fighters," said one. "I wonder what would happen if we had to face them again," said the other.

(These Russian soldiers gave themselves up fighting the freedom fighters. They sided with the patriotic movement. The white flags on their tanks indicated their surrender. But I still didn't trust them.)

Hearing their comments, I gained enough courage though to pass through them. I think it was the priest's blessing that cleared my way without being arrested.

* * *

By the evening, I reached my sister's house in Rackeresztur. At first, nobody recognized me until I pulled my hat off. They had no idea that I was fighting against the Secret Police, no idea how horrendous fighting on city streets felt like, and no idea of the trauma I went through when Zsizsi dropped dead on me. Hearing it explained, they thought I was faking myself. Now dressed in a rabbi's outfit, they were convinced that I was definitely a fake, making them disbelieve that I could do such things they saw only in films.

"Think what you want, Sister," I said. "Your world was always separated from mine by events that needed sacrifice on my part. You always doubted that I could endure any sacrifice to gain my personal freedom. Here I am and proved it again who I am. But soon, I won't be around, because now I am escaping the Russians. I don't believe them, not for a moment that they would let the *Magyars* shake their *Empire* and stop their quest from turning the whole of Eastern Europe into Communism. I only wanted to stop by you and say good-bye to Ella. Where is she, anyway?"

"Ella is somewhere in Budapest looking for you. Since she knew where you worked, she wanted to find a job there and be close to you. She left just before the trouble started. She should be back any day. Wait a few days here," Iren said.

"But only three days, Sister, and not a day more. I want to return home to the village I came from and wait there the outcome, whether the Russians would allow this country's freedom to stand, now that they were defeated in Budapest. Should they return to take back what they lost, I know they would capture me and kill me. But I have plans to prevent that, for I would not want to lose my life and my freedom, ever," I replied.

My comments finally convinced Iren that I was now on the run to save my life from being captured by the Russians.

*　*　*

Before I left my sister's house, however, I put on my own clothes and instructed Iren to send back Papa's suit to him. I never found out whether he received it or not, as the country quickly become gripped by anarchy. Although Hungary has been liberated from Communism for now, there is no governing body set up yet to replace the old regime. Without order, nothing functioned predictably. This was the time when the people everywhere were mopping up the old order at will, getting rid of all the symbols of Communism, and getting even with those who terrorized them. While they were doing that, the Russians were amassing the brutal Mongolian soldiers to mow Hungary to ashes. They were mobilizing these units outside the country on the Romanian border.

Now Ella had not returned as yet, so I left Iren's house knowing for sure that I would never see her again. I didn't conceal my identity any longer as there were no Russians and no Secret Police roaming anywhere on my way home. I had fifty more miles to walk before reaching Balatonkeresztur. I journeyed on the same highway that I so curiously watched when we moved home from Rackeresztur two years earlier. Even here at Szekesfehervar (about twenty-five miles from Budapest), the road was full of caravans of tractor-pulled trailers and horse-drawn wagons, bringing just about everything for the starving people of Budapest. I was so surprised seeing this much outpour of goodwill that suddenly I didn't know which way to go. I walked and waited and walked some more, but there was no end to the caravans. Finally I subdued my compassion and decided against going back to Budapest. I didn't believe that the Russians would stomach this much humiliation inflicted on them at the hands of a few thousand freedom fighters. Unless the West would suddenly invade Hungary to protect the country, I wouldn't stay in the country for any promise. The Russians were always liars and shall be always liars.

Nagy is the premier now. He declared the country's neutrality and negotiated with the Russians to leave the country. He sought help from the UN and the world at large to come to the aid of Hungary. But, instead of real help, only moral support came from all the nations. The big help that was promised during the uprising turned to abandonment, especially from the United States. And, with it, the whole world backed off also. So the Russians, emboldened by the inaction of the West, did what they wanted. While promising withdrawal from Hungary, they regrouped in Romania and reinvaded the country within days, with far more brutality and far more firepower than they ever had in Hungary before.

Now, as I was walking home and had only a few more miles to go, I heard rumors on the streets: "The Russians are coming back!"

How long would my personal freedom last? I asked that question again and again on my way home. The only answer emerged: Know who your enemies are. They are fearless and brutal; even the devil turns to them for advice. They are the Russians. They have the upper hand this time. This time there would be the greatest massacre in the whole country the world would ever witness. I don't want to be part of that. I concluded.

With this conviction, I prepared myself now for the greatest leap of faith in my entire life in order to hold firm onto my personal freedom. So I decided that I would run away from the Russians. The unanswered question yet was *where*. I still had a few more days left to think about that. The Russians weren't coming yet. It was only rumored that they were returning to Hungary.

Being home now and finding my unlocked bedroom the same way as I left it, I looked for Matild. I couldn't find her anywhere. Her animals were dropping dead from thirst and hunger. The few that were still living, I rounded and slaughtered and deep-fried. Some of it I ate while being home; the rest I prepared for my journey to the West. The rumor that the Russians were coming back turned out to be true. This reality sent shockwaves in everybody throughout the country. The sudden change of events filled the hearts and minds of everybody with fear and revulsion. It was not only I that had to decide what to do, but the whole nation had to.

The Russians reentered Budapest, and from there they spread throughout the countryside in order to reoccupy Hungary. In Budapest, they destroyed whole city blocks in order to kill every *revolutionary*. In the countryside, they rounded up the *instigators* and deported them to the *Gulags* in Russia. Some of the freedom fighters took shelter wherever they could find a vantage point to fight back. Eventually, they were pushed to the hills of Buda and kept fighting from there. Within a few days, Budapest had become the cemetery of the whole nation. The West turned its face the other way and let the freedom of Hungary die in the same cradle where the revolution was born. Some of the other freedom fighters, who realized that it was useless to fight the "Bear" with bows and arrows, gave up and escaped. I am one of them. But where?

It was now the 4th of November 1956. Hundreds of tanks and thousands of Attila-minded Russian soldiers were mercilessly killing and destroying everything in sight in Budapest to gain the upper hand. I was listening to all this being reported now on Radio Free Europe. I was at my old friend's house, Steve Fodor, the fish scooper. He was also devastated hearing what was happening. He was highly apprehensive for he did his share turning against the Communists in the village. In venting his anger, Steve knocked down every red star in the village and vandalized the local headquarters of the Communist Party.

So we were in a get-ready mood to run away before the Russians could nab us.

"Where?" Steve asked, being horrified.

"The only area that is still free is the western part of the country, so reported Radio Free Europe. But I hear now that the Russians are coming with an endless row of tanks to take over Sarvar, their biggest airport in the western part of the country. In order to take over Sarvar, these tanks have to pass through here, my hometown, as there is no other road leading to it from Budapest. If I don't leave now, they would capture me right here in this house and hang me right here on your walnut tree. And you could be hanging right next to me also, for your part in revenging the Communists for jailing your father is also unforgivable," I answered.

"Don't say that. Were you a freedom fighter in Budapest, or what else is it that makes you so scared?" he asked.

"Yes, I was. But now I have to do something else because my personal freedom is again at stake. Aren't you worried about your personal freedom?" I asked Steve.

"Well, yes. But what am I to do?"

"Come with me! We'll escape together."

"When do you think, we should do that?" Steve asked.

"Day after tomorrow at five o'clock in the morning."

* * *

Day after tomorrow was November 8, 1956. Being let down now to the lowest level, I was haunted by the total unknown that I'm facing. I would be without a country and without friends. There was nowhere else to escape except to the West—to Austria. Without knowing anybody there and not even a word of their German language, I would have to use everything else except my tongue in order to explain myself to the people.

Many other hurdles were tormenting my mind as well at this time. But the biggest was that I didn't know my way to Austria, except that the sun rested in that direction.

Therefore, I decided that I would go from town to town and ask the older folks directions, for the young like me was as ignorant as I was about where exactly Austria is. Under Communism, learning geography and Western culture was total fabrication and distortion of reality. Australia and Austria meant the same thing. One is about seven thousand miles from the other.

So on November 7 from early morning till late evening, I was preparing my mind for the strangest journey in my entire life. At the crack of dawn, I walked over to Steve and banged his door and opened it. He was still in bed.

"Get up and prepare yourself, for by this time tomorrow, we'll be on our way to Austria. Make no mistake about that. I leave you here if you aren't ready!"

And I left him. In truth, however, I was scared to make this long journey alone, and for that reason, I went to him to find out whether he was still coming. Steve was a type of person who rarely knew the difference between *yes and no* when it came to making a commitment. Even after he assured me, "No matter what, I'm coming," I went around town and coaxed five other *trustworthy* schoolmates to come with me to the West.

Convincingly, I persuaded them to join me for the otherwise fearful journey. Every one of them said "yes." This way, I thought if Steve changed his mind, these other friends would accompany me to Austria.

Being assured of companionship, I went back home and prepared plenty of food for the road and bundled the whole thing into a large canvass tablecloth.

It was time now to think about a few *forints* (Hungarian money) to take along. Since I had not even a penny in my pocket, I was going to a kind person to borrow some. I knew that this person always loved me and admired how I and Ella struggled earlier to support ourselves. This particular woman was Jewish. Her family operated a grocery store in the village before the Communists confiscated it in 1953. She had two daughters, Judith and Eva. Their father was in jail now for being a Capitalist merchant. This woman, who was as beautiful and compassionate as my mother was, fell on my shoulders the minute I stepped inside her house. She was bitterly crying for her daughters. They escaped the country two days ago.

"God only knows where they are now. The only thing I know is that they are heading to Austria, for a Jew has no future in this country under Communism." She was in tears.

"Neither do I. But have no fear, *dear mother*, for I'm going there also. I'll tell them how much you miss them. I'll ask them to send you word through Radio Free Europe. Keep listening to it."

"When are you planning to leave?"

"Five in the morning, tomorrow."

"Let me hug you one more time and bless you with the spirit of Abraham, for he sojourned himself in foreign lands also. Here, take some money with you in case you have to pay your way out at the border."

She turned her sad face and smiled, already hoping that I would meet her daughters in Austria and would let them know that their mother was waiting to hear from them.

So I had food and money now and was all set to leave. I grabbed the broom from the corner and broke off the handle and shoved it through the tied bundle of food and hurled the whole thing onto my shoulder. Now my feet were straddling the threshold between the kitchen and the bedroom. "One more look," I said to myself, "just one more look to make sure that I didn't forget anything."

As I was scanning my bedroom from wall to wall, my head suddenly stopped, and I could not move it any farther. A jolt entered my heart as I found myself gazing at the crucifix hanging on the wall. "Take me with you!" an inner voice commended.

"Oh yes, I'll take you with me! I have nobody else anyway, and I don't need anybody else," I responded and removed the crucifix and placed it in my left inner pocket. And I left without even shutting my bedroom door.

(That crucifix traveled with me everywhere as I journeyed from country to country. Today, it is still in my left side inner pocket, but not in my coat's pocket. It is deeper, much deeper. I hold him in my heart instead.)

As I stepped outside, I almost knocked Steve over. He was waiting for me there. "I don't want to miss you," he said.

"I see that you aren't bringing anything for the road. You think we are just going to the next town to visit your sister?"

"No. But I think that bundle on your shoulder has something in it for me also," Steve quipped and smiled.

"I sure have, knowing how lazy you are to cook for yourself. Let's go! There are five more kids waiting for us to be picked up. I invited them yesterday, and every one of them said 'yes.' You want to know something? I don't believe them. Their response to my invitation was too quick and without any thinking about what lies ahead. Soon, we shall see, whether they changed their minds."

As we passed their houses where they were to be picked up, not even one was waiting.

So we left town, going through the village without seeing anybody. It was five o'clock in the morning, still pitch dark. In my mind I knew the way already from a sketch given to me by the Jewish lady yesterday. I kept repeating each town many times in order to memorize what came after what. Then, I threw the sketch away. The reason why I did this was that in case I was arrested, the Russians wouldn't find the draft map on me, revealing to them that I was escaping.

We still had 105 miles to go to reach the border. In order to avoid the suspicion of fleeing, we walked mostly at night and slept during the day in hay or corn stacks. Twice during our journey we encountered peasants who were coming to collect the stacks that they used for animal feed during the winter. When we saw them sitting on their horse-drawn flat-bed wagons and coming toward us, we left the stacks and walked toward them instead of running away. They knew what we were up to because other fleeing kids did the same thing. In fact, they carried extra water and food with them to help us out.

As we approached Sopron, the last town before the border, we encountered more young people fleeing than the population of the town (ten thousand). It dawned on me then that freedom fighters were not only in Budapest but also in the whole country. Seeing this mass exodus, I thought that every remaining freedom fighter was fleeing the country.

Coming closer to the border, we saw a wide path of wild growth trampled by the thousands upon thousands of people who were heading to Austria. The border guards gave up patrolling, for they were part of the revolting people. But they did one smart thing. They lined themselves in a row before the crossover bridge to Austria and placed a wicker basket in front of them. They collected from the fleeing people all the Hungarian money they had. We all knew that the money was worthless in Austria. So I too, gladly emptied my pocket and dropped my money into the nearest wicker basket.

In this anxious moment in crossing this border bridge, I threw away my heaviest burden I ever had on my mind—the fear of being killed by the Russians. I think others had the same burden, for after crossing this now historic bridge, they hugged and kissed each other, lauding: "*Freedom! Freedom! Freedom* at last!"

* * *

By this time, the world realized that the Russians were lying as always. They reinvaded Hungary from Romania with beastly mobility to ensure brutality. Taking over Budapest was their first battleground. No stone was left unturned in their madness. Killing or deporting the freedom fighters was not merely uncommon. It was their solemn pledge to do so. The only safe haven to survive this ordeal was to look back from Austria, crying after those left behind.

The Western leaders suddenly realized the impact of the Hungarian revolution. Thousands upon thousands flooded the cities all around the world from Vienna to Sydney to New York, protesting and demanding action. It was, however, too late for military action. (If I ever want to look for gullible fools, I would go no farther than those occupying the White House.) They believed that the Russians left Hungary for good. They had not yet learned that lying was the key to their deception. And that the Communists (the Leftists) were the greatest practitioners of it, even today.

The Russians so quickly reoccupied Hungary that the slumbering West couldn't even agree how to condemn them at the United Nations before it was all over.

Not willing to punish the Russians, the West quickly rushed to the aid of the thousands of fleeing freedom fighters, now amassing in

Austria. Consulates were quickly opened in the huge refugee camp by Australia, Canada, the United States, and those of Western Europe, graciously welcoming into their countries the courageous freedom fighters and others fleeing the onslaught of the Russian barbarians.

Materially we had nothing, but intellectually we were the richest in the world. Doctors, lawyers, poets, philosophers, scientist, and those skilled in trades left Hungary in mass to seek freedom and liberty in these countries where democracy was constitutionally guaranteed. I had materially nothing either, but I had my trade, a tool-and-die maker.

Steve and I had to make now the monumental decision—where to go. For me, this decision-making step is already *tailor-made*. The words "Go to America because there was 'freedom there to do'" came back to life as Mr. Forro was tapping my head from his grave to remember it. At the time when he said these words, they were a mystery to me. But now, I must say the answer to it was right in front of me—the American consulate.

I arrived in the United States of America on December 1, 1956, on the very first military transport plane which landed at Camp Kilmer, New Jersey.

Steve stayed behind. He couldn't make up his mind where to go. Three months later, however, he, too, arrived on a boat into the New York City harbor. I greeted him there as if I were just liberated from a *Communist prison*. So good I felt seeing him. I embraced him and said, "*There is no place like America.*"

END

CPSIA information can be obtained at www.ICGtesting.com
Printed in the USA
BVOW08s2333140616

452096BV00001B/4/P

9 781681 973685